FREEDOM THROUGH VIGILANCE

HISTORY OF
U.S. AIR FORCE SECURITY SERVICE
(USAFSS)

Volume II

USAFSS Ground Sites in
Europe, Libya, Turkey
and Pakistan

Copyright © 2010 by Larry Tart
Cover designed by Larry Tart
Editing and proofreading accomplished by William G. Deister

ISBN 978-0-7414-6115-5

Printed in the United States of America

Published January 2013

INFINITY PUBLISHING
1094 New DeHaven Street, Suite 100
West Conshohocken, PA 19428-2713
Toll-free (877) BUY BOOK
Local Phone (610) 941-9999
Fax (610) 941-9959
Info@buybooksontheweb.com
www.buybooksontheweb.com

ABOUT THE AUTHOR

Larry Tart has lived the history about which he writes. He served in Air Force Security Service for twenty-one years, retiring from USAFSS Headquarters as a SMSgt. in 1977. Trained as a Russian linguist, he completed seven overseas tours—four at USAFSS ground sites and three in the command's airborne reconnaissance units. He also served as a special projects analyst in the Air Force Special Comm Center in Texas in the mid-1960's. Larry was inducted into the Air Intelligence Agency Hall of Honor in 2000. A year later, he published *The Price of Vigilance*, about the shoot down of USAFE C-130 60528 over Armenia in 1958.

SMSgt. Larry Tart receiving medals, HQ USAFSS, 1977, and at Prop Wash Gang Reunion, October 2009

i

Completing the Defense Language Institute's basic, intermediate and advanced Russian language courses, Larry Tart holds a BA in Russian from the University of Maryland. Commencing in 1956, he served fifteen years overseas, with tours in England, Germany, Japan and Greece. After ten years as a voice intercept operator, transcriber and traffic analyst at USAFSS ground sites, he flew reconnaissance missions for the next decade as an airborne intercept operator, airborne analyst and airborne mission supervisor—logging 3,000 flying hours aboard C-130 and RC-135 aircraft. His military awards include eleven Air Medals and three Meritorious Service Medals.

For 16 years in his post-Air Force career, he worked as a systems engineer and programs manager, building intelligence, surveillance and reconnaissance systems. As the protagonist seeking to honor a USAF C-130 reconnaissance crew that Soviet MiG pilots shot down over Armenia in September 1958, Tart is recognized as the "Father of the Aerial Reconnaissance (C-130 60528) Memorial," dedicated in National Vigilance Park, Fort Meade, Maryland, on 2 September 1997.

In 1996, Larry founded the Prop Wash Gang, a fraternal group of 800+ current and former USAFSS reconnaissance flyers. Under his guidance, the PWG helped with the creation of exhibits in National Vigilance Park and the National Cryptologic Museum in Maryland, and provided plaques and memorabilia to the Air Intelligence Agency Heritage Hall, San Antonio, Texas. In appreciation of their services, the Gang sends "care packages" at Christmas-time to those Air Force Intelligence, Surveillance and Reconnaissance Agency recon flyers who are away in the "sandbox" supporting the war on terrorism during the holidays.

Dedicated to family members who lost loved ones in the shoot down of C-130 60528 in 1958, Larry Tart wrote *The Price of Vigilance*. Published by Ballantine Books in June 2001, *The Price of Vigilance* pays tribute to airborne reconnaissance silent warriors who have paid the ultimate price. *Freedom Through Vigilance* is a follow-on project—honoring the men and women who served silently in signals intelligence during the Cold War and those currently supporting information warfare. For additional details, visit URL's: www.silent-warriors.com and www.larrytart.com.

IN MEMORIAM

Photograph courtesy of Airlee Owens

I dedicate *Freedom Through Vigilance* to departed friend and former Air Force Security Service veteran Airlee Owens, who passed away on 17 February 2010. Airlee photographed the eagle above near his home in Bandon, Oregon, in 2008. I regret that I was unable to get this USAFSS history into print in time for him and many other fallen USAFSS veterans to enjoy it.

I also inscribe *Freedom Through Vigilance* to Anthony P. Baciewicz, Leslie J. Bolstridge, Nathan C. Britt, William L. Burkhart, Henry N. Connors, John S. Deaver, Richard D. Ebersole, Roger K. Gavit, Arthur Gort, Walter D. Goss, Thomas C. Hyde, Robert C. Jones, Jerry S. Keaton, Barry Matthews, John E. Neeley, Hugh J. O'Brien, James B. Perleth, Albert Picard, James J. Reynolds, Roslyn L. Schulte, Edward E. Stacey, Robert F. Stark, Luther A. Tarbox, Joseph Tortorete and Richard A. Williams. A 2006 graduate of the Air Force Academy, First Lt. Roslyn Schulte died on 20 May 2009 from a roadside bomb near Kabul, Afghanistan, the first of our command's female airmen killed in the line of duty. The others had long distinguished careers in USAFSS; many were personal friends of the author, and several describe their part in USAFSS history in *Freedom Through Vigilance*. They are smiling down on us as they soar with eagles.

SPECIAL THANKS

I am especially indebted to William "Bill" Deister for his superb editing of *Freedom Through Vigilance*. Coupled with 24 years experience, 21 years as a Russian linguist (intercept operator, transcriber and analyst) with Security Service units in the Far East, Europe and at NSA, including a tour in the HQ ESC Alert Center and a 99-day cruise aboard the missile tracking ship USNS General H. H. Arnold, plus three years Defense Attaché staff duty overseas, Deister brought to the editing task 21 years of skill as a dedicated high school US History and Russian language teacher.

As a self-professed perfectionist, who takes great pride in his mastery of English grammar and how to write in clear, concise sentences, Bill has found and fixed misplaced and missing punctuation and grammatical, spelling and factual errors that even the most proficient editors sometimes overlook. I was most fortunate to link up with Bill just when he was retiring from teaching and searching for a challenging avocation. With his understanding of subject matter—he has lived much of the USAFSS history himself—and with his enthusiasm to see the best possible presentation of our history, I could not have found a better-qualified editor for the project.

Our friendship dates back to 1971 when Bill and I were classmates in Advanced Russian Language training at the Presidio of Monterey, California. Our tours at Wakkanai, Japan, also overlapped briefly in 1962. Security Service was indeed a small world. Thank you very much, Bill. The first copy off the press of *Freedom Through Vigilance* is yours—autographed of course. By the way, I take full responsibility for any errors that sneaked by our reviews; you did your editing masterfully.

I also thank the hundreds of USAFSS pioneers who have shared their experiences and provided military records and photographs used in documenting our Air Force Security Service history. I could not have completed this project without your assistance.

Lastly, I thank my wife Diane for 43 years of dedicated support. She and other spouses of career USAFSS personnel are the true heroes in our Security Service families. A special thanks to all of you.

TABLE OF CONTENTS

CONTENT

CONTENT

CONTENT

SILENT WARRIORS
by Russ Butcher[1]

What is the make-up of this special breed,
these strange and special few?
Where do they come from, year-on-year?
What is it that they do?

They are like shadows in the night
or vapor in the air,
so seldom seen and rarely heard
but rest assured, they're there.

They come not from a single place,
they come from far and wide,
the open plains, the city streets,
the rural countryside.

They are the farmer's little boy,
the little girl who lived next door,
the uncle of a high school friend
who gave his life at war.

They are the barber's youngest child
who heard his country call,
or friends with whom we laughed and sipped
whose names are on "THE WALL."

And what they do, you needn't ask
for none will ever tell,
in silence based on "need to know"
they proudly serve so well.

They're much the same as all before
who vanquished freedom's foe.
they are ones who fuel the fire
which keeps THE TORCH aglow.

---

[1] Dedicated to our Silent Warriors; printed with permission of author Russ Butcher, former USAFSS traffic analyst at Misawa, Japan (1961-63).

An army without secret agents is exactly like

a man without eyes or ears —

Sun Tzu — 2,500

years ago

_____

Bad Intelligence is worse

than no Intelligence —

Larry Tart —

2006

FOREWORD

While thinking of an opening for this foreword, I found myself imagining television's beloved Mr. Rogers asking, "Can you say, u-sahf-fuss?" Some readers may wonder why anyone would want to say such a strange word. But to thousands of Air Force veterans, USAFSS—the United States Air Force Security Service—was their home in the military, whether for one hitch or a long career. To a person they are proud to have served in the smallest major command in the Air Force—to them simply Command. For decades, they didn't talk about what they did. It was top secret. If people believed they were the Military Police, well, fine. In recent years, however, declassification has allowed much of the signals intelligence (SIGINT) mission of Security Service, and its successor commands and agencies, to be discussed openly.

In *Freedom Through Vigilance,* author and retired USAFSS veteran Larry Tart has given us a rare glimpse into Air Force signals intelligence operations. Although most of the book treats the Security Service years, the author follows the SIGINT mission through a succession of increasing responsibilities leading to new command designations: Electronic Security Command (ESC), Air Force Intelligence Command (AFIC), Air Intelligence Agency (AIA), and Air Force Intelligence, Surveillance, and Reconnaissance Agency (AFISRA).

Those responsibilities have grown through some seven decades to meet challenges posed by modernizing communications systems. When USAFSS was established in 1948, and for many years during the Cold War, its military targets communicated primarily by Morse code. Over time the use of voice radio became more common, and the book relates the history of operations to intercept and exploit both types of signals. Finally it introduces the mission of AFISRA, in an age of digital data and cell phones, in waging the global war against terror following Al Qaeda attacks on the United States on September 11, 2001.

In its breadth, *Freedom Through Vigilance* encompasses the establishment and physical building of units and bases, and it discusses all mission activities, including signals collection, radio direction finding, processing, analysis and reporting—sometimes

xi

during periods of national crisis and war. Much information about units is set out in clearly organized tables. While reading this incredibly detailed yet readable history, Security Service veterans will feel right at home with the vocabulary that once was everyday for them. Many personal accounts, obtained in interviews, from outside sources, and by email, support factual information while at times bringing excitement and humor to the history. Larry even shares a few amusing stories of his own about off-duty life in Europe. The text, written in a blend of formal and informal styles that flows smoothly, is enriched by an extensive collection of photographs.

The author felt that FTV's content called for an editor having certain skills and a knowledge of the mission and culture of Security Service, and Larry invited me to fulfill that requirement. Like him, I am a retired career Russian linguist, and more recently a retired high school teacher of social studies and Russian language. We are old friends, having been classmates in Advanced Russian at the Defense Language Institute, Monterey, for most of 1971. I had previously taken Basic and Intermediate at Syracuse and the 12-week RS-425 Advanced Special Russian Transcription course at Ft. Meade. My own assignments over 24 years primarily involved collection and transcription, with some target analysis at Spec Comm in my first term, three years out of Command well into my career and one year in HQ at Kelly in General Larson's brand-new Alert Center in 1979-1980. I served three two-year tours at the National Security Agency (NSA), three tours in Japan, and two in Europe, and I hold three career professionalization certifications from NSA. I knew many of the persons who shared their experiences with the author.

Freedom Through Vigilance pays public tribute to Air Force SIGINT veterans who have cherished in silence memories of their accomplishments, often performed under adverse circumstances or in remote and dangerous places. They will see themselves in this book, even if not named, as they read about the men and women, from airman to general, with whom they performed their vital mission. One of the standout personal accounts comes from the author's friend, Paul Strieby, who expresses his feelings about the importance of the mission in words that we all feel, even if we didn't get to be in on something so "hot." Also noteworthy for their inspiration are comments about making the most of opportunities offered by Chief Master Sergeant Suzan Sangster, currently serving in the Air Force Intelligence, Surveillance, and Reconnaissance Agency, today's successor to USAFSS. The book contains stories of many SIGINT airmen who did take the opportunities open to them and built very fine careers.

Readers of Larry Tart's new book, civilian or military, cannot help but be deeply impressed by the technical expertise, resourcefulness, bravery, and limitless devotion to duty of the airmen and officers who were Security Service.

William G. Deister
SMSgt., USAF, Ret.

Europe, N. Africa and West Asia

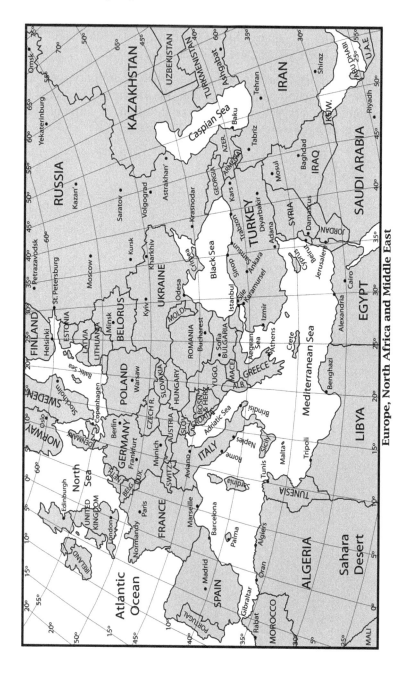

Europe, North Africa and Middle East

xiv

INTRODUCTION

FREEDOM THROUGH VIGILANCE
HISTORY OF SIGNALS INTELLIGENCE
IN THE U.S. AIR FORCE

USAFSS — The Beginnings

He cleaned out his desk, said his good-byes to old friends and headed for the front door of Air Force Security Service Headquarters at Brooks Air Force Base, San Antonio, Texas. Suddenly, he heard the inimitable voice of Colonel Robert H. Augustinus' secretary, "Lieutenant Harriger, the colonel must talk to you immediately."

It was a hot afternoon in San Antonio on 25 June 1950. Hours earlier, events began unfolding 14 time zones away in Korea that would change Russell "Hop" Harriger's life and the lives of hundreds of thousands of Americans forever. The North Korean army had invaded South Korea and was marching on Seoul, the South Korean capital. The United States Air Force Security Service (USAFSS) was about to go to war, and for the third time in a decade, Hop Harriger's plans to attend law school were put on hold. Faced with its first operational crisis, USAFSS had other plans for Lt. Harriger and other assigned personnel who were approaching the end of their active duty military commitments.[1]

Participation in the Korean War truly would be its baptism under fire for Security Service, a totally new command within the U.S. Air Force, which itself had been an independent branch of the United States armed forces only since 1947.

U.S. AIR FORCE — A BRIEF HISTORY

The United States Air Force had its beginning as the Aeronautical Division of the U.S. Army Signal Corps on 1 August 1907, and the Corps accepted the Army's first airplane two years later (2 August 1909).[2] Less than six months later (19 January 1910), a Signal Corps pilot dropped three two-pound bags of flour in an attempt to hit a target, the Army's first bombing experiment. Thirty-three years later, Signal Corps communications intelligence (COMINT) platoons were providing targeting information in support of Allied bombers carrying out bombing raids against Nazi Germany.

The Aviation Section of the Signal Corps was created on 18 July 1914, and five months later a couple of Signal Corps lieutenants demonstrated two-way air-to-ground radio communications. Thirty years later, Technical Sergeant Herman L. Roesler was flying as a voice interceptor (German linguist)—providing internal advisory warning support—during U.S. Army Air Corps B-17 bombing missions against German facilities in Europe. Japanese-American (Nisei) linguists performed similar airborne duties aboard Air Corps aircraft in the Far East, intercepting Japanese air force and air defense communications in 1945.

On 24 May 1918, the U.S. Army Air Service was organized, giving the air arm of the army parity with other army branches. After WW I, Brigadier General William (Billy) Mitchell and other airpower pioneers spoke out forcibly for an independent air force. Envisioning aviation as a separate strike force, they opposed the Air Service remaining an arm of the U.S. Army. For speaking out so vehemently, Mitchell was court-martialed in 1925, demoted, and he resigned from the service. Later he was vindicated and declared a hero by U.S. Air Force leaders.

Congress and the army rejected Mitchell's argument for an independent air force. However, on 2 July 1926, the Air Service became a separate combat arm—the U.S. Army Air Corps—equal in status with the infantry, cavalry and artillery. With the threat of world war looming in Europe and the Far East in 1938-39, the Air Corps budget grew dramatically. In 1939, the U.S. defense budget for fiscal year 1940 authorized $300 million to support an Air

Corps consisting of 6,000 planes, 3,203 officers and 45,000 enlisted troops.

With the buildup in airpower, on 20 June 1941, the War Department reorganized its ground forces and created as its air arm the U.S. Army Air Forces. However, from 9 March 1942 to 18 September 1947 the Army Air Corps continued to operate as a combatant arm of the Army Air Forces.[3]

The National Security Act dated 26 July 1947 created the U.S. Defense Department and laid out provisions for reorganizing the War Department. The Department of the Air Force was created on 18 September 1947, with Army Air Forces personnel, aircraft and facilities transferred to the new U.S. Air Force. Soon AAF troops wearing olive drab uniforms and brown shoes became Air Force airmen in blue uniforms and black shoes. However, the Army Air Forces radio squadrons mobile—the air arm's communications intelligence resources—remained in the Army Signal Corps as Army Security Agency resources until 1949 when the RSM's were transferred to the newly created U.S. Air Force Security Service.

U.S. AIR FORCE SECURITY SERVICE

AN OVERVIEW

The United States Air Force Security Service was created as a separate Air Force command on 20 October 1948; however, the history of USAFSS would be incomplete without addressing its predecessor entities and successor commands. Army Signal Corps radio intelligence companies (aviation) were activated in World War II expressly to intercept enemy air force communications and provide "radio intelligence" to American air force field commanders.

The signal radio intelligence company (aviation) evolved into the radio squadron mobile. An RSM was attached to and supported a numbered Air Force—for example, the 3rd RSM supported the Ninth Air Force in Europe from the D-Day Invasion at Normandy, France, until the end of the war. Other Signal Corps entities monitored American military communications— communications security or COMSEC during WW II. The mission that USAFSS inherited in 1949 was essentially those two activities—providing radio intelligence (aka communications intelligence and signals intelligence) and COMSEC support to Air Force commanders.

Over the years, the Air Force communications intelligence mission evolved to keep pace with technology and changes in enemy operations. Before World War II, almost all military communications by radio (audible comms) were transmitted using Morse code and fairly low level techniques to encrypt messages. However, as less bulky, more reliable radios became available—including mobile units—voice communications increased dramatically, creating an immediate shortage of trained linguists and voice interceptors. That linguist shortage exists to this day in the intelligence community.

The deployment of radar during World War II added to the complexities of the Air Force intelligence mission, as did the introduction of multichannel communications and computer-controlled weapons systems in the 1950's and 1960's. The signals intelligence (SIGINT) environment now included communications, electronic and data transmissions. By the late 1970's the Air Force SIGINT mission had expanded to include the use of command, control and communications countermeasures (C3CM),[4] and USAFSS became the Air Force Electronic Security Command (ESC) in 1979.

Further changes in communications technology—advent of personal computers, email and widespread usage of cellphones—and the end of the Cold War resulted in other changes in the signals intelligence mission and a realignment of the U.S. Air Force intelligence community. The Electronic Security Command was redesignated the Air Force Intelligence Command in 1991. After additional changes, the AFIC became the Air Intelligence Agency two years later. Finally on 8 June 2007, a newly activated Air Force Intelligence, Surveillance and Reconnaissance Agency (AFISRA) replaced the AIA. Thus, the lineage of U.S. Air Force signals intelligence runs from the Army Air Forces signal radio intelligence company (aviation) in 1942 to USAFSS (1948), ESC (1979), AFIC (1991), AIA (1993) and finally to AFISRA (2007 to Present).

BOOK LAYOUT

The majority of *FREEDOM THROUGH VIGILANCE* addresses the Air Force Security Service (1948-1979), with limited coverage of ESC, AFIC, AIA and AFISRA. "FTV" is divided into four volumes. Volumes I, II and III chronicle the U.S. Air Force Security Service SIGINT ground-site histories during the Cold War and females in USAFSS. Volume IV will address USAFSS airborne SIGINT reconnaissance operations.

The author struggled with formats, event groupings and layout that would most clearly present our USAFSS history, and in the end, settled on a hybrid approach. I also grappled with level of detail and number of photographs included in this product. The trade-off was to eliminate significant amounts of information (and photos) from the manuscript and publish a single volume or retain historic relevance and publish multiple volumes. I chose the latter option. To the extent feasible, events are covered geographically then chronologically by individual units (events) within a specified area.

Chapter Layout	
Volume I	
Chapter One	Army Air Forces Ground-based COMINT and COMSEC in WW II
Chapter Two	USAFSS — General History
Chapter Three	Female Contributions to USAFSS (and Successor Organizations)
Volume II	
Chapter Four	USAFSS in Germany (and Austria)
Chapter Five	USAFSS in Turkey, North Africa (Libya), Greece, Italy and Pakistan
Chapter Six	USAFSS in the UK (England and Scotland)
Volume III	
Chapter Seven	USAFSS in Alaska
Chapter Eight	USAFSS in Far East, including USAFSS Support in Korean War and Vietnam War
Volume IV *	
	USAFSS History — Airborne Operations
* Publication date for Volume IV is undetermined.	

While Volume I provides a general history of the Air Force Security Service command and female contributions to the

USAFSS mission, the real "meat" of Freedom Through Vigilance—the history of worldwide USAFSS field operations—lies in Volumes II and III. Appendix A of all three volumes contains a list of acronyms and abbreviations used in Freedom Through Vigilance, and Appendix B is a list of worldwide locations at which USAFSS units operated (1949-1979).

USAFSS Unit Locations List

Created by Air Force Security Service (or Electronic Security Command) Headquarters from official records about 1979, the USAFSS Unit Locations List (Appendix B) should be invaluable to USAFSS veterans desiring to refresh their memories regarding locations/units in which they served during the period 1949-1979. The units included in the list are valid, albeit the list is not all inclusive. For example, many of the early detachments created overseas by radio squadrons mobile in the early 1950's are not on the list, perhaps because copies of special orders activating those units may not have found their way to the USAFSS HQ archives used to create the list. We are indebted to retired USAFSS Major Frank Clark for providing a copy of this "Location/Unit/Date" listing for our USAFSS history. In 2010, Clark recalled that he had obtained the unclassified listing from the USAFSS history office shortly before he retired in 1980.

Index and Endnotes

Each volume also contains an index. Additionally, source documents and other clarification are cited in endnotes. The author takes responsibility for all errors.

Where to Purchase

Freedom Through Vigilance is available directly from:

the author (larrytart@aol.com), (www.larrytart.com) or

the publisher (www.buybooksontheweb.com).

Contributed by Tom Morris Jr.

Sergeant Thomas C. Morris, Jr.
December 1951
DET. D
2ND RSM

Shown in olive drab uniform, Sgt. Tom Morris Jr. served as a Morse intercept operator in Berlin in 1951-52. Later (in 1958), he flew intelligence-gathering missions aboard RC-47's in Korea.[5]

Germany during the Cold War

CHAPTER FOUR

USAFSS IN EUROPE, GERMANY-BASED UNITS

During the Cold War, the United States Air Force Security Service (and its successor commands) deployed intelligence gathering resources regionally in Europe, the Middle East, the Far East, Alaska, Panama and within the contiguous United States. Within Europe, USAFSS began operations in Germany in 1949 with an expansion program commencing in 1950 that fielded units in the United Kingdom, Libya, Turkey, Greece, Pakistan and Italy. In addition, USAFSS conducted limited operations during the 1950's in Newfoundland, Austria, and even Greenland. We begin our European USAFSS history with the 2nd Radio Squadron Mobile in Germany.

Tense East-West relations in Europe in 1948 and 1949 constituted a severe challenge for the U.S. Air Force Security Service as the command assumed responsibility for signals intelligence in the U.S. Air Force. As the newest member of the SIGINT community and a stepchild of the Army Security Agency, USAFSS faced the daunting task of concurrently fielding operational Air Force radio squadrons mobile in Europe, the Far East and Alaska. When USAFSS officially took control of the 2nd RSM in February 1949, the United States and the Soviet Union were embroiled in the first East-West confrontation of the Cold War.

BERLIN BLOCKADE—FIRST COLD WAR CRISIS

Soviet interference with Allied access to Berlin in the Eastern Sector of Germany caused the first major East-West confrontation of the Cold War. Under the Potsdam Agreement that divided defeated Germany into four occupation zones in 1945, Berlin had been divided into four sectors—Soviet Sector (East Berlin) and American, British and French Sectors (West Berlin). A four-power

Allied Control Council administered Berlin, but relations between the Soviet Union and its former World War II allies were antagonistic from the start. Moscow wanted the Western Allies out of Berlin.

Given Berlin's location deep within the Soviet-occupied zone of Germany (East Germany), the Soviet Red Army controlled surface access routes into West Berlin, although the Four-Power Agreement guaranteed unrestrained travel between West Germany and West Berlin. The agreement also provided for three air corridors connecting West Berlin to West Germany. West Berlin soon became a bustling capitalist island in a barren Communist wasteland, but the Western military garrisons in the city were dependent upon unrestrained travel through Communist-controlled East Germany for survival.

Trying to force the United States, Britain and France to abandon West Berlin, Joseph Stalin ordered a blockade of the city. On 24 June 1948, Red Army troops at checkpoints along the East-West German border blocked access to Autobahns, rail arteries and canals through Soviet-controlled territory to the Western Sectors of Berlin. Stalin intended to starve out the Western Allies by denying the delivery of life-sustaining essentials. The Soviet army commandant in East Berlin also announced that the Russians would not supply food to civilian residents in West Berlin.

On 25 June, the Allies began a massive "Operation Vittles" airlift of foodstuffs and coal to the besieged city. The Berlin Airlift operated around the clock (24/7) for eleven months, delivering some 2.3 million tons of food, medicine, fuel, clothing, raw materials and manufactured goods to 2.2 million grateful West Berliners. At the height of the airlift on 16 April 1949, an Allied cargo plane landed in West Berlin every minute—12,940 tons of freight were delivered that day. Failing to achieve their objective, the Russians lifted the blockade on 12 May 1949; however, the airlift continued at a reduced level through September, stockpiling supplies in the event of a future blockade.[6]

Harassment in Air Corridors

Allied transport aircrews entered the air corridors over East Germany at one to three minute intervals at a prescribed time and altitude. They followed radio beams to keep on course and maintained speed and interval within the stream of aircraft. Flights into Berlin encountered numerous problems: erratic weather, narrow flight approaches into Tempelhof Airport and Soviet harassment. The Allies also flew cargo into Gatow airfield in the British zone and Tegel Field, which Army engineers built in the French zone in only 49 days.

It was not uncommon for a pilot to leave Rhein-Main or Wiesbaden Air Base, Germany, only to find Tempelhof socked in by low overcast plus rain or snow that made it hazardous or impossible to land. A pilot literally had to fly between high-rise apartment buildings at the end of the Tempelhof runway for the landing, and had only one pass at the airfield—one opportunity to land. If weather or another factor prevented landing, the pilot returned to home base with his cargo and reentered the flying cycle.

Adding to treacherous flying conditions, Soviet forces harassed but did not attack airlift flights. The Allies logged 733 incidents of harassment in the air corridors from August 1948 to August 1949. Soviet fighter pilots buzzed planes in the corridors, flew in close formation with transports and fired off volleys in close proximity to but not at airlift planes. Releasing balloons in the air corridors, putting up rounds of flak, jamming radio frequencies and shining searchlights in pilots' eyes were other forms of harassment—the Soviet armed forces subjected the Allied airlift aircrews to virtually all types of intimidation except actual attacks.

Miraculously, no accidents or deaths were attributed to the Soviet actions, and airlift operations were surprisingly safe despite crowded flying conditions and bad winter weather. Nonetheless, while breaking the blockade, the Allies suffered some air crashes, resulting in the deaths of 31 American and 39 British patriots.

SIGINT Coverage of Berlin Blockade

The extent to which the 2nd Radio Squadron Mobile supported U.S. Air Forces Europe (USAFE) during the Soviet military harassment of Allied aircrews involved in the Berlin Airlift is unknown. When the blockade began in June 1948, the 2nd RSM belonged to the Army Security Agency, although Air Force officers were attached to the squadron to facilitate signals intelligence support to USAFE. After World War II, the 2nd RSM was retained in Europe as part of the Allied occupation force, but the first U.S. Air Force unit history for the squadron suggests that the squadron was providing little if any tactical signals intelligence in 1948-1949.

A unit of this type is normally primarily concerned with furnishing intelligence of a "strategic nature"; however, it is sometimes difficult to determine the exact value of specific radio intelligence.

Thus, the 2nd RSM appears to have provided tactical signals intelligence support only peripherally to USAFE during the Allied airlift. During World War II, the radio squadrons mobile devised innovative and effective tactical SIGINT support to air force commanders in the field, but all that expertise was lost in demobilization after the war. Developing tactical SIGINT direct support techniques in postwar Europe took years of trial and error traffic analysis and reporting by a new generation of intercept operators, linguists and analysts.

2ND RSM ACTIVATED IN GERMANY

The first U.S. Air Force unit history for the 2nd Radio Squadron Mobile covered the period 1 February 1949 to 31 July 1949. It describes the activation of the first operational USAFSS organization in Europe. Starting with a "chronological summary," the unit historian, First Lt. Wyatt E. Hines, provided background on the heritage and current status of the 2nd RSM.

The 139th Signal Radio Intelligence Company, stationed at MacDill Field, Florida, was reorganized and redesignated as the 2d Radio Squadron Mobile, Germany, on 16 March 1944. . . . . The Squadron on completion of a certain amount of training was sent to the European Theater. Historical records of its combat service are very poorly written and in no way complete; however, these records are being arranged and compiled for forwarding in future reports.

In preparation for the relocation of the 2nd RSM, the squadron underwent a special inspection in May 1944 (see Appendix C). Per War Department cable, the U.S. Forces, European Theater, transferred the 2nd RSM from the Army Air Forces to the

Department of the Army (Army Security Agency) on 13 December 1945 (see Appendix D). (For members of the squadron, their branch of service did not change; they continued to be part of the Signal Corps.) The 2nd Radio Squadron Mobile remained at Bad Vilbel, near Frankfurt, Germany, until early 1947 when the ASA relocated it to Herzo Base, Herzogenaurach, Germany.[7]

Contributed by Joe Mishkofski

2nd AAF RSM, Herzogenaurach, Germany, 1948

The ASA also had at least two other signals intelligence units— 6th Detachment, 2nd Signal Service Battalion and 114th Signal Service Company at Herzo Base in the late 1940's. Unit histories for the 2nd RSM while assigned to the ASA are not available. The initial Air Force unit history for the 2nd RSM described in detail the transfer of the squadron from the ASA to USAFSS.

2ND RSM TRANSFERRED TO USAFSS

Effective 1 February 1949, U.S. Army Headquarters transferred the 2nd Radio Squadron Mobile at Herzo Base to the Department of the Air Force, with further assignment to the United States Air Force Security Service (see Appendix E). Wording of the Army order effecting the transfer was ambiguous and later raised questions regarding the regular army personnel being transferred to the Air Force.

> *Department of the Army personnel currently assigned to this unit are hereby assigned to the Department of the Air Force for further assignment with that unit. No change in status, duty assignment or departmental status of personnel is involved.*

The joint Army-Air Force document that authorized the transfer of the squadron from Army to Air Force control dealt with the transfer of "troop basis spaces and civilian personnel authorizations." The Army personnel involved in the transfer were to be on temporary duty, not permanently reassigned to the Air Force. Air Force officers who had been serving with the ASA to participate "in certain operational and training activities of the Army Security Agency" were also transferred to USAFSS. When USAFSS assumed control of the 2nd Radio Squadron Mobile, the unit was barely functioning.

> *Prior to its departure from Herzo Base, the unit had been operational as well as conducting the Herzo Base Radio Intercept Operator School. However, when it was practically certain that the unit would be transferred, it was so cut in strength that its operations as far as intercept were severely curtailed.*

The minimally functioning 2nd RSM constituted Air Force Security Service's second SIGINT intercept operations in February 1949; the 1st Radio Squadron Mobile in Japan was operating in the Far East at approximately the same level of effectiveness.

Army Signal Corps Capt. Grady F. Bryan commanded the 2nd RSM when the squadron became an Air Force unit; Lt. Hines was the operations officer. The other two officers in the unit were First Lt. Carl J. Koehler (adjutant and executive officer) and First Lt. John D. Moors (motor pool officer). To build up operational expertise in traffic analysis before relocating, the squadron detailed two men to the Traffic Analysis Section of a colocated ASA intercept detachment. Planning began to move the 2nd RSM from Herzo Base to a new Air Force home in Germany.

2ND RSM RELOCATION

USAFSS informed USAFE that either Camp Pieri or Darmstadt—tentatively selected sites—would be acceptable for an intercept station and requested that USAFE take action to initiate relocation of the 2nd RSM. A USAFSS COMSEC unit, Detachment D, 136th Communications Security Squadron, was based at Camp Pieri (Freudenberg Kaserne), Wiesbaden-Dotzheim.

In a Movement Directive dated 25 February 1949 (Appendix F), USAFE directed the 2nd RSM commander to move the unit without delay on a permanent change of station from Herzo Base to Darmstadt, Germany. Movement was to be by vehicles organically assigned to the squadron. Traveling a day apart as two elements to maintain intercept operations, the 2nd Radio Squadron Mobile relocated to Ernst Ludwig Kaserne, a Darmstadt Sub-Post facility, on 26 and 27 February 1949.

Contributed by Joe Mishkofski

Darmstadt Sub-Post, Germany, 1949

2nd RSM Facilities at Ludwig Kaserne

The squadron moved into Building # 17, a large World War II multistory barracks that housed the entire squadron. Conditions were very crowded, especially since a major part of the attic of Bldg # 17 that was to be 2nd RSM Operations was uninhabitable. The basement housed Unit Supply, Squadron Headquarters and the administrative section. In addition, 2nd RSM enlisted personnel shared the lower floors of the building with another Air Force unit.

Operations occupied parts of the attic that were habitable, with Ops Administration sharing a small office with the Signal Center. The Intercept Section was cramped, and the traffic analysts worked in a small office that lacked table space and space to hang wall maps and charts. Upon completion of rehabilitation of a section of the attic on 23 May 1949, the space crunch eased somewhat for the CW Intercept and Traffic Analysis Sections, but the modifications to the attic dragged out into the spring of 1950. The troop billeting situation was remedied in June when the squadron occupied all of Bldg # 17.

The 2nd RSM established its main direction finding site about a mile from Operations, 500 yards west of the Autobahn on the Griesheim airstrip. A second DF set was installed in Bldg # 17 for training purposes. The squadron also had its own Communications Section, Installation Section (wire, antenna and power subsections), mess hall and motor pool. The unit motor pool set up its shop in buildings on the southwest corner of the Darmstadt Sub-Post.

The Darmstadt Sub-Post had two theaters, one in the Quartermaster School area and one on Ludwig Kaserne. There were also a snack bar, library and education center on post, but no post exchange and few other recreational facilities. Another snack bar and post exchange was located in the QM School area. The gymnasium, bowling alley, chapel and two Enlisted Men's Clubs were spread around the city of Darmstadt within a five-mile radius of the Sub-Post. Plans had been completed to install a small post exchange in the snack bar by the squadron.

Although one of the smaller tenants on a U.S. Army post, the 2nd RSM established a precedent during its first few months at Darmstadt that other USAFSS overseas squadrons later followed for decades. During the spring of 1949, the squadron furnished 70% of the Darmstadt Sub-Post baseball team. A substantial number of the post football team's members were also 2nd RSM personnel in 1949.

Responsibility to Higher Command

The 2nd Radio Squadron Mobile had dual chains of command. The commander reported to USAFSS Headquarters in Texas and USAFE Headquarters in Wiesbaden, Germany. Accepting tasking from either USAFSS or USAFE, the squadron provided copies of signals intelligence reports to both headquarters. USAFE provided the squadron logistic and administrative support, and the 2nd RSM functioned under the operational control of the USAFE Director of Intelligence. The squadron assigned an officer and two airmen to the USAFE Intelligence Division to facilitate the sharing of SIGINT with Headquarters USAFE. On 24 May, Air Force Director of Intelligence Maj. Gen. Charles P. Cabell visited the 2nd RSM operations compound, showing high-level interest in the squadron's mission.

CW (Morse) Intercept Section—February-July 1949

The CW Intercept Section was composed of one officer and 28 enlisted men in February 1949. Being the only officer in operations at the time, Lt. Wyatt Hines wore the hats of the operations officer, traffic analysis officer and DF officer, plus all other officer functions in operations. As additional officers arrived in the unit, Hines shed many of his secondary jobs. With 32 intercept operators and one clerk assigned at the end of July, the Intercept Section was still undermanned although the situation was improving. Intercept operators were arriving from radio school at Scott Field[8] with very good code speeds and a good knowledge of radio work. The squadron lost approximately one trick[9] (10 intercept operators) through the transfer of the Regular Army personnel back to ASA in July.

Traffic Analysis Section—February-July 1949

For security purposes, the squadron referred to the Traffic Analysis Section as "Traffic Center." Considered one of the most critical functions in Operations, the Traffic Analysis Section was probably least capable of performing the squadron mission. In February 1949, the T/A Section consisted of three unskilled men with about three months of training. By the end of July, the section had grown to one officer and eight enlisted men, plus a liaison officer and two analysts on detached duty in the USAFE

Intelligence Division. The personnel in the T/A Section had no formal training, and the unit history contained a statement that "men assigned to this section should be trained in the Zone of Interior prior to shipment overseas."

Planned 2nd RSM DF Net

The 2nd Radio Squadron Mobile's Darmstadt/Griesheim direction finding site was an outstation on the Army Security Agency DF network in Europe that included three Army DF stations. Because the Army continuously had high priority DF missions against Soviet military targets, the network seldom accepted DF missions from the 2nd RSM. To remedy this situation, the squadron decided to form its own DF net. The unit planned to drop out of the ASA DF network as soon as it could acquire the DF equipment and set up three operational DF stations of its own.

Mission and Obsolete Equipment Incompatible

As the unit historian pointed out in the first Air Force unit history for the 2nd RSM, the table of organization and equipment[10] that defined the make-up of the squadron had not kept pace with the unit's current mission.

The present T/O & E under which the radio squadrons mobile are organized is not adequate for present requirements and conditions. Most of the equipment listed under the T/O mentioned is now obsolete. More important is the fact that radio squadrons are no longer performing MOBILE MISSIONS as their PRIMARY OBJECTIVE. Mobile teams should by all means be retained, but stationary or SEMI-FIXED equipment should also be provided. One serious deficiency is noted in lack of teletype and modern, fixed-station intercept and recording equipment.

The equipment that the 2nd RSM inherited from the Army in 1949 was essentially the same portable huts, intercept receivers, radio communications gear, vehicles and field kitchen that shipped to Europe with the Army Air Forces 2nd Radio Squadron Mobile in 1945. The unit motor pool was authorized 46 vehicles, 27 of which were deuce-and-a-half trucks. Most of the 2 1/2-ton trucks hauled HO-28 or HO-17 huts that housed signal equipment in mobile operations, although most squadron operations were now accomplished in garrison.

Supply and Spare Parts Issues

The Squadron Supply Section was organized to issue both quartermaster and signal supply items. It functioned fairly efficiently as far as normal items of issue were concerned. However, scarce or critical items, especially repair parts for signal equipment, were nearly impossible to procure through standard channels and often had to be requested directly from USAFSS Headquarters.

Working with the unit's out-of-date table of organization and equipment posed a special procurement dilemma. The requisition of all items not included on the T/O & E had to be submitted in "project" form. Project approval constituted a waiver to the T/O & E. Using the project requisition process for both large and small acquisitions became the norm for years to come in Security Service.

Detachments and Other USAFSS Units

The 2nd RSM had no subordinate units or detachments through 31 July 1949, but its mobile equipment was used extensively later when it began fielding detachments. On a related note, the squadron was aware of, but had had "no relations with the 136th detachment"—the USAFSS COMSEC unit at Wiesbaden (Camp Pieri).

Personnel Actions and Squadron Strength

Air Force Capt. Charles D. Pryor assumed command of the 2nd RSM on 10 March 1949, replacing Signal Corps Capt. Bryan, who returned to the ASA at Herzo Base. Capt. Pryor immediately called for and was provided an inspection by the USAFSS Inspector General. In typical military style, the IG inspection emphasized personnel matters: Is each airman working in his designated MOS (military occupational specialty)? Is each airman's "201" file current? Are training records up-to-date?, etc. Little effort appears to have been spent inspecting how well or how poorly the unit performed its operational mission.

The most obvious change resulting from the IG inspection was a shuffling of officers to align them with the primary MOS reflected in their records. Capt. Gordon H. J. Fleisch, formerly the squadron executive officer, became the operations officer. Squadron special order # 70, dated 11 August 1949 (Appendix G) lists the officers in the squadron along with their primary duties and additional duties.

Squadron strength grew rapidly from four Army Signal Corps officers and 118 regular army (RA) enlisted men on 1 February 1949, when the 2nd RSM became an Air Force unit, to nine USAF officers and 196 airmen on 31 July 1949. Most of the new airmen—most of those who had not been part of the squadron in February—had arrived in the squadron after orientation training with the 8th Radio Squadron Mobile at Brooks AFB, Texas.

Squadron Morale and VD Rate

During the summer of 1949, there was heated debate between the ASA and USAFSS regarding the disposition of the RA personnel who initially transferred with the 2nd RSM to the Air Force in February. The drawn-out discussions adversely affected morale in the squadron according to the unit history ending 31 July 1949.

Morale is at present higher than in the month of June. Inasmuch as a great contributing factor to morale is Special Services Activities, these activities are encouraged. The Squadron Mess is another contribution factor. During the months from February to July, the VD [venereal disease] rate and delinquency rate were comparatively low.

Due to the uncertainty of pending transfers from the squadron to Army Security Agency, morale reached a new low in the month of July during the first two weeks. When the transfer situation was finally clarified, an almost visual rise in morale was observed. Over 100 men were affected by the transfers pending. It is found, however, that the majority of the VD cases and delinquents were largely responsible to a minority who are normally classed as "chronic offenders." Discussions have been held by squadron officers, and airmen in this category will be placed before appropriate boards for separation from the Air Force.

As a preventive against being infected with venereal disease, the Air Force offered VD Prophylactic Kits and condoms to its airmen for the asking at squadron orderly rooms.

Personnel Transfer Issues Resolved

There was disagreement between the Army and the Air Force regarding a transfer of the RA men assigned to the 2nd RSM. The Signal Corps wanted "their" troops back, while the vast majority of the RA soldiers found life in the new Air Force decidedly better than what awaited them if they returned to the ASA intercept site at Herzo Base, Germany. The 2nd RSM also needed the men to perform its signals intelligence mission. Ultimately, the men themselves cast the deciding vote.

Each Army man still serving with the 2nd RSM in July 1949 had the option of switching from the Department of the Army to the Department of the Air Force. Two of the Signal Corps officers, 1st Lt.'s Carl J. Koehler and Wyatt E. Hines, transferred from the Signal Corps to the USAF on 6 July and 25 July 1949, respectively. Remarkably, only nineteen of the 100-plus RA enlisted men chose to remain in the Army and return to Herzo Base. The nineteen soldiers transferred from the 2nd RSM back to the Army Security Agency on 26 July 1949. The remaining Signal Corps officer serving with the 2nd RSM, First Lt. Moors, transferred to the Air Force later in the summer. For the first time, the 2nd Radio Squadron Mobile had no Signal Corps personnel in its ranks.

Summary of Progress

The unit history summarized progress made during the 2nd Radio Squadron Mobile's first six months as a USAFSS organization. The squadron had probably undergone more changes during that period than it would encounter at any time in the future.

The transition period through which it is now progressing should be increasingly less difficult due to installations now completed, supply of men and materials being expedited, clearances being rapidly received, and many other factors <u>not</u> now considered problems to be solved.

Monthly historical reports were to be submitted in the future. The next unit history for the 2nd Radio Squadron Mobile that is available to the author covers 1-31 January 1950. However, several former members of the squadron have shared a wealth of individual memories and personal records that offer additional insight into the 2nd RSM history for the late 1940's and early 1950's.

Joseph A. Mishkofski—ASA to USAFSS

At age 17, Private Joseph A. Mishkofski received a letter on Army Security Agency letterhead dated 6 August 1947, welcoming him to the agency. The letter that was signed by Col. Harold G. Hayes, Chief, Army Security Agency, stated in part:

I have been advised that you have enlisted in the United States Army and have elected to serve with the Army Security Agency. I take this opportunity to welcome you to the Agency, and to hope that you will find your service interesting and profitable.

Neither Col. Hayes nor Pvt. Mishkofski could have imagined at the time that Joe Mishkofski would be transferring from the ASA to U.S. Air Force Security Service in 1949. Mishkofski enlisted in the Army on 18 July 1947. He learned Morse code in the Radio School at Fort Monmouth, New Jersey, before arriving at Vint Hill Farms Station, Warrington, Virginia, for intercept operator training in October 1948. With a shortage of intercept operators at all ASA intercept sites, Pfc. Mishkofski had his choice of ASA assignments upon completion of the radio intercept course.

- Vint Hill Farms Station
- Two Rock Ranch, Petaluma, California
- Germany
- Japan
- Hawaii
- Asmara, Somaliland.

Adventuresome and eager to see Europe, Mishkofski chose Germany and reported to the 2nd RSM at Herzo Base, Herzogenaurach, Germany, on 15 January 1949.

Contributed by Joe Mishkofski

Pfc. Joseph Mishkofski, Herzo Base, Germany, 1949

He had barely unpacked his duffel bag when alerted that the squadron was moving to Darmstadt. He traveled with the squadron to its new home on 26 February 1949. On 31 May 1949, the 2nd Radio Squadron Mobile published orders realigning the rank structure of both the Army and Air Force enlisted men assigned to the squadron.[11] Pfc. Mishkofski was redesignated as Cpl. Mishkofski. Air Force Pfc.'s likewise became corporals.

Being a natural athlete, Mishkofski fitted in well with the "jockstrap" culture at Darmstadt Sub-Post. He was one of thirteen squadron members who played on the post baseball team. On 16 June 1949, Mishkofski traveled back to Herzo Base for a pair of games against the Herzo Base team. On 4 July, a 2nd RSM baseball team beat a Quartermaster School Center team in a Darmstadt Sub-Post championship game in which the winning team members won a three-day pass. Life was good at Darmstadt, and the RA enlisted men wanted no part of returning to ASA duties at Herzo Base.

Contributed by Joe Mishkofski

Cpl. Joseph Mishkofski, Darmstadt, Germany, 1950

According to a corrected set of special orders that the 2nd RSM issued on 15 July 1949, Cpl. Mishkofski and 94 other Army enlisted men transferred from the Department of Army to the Department of Air Force with effective dates in early May 1949.[12] The late publication date of the transfer orders explains the related morale problems discussed earlier.

For some airmen, morale must have been really high in the squadron over the Christmas holidays in 1949. Recently promoted Sgt. Mishkofski was one of twelve 2nd RSM airmen who traveled to Garmisch-Berchtesgaden, Germany, on five days of permissive temporary duty "for the purposes of participating in recreational activities." Mishkofski accompanied another 2nd RSM group (nine enlisted men) to Garmisch on permissive TDY for five days in early April 1950. The Special Services Center at Darmstadt Sub-Post arranged the permissive TDY's.

DETACHMENT A, 2ND RSM, ROTHWESTEN

In July 1949, the 2nd Radio Squadron Mobile finally received requisitioned AN/CRD-2 direction finding sets that the unit needed to update its existing DF site at Griesheim and activate a new DF outstation at Rothwesten Air Base, near Kassel, Germany. Rothwesten was a former Luftwaffe pilot training base.[13] To expedite creation of a USAFSS DF net in Europe, Capt. Pryor obtained approval from USAFE and ASA to colocate a small cadre of Morse intercept operators (Detachment A, 2nd RSM) with an ASA station (Detachment A, 114th Signal Security Company) at Rothwesten. He designated First Lt. Arthur W. Banne as the commander of Detachment A—the 2nd RSM's first subordinate unit.

In July, Lt. Banne traveled to Rothwesten to work out details with the ASA detachment and the 601st AC&W Squadron to obtain support for a 2nd RSM detachment on base. As Rothwesten's USAFE host unit, the 601st agreed to provide billeting and mess facilities for the 2nd RSM detachment, as it was already providing for the ASA detachment. Detachment A, 114th SSC, made space available for a USAFSS operations center.

On 15 August 1949, Lt. Banne led a ten-man team of Morse intercept/DF operators that activated Det A, 2nd RSM at Rothwesten. Cpl. Joseph Mishkofski—a member of the initial team—served as a DF operator at the base for a month. In an email message to the author in 2006, Mishkofski described the layout of Det A, 2nd RSM at Rothwesten. They set up the DF site and their antennas near the runway, and opened an operations center on the second floor of the barracks. Their CW intercept position was an HF SCR-399 radio in an HO-17 hut mounted on a "6 x 6"—a deuce-and-a-half truck. "Cramped quarters."

The 2nd RSM controlled its detachment's operations—Morse intercept and DF only—at Rothwesten, while the ASA detachment, which included both Morse and voice DF and intercept operators, worked under the control of the 114th SSC at Herzo Base. Mishkofski returned to 2nd RSM Headquarters at Ludwig Kaserne in September 1949. A third 2nd RSM DF site was already in the planning stage.

DETACHMENT B, 2ND RSM, SCHLEISSHEIM

Located in the northern outskirts of Munich, about five miles east of Dachau, the 2nd RSM's next DF site was also established on a former Luftwaffe airfield. SSgt. Howard R. Colvin led a small 2nd RSM team that set up Detachment B, 2nd RSM at

Schleissheim airfield (aka Oberschleissheim) in late 1949. Sgt. Thomas P. Hunter and Cpl. Isaac H. Borland were also charter members of Det B, Hunter as a radio maintenance technician and Borland as a motor pool driver. Borland recalls installing the DF station between Christmas and New Year's Eve 1949.

As ASA Regular Army troops before transferring into USAFSS, all three men had arrived in Darmstadt with the squadron in February 1949. Borland still has a copy of the Christmas card that the squadron sent him in 1949—"the only Christmas card I ever received from a military outfit." In discussing his time with Detachment B, Borland remembers celebrating his 21st birthday in a gasthaus just outside the base in February 1950. He returned to Ernst Ludwig Kaserne in June 1950. First Lt. Daniel M. (Buster) Beadle assumed command of Detachment B during the summer of 1950. The 2nd RSM continued to operate a detachment at Schleissheim into 1951.

ADDING MORE RSM'S IN 1949

While expanding the capabilities of the 2nd Radio Squadron Mobile in Germany, Air Force Security Service was concurrently creating additional intercept squadrons in Texas. USAFSS activated the 3rd RSM and 10th RSM at Brooks AFB in the second half of 1949. The 3rd and 10th RSM's, which were ultimately deployed in Alaska and England, respectively, are addressed in later chapters.

2nd RSM Status—31 December 1949

All in all, the 2nd Radio Squadron Mobile ended 1949 on an upbeat note. Since its transfer to the Air Force, it had almost doubled in personnel, and its intercept operators and analysts were becoming proficient at their jobs. A five-page mimeographed Christmas Dinner Menu for the 2nd RSM, 25 December 1949, not only listed a traditional Christmas dinner—roast turkey with all the trimmings, plus cigars—it also included each person in the unit by rank and name. Still commanded by Capt. Pryor, the squadron strength was eleven officers and 225 enlisted men, including thirteen cooks who prepared the Christmas dinner. A list of officers by job title dated 11 August 1949 had changed little by December 1949.

2nd RSM Officers— December 1949		
Rank	Name	Title (Primary Duty)
Capt.	Charles D. Pryor	Commander, 2nd RSM
Capt.	Gordon H. J. Fleisch	Operations Officer
Capt.	Campbell Y. Jackson	Liaison Officer (USAFE DCS/IN)
Capt.	Kenneth R. Slater	Probably replaced Capt. Jackson
1st Lt.	Arthur W. Banne	Commander, Det A, Rothwesten
1st Lt.	William F. Fairchild	DF Officer
1st Lt.	Wyatt E. Hines	CW Intercept Officer
1st Lt.	Carl J. Koehler	Executive Officer
1st Lt.	John D. Moors	Motor Transportation Officer
1st Lt.	Edward R. Murray	Traffic Officer
1st Lt.	John Valersky	Communications Officer
2nd Lt.	Hollis A. Benson Jr.	Reported for duty in August 1949

With a shortage of officers, most were in charge of ancillary functions in addition to their primary duties. Like their officer counterparts, the key enlisted men in the table that follows had only limited military experience in July 1949, but they were "seasoned veterans" by the end of the year.

2nd RSM Key Enlisted Personnel—July 1949		
Rank	Name	Title (Primary Duty)
TSgt.	Jose E. Gutierrez	CW Intercept Operator
TSgt.	William Turner	CW Intercept Operator
TSgt.	Charles E. West	CW Intercept Operator
Sgt.	Gordon L. Younts	Personnel
SSgt.	Glen E. Wright	Medical
SSgt.	Bronislaw Netowski	Motor Transport
SSgt.	Charles J. Riccio	Supply
SSgt.	Howard R. Colvin	CW Intercept Operator/DF
Sgt.	Robert G. Trowbridge	CW Intercept Operator
SSgt.	Salvatore J. LoGatto	CW Intercept Operator/DF
SSgt.	Earl Kennard	Mess
SSgt.	John W. Fleming	Outside Maintenance
SSgt.	Walter Kenney	CW Intercept Operator

The 2nd RSM was becoming a professional organization but lacked experienced leaders. Not surprisingly, after only eleven months of signals intelligence operations, USAFSS had a dearth of

NCO's in the top-three grades. TSgt. Walter G. Soucy (later promoted to MSgt.) joined the unit in the latter half of 1949 as squadron first sergeant. In December 1949, the 2nd RSM had no master sergeants or warrant officers, and only seven technical sergeants and eighteen staff sergeants. For the most part, the USAFSS experts in the operational career fields—Morse intercept operators, linguists, traffic analysts and cryptanalysts—in 1949 and 1950 were SSgt.'s and Sgt.'s. Many of the 2nd RSM's officers and airmen later became USAFSS experts in their fields.

2nd RSM USAFSS Operations—Year II

Going into 1950, the Western Allies, and by extension the 2nd Radio Squadron Mobile, were convinced that a Soviet military invasion of West Germany was imminent. The threat had steadily gained credence since Britain's wartime Prime Minister Winston Churchill made his famous "Sinews of Peace" address in Missouri on 5 March 1946.

From Stettin on the Baltic to Trieste in the Adriatic, an iron curtain has descended across the continent.

As Churchill explained, behind that curtain Russia had established a sphere of influence over Eastern Europe and was planning a march on the West. Communist seizure of power in Czechoslovakia in February, followed by the Soviet blockade of Berlin in June 1948 and the Soviet explosion of its first atomic bomb in September 1949, added to the hysteria. The Truman Administration responded with increased budgets for intelligence gathering, and the 2nd Radio Squadron Mobile was at the forefront of the largest Air Force build-up of signals intelligence capabilities in history.

2nd RSM Unit History—Jan-Feb 1950

The 2nd Radio Squadron Mobile personnel strength remained stable in January and February 1950 with twelve officers and 219 airmen assigned in January, and fourteen officers and 214 airmen on 28 February. Charles D. Pryor, the commander, was promoted to major on 1 March 1950. The chart that follows shows the allocation of unit members available for duty on 31 January by section.

2nd RSM Personnel by Section—Jan 1950			
HQ	Supply	Mess	Medical
2 Off	2 Off	0 Off	0 Off
12 Amn	8 Amn	12 Amn	1 Amn
Operations	Motor Pool	Traffic Cen	Maint.
2 Off	1 Off	0 Off	0 Off
53 Amn	21 Amn	9 Amn	12 Amn
Control Sec	Wire Section	Signal Ctr	Guard
1 Off	0 Off	1 Off	0 Off
12 Amn	2 Amn	10 Amn	5 Amn
Sqdn Duty	Comm	Switchboard	Unassigned
2 Off	1 Off	0 Off	0 Off
2 Amn	1 Amn	6 Amn	0 Amn

The 53 airmen in Operations included CW intercept and DF operators plus a clerk. An additional 48 personnel were away from base on temporary duty—including two airmen at USAFE/IN, and CW intercept and DF operators serving at Rothwesten and Schleissheim, plus some attending schools away from Darmstadt.

Later in the year, the unit experienced a population explosion, paving the way to field additional detached units and activate additional USAFSS squadrons in Europe. The squadron roster at the end of 1950 included 35 officers and 467 airmen.

With another year's signals intelligence experience on the books, squadron officer leadership had increased dramatically by December 1950. The unit now had three majors, twelve captains, fifteen first lieutenants and five second lieutenants. In the top three NCO grades, there were seven master sergeants, eleven technical sergeants and forty-seven staff sergeants. In addition, many of the 133 sergeants and 152 corporals had become seasoned professionals in the past year. Among the airmen were several Russian linguists who were available for voice intercept duty after completing six to twelve-month courses in Russian.

Facilities Status—January 1950

Providing an update on squadron facilities in January 1950, the unit historian reported that a small PX (post exchange) had been opened on Ludwig Kaserne and that it carried "necessary items for the airmen." Regarding operations facilities, the German contractor did not complete the attic rehabilitation according to the plan. There were incomplete wiring, incomplete installation of heating equipment and light fixtures, a leaky roof, cracked plaster walls, and incomplete paint work—all of which had to be rectified before the area could be occupied. Finally, some good facilities news—the third DF site was now operational at Schleissheim.

2nd RSM DF Net Established

With the activation of the DF outstations at Rothwesten and Schleissheim, plus its primary Griesheim DF site, the 2nd Radio Squadron Mobile was able to triangulate DF target bearing results to pinpoint enemy targets. Now capable of operating as a standalone center, the squadron took the Griesheim DF outstation out of the ASA DF net and began operating the USAFSS European DF Net. Commencing in January 1950, the three DF sites in the 2nd RSM's DF net were referred to as Site # 21 (Griesheim), Site # 22 (Rothwesten) and Site # 23 (Schleissheim). Later in 1951, Air Force Security Service adopted numeric detachment designators for each squadron's detachments.

William M. (Bill) Baker, who served with the 2nd RSM (1950-1952), recently recalled his association with the unit's DF sites. As a DF operator, he spend time at all of the squadron's DF sites. He remembers the 2nd RSM's original DF Net by the three stations' codenames. Griesheim (Main Darmstadt DF site) was "Sawdust"; Rothwesten was "Hammerhead"; and Schleissheim was "Rocket."

DF Net Status—January 1950

The unit history for January 1950 provided an overview of the 2nd RSM's DF net personnel and DF site facilities. One officer and 33 airmen were assigned against unit authorizations for three officers and 95 airmen. Ten operators (five DF operators and five intercept operators) were on TDY at both Rothwesten and Schleissheim. The operators could support requests for DF bearings, but the number of "Control" (DF evaluation) personnel was not adequate to fully evaluate mission results and perform reporting with graphs and charts.

The DF Section had three sites operating around the clock. At the end of January 1950, the three-station net was complete, but many improvements needed to be made to produce an effective, highly efficient DF operation.

The squadron was in the process of using an SCR-399 radio in an HO-17 hut mounted on a deuce-and-a-half truck to travel around the "zone" as a transmitter that would send test messages from known locations. These test transmissions would facilitate the calibration of each site's DF equipment and would maintain a continuous check on the operation of the 2nd RSM DF net.

FIRST VOICE INTERCEPT OPS IN USAFSS

During its first operational year (through January 1950), the United States Air Force Security Service's signals intelligence mission involved the interception and exploitation of CW (Morse) traffic only—no voice intercept mission. The American military services had trained German and Japanese linguists and had a voice intercept mission in the final years of World War II, but did not begin training Russian linguists-voice interceptors until the late 1940's.[14] Former Morse intercept operators in the 2nd Radio Squadron Mobile, SSgt. Walter Kenney and Sgt.'s Robert E. Draughon and Virgil C. Fordham, graduated from the army's Russian Liaison Agent and Interpreters School, Oberammergau, in the German Alps in early 1950. They became the first voice intercept operators in USAFSS.

For the first time, the personnel chart in the unit history (February 1950) reflected the existence of a 2nd RSM radio-telephone (R/T) voice intercept mission. In addition, the strength of the Intercept Section (primarily Morse intercept operators) had almost doubled in six months—33 assigned in July 1949 and 65 in February 1950.

Intercept Section Personnel—28 Feb 1950			
Duty Status	CW	R/T	Total
TDY Rothwesten	5	0	5
TDY Munich/Schleissheim	5	0	5
On Leave in ZI	0	1	1
TDY to another duty station	2	0	2
Clerks (MOS 405)	4	0	4
Present for duty (Intercept Operators)	44	2	46
TDY Language training at Oberammergau	0	2	2
Total personnel assigned	60	5	65

TSgt. Allen E. Schrock, a communications chief (MOS 542) in training for his radio intelligence control chief specialty (543), was the NCOIC of the Intercept Section, while other enlisted men were being assigned to the unit's new Control Section.[15]

2ND RSM—FIRST RUSSIAN LINGUISTS

According to the unit history, SSgt. Kinney, NCOIC of the Voice Intercept Section, recently upgraded as a skilled voice intercept operator (MOS 538)—months later, he was not listed as a member of the organization. SSgt. Fordham had upgraded to the translator-linguist MOS 267 and was in on-the-job training as a "538." Sgt. Draughon, also a 267, would enter training as a 538 after he returned from leave in America.[16]

Cpl. Edward C. Rye and Pfc. John L. Stief, who recently arrived from Army Language School, Monterey, California, were 267's in OJT. SSgt. Ambrose H. Jackson and Sgt. Norman R. Opitz were currently in language training at Oberammergau. Having arrived as Morse intercept operators, both were to be assigned to the R/T Section upon return to the squadron.

Other Early Key Linguists in the 2nd RSM

Other NCO's who became voice intercept operators in the 2nd RSM in 1950-1951 included: TSgt. Gordon D. McKenzie and SSgt.'s Henry P. Stacewicz, Stanley E. Kresge, and Louis J. DuLong. In a discussion with the author in February 2006, retired Chief Master Sergeant McKenzie explained how he became a Russian linguist and recalled voice intercept operations in the 2nd RSM in the early 1950's.

While working in personnel in California in 1950, TSgt. McKenzie responded to a bulletin seeking volunteers to train as Russian linguists. Believing he would attend the Army Language School in Monterey, California, he volunteered, left his wife Dorothy in California and proceeded to Brooks AFB, Texas, to await a language class.

The USAFSS quota for his preferred class at ALS at Monterey was filled, so USAFSS offered him a class slot in a Russian language course in Oberammergau, Germany. SSgt. Stacewicz had volunteered for the same over-quota class at Monterey. Stacewicz and McKenzie became close friends while they awaited reassignment at Brooks AFB. They reported for duty in the 2nd RSM at Darmstadt in early July 1950. TSgt. McKenzie began language classes at Oberammergau right away and became NCOIC of the squadron's Voice Intercept Section shortly after graduating from the language course in early 1951. By that time, the squadron operated four voice intercept positions on the fourth floor (in the attic) in Bldg # 17 on Ernst Ludwig Kaserne.

Pending receipt of his special access clearance, SSgt. Stacewicz served as NCOIC of the 2nd RSM Air Police Section. He attended the next Russian class at Oberammergau. After graduating in the fall of 1951, Henry "Hank" Stacewicz joined the other linguists in the 2nd RSM's Voice Intercept Section at Darmstadt.

SSgt.'s Kresge and DuLong reported to the 2nd RSM in 1951 after completing the six-month Russian course in Monterey. This cadre of Russian linguists played a major role in developing the voice intercept missions of new USAFSS units that evolved in Europe during the 1950's.

SSgt. Richard "Dick" Gorman also attended a Russian course at Oberammergau but failed to graduate. He cross-trained to the cryptanalysis career field after returning to the 2nd RSM and later served as a division chief in the Air Force Special Communications Center at Kelly AFB, Texas, as a civil servant.

DET C, 2ND RSM, BREMERHAVEN

In the spring of 1950, Second Lt. Hollis Benson Jr. and TSgt. Charles E. West led a team north from Darmstadt to the port city of Bremerhaven, Germany, to activate the 2nd Radio Squadron Mobile's third detachment—Detachment C, 2nd RSM. The detachment's home was in the "Staging Area" at the Carl Schurz Kaserne, a former Luftwaffe airfield.

Bremerhaven—"Zeppelinhafen"

Located on the North Sea in northwestern Germany, Bremerhaven lies on the east bank of the mouth of the Weser River. It was one of Nazi Germany's most important harbors and continues to be one of Europe's busiest ports. By 1939, the Kriegsmarine (German Navy) had outfitted Bremerhaven as a "Zeppelinhafen"— a port capable of accommodating an aircraft carrier.

Cargo Ship at Dock, Bremerhaven, 1961

The fourth largest container port in Europe (16th largest in the world), Bremerhaven imports/exports more automobiles than any city in Europe except Rotterdam.[17] Most service personnel with auto-shipping privileges who have served in Germany shipped a car through the Bremerhaven Port.

American Auto being loaded on a Cargo Ship,
Bremerhaven, 1961

The Kriegsmarine laid the keel of the *Graf Zeppelin*, an aircraft carrier, in Kiel in 1936, and Bremerhaven was destined to become her homeport. The *Graf Zeppelin was l*aunched in 1938, but infighting within the Nazi regime intervened. Although 95 percent completed, the *Graf Zeppelin* was never completed and commissioned.[18] Allied bombers pretty much destroyed the city of Bremerhaven during World War II, but deliberately spared vital port facilities to provide useable Allied harbor supply capabilities after the war.

Carl Schurz Kaserne—Staging Area

Situated in the heart of the port area in the Weddewarden District of north Bremerhaven, the Carl Schurz Kaserne with its grass airstrip was built in 1927, and the Luftwaffe took over the airfield in 1935. During World War II, the Luftwaffe conducted mine search missions and other air operations from the Kaserne, and in April 1945 moved its missile and rocket test and development facilities from Peenemünde to Bremerhaven.

At the end of the war, the Allies captured much of the missile technology in hangars at Schurz Kaserne. Five years later, Air Force Security Service established an intercept site in one of the hangars. While Bremerhaven is located in what became the British Occupation Zone in 1945, the U.S. Army took control of the port facilities and Schurz Kaserne. Located next to the passenger and cargo port terminals, the U.S. Army used the Kaserne as its "Staging Area" to accommodate military personnel arriving and departing Germany by ship. Hence, the derivation of Staging Area.

Det C, 2nd RSM Operations

The Detachment C men erected their antennas and parked their DF van by a former flight line, across the runway from where they created their operations compound. They set up their intercept equipment—a couple of receivers initially—in Bldg # 103 (an unused combination hangar and control tower). Bremerhaven had won out over Bremen in a trade-off to determine where to establish the 2nd RSM's newest intercept site. Det C personnel were billeted in a separate Kaserne at the "Marine Barracks."

Marine Barracks, Bremerhaven, 1951

Detachment C was operating "full blast" in August 1950 when SSgt. Harold E. Bly reported for duty. Bly discussed his 2nd RSM assignments with the author in 2006. After completing Morse intercept operator training at Brooks AFB, he reported for duty in the 2nd RSM at Darmstadt at the start of the Korean War and had barely completed in-processing when the squadron transferred him to Detachment C. (Detachment C was later redesignated Detachment 23.) The unit was operating about five Morse intercept positions in the hangar compound when he arrived.

The Staging Area was a beehive of activity as thousands of new Army troops arrived by ship, marched in formation to the cavernous troop mess hall for a meal and boarded a troop train in the Staging Area for movement to their next duty station. Bly did not use the troop mess hall; instead, he ate his meals in the Army NCO Mess located in the Staging Area building that later became the new USAFSS operations compound.

The 2nd RSM transferred SSgt. Bly and other Det 23 personnel to the 41st RSM, and Bly served a three-year tour in Bremerhaven. In 1953, TSgt. Bly volunteered for language training, a six-month Russian Language Course at the Army Language School, Monterey, California. USAFSS reassigned him to the 2nd RSM at Darmstadt when he completed the language training. In 1955, TSgt. Bly contracted polio and was discharged from the Air Force on disability.

The entrance to the Detachment 23, 2nd RSM secure compound is shown in the photographs below. This former hangar and control tower housed a snack bar, small BX, gym and other support facilities in the early 1960's.

Contributed by Keith Barkley

Det 23 Compound in former hangar, Bremerhaven, 1951

Contributed by Keith Barkley

Det 23 (Det 3, 2nd RSM), Bremerhaven, Germany, 1951

Detachment 23, 2nd RSM veteran Keith Barkley (1951-54) returned to Bremerhaven on vacation in 2001.

Keith Barkley by Marine School, Bremerhaven, 2001

The former Marine Barracks (facility that served as 2nd RSM billets in the early 1950's) housed the German Marine School, when Keith Barkley toured Bremerhaven in 2001.

Marine School, Bremerhaven, Germany, 2001

NSG JOINS USAFSS IN BREMERHAVEN

In early 1951, Detachment C was redesignated as Detachment 23, 2nd RSM. Det 23 continued performing its mission in Bldg # 103, and was joined by five Naval Security Group communications technicians later in the year. In June 1951, NSG detached the five CT's to the ASA facility at Herzo Base. Later in the fall, they relocated to Bremerhaven, attached to Det 23, 2nd RSM. Thus began a joint USAFSS-NSG operating relationship that endured in Europe for decades. Detachment 23 was deactivated in late 1951, replaced by the 41st Radio Squadron Mobile. Discussion of the 41st RSM continues later.

Soviet Jets Deployed in East Germany

The next USAFSS expansion in Europe was associated with the movement of Soviet jet fighter and bomber regiments into Soviet-occupied eastern Germany. In April-May 1950, Josef Stalin began replacing less capable propeller-driven Soviet aircraft in Germany with MiG-15 Fagots and IL-28 Beagles. To the USAFE Director of Intelligence, Brig. Gen. Millard Lewis, the logical response was to covertly deploy an Air Force SIGINT team to Berlin.

DETACHMENT D, 2ND RSM, BERLIN

With the Russians using most means short of armed attack to coerce the Allied Powers to leave Berlin, and with Berlin surrounded by Soviet air and ground forces armies, the city was a covetous location for Allied listening posts. Conversely, the Four-Power Agreement on Berlin placed on the military occupation forces limitations that forced signals intelligence gathering from West Berlin to be accomplished clandestinely. The Allied agreement limited the size of each ally's Occupation Force, the occupiers wore military uniforms at all times, and each military person traveled to Berlin on military orders written in both English and Russian. These were the rules under which Maj. Pryor established Detachment D, 2nd Radio Squadron Mobile in West Berlin in July 1950. Even references to Detachment D were classified, and "Detachment D" was not included in associated bilingual military orders or discussed outside secure signals intelligence compounds. At the end of 1950, the 2nd Radio Squadron Mobile had four operational detachments.

2nd RSM Org Chart—31 Dec 1950	
2nd RSM Darmstadt, Germany 1949-55	
Det A, 2nd RSM Rothwesten, Germany 1949-51	Det B, 2nd RSM Schleissheim, Germany 1949-51
Det C, 2nd RSM Bremerhaven, Germany 1950-51	Det D, 2nd RSM * Berlin, Germany 1950-54
* Unclassified cover in Berlin was 7350th Base Complement Sqdn.	

Lt. Pearsall and Sgt. Fordham, Berlin Pioneers

During the last decade, the author researched the activation of Detachment D, 2nd RSM in a series of emails and phone calls with former Second Lt. Kenneth F. Pearsall and former SSgt. Virgil C. Fordham. Pearsall and the author also enjoyed a sit-down discussion of early USAFSS operations in Berlin in 2006. Reminiscing about the 1950's, Pearsall and Fordham are amazed and justifiably proud that USAFE Headquarters entrusted and empowered them—a lowly Second Lt. and a junior NCO—to open a super-sensitive USAFSS intercept station in Berlin.

Fordham—the Juvenile Army Draftee

As explained by Virgil Fordham, the U.S. Army drafted him in January 1946 when he was a mere 16 years old. Hesitant initially to discuss his fraudulent early years in the Army, in June 2006 he volunteered that, "Perhaps some background is in order."

In the spring of 1944, my parents moved the family from Paducah, Kentucky, to Abilene, Texas. World War II was in full swing; I was 15 years old, and my older brother was in the Navy. Shortly after starting in the 10th grade at Abilene High School, I received a "Dear John" letter from my Kentucky girl friend, and that evening my Dad leaned on me a bit too hard about joining the church. Our argument resulted in my refusing his punishment, quitting school, and leaving home with my meager savings to make it on my own at age 15.

I ended up in Louisville, KY, working as a pressman for a printing company. World War II was quickly winding down and was going to pass me by. After several attempts to enlist in the service had failed due to being underage for the Army and Navy and no parental consent for the Merchant Marines, I registered for the draft, adding a couple of years to my age, of course. I received my induction call in the fall of 1945 and after Christmas of '45 reported to Fort Lewis, Washington, for basic training, at age sixteen.

After enduring 18 months in the Army with the "age lie," Fordham was discharged in July 1947. His civilian career was short-lived.

Fordham—Intelligence Guru

Allowed to retain the rank of corporal, he decided to reenlist.

In August 1947, I re-enlisted in the Army, this time giving my correct age and everything. At the induction center, we took a series of tests to see what career we might best fit. Three others and I were selected for the Army Security Agency (from which the USAFSS sprung—no Air Force in 1947), and awaited orders to Arlington [Hall] or Vint Hill [Farms], Virginia. We each were given a welcome flyer from the Head of ASA, a general officer.

The induction center sent the enlistees to Camp Holabird, Maryland, mistaking the Army Counterintelligence Division School at Holabird for the Army Security Agency that the recruiter had promised the men. Since none of the four had the requisite college degree required to enter the CID School, Fort Holabird issued reassignment orders after a few weeks. The Army reassigned Fordham and one of the others who had military police experience—not to ASA—but to Camp Gordon, Georgia, to be prison guards.

On arriving at the prison, they told us that we were too young to be a prison guard (minimum age being 25). Again we awaited orders. Mine was to Fort Benning, GA, to the Military Police unit. I was put on a guard post in the most remote area of the reserve. By this time I was a bit pissed, so in looking over the "Welcome Flyer" from the ASA general, I noticed that it had an address for him.

At my guard post I had plenty of time to write and rewrite (over and over) a letter to the general. I finally mailed him my masterpiece "letter" and included my copy of the welcome flyer and all the reassignment orders since. A week later, I received a special delivery letter personally from the ASA general. It was short but sweet—an apology for the screw-up, a statement that he would personally fix it, and that within a week I would have my orders for transfer to ASA, Vint Hill, Va.

The orders arrived as promised, and Cpl. Fordham arrived at Vint Hill Farms, Virginia, on a cold evening in December 1947.

Within a few days, all three of the other guys on the original orders to Camp Holabird also arrived. They had come from all over the U.S.—all very happy in their assignments and the locations they had ended up at. I wouldn't dare let them know that I was responsible for their ending up at Vint Hills. My start in the business!

Contributed by Gordon Wicklund

I.G. Farben Building, Frankfurt, Germany, early 1950's

580

Fordham—Morse Intercept Operator

After completing Morse code training and intercept school, Fordham reported to ASA Europe Headquarters in the IG Farben Building in Frankfurt, Germany, in February 1948. He had an enjoyable, but brief respite at Gibbs Barracks, Frankfurt.

I was sent to Detachment 6 at Herzogenaurach (Herzo Base) the next month. Did CW intercept with Det 6 for several months, and volunteered for assignment to a small unit called 2nd Radio Squadron Mobile at Herzo Base as a CW intercept operator. When the Air Force was created from the Army Air Corps (or a short while later), all members of 2nd Radio were given our choice of transferring (in service) to the USAF and staying with 2nd Radio Squadron, or being reassigned to Detachment 6.

Sgt. Fordham elected to stay with the 2nd RSM and moved with the squadron to Darmstadt. He upgraded to a 7-level CW intercept operator, and a few months later, was a SSgt. in charge of a shift—a Trick Chief. He also became interested in and developed a knack for traffic analysis.

I was never satisfied with just copying a target, I wanted to get in on the traffic analysis part. The T/A guys didn't like us getting into their business, but in the '40's and '50's they always seemed to be late getting us information we needed, like frequency and callsign changes. So, I kept my own card file (in a metal candy box) at the trick chief position.

Anyone with a little sense and a good ear could do the same. I always thought the T/A guys should have been working closer with the intercept operators. Even when operating in the late 1940's at Herzo base, I was often able to predict callsign and frequency changes ahead of the T/A folks.

The Traffic Analysis guys didn't like what I was doing one bit, and I got talked to a couple of times about it—that was one reason why I decided to go to language school; I didn't like the blinders.

Fordham—Russian Voice Intercept Operator

When the squadron received a quota for the Russian language school at Oberammergau, Virgil Fordham volunteered.

I volunteered and six months later returned to 2ⁿᵈ Radio to start our voice intercept operation. A while later we received voice operators from stateside schools, and sent others to the Oberammergau school. I headed up the Voice Intercept Section at Darmstadt (as Staff Sergeant).

Taught by Russian displaced persons from World War II, Sgt. Fordham's Russian class graduated at Oberammergau in November 1949. In June 2006, Fordham spoke very highly of his Russian teachers and the language course taught in the German Alps.

I thought the six-month course taught at Oberammergau by the Russian DP's turned out better language guys than the year-long courses at Syracuse and Monterey. At Oberammergau we not only got a good grilling in the language and background courses, but our favorite Russian instructors (like Gospodin Sorokin and his wife) would invite us over to their apartment a couple of times a week for their parties, including lots to eat and drink, and lots of Russian singing.

Our parties usually consisted of four or five Russians and three or four students. We were not allowed to speak English and were practically forced to drink vodka Russian style (toast after toast). I believe I learned more Russian at their parties than in the classroom. I wonder if everyone who went to Oberammergau experienced the same.

Understanding intercepted voice communications was only half the battle; the traffic analysts wanted the Russian linguists to include every spoken word in each transcript. As Fordham describes the problem, attempting to write down intercepted Russian traffic in real time proved to be a "real challenge."

So, I took a quick course in Greg shorthand and adapted the techniques to Russian intercepts. I created a Russian intercept (typical air dialog) dictionary with shorthand symbols adopted from Greg. We took our intercepts down in script and this make-shift shorthand and later transcribed it on Russian typewriters [U.S. military standard typewriters with a Russian Cyrillic keyboard]. It was a hell of a lot easier to use the shorthand on 80% of the intercept and concentrate on getting the rest of it right.

At reunions five decades later, former USAFSS Russian linguists whom Virgil Fordham had never met recalled using "Fordham Shorthand" to produce hand-scans of intercepted communications.

SIGINT Data Fusion in Berlin

As the 2nd RSM's linguists gained proficiency copying voice communications, the unit's tasking began to take on more of a tactical role. At a 2nd RSM reunion in 2006, Virgil Fordham discussed with the author events leading up to expanded USAFSS operations in Europe. The USAFE Director of Intelligence wanted to deploy a voice intercept capability in Berlin.

In July 1950, Major Pryor sent 2nd Lt. Pearsall and me to Wiesbaden to meet with the AF Director of Intelligence [USAFE/IN] (General Lewis, I believe). I was the intercept operations guy and Pearsall was the communications officer (no intercept experience).

Maj. Gen. Millard Lewis later served as Commander, USAFSS.

When we got to the general's office it was just the three of us. He explained what he would like us to do. First, we were to talk to no one about what we were to be doing. He wanted us to go to Berlin, Tempelhof Air Base, and do a survey of Russian air and air base communications intercept, and to get base operations to place a remoted radar scope (terminal) in a secure area where we could set up operations.

They discussed the possibility of merging (fusing) radar tracks with voice intercepts in real time, and what might be gained by this process.

I was to monitor and plot Russian air activity on the radar scope, try to intercept their ground-to-air and air-to-air communications, and tie the communications to the radar plots.

With minimal discussion, General Lewis sent Lt. Pearsall and Sgt. Fordham on their way. They developed a plan and proceeded to Berlin to determine the viability of creating a SIGINT intercept site in the heart of the occupied eastern zone of Germany.

A week later Pearsall and I loaded some radio equipment and antenna wire on a plane and headed for Berlin. When we got to Tempelhof, we found that the CPS-5 radar scope could only be operated in the local air operations center in the control tower (due to available cable lengths and line amplifiers). The air ops center was located in a room in the control tower and had 24-hour operations with British, French, and American military air controllers (working the corridors into Berlin).

We were given a small room (closet size) off the ops center, and a cable was run through the wall to our single radar scope. While they were installing our radar scope, we strung our own radio antennas from tower to roof and set up an intercept position using a small table, a chair, and a small safe. That just about filled the room/closet. We had base facilities install locks on the door, after which we allowed no one access—we had carbines/pistols and provided our own security.

Convinced that they had gathered more than adequate data to prove effectiveness of SIGINT collection operations in Berlin, Pearsall and Fordham couriered their classified materials home to Darmstadt and briefed Gen. Lewis at Wiesbaden. Gen. Lewis directed the 2nd RSM to activate an intercept site in Berlin as soon as possible. Fordham and Pearsall returned to Berlin and set up intercept operations in August 1950.

Original USAFSS Intercept Site in Berlin

In 2006, Virgil Fordham described the original intercept site that he and Ken Pearsall set up at Tempelhof Air Base in the American Sector of Berlin.

We were located on the top floor and got there by riding a continuously running three-man lift (elevator) at the end of the hall (you jump on and jump off). Our ops area was the first door on the right as we exited the elevator and started down the hall. Our intercept ops room had one (later two) PPI consoles, and we had tables with HF receivers next to the PPI consoles so we could hand-copy transmissions while viewing the PPI targets. We could do this with one operator, sometimes with two per position.

I believe we had only two PPI/intercept position combos when I left. We did have a couple of other tables/receivers for HF intercept without PPI consoles. While I was there, the radar PPI consoles were placed in the one operations room next to our intercept receivers. . . . . Before I left, we received a VHF receiver for search and a tape recorder. I don't believe we made much use of the recorder while I was there but heard they later connected it for remote control from the intercept positions.

Living quarters for the intercept operators and the first Detachment D, 2nd RSM operations facility in Berlin were conveniently located adjacent to each other.

Our operators' quarters (beds & footlockers) were next door to the operations room with a connecting door and would sleep five or six persons. I believe next door, down the hall, were a couple of smaller rooms for NCO's. . . . . It was strictly a no frills secure operation—all areas "need to know" entry.

From these humble beginnings, Det D, 2nd RSM evolved into one of Security Service's most important intercept squadrons, operating dozens of COMINT, ELINT and RADINT intercept positions and conducting associated analysis. As Detachment D's mission grew, its original operations area expanded into a four-room complex within the control tower complex.

Ken Pearsall's Recollections of Det D

Using old temporary duty orders, in June 2006 Ken Pearsall reconstructed milestones involved in the startup of Air Force Security Service operations in Berlin. After Gen. Lewis gave the order to determine the feasibility of setting up an intercept site at

Tempelhof, Maj. Pryor assigned the task to Second Lt. Pearsall, apparently with some misgivings.

> *My being the only bachelor officer in the unit, I was selected to travel to Berlin to discuss with the base commander what had to be done. The Commander, 2nd RSM, was reluctant to send me, but he had no choice. I guess he thought I was a "wet-behind-the-ears" 2nd Lt. He didn't seem to know that I had spent 2 1/2 years as a radar mechanic/operator for the ground controlled approach system.*

Before attending Officer Candidate School in 1949, Airman Pearsall had worked as a GCA technician at Andrews AFB, Maryland (1946-48). He traveled alone to Berlin to coordinate plans for the site survey.

Contributed by Kenneth Pearsall

Berlin Tempelhof, July 1950

> *I went to Berlin on TDY 4-7 July 1950.[19] I visited the 7350th Base Complement Squadron and base commander, Colonel John Barr, to discuss setting up the site. He had previously been briefed by General Lewis to cooperate with me. Col. Barr told me to look around to find a site for this operation and report back to him.*

I located four (4) rooms on the 5th floor of the main building down the hall from the CPS-5 radar system, which we were going to tap into to gather flight tracks. I presented my findings to Col. Barr, and he directed his base installations officer, Capt. Malcolm Menghini, to prepare the rooms for my occupancy whenever I asked him.

Pearsall told Col. Barr that the initial step was to conduct a preliminary collection survey and that he would keep him informed. Pearsall continued his recollections.

On 17 July 1950, SSgt. Virgil Fordham and I traveled to Berlin to make the survey.[20] Maj. Richard S. Griffith, Commander, 1946th AACS Squadron, allowed us to operate a receiver and radar indicator (PPI) in a secluded area within the Radar Approach & Control (RAPCON) Center within the control tower complex. As I had expected from my previous experience with radars and communications, we hit a virtual "gold mine." Sgt. Fordham was flabbergasted with what he was hearing. There was no doubt in our minds this was the place to set up an intercept site if we wanted to monitor Soviet and East German flight activity in East Germany.

We returned to Darmstadt and presented our findings to the 2nd RSM commander, and he made arrangements for me to brief Brig. Gen. Lewis. I briefed Gen. Lewis, and he immediately directed an intercept site in Berlin. Thus began the saga of the Berlin intercept site.

Initially scheduled for three days, Virgil Fordham remembers that the site survey lasted a couple of weeks, with Pearsall and Fordham returning to the 2nd RSM in early August.

Det D Operations Commenced August 1950

Back in Darmstadt, Pearsall and Fordham scrounged enough equipment from 2nd RSM supply to activate a new intercept site at Tempelhof Air Base. Arriving back in Berlin, the Tempelhof base housing officer issued Pearsall keys to a good-sized room on the top floor of the base control tower building. An adjacent room became quarters for Sgt. Fordham and other enlisted men who arrived later on temporary duty from the 2nd RSM.

> *On 25 August 1950, SSgt. Virgil Fordham and I again went TDY to Berlin to begin setting up the operation.[21] We carried with us receivers, antennas, etc. to begin the operation.*

Contributed by Kenneth Pearsall

Airlift Memorial Dedication, Berlin, 10 July 1951

By late 1951, Det D, 2nd RSM had outgrown its one-room operations facility. Lt. Pearsall arranged to expand Operations into a four-room secure vault complex.

> *I arranged with Capt. Menghini to secure the rooms. On three of the four rooms, the entrance doors had to be bricked up, leaving only one main entrance door.*

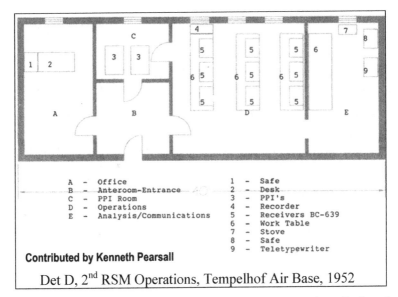

A - Office
B - Anteroom-Entrance
C - PPI Room
D - Operations
E - Analysis/Communications

1 - Safe
2 - Desk
3 - PPI's
4 - Recorder
5 - Receivers BC-639
6 - Work Table
7 - Stove
8 - Safe
9 - Teletypewriter

Contributed by Kenneth Pearsall

Det D, 2nd RSM Operations, Tempelhof Air Base, 1952

Next, Pearsall arranged to have two PPI scopes installed and interfaced to the CPS-5 Radar. Support on Tempelhof for their project was outstanding, especially after Lt. Pearsall became a favorite golfing partner of Col. Barr. The colonel treated Lt. Pearsall as a 7350th squadron staff member, with Pearsall attending 7350th staff meetings, serving as the Base Officer of the Day, etc. A half century later over a beer in the Officers Club at Wright Patterson AFB, Ken Pearsall regaled Virgil Fordham with a Berlin support services story. Here's Virgil's version of the story.

He related one incident where the base materiel officer complained at a staff meeting that 2nd Lt. Pearsall was wanting him to construct operating positions (to our drawings) and due to workload he wouldn't be able to get to it for a few months. The base commander, who by then was a friend and fellow golfer of Ken, told the materiel officer to make Pearsall's request his # 1 priority—"Don't ask questions; make the tables."

None of the Tempelhof people knew what Pearsall did or who he worked for, just that he carried a lot of weight. Of course, the base commander had his orders from higher up (Wiesbaden) to support us fully.

Within secure USAFSS channels, the site was designated Detachment D, 2nd Radio Squadron Mobile, but Pearsall does not recall the operation ever being called Detachment D. For the three years that he served in Berlin, he was always assigned on temporary duty to the 7350th Air Base Complement Squadron.

Security was so tight—at least initially—that few in the 2nd RSM in Darmstadt knew about the unit's detachment at Tempelhof. And no permanent party personnel in Berlin, including the base commander, were authorized access to Det D's operations area. Pearsall and Fordham supposedly held the only keys to their area. The door to the USAFSS facility was locked at all times, and whoever was on duty served as security guard.

Overzealous Base Housing Officer

Having phantom airmen operating incognito behind a locked door in a facility that he controlled did not sit well with the Tempelhof housing officer, so he surreptitiously paid a visit one Sunday morning when he expected their facility to be unoccupied. Hearing a key unlock the door, an airman on duty informed the unfamiliar Air Force captain in the doorway that the facility was off-limits. Identifying himself as the base housing officer, the captain intimated that he had authority to go wherever he wanted. However, observing the loaded Colt .45 in the airman's holster, he closed the door and departed.

Learning the next morning about the unauthorized entry, Lt. Pearsall stormed into the Col. Barr's office and demanded that the housing officer give up all keys to the space controlled by Pearsall. The base commander summoned the housing officer into his office and ordered him to surrender the keys. As word of the incident spread, Pearsall's already significant clout with other base officials seemed infinite. Pearsall was promoted to First Lt. in January 1951 and redeployed from the 2nd RSM in August 1953—reassigned to the USAFSS Inspector General's Office.

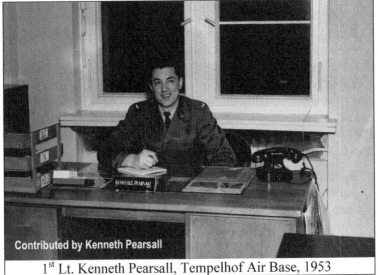

Contributed by Kenneth Pearsall

1st Lt. Kenneth Pearsall, Tempelhof Air Base, 1953

Pearsall's Post-Berlin Career

"Hating" his duties with the USAFSS IG, Pearsall volunteered to command a USAFSS detachment (Det 9, 8th RSM) that was colocated with an air control and warning (AC&W) squadron in Montauk, NY. Then after attending the SIGINT school at Kelly AFB and a brief assignment to the 6901st Special Communications Group, Zweibrücken, Germany, the Air Force selected Capt. Kenneth Pearsall for air attaché duty in Moscow. After learning Russian at Syracuse University, he served with the U.S. Air Attaché Office in Moscow, followed by duty tours with the Air Force Foreign Technology Division, Wright Patterson AFB and the European Security Region (USAFSS), Frankfurt, Germany. From 1963 to 1966, Maj. Pearsall was ESR's staff officer for the European ACRP (Airborne COMINT Reconnaissance Platform) program, coordinating aerial recon activities of the 6916th Security Squadron at Rhein-Main. Retiring from active duty as a major in 1966, Kenneth Pearsall worked in civil service with the FTD at WPAFB, retiring again in 2001. Now fully retired, he visited with the author in State College, Pennsylvania, in 2006.

Det D Staffing—the Early Years

Mindful that agents of the Soviet GRU (military intelligence) were on the lookout for U.S. intelligence activities in Berlin, the 2nd RSM increased the number of voice intercept operations in Det D gradually. Pearsall and Fordham worked alone for about three weeks in Berlin pending the arrival of additional Russian linguists, ostensibly on temporary duty with the 7350th squadron. In June 2006, Virgil Fordham provided the names of the earliest cadre of Detachment D airmen.

In early Sept '50, 2nd RSM Darmstadt sent us the following personnel—all Russian language intercept guys; SSgt. Ambrose H. Jackson, SSgt. Robert E. Draughon, and Sgt. Norman R. Opitz.[22] Draughon and Opitz went back to Darmstadt by the end of Nov '50. Jackson left us the first week of December 1950 to set up the AFSS station at Chicksands, England.

At my request, Darmstadt sent us two additional Russian language intercept guys whom I had worked with in Darmstadt, and whose intercept capabilities I knew. Cpl. Jack W. Dukes was sent to us on 1 Oct '50, and Cpl. John L. Stief arrived on 1 Nov '50. Both stayed in Berlin for the rest of their tours and were there when I left at the end of June '51. We had six or eight voice intercept operators when I left Berlin.

Sgt. Darral H. Hanson joined Det D in Berlin in December 1950, and still others arrived in Det D in 1951.[23] Promoted to SSgt. in February 1951, Hanson became the NCOIC of voice intercept when Fordham departed the 2nd RSM. A "fast burner," Hanson made TSgt. in June 1952 and completed his tour with the 2nd RSM in June 1953. With five Russian linguists on duty in Berlin at the end of 1950, the 2nd RSM increased the number of voice intercept operators at Tempelhof by an order of magnitude by 1953 per statistics provided by Kenneth Pearsall.

When I departed on 1 August 1953, there were 50 personnel (two officers, two EM [enlisted] analysts, one EM maintenance and 45 EM voice operators) assigned TDY to the site.

Soviet WW II War Memorial, Berlin, 1951

In a rare breach of operational security in which the USAFSS unit in Berlin was listed publicly by its true designator—Detachment D, 2nd Radio Squadron Mobile—the Berlin Tempelhof Air Base special menu for Thanksgiving 1952 named all assigned units and their personnel. The menu identified Lt. Pearsall as Det D's commander and listed 27 enlisted men in the detachment.[24]

Overview of Det D Operations—1953

Pearsall provided the following overview of USAFSS operations in Berlin during the mid-1953 era.

We were operating two radar PPI positions and nine voice operator positions on a 24-hour operation. Not all nine positions were manned around the clock. It varied by the extent of activity (i.e., daytime, evening or later). All of the EM assigned were very eager to operate in this environment, which increased their language skills, and they enjoyed being assigned to Berlin as there were many more activities in the city compared to Darmstadt.

Because there was no Berlin Wall at the time—only a sign stating, "You are entering the Soviet Sector"—Pearsall had instructions to return to Darmstadt immediately anyone who did not want to stay in Berlin or had disciplinary problems. None of his troops got into disciplinary trouble, but one airman asked to leave Berlin early because he did not "like being surrounded by Russians."

> *I asked him where he saw so many Russians. He said they are all around. I told him I had been there for 18 months, and the only Russians I had seen were the guards at the Russian memorial near the Brandenburg Gate.*

The airman departed Tempelhof on the next C-47 courier flight bound for Wiesbaden.

Courier Flights

During early USAFSS operations in Berlin, Lt. Pearsall served as a courier once per week to deliver intercept records to the 2nd RSM and to brief Gen. Lewis at Wiesbaden once per month. Unbeknownst to Sgt. Fordham, Pearsall also dabbled in human intelligence while transiting the air corridors to/from Berlin.

> *One time when Pearsall wasn't available to make the courier run, I made it for him. I strapped on his 45-Colt, took his courier bag, and boarded the C-47 courier plane. Now, what I didn't know was that Ken had been doing some added surveillance from the courier plane. After we were airborne out of Tempelhof, the copilot came back to the passenger compartment and took me up front for my aircraft surveillance task.*

> *Well, I acted like I knew what it was all about and quickly learned what I was to do, without letting them know that I knew nothing of what Pearsall had been up to. The C-47 pilot flew the plane over every Russian air base within the corridor, and I caught on that I was to count the airplanes by numbers and types using the binoculars the crew provided. The copilot helped me with the count, types, and the name of the air base.*

> *We did a good job recording the aircraft by air base; however, I had no idea what I should do with the data. When we landed at Wiesbaden I delivered the courier package of RADINT and SIGINT, and went to the bathroom and flushed the "out of scope" aircraft count. I*

never told Pearsall of my one-time involvement in his aircraft count and he never mentioned it.

When asked about his extracurricular HUMINT aircraft counts in 2006, Pearsall smiled and nodded affirmatively that he had passed the information to a USAFE Intel officer.

Cyrillic Typewriters and VHF Intercept

Virgil Fordham discussed Cyrillic typewriters that Detachment D linguists used to transcribe intercepted voice traffic. He also recalled searching the VHF spectrum for Soviet air force communications in the Berlin area.

The MC-88's do sound familiar, and they were uppercase Russian Cyrillic type. Not sure of the nomenclature. It took us about four or five months to get them at the Berlin operation. We were using them back in Darmstadt before we opened Berlin but didn't have many.

We didn't get tape recorders until mid-1951, I believe. They came about the same time they sent us a VHF receiver for searching the bands for any Russian traffic. We put in lots of man-hours searching the VHF bands but don't believe we picked up any Russian traffic. I believe they didn't start using VHF out of country until after 1951 (needs verifying). All of our product was from HF transmissions during 1950 and 1951.

Donie G. Heavner (left) and Thomas C Morris Jr.,
Brandenburg Gate, Berlin, 1951

Using some of his clout in Berlin, Lt. Pearsall even went outside
USAFSS channels to borrow a VHF receiver in an attempt to
intercept Soviet VHF communications that were not yet being
used in East Germany. He discussed the receiver with Fordham in
2006.

*Do you recall the designation of that 'piece of junk'
receiver that 2nd RSM gave us to operate with; how
unstable it was and had such a narrow bandwidth that you
could go past a signal and not hear it? I thought it was R-
400. Also, how I borrowed the 'nice' BC-639's from AACS
Sq on base? I caught 'hell' for doing that, but I didn't care.*

Today, Fordham and Pearsall differ in their opinions of when
the Soviet aircraft began communicating in the VHF (100-150
MHz) spectrum in Germany, with Pearsall believing that MiG-
15's and IL-28's used VHF in 1950. Fordham is most likely
correct—the first observed Soviet usage of VHF air-to-ground
communications occurred in August 1952 in Korea, and involved

Soviet air force MiG-15's in combat against American F-86's during the Korean War. Lt. Pearsall did acquire some BC-639 VHF receivers at Tempelhof, but that probably occurred after Fordham departed in the summer of 1951.

I checked with the 1946ᵗʰ AACS Squadron Supply Officer, Capt. Robert Trapp, and asked him about some BC-639 receivers. He took me to a hangar and showed me all the equipment that was sent to Berlin during the Berlin Airlift. I checked out on a hand receipt nine (9) BC-639 receivers. Those receivers had a nice wide bandwidth, and when tuned to frequency could be locked on it. The operators were elated when we installed this equipment.

Conversely, HQ USAFSS was none too thrilled that a lieutenant in the field had begun using non-approved intercept equipment.

Fordham—Post-Berlin

To no one's surprise, Detachment D collected unique and significant SIGINT that was unavailable from other sources. The deployed voice intercept operators were literally surrounded with their signals of interest, and having access to the collateral Allied radar coverage of East Germany further enhanced the USAFSS mission. Sgt. Fordham's protégés in Berlin continued to expand the Detachment D mission after he departed. With few jobs available for Russian linguists back in America, the USAFSS reassigned Fordham as a Morse code instructor at Keesler AFB, Mississippi.

When I came back to the U.S., I had a 7-level MOS in Voice Intercept and a 7-level MOS in CW intercept. I also had some electronics experience from being a ham operator for a number of years. Back in my CW days, I could find and hang-in with signals that no one else could copy. Old MSgt. Charlie West was the best I've seen at that. I was assigned to the USAFSS intercept course at Keesler [AFB, Biloxi, Mississippi] along with several others from 2ⁿᵈ RSM, Jack May being one I remember.

Fordham taught in the Morse intercept operator school for about a year before entering Officer Candidate School. Serving as an electronics officer in commands outside USAFSS, Maj. Fordham retired from the Air Force in 1966. He hired on with Rockwell International as the program manager on a massive international project for the government of the Shah of Iran—"Project Ibex"—providing Iran with SIGINT ground-based systems and airborne platforms.

Virgil Fordham renewed acquaintances with former Darmstadt and Berlin comrades at a 2nd RSM reunion in 1998. He also discussed his 2nd RSM experiences during a 2nd RSM reunion in Arlington, Virginia, in 2006. As it turns out, former 2nd Radio Squadron Mobile Morse/DF operator Bill Baker lives only ten minutes from Virgil Fordham in California.

Detachment D's DF Capability

Unlike the other detachments, in 1950 and 1951 Detachment D in Berlin had a primary mission of collecting Soviet air force voice communications, and it did not have a direction finding capability. In January 1952, SSgt.'s William M. Baker and Dallas D. Clark flew into Tempelhof Air Base aboard a C-82 transport with a DF system. The camouflaged system was housed in a standard HO-17 hut. Radio maintenance technicians had mounted a regular aircraft radio compass on the HO-17's roof; the intercept receiver was inside the hut. With the HO-17 hut placed on the ground near the end of one of the parallel runways, they were quickly in business. According to Baker, the DF mission was against HF beacons, not enemy voice transmitters.

> *The idea was to monitor all the Eastern radio beacons and record their bearings, using the radio compass, almost continuously. We operated 24 hours a day. In our slack time we would act as CW intercept operators and copy any callsigns that we found of interest.*
>
> *I don't know if you were ever acquainted with the slide rule [slip stick] developed by the British, but that is what we used to determine the callsigns of interest. At that time the results of the slide rule manipulation was called a "book." DF sites were usually manned by one person, unless there was some training being done, so it was pretty lonely out there. Especially the midnight-to-8 a.m. shift.*

Baker described Detachment D's living quarters and operations as being "on the fourth and fifth floors of a building that was to the right as you faced the Airlift Monument"—the Tempelhof control tower. Baker was fascinated with the German version of the elevator in the building.

> *I do remember we had a continuous elevator on that end of the building that took us up to our floors. It was a series of open cages that you stepped on and off as it came past your floor. It's kind of hard to explain, but it was just a continuous loop with the cages going up one side and down the other.*

The "elevator" that Bill described was a "Paternoster." The IG Farben Building in Frankfurt had a similar system. In fact, some Paternosters are still in use in Germany.

Forty-seven years later, Bill Baker recalled some events that illustrate the tense situation in Berlin during the early years of the Cold War:

> *We had a recon flight that came over practically every evening. It was a twin jet (probably light bomber), and I'm sure it was taking photos to see if anything had changed at Tempelhof since the day before. I'm sure they had quite a conference when they got the first picture of our little HO-17 out by the runway! Anyway, that was frustrating, too, since we were not allowed to have any combat aircraft at Tempelhof or even fly them up the corridors. I think the first years of the "Cold War" were probably the most trying for the military folks, especially in places like Berlin. Of course they told us when we volunteered to go up there that we were expendable.*

The light bomber was probably one of the Soviet air force IL-28 Beagle bombers brought to East Germany in 1950. Bill Baker also recalled another incident that illustrates the viciousness of the Soviet military towards Western aircraft overflying Soviet-controlled territory,

> *An Air France DC-6 was shot at coming up the south corridor in April 1952. That was my first experience at seeing the size of hole a 20 mm cannon shell can put in an airplane, and there were quite a few of them. I wish I*

could explain the anger and frustration I felt when I looked over that airplane.

This was one of the many air incidents occurring over the Allied air corridors linking Berlin to West Germany during the Cold War. All military forces in both Berlin and the "Zone" (West German Occupation Zone) were still required to wear uniforms both on and off duty when Bill Baker returned home in June 1952.

Period of Transition—Flughafen Tempelhof

Dr. Alfred Leinweber, a retired Air Force colonel, made available an essay that he penned in 2002, which was the 50th anniversary of his assignment as a Russian linguist with Detachment D in Berlin. In the essay Dr. Leinweber reminisced about the Berlin that he knew in 1952-1953.

It was a time of transition for Flughafen Tempelhof 50 years ago. Eisenhower was just then forming NATO. The Korean War was going full blast. Joe Stalin was still alive, and had only recently desisted from his attempted strangulation of Berlin. The Air Force was only about three years old, and lots of us were still in OD uniforms and had to polish gold-colored brass.

The recently-departed Red Army had tried to burn everything above ground in the great arc of an operations building at Tempelhof (largest building in Europe?), which we all came to know so well. They flooded the subterranean floors where Luftwaffe fighters were kept. I never could find out how many levels were below ground. Stone and steel don't burn very well, so quite a lot of the building was left—about 3/4 of a mile of it.

Detachment "D" of the 2nd Radio Squadron Mobile occupied one long room "am vierten Obergeschloss," with a glass-lensed peephole in the door, so that one could be eyeballed from within before he entered. Thirty years later, someone knowledgeable told me that peephole was still there. Also, the three-man elevator boxes [Paternoster] were still said to be continuously running, carrying voice and CW operators to their workplace.

Leinweber identified the detachment's intercept receivers as "numbers of Collins 51J and Hammarlund receivers, along with 'Bendix washer' radar sets." Slaved to the Allied air traffic control radar at Tempelhof, Det D intercept operators used their radar displays to correlate intercepted communications to air activity reflected by the radar.

Det "D" comprised about a dozen of us, voice and CW operators, covering all shifts. TSgt. Darral Hanson and 2nd Lt. Kenneth Pearsall were our authority figures. The guys were a multitalented bunch. One had been a ghost writer in New York City; another had been a superintendent of schools; and another was an electrical engineer. The latter was probably the most valuable man on Tempelhof. He could fix any of our electronics, though he was there as a voice operator. All of us were in our early '20's.

In the late '40's, there were three-year enlistments. One of our guys, Dallas Clark, was approaching the end of his enlistment and was actually enroute to the port of Bremerhaven for his voyage back to the land of the Big PX. He was involuntarily extended for another year due to the NATO buildup, and he was turned around and sent back to us. I've always admired the good grace he exhibited, ever a cheerful and responsible member of the outfit.

President Truman extended Clark's enlistment (and enlistments of thousands of others) by executive order in June 1952, citing issues related to the ongoing Korean War.

On my arrival in January 1952, I was shown a smoke-blackened room, about 50' x 50', where I was to be billeted. It was just a few steps from the operations room, but that was the only attractive thing about it. I set up my folding metal G.I. cot in one corner, drew bedding from supply, and I was then in residence, with all my worldly possessions in my footlocker and barracks bag. Later, some other guys moved in with me, and painters finally came and brightened up the place.

Berlin had been destroyed over its wide areas, as no other comparable place had ever been done in. The Kaiser Wilhelm II Gedächtniskirche [Memorial Church) on the Kurfuerstendamm was blasted as it now stands, only it had not yet been stabilized for safety, and entering it was dangerous. The huge cast-metal statues in the Tiergarten were still full of Red Army bullet holes. . . . . The monument depicting the three air corridors had already been erected on Platz der Luftbrücke. An eagle facing it across the quadrangle had already had the swastika blasted from its claws.

Now a little about the beginning of it all—Brooks AFB was Security Service HQ with a wire-enclosed compound where we mounted guard all too often. The big outfit there was a giant "casual" squadron, with about 2,000 of us going to schools or waiting for shipment elsewhere. Naturally, everything was overseas except for the schools.

I lived in a 200-man barracks with holes in the roof, where Eddie Rickenbacker had lived when he was a cadet in 1916. In this setting, we went through two weeks of English grammar instruction, then two weeks of Russian language, during which we mastered the Cyrillic alphabet and got a good start on Russian grammar, and of course, some vocabulary. Then came the Army Language School at the Presidio of Monterey, CA.

There was a year-long Russian course, but we were in a six-month course, which had its genesis when Russian voices were heard flying air cover for North Korean troops. It was an all-Air Force program—designed to quickly get us into the Aleutian Islands, to assorted places in Europe and to some small islands in the Sea of Japan, all surrounding the Soviet landmass. I was in R6-3 (Russian, 6 months, 3rd group to start). R6-1 was still there and in session at that time. Twenty-three languages were being taught, but half the resources and students were there for Russian language study.

Our day was split up into times for vocabulary study, speech patterns, conversations, dictation, and some other things, with a different instructor every hour. There was a language lab, the first I'd seen. Tape recorders hadn't come along for personal use just yet, but there were wire recorders. R6-3 was divided into sections A, B, C and D. The group in D section were just hanging on, maybe including some guys from the deep south who couldn't quite get their tongue wrapped around Russian vowel sounds. The guys in section A contrived to look bored, while they fondled their Phi Beta Kappa keys. Every two weeks there was a large oral and written exam and a reshuffling of the sections, with now and then, someone being sent off, presumably to learn another trade.

Pre-language training at Brooks AFB in 1951 changed very little by January 1956 when the author attended pre-lang training across town at USAFSS Headquarters at Kelly AFB. Likewise, the author's Russian course (R6-33-56) at ALS, Monterey, followed to a "T" the R6-3 lesson plan from five years earlier. Although not in Berlin for the occasion, Dr. Leinweber attaches special significance to the building of the Wall in 1961.

In 1961 when the Berlin Wall went up, the jet age was upon us with full force. Fighter-plane reflex time was needed against the East, which brought into being a string of hitherto unused bases well back of the Rhein, mostly in eastern France. I had recently qualified in dentistry and settled into a small-town practice in Missouri. Almost overnight, I found myself Chief of Dental Services at Etain AB, very near the Argonne (Sergeant York) Battlefield area of WW I. I got some leave time, and burning with curiosity, made my way to Berlin and Tempelhof.

There, I was greeted by (my jaw dropped) a major. I realized that I no longer had a proper clearance and "need to know," but I explained my curiosity to him, and he was most cordial, without telling me anything. He said I'd be surprised at some of the new technology.

Dr. Leinweber made a career of the Air Force, serving his last overseas tour in 1971-1972 as an advisor to the Chief of the Republic of Vietnam Military Dental Corps. Now retired, Dr. Leinweber has never forgotten his USAFSS roots. He strives to attend all the annual USAFSS Berlin alumni association reunions, including a reunion in Berlin in 2001.

Detachment D, Changing of the Guard

There was a change in leadership in Detachment D in Berlin in 1953. Sam C. Herrin, a former USAFSS Russian linguist, reported for duty with the 2nd Radio Squadron Mobile in August 1952. His duty station was to be Detachment D, 2nd RSM in Berlin. In October, the squadron attached Herrin on temporary duty with 7350th Air Base Complement Squadron in Berlin for 90 days, and that TDY was later extended to an indefinite period.

First Lt. Pearsall was the Detachment D Commander when Herrin arrived but was soon replaced by Lt. Clarence W. Blanford. Herrin was promoted to SSgt. and became Det D's NCOIC of voice intercept in 1953, replacing Darral Hanson. Herrin's pastime during off-duty hours was "sightseeing" around Berlin as an observer on training flights.

> *I used to bum rides with any pilot assigned to Berlin who kept his flying currency up by flying circles in the small open area over the city. Just for fun, I'd count MiG's and IL-28's on the ground at the Soviet bases that we could see without actually flying into Soviet-controlled space. Probably broke a couple of rules doing that ;>), but it was fun.*

SSgt. Herrin and his Detachment D comrades were absolutely forbidden to engage in any nefarious activities that might get the attention of the Soviet forces in Berlin. During an incoming briefing, Detachment D First Sergeant Erickson personally briefed each airman on "DO's" and "DON'T's" and provided each airman a one-page guide to getting along in Detachment D. Here's Erickson's one-page plan for newcomers.

INFORMATION TO NEWCOMERS TO THIS DETACHMENT

1 *First of all, and of utmost importance is to neither say, write nor do anything which might, in any manner, connect your work with the 2nd RSM.*

2 *We're very close to the Russian Sector, so act accordingly. In event you're unlucky enough to be caught on the wrong side, give only your name, rank and serial number, and demand to see the U.S. Military Authorities of the U.S. Consul.*

3 *Your address as far as Berlin is concerned, is "Detachment D."*

4 *Your mailing address while here is "Name, Rank, AFSN, 7350th Base Complement Squadron, APO 742. U.S. Army," Note: the "A" as listed on your orders in the APO number is missing.*

5 *Linen will be exchanged and laundry will be turned in on Fridays.*

6 *Chow hours are 06:30, 11:30 and 17:00 hours.*

7 *Drilling and AI&E [Air Information & Education] lectures on Friday afternoon and Saturday mornings. These are not for us, though, if you keep entirely out of sight while on the base during these periods. Remain in your room if necessary, but do not make yourself conspicuous by roaming around to the P.X, coffee shop, post office or anywhere else during these two (2) periods.*

8 *You will be given eight overnight passes per month only upon written approval of your trick chief. This is a new innovation which can very easily be taken away upon receipts of DR's [discrepancy reports], etc. You are working for the trick chief, and not for me. Therefore, any complaints, suggestions, etc. must go thru him before going further along the chain.*

9 *There will be room inspection each Thursday at 10 hours. This will be held by either the detachment commander or the undersigned. Cleanliness and neatness is of primary importance. Inasmuch as this is only a weekly occurrence and informal, it shouldn't be difficult to comply with.*

10 *Even though the janitor can be employed to keep your room clean, this does not absolve you of the responsibilities for same.*

S. Erickson
Erickson

To no one's surprise, Sam Herrin has high praise for Sgt. Erickson. Herrin never questioned his policies, but he thought some operational requirements went overboard.

The restrictions we had in those early days seem funny now but were frustrating at the time. There was a strict prohibition about doing ANY analysis. Operator notes were not allowed because it would upgrade classification of the traffic. We had a direct feed from the Tempelhof radar to a scope in a room adjacent to voice operations. We sketched the screen picture of targets and sent that in, but we were not allowed to correlate anything! Strictly collection and forwarding under CONF [confidential] classification. Would really have loved to see how it all grew and developed by the 1960's and 70's.

Transcripts of intercepted communications without any evidence of analysis were classified Confidential in the SIGINT community for decades.

SSgt. Herrin left Berlin and the Air Force in January 1954 but reenlisted in mid-1955. After a tour with USAFSS in Japan and completion of Officer Candidate School, he was commissioned as an Air Force Second Lt. in 1959. He spent the next decade in USAFSS assignments, including serving as USAFSS site commander on Monkey Mountain outside Da Nang, Vietnam, in 1968-69. He finished his Air Force career as an intelligence career development officer at Randolph AFB, Texas, retiring in 1971. Since 1988, Sam Herrin and his wife have been involved in missionary work (Project Cross) in the former Soviet Union (still the USSR when they started). Detachment D and renamed incarnations of the detachment continued performing a signals intelligence collection mission in Berlin throughout the Cold War.

The photograph on the next page shows Virgil Fordham, Clarence Blanford and Kenneth Pearsall enjoying a mini-reunion in California in 2007.

Contributed by Virgil Fordham

Virgil Fordham, Clarence Blanford and Ken Pearsall, 2007

FIRST COLD WAR SHOOT DOWN CASUALTY

In September 1949, Joseph Mishkofski became involved in the 2nd Radio Squadron Mobile's monitoring of U.S. recon missions along the Soviet Union and East European borders. On 8 April 1950, Soviet fighters shot down a U.S. Navy PB4Y-2 "Privateer" mission near Bornholm Island over the Baltic Sea—the first Soviet shoot down of a U.S. aircraft during the Cold War. Even with a cooperative U.S.-Russian investigation in the early 1990's, that mission's ten-man crew has never been accounted for.

Mishkofski vividly recalls that shoot down incident. Recently promoted to Sgt., his intercept assignment was to copy Morse traffic from the U.S. Navy "ferret" (recon) mission. It was normally a fairly routine operation with the mission aircraft using a fixed callsign (Metro-43 implying a weather mission) and broadcasting unencrypted in-flight reports in Morse code on a fixed frequency of 1002 Kilohertz. Mishkofski had copied several earlier in-flight reports, but the mission aircraft failed to send its next report as scheduled.

The 2nd RSM also monitored Soviet communications related to recon missions. Its highest priority intercepts during recon missions were the Soviet air defense (PVO) nets that passed information regarding the missions. The author addressed the 8 April 1950 shoot down incident and other attacks on American reconnaissance aircraft during the Cold War in "*The Price of Vigilance.*"[25]

New 2nd RSM Operations Compound

Having outgrown its Operations workspace in the attic of Bldg # 17 at Ernst Ludwig Kaserne, the 2nd Radio Squadron Mobile built a new operations compound near its DF site at the Griesheim Airstrip. Retired Air Force Chief Gordon McKenzie dates the move to the new compound as soon after he returned to Darmstadt from language school in early 1951. In the fall of 1951 (September or October), Lt. Col. Jack P. Van Tuil assumed command of the 2nd RSM, replacing Maj. Pryor. Later—in the first half of 1953— the 2nd RSM relocated across town to Cambrai Fritsch Kaserne. USAFSS units continued operations at Cambrai Fritsch until 1972.

DETS ASSIGNED NUMERIC DESIGNATORS

By 1951, Air Force Security Service detachments had proliferated to the extent that an easier and more descriptive way was needed to differentiate between detachments of its squadrons.

New Detachment Designators *		
February 1951		
Old Designator	New Designator	Location
Det A, 1st RSM	Detachment 11	Misawa, Japan
Det B, 1st RSM	Detachment 12	Ashiya, Japan
Det C, 1st RSM	Detachment 13	Taegu, Korea
Det A, 2nd RSM	Detachment 21	Rothwesten, Germany
Det B, 2nd RSM	Detachment 22	Schleissheim, Germany
Det C, 2nd RSM	Detachment 23	Bremerhaven, Germany
Det A, 3rd RSM	Detachment 31	Adak, Alaska
Det B, 3rd RSM	Detachment 32	Nome, Alaska
* Only 1st, 2nd and 3rd RSM's had detachments in February 1951.		

Detachment 21 was a simplified and shortened unit designator for Detachment A, 2nd Radio Squadron Mobile; Detachment A, 1st RSM in the Far East became Detachment 11, etc. Effective 1 February 1951, USAFSS directed that all RSM detachments be renamed using numeric designators.[26] (Detachments of squadrons with double-digit identifiers had a three-digit identifier, e.g., the 12th RSM had detachments 121 and 122. Later—in 1952 or '53—detachments were identified by single digits; for example, Detachment 2, 12th RSM.)

The 2nd Radio Squadron Mobile's detachment in Berlin continued to operate covertly as Detachment D without any reference to the 2nd RSM. However, Detachment 24 may have been allocated to the detachment in Berlin, although not observed in open source traffic.

Det 21 Moved to Linz, Austria

Site # 21 (Rothwesten) was producing poor direction finding results, and the 2nd RSM wanted to relocate the DF equipment to a new location in January 1950.[27] However, the colocated CW intercept position was copying some high interest signals, and USAFE/IN wanted the squadron to retain the intercept position at Rothwesten for the time being.

Given USAFE's objections to abandoning Rothwesten, the 2nd RSM began looking in other areas including Bremen for a desirable location for a fourth DF site that the 2nd RSM would create as soon as adequate equipment became available. The date of the move is not firm, but Det 21, 2nd RSM was compromised as being located at Linz, Austria, on 18 June 1951.[28] The relocation from Rothwesten to Linz occurred in either late 1950 or early 1951.[29]

Few official details are available regarding the 2nd RSM detachment at Linz. Bill Baker participated in the set up of the detachment although he is not positive of the date. Then Cpl. Baker recalls spending a few days at Schleissheim (Detachment 22) enroute from Linz back to 2nd RSM headquarters at Darmstadt. The name of the unit (detachment designator) at Linz changed as USAFSS added additional squadrons in Europe in 1951. A USAFSS unit continued operating at Linz until 1957.

DET 25, 2ND RSM, LANDSBERG

In searching for available facilities in Germany where Air Force Security Service could activate a new radio squadron mobile with space to add processing capabilities later, USAFE identified

Landsberg Air Base, a former Luftwaffe base in the Alps near the small city of Landsberg am Lech (on the Lech River). Landsberg is located 23 miles south of Augsburg and 25 miles west of Munich. Ironically, Adolph Hitler wrote Volume One of *Mein Kampf* in 1924 while imprisoned in Landsberg.

Contributed by Ray Thompson

Landsberg Air Base, Bavaria, Germany, circa 1951

USAFSS operations commenced at Landsberg in March 1951 when the 2nd Radio Squadron Mobile dispatched a new detachment—Detachment 25—to the base.[30] Det 25 was a holding unit for "Earmarked Personnel" to be assigned to the 12th Radio Squadron Mobile that was being assigned to Landsberg. Detachment 25 was discontinued on 7 April 1951, with its assigned officers and airmen being reassigned to the 12 RSM.[31]

12TH RSM ACTIVATED AND SHIPPED TO GERMANY

The first unit history for the 12th Radio Squadron Mobile addresses the origin of the squadron. Additional unit histories—issued quarterly—offer insight into the methodology used to activate new USAFSS squadrons. As was the approach for fielding new squadrons from 1949-1951, USAFSS activated the 12th RSM at Brooks AFB, Texas, in the fall of 1950. On 31 December 1950,

Lt. Col. Edgar H. Heald commanded the squadron, and its strength was four officers and 16 airmen.[32]

One problem was obtaining qualified personnel for the unit. Like most all the other squadrons of the Command during the early stages of organization, personnel were obtained from other organizations by means of discussions, volunteers, and assignment through the Headquarters Classification Section.

Oberpfaffenhofen, Ger. (LAT 48.08 N, LONG 11.28 E, ELEV 600 m) (Landsberg Air Base) was to be the headquarters location of the squadron. Capt. Charles S. Willis was assigned to the 2nd Radio Squadron Mobile, Darmstadt, Ger., on 10 Jan 1951 for the purpose of preparing for initial operating positions and drawing necessary equipment. Preparations were made, and an installation team was soon dispatched from Headquarters USAFSS to install the equipment and antenna farm.

Recently promoted, Lt. Col. Heald and MSgt. Herbert P. Geilert departed Brooks AFB in February 1951, assigned to the 2nd RSM, Darmstadt, for the purpose of making ready quarters and mess facilities for the oncoming unit. On 19 March 1951, the unit departed San Antonio, Texas, by rail to Fort Dix, New Jersey. On 26 March, the unit continued to the New York Port of Embarkation and boarded the USNS Alexander M. Patch. The ship sailed the following day and arrived in Bremerhaven, Germany, on 5 April 1951.

Col. Heald and 1st Sgt. Geilert met the squadron at the port in Bremerhaven. After debarking, the unit moved by rail to Landsberg, arriving on 6 April 1951.

Much to the surprise of the unit, they were welcomed by members of Detachment "25" of the 2nd Radio Squadron Mobile, who all later became members of the 12th Radio Squadron Mobile. The unit was attached to Headquarters, 7030th Support Group, for logistical support.[33]

A total of six officers and 92 airmen who had previously been assigned to 2nd Radio Squadron Mobile, earmarked for the 12th Radio Squadron Mobile, had been assigned to Landsberg as Detachment 25 since 20 March 1951. The

Det 25 men had made ready quarters for the arrival of the 12th Radio Squadron Mobile.

With the 12th Radio Squadron Mobile absorbing the men of Detachment 25 on 7 April 1951, squadron strength stood at eight officers and 118 airmen. The 2nd RSM deactivated Detachment 25, 2nd RSM the same date.[34]

Landsberg Air Base was named after the town of Landsberg, located about five miles south of the base. Built between 1937 and 1939, the base had been home to the 3rd Group and staff of the Luftwaffe Alpengeschwader or Alps Bomber Wing during World War II. Bombed extensively between March 1944 and April 1945 by the Allies, the base was captured by the American 12th Armored Division on 26 April 1945. Various U.S. units occupied the base before the arrival of the 12 RSM. The 12th RSM personnel were housed in two-story buildings with basements and large attics.

Prior to the arrival of the 12th RSM, Capt. Charles S. Willis, CO of Det 25, had arranged for the USAFSS Installations Team to construct an antenna farm. The team (two officers and ten airmen) used 66 poles and 75,000 feet of wire on the antenna farm project. The antenna farm was completed on Mar 23, 1951, with all lead-ins to the operations area completed by 5 June 1951.

Capt. Willis assumed duties as the 12th RSM operations officer when the unit arrived at Landsberg. Capt. George V. Carroll, who had accompanied Capt. Willis and Det 25 to the base, was the unit's control officer.

The unit, as Det 25, went into 24-hour operation at 0800, 21 March 1951, using CW positions. At that time, Operations and Control were operating as one with the prime mission of training operators for use as future trick chiefs and control chiefs.

Control Section

On 9 May 1951, the Control Section came into being for the first time as a separate section with the assignment of control chiefs and assumption of responsibility for the preparation of the Daily Coverage Report and other administrative duties.

A series of meetings were held by the operations officer and the traffic analysis officer to brief and instruct the trick chiefs and control chiefs in the use of mission assignment cards and other data pertaining to operations and traffic analysis. These meetings were decisive in clearing up errors that were occurring as a result of the insufficient knowledge held by the trick chiefs and control chiefs using the information.

With the establishment of the Traffic Analysis Section in the 12th RSM, the speed and accuracy of [traffic] identification increased very noticeably. There had been quite some trouble encountered in using the teletype link with the 2nd RSM because of excessive line outage and the delay encountered in receiving identifications from them after they had been sent in.

In June 1951, the Control Section moved into new, permanent space in the attic of building # 6 where the section employed and trained airmen arriving in the squadron without special access security clearance.

These airmen were placed on duty in the Control Section with the control chiefs. These airmen helped edit traffic, maintained the control logs, and became familiar with the handling of [traffic] identification from the Control viewpoint. Thus, when the airmen did move into their section after receiving their clearances, they took with them an overall picture of how things worked between the two sections. The T/A officer reports that the experience these airmen received greatly aided them in their jobs.

The manner in which the Control Section operated at a confidential level as described in the unit history certainly must have bordered on a security violation.

Intercept Section

First Lt. Gordon G. Bandow and 27 airmen from Det 25, 2nd RSM activated the Intercept Section on 21 March 1951 in interim positions—temporarily using "flat top antennas" that produced much interference to their intercept mission.

The 27 operators were graduates of the Intercept School at Brooks Air Force Base and had spent approximately two weeks at the 2nd RSM before arrival at Landsberg. "Needless to say, utilizing these operators as trick chiefs and operators did not produce the desired results immediately and it was several weeks before one could be distinguished from the other from a point of view of supervisory personnel selection."

Traffic identification was moved to the Traffic Analysis Section on 5 June. In addition, the Intercept Section moved to its permanent location in the attic of Building # 23 after receiving additional equipment on 5 June 1951.

An intensive training program was conducted, especially for supervisory personnel after selection. During this training period six of the most well-trained supervisors were transferred to the Control Section and one to the DF Section as NCOIC along with nine operators.

At the close of the quarterly history (30 June 1951), the Intercept Section had 81 airmen assigned against an authorized strength of one officer and 168 airmen.

Traffic Analysis Section

Formed on 9 May 1951, the Traffic Analysis Section consisted of six airmen. With no officer available to manage the section, the operations officer supervised work in the analysis section.

The section was then located in an area offering minimum acceptable physical security and to adequately safeguard this information it required four to six airmen posted on rotating shifts as armed guards.

First Lt.'s Leonard C. Hess and Edgar M. Greene arrived from the 2nd RSM on temporary duty on 15 May 1951 to help establish operating procedures for the T/A Section. Lt.'s Hess and Green were permanently reassigned to the 12th RSM on 2 June 1951 as the traffic analysis officer and assistant T/A officer, respectively.

On 19 May 1951, the T/I [traffic identification] branch of this section was organized using the analysts who had been previously assigned as guards. From 3 to 15 June, traffic which the T/I branch could not ID was sent to the 2nd RSM for verification. They were considered fully qualified on 15 June and request for ID to the 2nd RSM was discontinued.

With the Traffic Analysis Section in place, the 12th RSM no longer had to depend on the 2nd RSM for operations support. One airman was assigned primary duties in "spot analysis of traffic" on 25 May 1951, and HQ USAFSS authorized the squadron to issue "item wires" to headquarters in lieu of daily reports required by current directives. By 28 June 1951, the T/A Section had achieved its authorized strength of 23 airmen.

Direction Finding Section

Lt. Ernest L. Taylor, who arrived on 8 May 1951, had the task of setting up the unit's Direction Finding Section. He activated the 12th RSM's DF station on the southeast side of Landsberg AB. Using an SCR-291 DF system, the squadron's DF Section began operations on 25 June 1951; none of the operators had any DF experience. The DF Control Office was located in the attic of Building # 6. At the end of June 1951, ten airmen were assigned versus an authorized seventeen operators. Nonetheless, they were satisfying requirements "with great success."

Supply Section

The 12th Radio Squadron Mobile's Supply Section experienced typical start-up problems. Receiving 72 boxcar loads of equipment in the first 23 days, the section's officer and five assigned airmen were overwhelmed, and available storage space was inadequate. Squadron airmen augmented the supply specialists, and some equipment was stored in tents, under guard at night to prevent pilferage. In addition, the squadron had to borrow some equipment from the Army Security Agency, Europe, until it received requisitioned items through normal supply channels.

Transportation Section

Lt. Fambro L. Kendrick and seven airmen activated the Transportation Section on 7 April. They received the first shipment of 33 two-and-a-half-ton trucks and fourteen one-ton trailers on 20 April before space had been allocated to the squadron for a motor pool. With regulations stating that each base would have only one motor pool and with the 12th RSM being a mobile unit that had its own personnel and transportation section, Col. Heald had to work out a plan with the air base support group. The group allocated space for an auxiliary motor pool for the squadron.

Air Police Section

Having no Air Police Section for the first three months, the operations officer had the responsibility of providing temporary guards to secure all areas where signals intelligence work was accomplished. Upon his arrival on 8 June 1951, TSgt. Cecil O. Gilleland became NCOIC of the Air Police Section, with the task of forming a guard force. By the end of June, Sgt. Gilleland had created guard posts, the section was fully staffed, and all personnel with special access clearances had been issued permanent-type badges. He continued to report to the operations officer.

Squadron Armory and Mess

The Squadron Armory was also neglected until Sgt. Gilleland's arrival on 8 June. Assigned additional duties as NCOIC of the armory, he established the armory in the basement of building # 23. Requests to establish the squadron's own mess hall were disapproved. Col. Heald assigned the 12th RSM cooks on special duty with the base consolidated dining hall.

Recreation and Education Facilities

The men of the 12th RSM had access to numerous on-base recreational facilities—gym, swimming pool, tennis courts, ball diamonds, Airmens Club, theater, bowling alley and service club. A 12th Radio Squadron Mobile softball team immediately became base champs. A branch of the University of Maryland offered courses that airmen could take to further their education.

Headcount September 1951

Total personnel assigned to the 12th RSM at the end of September 1951 were nineteen officers, 402 airmen and 25 civilians, some of whom were German nationals. The large staff build-up included newly trained specialists earmarked for other USAFSS squadrons that were being deployed in Europe.

12th RSM Key Personnel, July-Sept 1951

The unit history (1 July 1951-30 September 1951) included a roster of key personnel.

12th RSM—KEY PERSONNEL—Sept 1951			
Rank	Last Name	First Name	Title
Lt. Col.	Heald	Edgar H.	Commanding Officer
Capt.	Lindstrum	Donald	Executive Officer
Capt.	Johnson	Jesse H.	Adjutant
MSgt.	Geilert	Herbert P.	1st Sgt.
2nd Lt.	Cummins	Grayson L.	Personnel Officer
TSgt.	Denman	Preston L.	NCOIC
Major	Goff	Thomas	Operations Officer
Major	Willis	Charles S.	Ass't Operations Officer
MSgt.	Butler	Donald K.	NCOIC
Capt.	Carroll	George V.	Control Officer
MSgt.	Wilkinger	Weslie	NCOIC
Capt.	Nicholson	Donald	Intercept Officer
TSgt.	Reid	William L.	NCOIC
1st Lt.	Taylor	Ernest L.	Direction Finding
SSgt.	Boyd	Donald F.	Officer
			NCOIC
1st Lt.	Greene	Edgar M.	Traffic Analysis Officer
SSgt.	Hodges	Jr.	NCOIC
		James O.	
1st Lt.	McGinnis	Raymon L.	Communications Officer
TSgt.	Thrailfill	Harold E.	NCOIC
Capt.	Peacock	Lester	Technical Service Officer
MSgt.	Starwaud	Joseph K.	NCOIC
Capt.	Howerton	Paul A.	Supply Officer
SSgt.	Allen	William	NCOIC
1st Lt.	Kendrick	Fambro L.	Transportation Officer
MSgt.	Ford	George	NCOIC
1st Lt.	Miller	Americus V.	Det 121 Commander
SSgt.	Henrie		1st Sgt.
1st Lt.	Edson		Det 122 Commander
TSgt.	Odermatt		1st Sgt.

Det 21 and Det 22 Became Det 121 and Det 122

The arrival of the 12th Radio Squadron Mobile at Landsberg Air Base brought about a re-subordination of Detachment 21 (Linz,

Austria) and Detachment 22 (Schleissheim, Germany). On 1 August 1951, per HQ USAFSS direction, the 12th RSM published a general order redesignating Det 21 as Detachment 121 with an authorized strength of one officer and 40 airmen. Det 21 personnel were reassigned from the 2nd RSM to the 12th RSM and continued their assignments at Linz.[35]

On 17 August 1951, the 12th RSM published another general order redesignating Det 22 as Detachment 122, 12th RSM, with an authorized strength of one officer and 40 airmen. Unlike the switchover involving Det 21, only three of the airmen on detached duty at Schleissheim remained with Det 122.[36] The 2nd RSM issued orders on 9 August 1951 ordering seventeen airmen currently on detached duty with Detachment 22 at Schleissheim to return to Darmstadt for duty with the 2nd RSM. Departures from Schleissheim for the seventeen men were to occur incrementally between 15 and 25 August.[37]

12th RSM Field Exercise

At the direction of the Commander in Chief, USAFE, the 12th Radio Squadron Mobile conducted a field exercise between 3 and 6 September 1951 at Oberpfaffenhofen Air Strip, a 35-minute trip from Landsberg Air Base. Col. Maury from HQ USAFSS inspected the squadron in the field at Oberpfaffenhofen on the final day of the exercise. Lt. Col. Heald served the USAFSS visitors lunch at the squadron's mess in the field. Results for the field exercise and inspection were not included in the unit history.

12TH RSM PERSONNEL EARMARKED FOR 41ST RSM

As revealed in the unit history, an unspecified number of 12th RSM personnel were earmarked for transfer to the 41st Radio Squadron Mobile, which was being transferred from Brooks AFB, Texas, to Bremerhaven, Germany. On 22 September 1951, Maj. Glen E. Pennywitt from HQ USAFSS visited the squadron to observe operational procedures and inspect the physical arrangement of the squadron area. He also made a side trip to Sonthofen to observe the Sonthofen processing station's procedures and coordinate the processing of 41st RSM personnel there.

Earlier, all military troops arriving in Germany—including USAFSS personnel—had to process through a U.S. Army replacement depot at Marburg, Germany, but a large influx of personnel in 1950 overtaxed Marburg's facilities. About November 1950, the Army's 7720th European Command Replacement Depot moved from Marburg to Burg Kaserne in Sonthofen, Germany's southern-most town. On 24 September, Maj. Pennywitt went to Sonthofen to observe processing methods at Burg Kaserne. After discussing personnel earmarked for the 41st RSM with 12th RSM staff, Pennywitt caught the courier flight to Wiesbaden on 25 September.

12TH RSM PERSONNEL EARMARKED FOR 34TH RSM

From March 1951 forward, HQ USAFSS had been shipping large numbers of uncleared men to the 12th Radio Squadron Mobile, posing problems for the squadron in the utilization of airmen without crypto clearances. As of 30 September 1951, 56 airmen had arrived who were earmarked for the 34th Radio Squadron Mobile. The 12th RSM employed those with appropriate clearances in their operational job areas; those pending clearance action performed in less challenging jobs outside the operations compound. On 15 October 1951, Technical Services was scheduled to start the installation of CW positions at Detachment 122 (Schleissheim).

All equipment necessary for the installation is on hand with the exception of racks, MT 453A/F. This installation is for the purpose of training 34th Radio Squadron personnel.

No additional 12th RSM unit histories are available, and the number of airmen transferred to the 41st RSM and 34th RSM is unknown.

12th RSM Visitors—1951

Visitors to the 12th RSM during the period March-June 1951 included Maj. Gen. Charles P. Cabell, Deputy Chief of Staff, Intelligence/USAF and Brig. Gen. Millard Lewis, Chief of Intelligence at USAFE. In addition, on 6 July Maj. Gen. Roy H. Lynn, who had assumed command of USAFSS in February 1951, visited the squadron. The squadron hosted a special Bavarian "Wiener Schnitzel" lunch for Gen. Lynn at the Officers Club. Later in November 1951, a party of senior USAFSS officers and Mr. William Friedman, renowned Army Security Agency cryptologist, visited the 12th RSM at Landsberg.

USAF Photo

William Friedman (3rd from left) visits 12th RSM, Landsberg, Germany, 23 Nov 1951

"The Man in Black"

Johnny Cash was the man in blue—Air Force Blue—before he became "The Man in Black." Talk to any USAFSS veteran who served in Landsberg, and the odds are in your favor that Johnny Cash's name will surface. Before John R. Cash gained fame and fortune as a rumbling bass baritone, he chased dits and dahs as a Morse intercept operator with the 12th Radio Squadron Mobile during the early 1950's.

J. R. Cash, as he was known by family and close friends, grew up as a sharecropper's son in the cotton fields of the Mississippi delta. Into gospel music but playing no musical instrument when he arrived in Germany, Cash bought a guitar in the BX at Landsberg, taught himself to play it, then formed his first band, the

"Landsberg Barbarians." Soon, the Barbarians were entertaining at the NCO and Officers Clubs. Chester (Chet) Force, a fellow Morse intercept operator in the unit, sometimes picked and sang with Cash in the barracks but was not a Barbarians band member.

I was in 12th RSM '53 and '54; worked the C and the B shifts. Played a little guitar with Johnny. We got together and picked and sang a few times in his room. He had written a few gospel songs at the time, and that's about all he was interested in. This lasted about 6-8 months, and I transferred to England.

I know he put some guys together after that and played some clubs. His work habits were good to my knowledge. He like myself sat there with a couple of receivers and monitored the airwaves. He was enjoyable to be around and had a lot of laughs.

Gayle Stelter, another Morse intercept operator in the squadron, did not know John Cash, but found out later that he had cleaned up the barracks after their guitar playing sessions.

I didn't know Cash personally. I had to police the day room in Landsberg waiting for my clearance and had to clean up after a crew had been picking and using an old reel-to-reel tape recorder. I was later told that it was Cash.

Discharged from the Air Force in 1956, Stelter earned a PhD and spent 28 years in the teaching profession, retiring in 1997. Tongue in cheek, he contrasts his achievements in the Air Force to how quickly he became a tenured college professor.

My claim to fame is that it took me only 24 months to make Full Professor compared to the 33 months to make A1C [in the Air Force].

Gayle Stelter is proud of his USAFSS service and organized the 6912th alumni reunion in 1999. His initial master list of squadron alumni has grown from a mere handful of names in 1997 to a current roster in 2006 of 550 members who served at Landsberg, Bingen, Hof and Landshut, Germany, and Linz and Vienna, Austria. We are indebted to Dr. Stelter for making possible contact with several squadron alumni who have contributed to the history of the 12th and 6912th Radio Squadrons Mobile.

Johnny Cash Roots and Legacy

Discharged from the Air Force in 1954, John R. Cash became Johnny Cash in the entertainment industry. Over the years, he has neither flaunted nor tried to hide his veteran status, and few fans realize the role that the Air Force played in his personal life and musical career. J.R. Cash met his first wife Vivian Liberto while training at Brooks AFB in 1950. Using money from his Air Force paycheck, he bought his first guitar and began his musical and song-writing careers at Landsberg. He married Vivian after his discharge in 1954.

Johnny Cash had an uncanny ability to mentally compose songs while engaged in other activities and turn life experiences into country and pop music hits. He worked out the arrangement "Hey Porter" in his head while polishing his boots at Landsberg. At his first audition—primarily gospel music—a year later, Cash failed to land a recording contract. The record producer told Johnny to "go home and sin, then come back with a song I can sell." Johnny returned with "Hey Porter" and "Cry, Cry, Cry," and landed a contract with Sun Records in 1955. His first # 1 hit, "Walk the Line," followed in 1956.[38]

During five decades in music, Johnny Cash recorded more than 1,500 songs, including an untold number of country and pop hits. In 1969, he sold more records than the Beatles and swept the Country Music awards. He also had his own TV show from 1969 to 1971 and in 1980 became the Country Music Hall of Fame's youngest living inductee at 48. The Rock and Roll Hall of Fame added to Johnny's accolades when it inducted him in 1992. Finally, Johnny Cash received Grammy awards in 1994, 1996, 2000, 2002, 2003 and 2004—the latter being awarded after his death on 12 September 2003.

Ironically, Air Force veterans representing several USAFSS alumni groups, including the author, attempted to contact Johnny Cash and reintroduce him to his Air Force Security Service roots, but to no avail. Whether an assistant intercepted his correspondence without Cash's knowledge or Cash chose not to reconnect with his Air Force past is unknown.

Johnny Cash was not a fan of the Vietnam War, but he did not protest the war as did many entertainers. During the 1960's, he and wife June Carter Cash toured overseas with the United Service Organization (USO), entertaining American troops in the field. In typical style, Cash penned the song, "Drive On," capturing his version of life of a G.I. in combat after a series of USO shows in Vietnam.

During a USO tour of the Far East in 1962, Johnny and June Carter did afternoon and evening shows for Air Force Security Service personnel at Wakkanai, Japan. Serving with the 6986th RGM at Wakkanai at the time, the author attended both performances. Asking if there were any intercept operators in the audience, Johnny Cash joked, "I know what you guys are doing back at Operations. I spent 12 years in Security Service—between 1950 and 1954." The audience howled!

41ST RSM ACTIVATED IN 1951

In line with its intercept site expansion plans for Europe, Air Force Security Service activated the 41st Radio Squadron Mobile at Brooks AFB, Texas, on 1 June 1951. Maj. Gen. Lynn, USAFSS Commander, selected Maj. Glen E. Pennywitt to command the 41st RSM. In February 2006, 90-year old retired Air Force Col. Pennywitt discussed his involvement in the development of USAFSS capabilities in Europe in the early 1950's. He and his staff built up the 41st RSM in an old hangar at Brooks, where they cobbled together intercept equipment to outfit the new unit. The nucleus of the squadron was formed at Brooks, but the 2nd RSM at Darmstadt and the 12th RSM at Landsberg provided most of the operations personnel for the 41st.

In September 1951, Maj. Pennywitt conducted a site survey of the Bremerhaven Staging Area that was to be home to the 41st RSM. The 41st RSM was replacing Detachment 23, 2nd RSM in Bremerhaven, and he coordinated the squadron's future move with Lt. Benson, commander of Detachment 23, 2nd RSM.

While in Europe, Maj. Pennywitt also visited the 12th Radio Squadron Mobile in Landsberg in the German Alps, as well as the recently relocated 6910th Security Group Headquarters in Wiesbaden. In November 1951, the 41st RSM relocated from Brooks AFB aboard a Liberty ship from New York to

Bremerhaven. In 2006, retired Col. Pennywitt recalled that the only major problem that the unit faced in setting up operations in Bremerhaven was installing antennas. Engineers specified a requirement for 100-foot tall antenna masts for stringing Rhombic antennas that could monitor targets of interest, and the low sea level and high water table in Bremerhaven made it almost impossible to erect such tall antennas.

With the 41st RSM fully operational, in 1952 USAFSS reassigned Maj. Pennywitt as the Executive Officer of the 6910th Security Group in Wiesbaden, replacing him as 41st RSM Commander with Lt. Col. Heald, who had been the 12th RSM's first commander. A year later, Maj. Pennywitt assumed command of the 12th RSM at Landsberg. Shortly before he rotated home to America from Landsberg in August 1954, he participated in a site survey in the Bingen area, but departed the squadron before the 12th RSM moved to Bingen.

41st RSM Operations—First Traffic Analysts

Whereas Detachment C (aka Det 23), 2nd RSM had been dependent upon the 2nd Radio Squadron Mobile for traffic identification and traffic analysis, the 41st RSM brought its own traffic analysts to Bremerhaven. After a circuitous journey, former USAFSS SSgt. Keith Barkley arrived in the port city with the first group of 41st RSM T/A specialists in late 1951. In July 2006, Keith reminisced about how he became a USAFSS traffic analyst and pioneered T/A in the 41st RSM from 1951 to 1954.

> *I arrived at Lackland about 5 January 1951, just in time to take very temporary residence in "tent city." They were so overcrowded with other "heroes" like myself that they hardly knew what to do with us. We had about 2 weeks of training—to get haircuts and try to teach us left from right I think.*

> *We were then assigned to our first duty station. I should say that I was a farm boy and wanted to fix airplanes or at least do something mechanical. Tests were easy for me, and I tested near perfect scores on my AFSC [air force specialty code] exams. With the start of the Security Service, they needed my brain more than they needed my body, I guess, so when they skimmed the top scores off of*

these tests, I was selected for crypto training. I was pretty disillusioned when they loaded me onto a school bus and announced that we were going across town to Brooks AFB.

At any rate, quite a number of us ended up at Brooks, in the USAFSS. The three main choices there were, Chinese language at Monterey, Russian at Syracuse or crypto right there at Brooks. After several weeks of crypto training, we were put to work in the "Compound" (a fenced operations area at Brooks). Actually we didn't know much, and I don't know that we learned much, but we did get some hands-on experience with intercepted radio traffic.

From Brooks, USAFSS reassigned A2C Barkley's group of traffic analysts to the 12th RSM at Landsberg AB, Germany. According to Barkley, after training for 18 weeks as "crypto experts—202 traffic analysts," the Air Force reassigned his group of eight to ten men to a USAFSS unit in Libya, granting the airmen a delay-enroute leave.

We went home for 30 days leave about the first of November 1951. At this point our luck took a turn for the better. While we were home on leave, 41st RSM in Bremerhaven was activated, and our orders were all changed to that station.

After the 30-day leave and a slow processing adventure at Camp Kilmer, we headed for Bremerhaven on the USS Eltinge—a Victory ship that had few creature comforts! We arrived in B'haven about 10 days later thinking—here we are—but we underestimated the efficiency of the Air Force. We were loaded onto a train (actually extra fine accommodations) and shipped to Sonthofen in the Austrian Alps for processing. This was a beautiful location. (one of Adolph's Youth Camps). [Note: Sonthofen is actually Germany's southern-most town.]

We were then sent back north. Next stop was Darmstadt— home of the 2nd RSM, which was designated as "group" to us at 41st. I think we spent the actual Christmas day there. I have no idea what this 2-day stopover in Darmstadt accomplished!

Finally, the 41st RSM's first group of traffic analysts arrived in Bremerhaven during the last week of December 1951.[39] Keith Barkley elaborated on the arrival.

> *B'haven wasn't quite ready for us either. We were billeted in the Marine Barracks—formerly a submarine training facility for the Germans. Our first duty there was to unpack Carbines (M-1's I believe) and wipe the cosmolene off of them, clean them and make them usable—to defend ourselves, I guess. Eventually we were put to "work" at the operations area at the Staging Area.*

Det 23, 2nd RSM and the 41st RSM were still conducting intercept operations in hanger # 103 when Barkley's group set up the 41st RSM's traffic exploitation section—traffic analysis was too sensitive for a section name. While training at Brooks and Landsberg provided some sense of direction, there were essentially no formal directives or technical aids to facilitate traffic exploitation.

> *We did learn fast, though, and to our credit became a very highly respected group of analysts. Our next duty move was into another hangar, much better equipped for our operation. I think we must have been in that building for over a year, until the beautiful headquarters building was readied for us.*

The 41st RSM moved from its temporary operations area in a hangar to its new operations compound in 1954. Keith Barkley correctly deduced that the initial cadre of USAFSS officers and senior NCO's lacked experience in signals intelligence operations.

> *We became exposed to a variety of noncoms and officers over the next 3 years. Most of them were not exactly trained for the job they were required to do at the 41st. They were WW 2 vets, most of them. The Sgt.'s had been radio operators I suppose. The best officer, and man, I have ever known was Lt. Charles Culpepper. I think he had been a pilot. He was a tall broad-shouldered man. We would have done anything for him—or to make him look good. I mean no disrespect to the other officers as I am sure they did their jobs well, but none of them were really trained to be crypto analysts.*

Keith Barkley was proud of his contributions to the USAFSS traffic analysis mission.

My eventual job after I became SSgt. was to head the Long Range Bomber Section. I think we had the distinction of being the best at that in the Command. I know that when I sent in information or analytic conclusions I was always greeted with "We Concur." I remember getting a Commendation from Col. Stroot,[40] I believe. He commended me on my work—expressed special interest, wanted me to brief him personally someday, etc., etc. Then he stamped it "Confidential" and sent it to me through the mail! I would have loved to keep it, but it contained "TS" material—I burned it! ((Perhaps indicates how little some of our officers really knew about what we were doing.))

Barkley served in the 41st RSM for three years and received his discharge from the Air Force in late 1954. He was nonplussed that no one in the squadron encouraged any of the analysts who arrived in the 41st RSM in 1951 to reenlist.

Our tour of duty was over in November 1954. Of my original 202 group, none of us stayed in the Air Force. A couple of them, including Lt. Culpepper, did work for NSA for a time. I really wonder why some of us were not approached and encouraged to stay in the USAFSS and use what they had taught us—maybe we weren't as valuable as I remember us being!!

Returning to Nebraska, Keith Barkley built the family farm into a "pretty fine dairy and general farming operation."

I used much of the leadership training I got in the Air Force in filling many of the non-paying jobs in the county as well as serving on various more prestigious boards of directors. The AF was good for me, and I have many great memories.

In 1984, Barkley contacted former 41st RSM members, organized the first squadron alumni reunion and has attended most subsequent reunions. Thinking back on 41st RSM personnel, he recalled that MSgt. Robert A. Suplick served as the first NCOIC of Traffic Analysis in the 41st RSM, probably in 1952. During a second tour in the port city, SMSgt. Suplick also served as the NCOIC of the T/A shop from 1960-1964.

41ˢᵀ RSM BECOMES 6913ᵀᴴ RSM

In May 1955, the 41st Radio Squadron Mobile became the 6913th Radio Squadron Mobile, part of a major USAFSS reorganization. The 41st RSM personnel officer issued special orders reassigning all assigned personnel to the new organization with no change in duty station—otherwise, it was business as usual in the squadron.

41st RSM DF Operations

After Detachment 23, 2nd RSM operations was merged into the 41st RSM (late 1951-early 1952), the 41st moved its direction finding site from the Staging Area into the country south of Bremerhaven. Robert Burnside, a Morse intercept operator who worked at multiple 41st/6913th RSM DF sites from 1953 to 1956, estimates that "DF Bremerhaven" (41st DF site) was 15-18 miles from the Staging Area—in a field between the Bremerhaven-Bremen road (old Route 6) and the Weser River. Burnside knew the sites by given names: DF Bremerhaven and DF Landsberg initially, and later, DF Fassberg and DF Schleswig.

DF network control was located at Landsberg (12th RSM). The sites used both CW and teletype to communicate with DF control. One Morse operator trained in DF and one Russian linguist per shift worked around the clock at each DF site—typically 10-12 total airmen were assigned at site. Bremerhaven DF personnel commuted to the site, initially from the Marine Barracks and later from the Staging Area. There was a small Navy Ships Store at Marine Barracks, but no BX or commissary. In June 2006, Burnside described 41st RSM DF operations to the author.

When in Bremerhaven we had a landline phone to the unit in case we needed anything. Sometimes we did since on occasion the Communist Party would try to disturb the site, and we would need to call for some backup. That happened on two occasions while I was on duty there during midshifts and once during a dayshift. As long as I worked the sites, control of the sites remained with Landsberg (as net control). Any mission could be called in

from anywhere needing our services but had to go through
net control (or one of our sites) before action was taken.

Completing a 12-month Russian language course at Syracuse University, Jack Sharp served as a linguist/DF operator with the 41st RSM from 1953 to 1956. On slow shifts, Jack often chatted with Bill Smith, another Russian linguist/DF operator at Landsberg. Smith had also learned Russian at Syracuse. After Landsberg, Smith became an actor in Hollywood, usually playing a villain such as his role as a Russian army major in the movie *Red Dawn*.[41] He also had bit parts in TV hits—Hawaii-Five-O, Rockford Files, Dukes of Hazzard, et al. Ironically, although he preferred "Bill," his screen credit always read "William Smith."

41st RSM DF at Detached Locations

Commencing in its second year of operation, the 41st RSM created a second DF site about 120 miles southeast of Bremerhaven, later replacing that site with one to the north of the port city. None of the traditional U.S. support facilities—family quarters, commissary and PX, or medical and dental facilities—existed at the detached DF sites; thus, only single enlisted personnel served at those sites. A squadron officer visited each detached site once per month to pay the troops and deliver mail. In addition, the detached airmen picked up mail and made purchases in the BX and commissary in Bremerhaven during courier runs to 41st RSM Operations.

At their remote sites, the airmen had a couple of jeeps and a 3/4-ton truck at their disposal, and hauled gasoline and power unit spare parts from Bremerhaven to support their transportation and power needs. In addition, some of the airmen owned automobiles. Although he did not help activate the 41st RSM's DF site at Fassberg, Germany, Bob Burnside served there for about a year in 1954 and 1955.

DF Fassberg Site

In late 1953, the 41st Radio Squadron Mobile activated its second DF site (Det 1, 41st RSM) on RAF Fassberg, a Royal Air Force fighter base in the British Occupation Zone about 60 miles south of Hamburg. Located too far from Bremerhaven for daily commutes (120 miles), the 41st RSM arranged for the DF Fassberg airmen to live in RAF Sergeants' Quarters and paid the detached men per diem for rations.

Contributed by Robert Burnside

Setting up DF Site at Fassberg, Germany, 1953

The RAF quarters were WW II-era barracks, perhaps former Luftwaffe pilot billets. Each airman had an individual room on the second floor, while RAF sergeants occupied the first floor. As explained by Bob Burnside, the Fassberg DF team had the option of purchasing meals from the RAF or preparing their own food.

> *Our barracks had a kitchen, so we prepared a lot of our own meals since the food at the Sergeants Mess was pretty bad. There was an RAF sergeant in charge of quarters, and he was a nice sort with whom we had a good relationship—no problems.*

> *We paid the sergeants' monthly fee for living and eating there although about the only meal we ate there, at Fassberg, was breakfast. And then if you wanted two eggs, you had to bring the second one to be cooked since you were only allowed one.*

Bob Burnside and other 41st airmen serving on the RAF base never acquired a taste for the "bangers" (British sausages), sliced bread fried in sausage grease and baked beans that were staples on the RAF breakfast menu. And bringing your own egg to enjoy a two-egg breakfast was bothersome. Likewise, they tired quickly of mutton that the Sergeants Mess served often for dinner. As an alternative, Burnside and his comrades quietly stocked the refrigerator in their kitchen from the commissary and a German Metzgerai (butcher shop) and took pride in preparing their own meals. The RAF also had a small NAAFI (camp store) on base, but it offered little of interest to the Americans who went out of their way to minimize the appearance of extravagance around their British hosts.

We all received TDY pay which was $9.00 a day plus our regular pay. I mention this since it necessitated that we be very careful of not flaunting our affluence in front of the British troops, since most of us as airmen first class, SSgt.'s and up were making more money per month than their higher ranking officers.

The Site Mascot

As is typical with the American military overseas—in war and in peace—the airmen at the Fassberg DF site acquired a mascot. Bob Burnside elaborates.

While in Fassberg we somehow came to adopt a small, black female puppy. We named her "Spook," and she lived at the site with us (on the site and in the vans). She was a great little dog, and when she became pregnant we were all excited and of course helped her raise the pups.

All the pups were given names that were current radio terms we used daily. We found homes for them all but kept Spook. The plan was that the last guy to leave, to rotate from the site was the one to take Spook with him. I do not know if in fact that happened since I was not that person. I like to believe it did happen because we all loved that little dog, and she filled a real void in our lives.

Fassberg After Hours

With a horseshoe pit constructed by the DF site airmen, a recreation room with a card table and a record player on their floor of the barracks and numerous dart boards, the RAF base offered some recreational opportunities, but tiny Fassberg village had only one bar. As Fassberg's only watering hole where one could have a "cool one," Pop's Place served beer that rated high above the warm beer available in the RAF Sergeants Mess. According to Jack Sharp, Pop also served a rather tasty Apfel Korn Liquor and a rot-gut schnapps called Ratzeputz. His comrades tricked him once into downing a double shot of Ratzeputz, all the while believing it was Korn. Almost took his breath!

On one occasion, Bob Burnside visited the former Bergen-Belsen Concentration Camp, which was located 10 miles from Fassberg. He did not know the "Anne Frank Story" at the time, and that she had died at Bergen-Belsen. Nonetheless, viewing the graves and what had happened there stunned him and affected his sleeping for months afterward.

Being isolated from U.S. military facilities had its pros and cons. Receiving per diem pay in lieu of a meal card authorizing gratis meals in a U.S. Army mess hall was a definite plus, as was the general laxity of daily living—no personal inspections, commander's calls or other mandatory formations. At the same time, site personnel did not have ready access to creature comforts and recreation facilities available back at headquarters—movie theater, service club, hobby shops, team sports, wider selection of gasthauses and restaurants, etc. All the detached DF site staff were volunteers, and no one complained. In fact, according to Burnside, morale and esprit de corps were sky-high.

> We did maintain a military appearance and bearing and when living in the sergeants mess, maintained our quarters appropriate for inspection, not only by our own NCOIC, but also the RAF NCO in charge of quarters. We also prepared ourselves appropriately for paydays. That's when an officer from Bremerhaven would show up with our pay, mail and other goodies, etc.

> We all had a deep sense of pride in doing what we were doing and doing it well. The nature of the job made it even more important to us—so, yes, we maintained our military bearing for we were not only proud of doing our job well; we were representing our service and our country not only to the British soldiers and their officers but also to the German people. I think we all felt this responsibility and acted accordingly.

The 41st/6913th RSM phased out the Fassberg DF site in 1956, replacing it with a new DF site (Det 2, 6913th RSM) at Schleswig in Schleswig-Holstein state.

Schleswig DF Site

The Schleswig DF site was located on RAF Schleswig—perhaps 100 miles northeast of Bremerhaven as the crow flies, but roughly twice that distance via a circuitous route for 41st RSM personnel. Normally transporting classified materials, from Bremerhaven they drove south to Bremen, then east to Hamburg before heading north to Schleswig—a five- to five and a half hour trip.

In July 2006, James (Jim) Miller discussed 41st/6913th DF operations. During his time with the squadron, MSgt. Francis (Frank) M. DeLauis Jr. was the NCOIC of Operations. Miller, NCOIC of the Fassberg DF site, played a major role in the activation of 6913th RSM DF operations at Schleswig. On 29 August 1955, he participated in a coordination meeting at the 6900th Security Wing in Frankfurt to finalize plans to open the Schleswig DF site, A week later, he accompanied Capt. Hollis A. Benson and an advance party to Schleswig to work out arrangements with the British for the soon-to-arrive detached DF team. (Having brought Security Service—Det C, 2nd RSM—to Bremerhaven in 1950, Benson was now on his second USAFSS tour in the port city.)

TSgt. Richard G. Scarboro arrived in Schleswig during the first half of September 1955 with a 6913th DF team and intercept gear to begin direction finding operations at RAF Schleswig. Initially, the DF team lived in the Hotel Schleswig, later moving into a barracks on the British base. As at Fassberg, the USAFSS DF team received per diem in lieu of meals while living in Sergeants Quarters at Schleswig. Bob Burnside was a member of Sergeant Scarboro's team that opened the DF site at Schleswig. Having served earlier at the Fassberg and Bremerhaven DF sites, he was partial to the Schleswig site.

The food at the Sergeants Mess at Schleswig was much better. The quarters were better, the dining hall better, and they had their own bar and rec [recreation] room. It really was a pleasant assignment. I also felt the relationship with the British sergeants was excellent. We never had the camaraderie at Fassberg that we had at Schleswig—don't know why.

Military orders during the first few months of detached duty at Schleswig stated that the airmen were performing a site survey— probably until the 6913th shut down the Fassberg DF site in early 1956. DF work at RAF Schleswig ceased probably in 1967.

41st RSM/6913th RSM Mission

The 6913th RSM (and its predecessor 41st RSM) was a major component of USAFSS coverage of Eastern Europe. In addition to its high frequency (HF) Morse and teleprinter targeting, the 41st RSM/6913th RSM had an extensive HF voice communications intercept mission. The author served with the 6913th as a Russian voice intercept operator on Baker Trick during 1960 and 1961.[42]

Bremerhaven—Leisure Time

Compared to other "garden spots" to which USAFSS assigned airmen during the Cold War, Bremerhaven rated perhaps in the middle of the pack. Cold, damp winds off the North Sea penetrated the air during much of the year, convincing many U.S. military personnel who only saw the area when they picked up or shipped their private autos at the port that an assignment to Bremerhaven was to be avoided. However, USAFSS airmen who served in the 41st RSM or 6913th RSM look back with fondness on their assignments in the port city.

Bremerhaven is off the beaten path and lacks significant tourist attractions. Nonetheless, it had adequate bars, gasthauses and restaurants in the 1950's and 60's to satisfy most tastes, and shift workers found it convenient to visit metropolitan centers during a long, 96-hour break every eighteen days. (Work schedule was four swingshifts and 24 hours off, four midshifts and 24 hours off, four days and 96 hours off; then repeat.) Some of the frequently mentioned local hangouts included the Odeon, Otto's, Blue Angel, Red Angel, Rio Rita, San Souci, Red Mill and Nord Pole—the latter being on the road north to Cuxhaven.

A number of the bars—for example, the Blue Angel and Red Angel—remained open on overlapping schedules to accommodate USAFSS shift workers (and visiting sailors when U.S. Navy and Merchant Marine ships were in port). Others closed two to four hours for "cleaning." With Class A liberty passes, the airmen only had to report for duty per work schedule, and some were known to take their shaving kits to town with them on their long breaks—catching an hour of sleep here or there in the back booth of a bar. And early morning "roll call" at one of the watering holes after working a midshift was a popular event. A few, including the author, prided themselves in getting away for their long breaks.

Contributed by Ron Fandrick

Red Mill Bar, Bremerhaven, Germany, 1960's

Amsterdam Odysseys

Airmen stationed in Bremerhaven during the 1950's and 1960's could travel cheaply by auto to Copenhagen, Denmark, Amsterdam, Holland, or Frankfurt, Germany, in a matter of hours. Copenhagen was the most difficult to reach due to auto ferry schedules. The author visited Copenhagen once before settling on jaunts to Amsterdam. Just days after joining the 6913th RSM in August 1960, a Marine Sgt. from Naval Security Group gave me a 1959 red Renault Dauphine to assume his monthly payment of $69.00. That car, which my Air Force comrades dubbed the "Frog Car," soon learned its way to Amsterdam with minimal driver assistance.

Frog Car—with a sliding sunroof, no less—was a ticking time bomb, an accident waiting to happen. It is amazing that we survived those trips to Amsterdam and its environs. With ESSO gasoline purchased through the PX at $.12 per gallon costing several times less than local civilian gas, most G.I.'s in Germany carried in their car trunk at least one spare five-gallon jerrycan of PX gasoline. Two jerrycans of highly flammable fuel fitted side-by-side in the Dauphine's trunk, with adequate space remaining to haul changes of clothes for three merry travelers. Recalling that a Dauphine's trunk was in the front like a VW Beetle, the author cringes to think about what would have happened in a head-on collision. But we were young and felt invincible!

"Frog Car" (1959 Renault) in Amsterdam, Spring 1961

Three of four Baker Trick voice intercept operators—the author, Thomas (Billy) Burke, David de Wey and David Thorsen—formed a traveling trio that made many unforgettable journeys to A-Dam. Frog Car had room for only three vagabonds because one passenger shared the rear seat with a case of refreshments. The routine was always the same—top-off the gas tank, buy a case of beer for the trip at the PX, pick up 96-hour passes at the 6913th RSM orderly room, and pack the car during lunch hour on the last dayshift.

Each odyssey adhered to a schedule that would have made a German train conductor proud. Finishing the last dayshift at 16:00 hours, the Frog Car "took off" at 16:30 sharp for Amsterdam.

Whoever rode in the backseat popped the caps on three beers as soon as we exited the Staging Area. Our route called for an Auto Fahre ride across the Weser River near Nordenham to shave minutes off an otherwise less direct route via Bremen. The Auto Fahre left the east bank of the Weser at precisely 17:15. We dined on bratwursts during the 12-minute crossing. Missing the 17:15 Fahre—which we did once—added an hour to our journey, causing us to miss "last call for alcohol" in Amsterdam.

Pit-Stops

With the pedal to the metal, at maximum RPM Frog Car cruised at 115-120 KPH—we may as well have had a fuel toggle switch in lieu of an accelerator as we hummed into the night at top speed. Amsterdam was (is) about 250 miles from Bremerhaven by car, with the Dutch border by Nordhorn, Germany, approximately the halfway point. Barring any road construction delays, we normally made our first pit-stop at a Dutch restaurant/gasthaus by the border at 20:00 hours.

After two to three trips, the Dutch immigration troops readily recognized our red Frog Car with green "USA" (U.S. Forces, Germany) license plates and only summarily glanced at our Air Force passes before welcoming us to the Netherlands. During one trip, ole Billy Burke realized as we approached Holland that he had left his pass in Bremerhaven. While searching for the pass in his wallet, he pulled out a PX laundry ticket with his name on it. Glancing at Billy's ID card and laundry slip, the border guard waved us through the border crossing and wished us a happy holiday in Amsterdam.

Our next pit-stop called for refueling and tapping a kidney about 22:30—little of our original case of beer remained as we approached A-dam. Leaving Bremerhaven with a full tank of gas (eight gallons), our Dauphine would coast into Amsterdam's outskirts before flaming out. More often than not, Frog Car would splutter heading onto a major bridge leading into the city. Being a well-lighted, multilane bridge, this point became our preferred refueling stop. We topped off the Frog Car fuel tank again immediately before heading back to Germany. The two jerrycans of gas were more than adequate for three days' driving in Amsterdam and the return trip to Bremerhaven.

Amsterdam—On Leave

The author fell in love with Amsterdam even before he joined the 6913th RSM in 1960. Only five years my senior, my Uncle Robert McLamb had been a U.S. Air Force NCO at Soesterberg Air Base, 20 miles south of Amsterdam in the late 1950's.

Robert McLamb and Larry Tart, Heineken Brewery, 1959

Standing 6 ' 7 " and very muscular, "Big Mac" as he is known, was Holland's most eligible bachelor—Dutch ladies went out of their way to practice their English with Big Mac, and he did his part to further Dutch-American relations. During a 10-day leave in 1959, he introduced me in the best hangouts in Amsterdam. I became "Big Mac's Nephew" to his acquaintances. Big Mac had rotated from Holland by the time our trio began visiting Amsterdam from Bremerhaven in 1960.

Author's Collection

Canal Tour, Amsterdam, 1959

Mom's Place

The first Amsterdam journey for the author, Dave de Wey and Dave Thorsen in the fall of 1960 established a standard for future trips. Roads into central Amsterdam (Centrum) are marked clearly, and Frog Car took us to Rembrandt Square with no difficulty. We parked on a side street along a canal—mere steps from the front door to Mom's Place, a small hotel-bar located on the square.

Mom's Place was a typical bed-and-breakfast hotel in Amsterdam, with a cozy bar at street-level and a few tourist rooms on its second and third floors. Catering to all tourists but remembering her WW II liberators, the matronly hotel owner was especially partial to Americans. Drink a couple too many beers in her bar, and Mom would confiscate your car keys, put you to bed upstairs and settle up for your room the following morning. (For airmen from nearby Soesterberg Air Base, Mom would roust them in the morning, insuring that they got to work on time.)

We strolled into Mom's bar at 23:00, a full hour before closing time. Anka, barmaid on duty, shouted, "Big Mac's Nephew!" as she served us three Heinekens—the first three were on the house. We returned to Frog Car for our luggage only after the bar closed.

Anka and Monique were Mom's live-in barmaids—they lived upstairs and frequently hung out with customers. Part Indonesian,

Anka had the salient features and personality of a Polynesian dream queen, and Monique was a look-alike for screen goddess Kim Novak. Anka and Monique were not hookers, but if they cottoned to you, you were good to go. Having frightful memories of World War II, neither liked Germans, but catered to them, nonetheless. Business was business!

A-dam Memories—The Author

One afternoon as de Wey, Burke and I sat at the bar, Anka kept setting free Heinekens in front of us for perhaps three hours. A free beer now and then was the norm, but after many free rounds, I asked Anka, "What is the special occasion?" She replied, "You see the men at that table in the corner; they're Germans, and I hate Germans." "Every time they order a round, I charge them for your drinks also." Dave, Billy and I nodded and yelled, "Prost!" to the Germans and slipped Anka a nice tip.

On another occasion, sitting at the bar nursing a hangover one morning, I was picking at the nail on my right thumb—I had caught something under the nail the preceding night and it was painful. Watching me from behind the bar, Anka said, "Let me see; what is wrong?" Inspecting the thumb, she hesitated momentarily and said, "I do not know how you call it in English, but in Dutch, we say that you have a 'splinter' under your nail." Picking myself up off the floor from laughter, I explained to her that Americans also call that sliver of wood a splinter. With a pair of tweezers, she nursed the thumb back to good health.

It seemed that Anka was always bailing out the author. Leaving Dave and Billy at Mom's Place one Saturday night, I made the rounds of several watering holes, some farther from Amsterdam Centrum than I normally ventured. Ended up a few miles from Mom's Place at midnight. Losing my way and too tired to drive, I parked along a main, multilane street and dozed off in the driver's seat of Frog Car. A Dutch policeman who was walking his beat awoke me, and correctly observing that I had been drinking, confiscated my car keys and driver's license without arresting me. Asking if I had a hotel, he hailed a taxi and sent me back to Mom's Place to sleep it off—telling me to go to the police station in the morning to retrieve my car. On Sunday morning, I asked Anka to accompany me to pick up Frog Car.

The policeman provided me no paperwork for my car keys and license. However, from my description of the area where I had been bar-hopping, Anka directed a taxi driver to the correct police precinct station. After identifying myself to the desk sergeant, the sergeant returned my keys and license. When I asked where my car was stored, the Sgt. replied that the police had left it on the street where I had parked it. Without further adieu, I thanked the desk sergeant and we departed.

Outside the station, on a Sunday morning when streets were deserted Anka commenced an interrogation, "Describe the street where you left the car." We walked a few blocks on a main avenue; it did not look familiar. Reversing course, Anka led us to a boulevard a block away. Looking left then right, 500 meters away on a six-lane thoroughfare sat a small, red indiscernible type car. As we walked toward it, Frog Car never looked better! It took awhile to live down that episode.

A-dam Memories—Dave de Wey

In July 2006, I queried Dave de Wey about our Amsterdam odysseys. Dave's response:

How dare you tax an old man's brain! I can barely remember what I had for dinner last night.

Ah, Amsterdam. We did have some fine times there. Sad to say that we didn't go there for the cultural aspects. After long hours at a radio console it was time to party! Understandably then, much of our time there is a blur. A couple of things I do remember.

We always stayed at a very tiny hotel on Rembrandt Square, two dollars per night as I recall. The old woman who owned it would fix us fresh eggs, ham and cheese in the mornings. The rooms were sparse at best and cleaning was questionable. As a safety precaution I (as did many other G.I.'s) would toss my wallet under the mattress upon retiring. A couple of weeks after one weekend's visit to the hotel I was approached by a fellow airman back at the base who was kind enough to return my 4-Day-Pass and my Immunization Records which he had found "under the mattress in a small hotel on Rembrandt Square." Some coincidence!

By midnight or so, most of the restaurants in Amsterdam would be closed. And, late night imbibing would lead us to a powerful hunger. Fortunately, an old Chinese man toured the watering holes carrying what looked like a large black tool box. Inside was a base of hot charcoal on which he broiled small meat kabobs on a stick.

They were quite tasty as well as very inexpensive. I had partaken of these delicacies on several of our forays to adventure-land with no adverse side effects. My desire for these tasty tidbits ended, however, when upon returning to our base in Germany it was pointed out to me that there were <u>no stray dogs or cats</u> in the city of Amsterdam! Hmm.

Now retired in South Carolina, Dave de Wey went on to ask if I had accompanied him and Dave Thorsen to Paris.

I seem to remember driving down the Champs-Elysées with the moon roof open, smoking huge cigars. Paul (Turk) Hunn might have been with us as well...seems to me he picked up a chick from Cuxhaven at the Eiffel Tower. What times those were!!!

Never a Francophile, and abhorring Charles de Gaulle, I limited my travel in France and never visited Paris.

The Journey Home

After three and a half days of more or less continuous partying in Amsterdam, our trio's bodies were drained—time to return to work and rest up. Enjoying a 96-hour break after working our last dayshift, we always drove back to Bremerhaven the morning of the day we were scheduled to work our first swingshift at 16:00. Typically, we'd pull out of A-dam no later than 7:00 a.m., and our route home varied, depending on available time and hunger level.

Our stay in Amsterdam had been a blur, with never enough time to eat a balanced meal. The continental breakfast at Mom's Place went only so far in replenishing our stamina. For the remainder of each day, we survived on a kabob here or there and other junk food. Billy Burke's philosophy—there's a pork chop in every bottle of Heineken—only fools the body momentarily. By the time we departed A-dam, each of us longed for a couple of tall glasses of cold milk and a hearty meal.

Options included detouring by Soesterberg AB for a satisfying American breakfast at the snack bar or having a full meal at the Dutch restaurant at the German border. Diverting by Soesterberg added about 30 minutes to our trip, but it also had its advantages. A couple of Western egg sandwiches and two large milks did wonders preparing the body for the trip home. In addition, the base exchange shoppette sold 24-bottle cases of Heineken for $.90 per case plus $1.05 deposit on the bottles—beer bottles cost more than the beer that filled them.

Dining enroute at the Dutch-German border usually won out as the preferred option, especially after ole eagle-eye Dave de Wey spotted a Milch (milk) vending machine as we transited Amersfoort—30 miles from A-dam and about 90 miles from the German border. Located in front of a small Dutch market, the vending machine offered 300 milliliter cartons of ice-cold milk for a Dutch quarter ($.07). Ironically, the Dutch quarter coin is the size of a U.S. penny, and you are probably guessing where this anecdote is heading—stand by!

The U.S. military did not use the American copper penny on bases in the Netherlands in deference to the host country's quarter coin that was used in vending operations. However, the penny was used in commissaries and base exchanges in Germany. Our traveling trio learned during one of our first visits to Mom's Place that American pennies worked fine in the bar's jukebox—a song for a Dutch quarter (or one U.S. penny). We stocked up accordingly on pennies for future trips. The milk machine in Amersfoort also accepted pennies. The best part of the story follows.

Having literally milked that vending machine on several earlier trips at a penny per milk carton, we parked at the curb by the Dutch market on a bright, quiet Monday morning. The author had "purchased" six cartons of milk for six American pennies and turned to walk back to Frog Car when the market proprietor shouted at him. Postulating that the jig was up—that the shop owner was on to the milk filching scheme—I stopped in my tracks, prepared to accept the consequences. The Market Meister smiled and announced in perfect English, "You forgot straws," and handed me six straws from a dispenser on the side of the vending machine. We subsequently bypassed that milk vending machine for a few trips.

A brunch at the Dutch restaurant by the German border was always an "experience." Walter, the Dutch waiter, was overly friendly and had a few feminine traits, but he was generally efficient, and we were always in a hurry. Dave de Wey and I always joked to Billy Burke that Walter was putting the make on Billy. The restaurant was fairly clean, but had no screen doors, so flies often buzzed the guests. During one of our meals, a plump fly landed on the lip of Billy's half-full coffee cup. Billy swatted at the fly, and it nosedived into his cup, ending up floating in Billy's coffee. Motioning to Walter and pointing at his cup, Billy sat there expecting a new cup o' Jo. Peering into Billy's cup, the waiter announced without skipping a beat, "Ah, a flying Dutchman," laid our bill on the table and walked away.

Billy Burke's Dark Storm Cloud

Now a final Billy Burke tale! One of the friendliest, most pleasant NCO's in the 6913th RSM, SSgt. Thomas Burke seemed to live under a dark cloud—even while he slept. He and A1C Ray Kalinowski, who shared a room in the Baker Flight barracks in the Staging Area, never had a cross word with each other, but tended to "run" in different circles. An athlete extraordinaire and star on the post baseball team, Ray might be found lifting weights at the gym during off-duty hours, while Billy Burke would more likely be lifting a Beck's beer at the NCO Club. Occasionally, Burke ventured downtown between trips to Amsterdam.

While working our four dayshifts, Billy accompanied the author for a few brews on Lessingstrasse (aka Red Light District) in Bremerhaven. Finishing the night at the Blue Angel Bar and returning to the barracks by 11:00 p.m., Billy said goodnight in the barracks hallway and entered the room he shared with Kalinowski. Just another uneventful night in Bremerhaven—at least, at that point.

The next morning, Billy showed up at work, looking well refreshed except that he wore a classic shiner—his right eye was swollen almost shut and was deep purple and black. It was obvious that someone had cold-cocked him, but who? And why? Billy alibied that he had walked into a wall in his sleep, but on the next Amsterdam odyssey, Heineken beer loosened his lips and the truth came out.

In the wee hours of that mysterious night, Billy got out of bed, walked down the hall to the latrine, raised a commode lid and was relieving himself when tragedy struck. At least, that was the routine he had followed so often that he could do it in his sleep. In reality, Billy Burke was sleep-walking when he received his black eye. Each airmen living in the barracks had a footlocker on a stand at the foot of his bed. Being perhaps half awake, but unaware of his actions, Billy left his bed, walked to the foot of roommate Kalinowski's bed, raised the perceived commode lid and let go with a golden stream into Ray's footlocker. Waking up in total darkness to find someone urinating in his footlocker, Ray landed a solid right hook on his roommate's face. The incident actually drew Billy and Ray closer together. The author would love to know if that dark cloud still hangs over Billy Burke. He'd love to reminisce with Billy about their Amsterdam sagas, but Billy's fate after Bremerhaven is unknown.

6913th RSM Traffic Exploitation (1960's)

The 6913th Radio Squadron Mobile's traffic analysis mission had grown immensely since the squadron's first traffic analysts arrived in Bremerhaven in late 1951. By the time Capt. Bruce D. Strotman arrived as a newly anointed USAFSS signals intelligence officer in 1962, the 6913th Traffic Exploitation shop, as it was called, sat in the back of Operations—up a couple of steps in a large elevated room called the "upper deck." Climbing the steps into a T/E job was a formidable challenge for Strotman, a somewhat disillusioned ex-pilot whom the Air Force had cross-trained involuntarily into SIGINT. In 2006, retired Col. Bruce Strotman discussed with the author his tour with the 6913th—his introduction to USAFSS.

That was an amazing assignment for me. I will admit that I was a pretty unhappy camper being stuck in northern Germany as a pilot, and I never saw an airplane unless we happened to go to Frankfurt.

But it turned into a terrific education for me...I worked shift for quite some time and was told by the Ops officer that I would always be a shift worker because I was new in command and did not have the experience/knowledge to be the OIC of one of the day shops. My T/E Controller, Bill Donnelly, was a TSgt., and he wanted to make MSgt. as badly as I wanted to make that Ops officer eat his words.

Anyway, Bill used to have big time plotting, reporting, and T/A drills on mids. He told me that if I was going to be in charge (he meant only when HE went down to the snack bar or to the head), I was going to have to know what was going on and what to do!! So he got me some crayons and put me on the board with the A/D [air defense plotting] guys...one was Curt Dorsey!! We used to do lots of STUFF.

At the time, Capt. Strotman's role model was the current Traffic Exploitation Officer.

The Capt. in the T/E shop before me was probably the smartest guy at Bremerhaven. He spoke Russian and German (and) knew the business inside and out.

Strotman set his sights on the T/E Officer position. To qualify for a move to the upper deck, he determined to become the most knowledgeable and experienced of the unit's four flight commanders. Working alongside his analysts on shift—plotting flight activity, breaking codes, and performing situation analysis and reporting—Strotman achieved both objectives. When the T/E officer rotated, the operations officer acknowledged Strotman's accomplishments by designating him the new Traffic Exploitation Officer.

Bruce Strotman's tour of duty with the 6913th equipped him with SIGINT basics that he molded into an illustrious career in Air Force Security Service and the Electronic Security Command. Finishing his Air Force career as commander of the 6949th Electronic Security Squadron and Project Director, Rivet Joint RC-135, Block III Development, he was inducted into the Air Intelligence Agency Hall of Honor in 1996.

41ST/6913TH HERITAGE

Although the unit designator changed over the years, USAFSS maintained an intercept site in Bremerhaven from 1950 to 1968. The lineage of the unit follows.

Lineage of USAFSS Unit at Bremerhaven	
Unit Designator	Action/Comments
Det C, 2nd RSM	Activated in Spring of 1950
Det 23, 2nd RSM	Det C, 2nd RSM redesignated 1 Feb 1951
41st RSM	Arrived Nov 1951; Det 23 deactivated
6913th RSM	41st RSM redesignated 8 May 1955
6913th Security Sqdn	6913th RSM redesignated 1 July 1963
6913th Security Gp	6913th SS redesignated 1 October 1964
Det 1, 6950th Scty Gp	Redesignated July 1967
Det 1, 6950th Scty Gp	Deactivated 31 March 1968.

With the mission of Detachment 1, 6950th Security Group transferred elsewhere, the unit was deactivated on 31 March 1968.

USAFSS Intelligence Production

From the start, Air Force Security Service's operational mission involved the collection and exploitation of signals of interest for the U.S. Air Force. In April 1950, the Secretary of Defense and the Air Force Chief of Staff approved the USAFSS plan for the production of tactical intelligence.[43] Intelligence production was/is the process of developing raw data into finished intelligence for consumers—for the USAFSS—it involved converting intercepted signals into air intelligence for Air Force commanders.

USAFSS used a multistep intelligence production process. Air Force commanders defined air intelligence requirements, and USAFSS mission managers planned and directed the overall mission. Intercepting target signals, radio squadrons mobile processed raw signals into typed pages of traffic, logs and transcripts—in formats usable by analysts. Traffic analysts and cryptanalysts evaluated, analyzed and integrated the basic information into finished air intelligence reports that were disseminated to user commands and agencies.

In its original operations concept, USAFSS delegated responsibility for the execution of intelligence production to security groups that resided overseas with subordinate radio squadrons mobile. Under the ops concept, a security group in Europe and another in the Far East was the senior USAFSS authority in its Theater. Each security group's mission involved interfacing with local commands, managing the RSM's and USAFSS intelligence production within its area, and traffic exploitation—analyzing, reporting and disseminating intelligence products. Although traffic exploitation responsibility moved from the security group to another newly created organization later, this was the concept of operations that was in place in 1951 when the command activated its first security group.

6910TH SECURITY GROUP ACTIVATED

With war raging in Korea and threats of a Soviet invasion seemingly looming in West Germany, Air Force Security Service expedited the expansion of its signals intelligence capabilities in Europe and the Far East. On 23 May 1951, USAFSS activated the 6910th Security Group at Brooks AFB, Texas—the command's first operational group-level organization.[44] Struggling to staff the 6910th and to put together a management plan for USAFSS operations in Europe, the command rushed the 6910th SG to Germany.

6910th SG—Crowded Facilities in Germany in 1951

In 1999, retired former USAFSS Chief Warrant Officer William Carlton discussed the 6910th relocation to Germany.

On 28 Jul '51, Colonel Maury, Major Chester A. Murgatroyd, Capt. Raymond W. Pahutka and I took the 6910th to Wiesbaden, which at that time was the headquarters of USAFE. The city and its bases were severely overcrowded and it was necessary to split the group, with Headquarters at # 7 Beethovenstrasse in Wiesbaden and Operations at Darmstadt. The group was then deactivated at Brooks and reactivated at Wiesbaden, with an Operating Location at Darmstadt.

Carlton recalled the good and bad aspects of Wiesbaden circa 1951.

The headquarters building in Wiesbaden was a fabulous old three-story mansion located near downtown. It looked like a movie set, with a cathedral entry, a marble fireplace, a grand staircase and a sunken bathtub. The city itself would make everyone's list of the best places. It had been a resort for centuries and had sustained very little war damage. The location is excellent, with swift access to the rest of central Europe. German food was five-star; the beer and wine were better.

It would have been a great assignment except for the shortage of the most basic military facilities and services. We had no vehicles and no military bus service. Supplies of any kind were rare and we mostly bought our own. Airmen were initially billeted at Camp Pieri, a scruffy little artillery Kaserne in the boondocks. It had little to recommend it, although I do not recall the food being as bad as other correspondents have reported. Later, we moved to Lindsey Air Station, which was closer to work but not much of an improvement otherwise.

The lack of family housing for married 6910th personnel also posed severe problems.

Many new arrivals had to accept remote family quarters in Bavaria and see their families via weekend flights known as Hubby Hops. Remotely-housed wives were forbidden to enter Wiesbaden but it was rumored that a wife or two were hanging around the BOQ posing as Schatzies [girlfriends], surely the first time for that particular deception.

The 6910th Security Group Headquarters managed the intelligence production cycle in Wiesbaden while its analysts carried out the group's traffic exploitation mission in Darmstadt. According to Carlton, the 6910th activities at multiple locations created much confusion back at USAFSS Headquarters in Texas.

Many members of the command actually did not know where the 6910th was located. This led to a rather hectic trip in November 1951 for the commander's secretary, who was the very first civilian employee ever sent overseas by USAFSS. She was Annette Jones who later became my wife.

The civilian personnel office had enough trouble figuring out how to send someone overseas and almost gave up when no one would tell them where the group was located. They finally launched her towards Germany with instructions to try Wiesbaden. If the 6910th was not there, she was to continue to Darmstadt. She was supplied with home phone numbers in case of trouble along the way.

Ms. Jones joined the 6910th SG at Wiesbaden, becoming Col. Maury's secretary.

6910th SG—Retroactive Duty Assignments

The transfer of the 6910th Security Group from Texas to Germany happened with such haste that original orders had to be cancelled. Finally, the group commander and his staff were appropriately designated in special orders dated 10 September 1951.[45]

The orders stated that the following USAF personnel, this headquarters and station, having reported to the 6910th SG in accordance with competent authority are assigned duty on the effective date indicated.

6910th Security Group Assignments—1951			
Name	Eff. Date	Department	Duty
Col. Dabney H. Maury	28 Jul 51	Command	Commanding Officer
Maj. Chester A. Murgatroyd	28 Jul 51	Operations	Comm Officer
Capt. Raymond W. Pahutka	28 Jul 51	Materiel	Air Installations Off.
MSgt. William E. Carlton Jr.	28 Jul 51	Adjutant	Sgt. Major
Lt. Col. Merle C. Brown	3 Aug 51	Command	Deputy Commander
2nd Lt. Lawrence J. Johnson	7 Aug 51	Adjutant	Adjutant
Capt. Thomas D. Toyn	14 Aug 51	Operations	Assistant Comms Off.
1st Lt. Burton A. Peterson	14 Aug 51	Command	Unit Officer/Scty Off.
1st Lt. William E. Glass	14 Aug 51	Operations	Air Intel Officer
WOJG John T. Danforth	14 Aug 51	Operations	Comm Supt Officer
Maj. Ralph J. McCartney	15 Aug 51	Operations	Operations Officer
Cpl. Herbert E. Blanton Jr.	20 Aug 51	Adjutant	APR Clerk
1st Lt. Robert E. Duvall	27 Aug 51	Operations	Intel Eval Officer
Capt. James L. Monahan	5 Sept 51	Personnel	Personnel Officer
TSgt. Arthur H. Cherry Jr.	5 Sept 51	Personnel	Personnel Supervisor

Col. Maury designated Lt. Peterson the group's Class A Finance Officer for the purpose of paying officers and airmen assigned to the 6910th SG at Wiesbaden, Germany. Officers Murgatroyd, Toyn, Glass, Danforth, McCartney and DuVall were in Operations at Darmstadt; the remainder were based with headquarters at Wiesbaden. All of the USAFSS squadrons in Europe reported to Col. Maury (6910th SG Commander); see organization chart on the next page.

6910th SG Org Chart—31 Dec 1951	
6910th Scty Gp Wiesbaden, Germany (HQ) Darmstadt, Germany (Operations) 1951-53	
2nd RSM Darmstadt, Germany 1949-55	41st RSM (1 Bremerhaven, Germany 1951-55
Det 21, (Det 1, 2nd RSM) Rothwesten, Germany 1949-51	12th RSM (2 Landsberg, Germany 1951-55
Det 22, (Det 2, 2nd RSM) Schleissheim, Germany 1949-51	Det 121, (Det 1, 12th RSM) Linz, Austria 1951-54
Det 24, (Det 4, 2nd RSM) Berlin, Germany 1950-54	Det 122, (Det 2, 12th RSM) Schleissheim, Germany 1951-52
Det 25, (Det 5, 2nd RSM) Landsberg, Germany 1951-51	
10th RSM (3 Chicksands, England 1950-55	34th RSM (4 Wheelus AB, Libya 1951-55
	Project Penn (5 Ankara, Turkey 1951-53
1 Replaced Detachment 3, 2nd RSM. 2 Replaced Detachment 25. 3 10th RSM discussed in Chapter Six. 4 34th RSM discussed in Chapter Five. 5 Project Penn discussed in Chapter Five.	

6910TH SECURITY GROUP OPS

When the 6910th deployed to Germany in 1951, the entire organization—headquarters and operations—was to be located at

Wiesbaden, but lack of adequate space in Wiesbaden caused a change of plans. As explained by Bill Carlton, who helped create the original plan, a cadre of 2nd RSM analysts were to be transferred from Darmstadt to Wiesbaden, forming the nucleus of 6910th Operations. However, a severe space crunch in Wiesbaden resulted in splitting the 6910th into Group Headquarters in Wiesbaden and 6910th Operations colocated with the 2nd RSM at Ernst Ludwig Kaserne in Darmstadt. The cadre of 2nd RSM analysts transferred in place to the 6910th SG, and new 6910th analysts were diverted from Wiesbaden to Darmstadt.

Likewise, the 6910th SG Headquarters Squadron Section was activated at Darmstadt instead of Wiesbaden since the 6910th operational mission and most of its personnel were being assigned to Darmstadt. Maj. Louis R. Lammie, who had been commander of the USAFSS HQ Squadron Section at Brooks AFB, became commander of the 6910th HQ Sqdn Section at Darmstadt. Retired USAFSS Col. Duane E. Russell discussed 6910th Darmstadt Operations in 1999.

As I recall, I hit Wiesbaden with Capt. Floyd Cross and Lt. Bill Roche in March-April 1952. There, they told us to go to Darmstadt. Wiesbaden was the HQ, with Dabney Maury, and Darmstadt was the second-echelon processing, with Maj. McCartney as the Ops Chief. Maj. Russell Smith was the assistant. Various of us were the T/A [traffic analysis] officers, with me assigned to the voice problem, under Capt. Bob Duvall.

We were cohabitants with the 2nd RSM, and it was quite a learning process for all of us. Col. Dick Small, Maj. Glen Pennywitt, and others helped make our time productive, and enjoyable. One other item. As I began my tasks at Darmstadt, as a new R/T [radiophone] officer, I was led into a room where there were bales of paper strewn around. It was copies of handwritten traffic—no Cyrillic typewriters and no tapes. For weeks I waded through all this, with few fundamentals other than my personal logic to aid me.

Believe it when I say I was able to pull out some specific targets, and they were given to me to work and process. Don't believe I should identify the targets. I did go to the

2nd RSM, and spend time with the R/T operators to learn their skills. This helped me a great deal, and I relied on it a lot later on in the airborne program. [Later, Col. Duane E. Russell was revered for his contributions to the USAFSS airborne reconnaissance program.]

In a philosophy inherited from the Army Security Agency, second echelon analysis in the 6910th Security Group (and the 6920th SG in Japan) in the early 1950's was the domain of intelligence officers, assisted by enlisted analysts. Officers continued to head individual sections within second echelon processing centers, but USAFSS NCO's and airmen soon became the dominant work force, not only in traffic exploitation but throughout operations. Naming several other 6910th traffic analysts, some of whom may have joined the group later at Landsberg, Russell spoke highly of the 6910th NCO's.[46]

We had a number of excellent airmen and NCO's. One of the best that I recall is Maurice Malo. I worked in the T/A shop until the Fall of '52, and then moved into Mission Control under Maj. Smith.

Maurice Malo discussed his USAFSS tour in an email in 2006. He was one of the first enlisted traffic analysts in the 6910th Security Group. Enlisting in the Air Force right out of high school in 1950, Malo completed traffic analysis ("202") training later in the year and arrived in the 2nd RSM at Darmstadt in early 1951. Maury Malo was among the cadre of 2nd RSM analysts who formed the nucleus of the 6910th Security Group traffic exploitation section in the fall of 1951.

I was folded into 6910th when it was formed and had visions of re-siting to the French coast but ended up in Landsberg.

Maury Malo relocated with the 6910th to its new home in Bavaria in mid-1953.

Biarritz, France new Home for 6910th SG?

When the unit was forced to give up its facilities in Wiesbaden, serious consideration was given to relocating the 6910th Security Group to France, as Bill Carlton recalls.

*In 1952, a pullback of U.S. forces across the Rhine River
began. The 6910ᵗʰ was slated for a site in Biarritz on the
Atlantic coast of France. Serious preparations were made
for the move, including mandatory French lessons. In
early 1953, the Biarritz move plans were quietly scrubbed,
with no explanation.*

The plan to relocate the 6910ᵗʰ SG to France did not reach
fruition, but the romance that started between Bill Carlton and
Annette Jones at Brooks AFB, Texas, ended in wedding bells.

*On 20 Sept 1952, Annette and I were married in the first
overseas wedding of USAFSS personnel. The wedding
party was all-USAFSS; the Group Commander gave the
bride away, and the reception was held in Group
Headquarters.*

In early 1953, Col. Maury returned to the United States and
retirement, replaced by Col. Robert H. Augustinus as 6910ᵗʰ
Security Group Commander.

6910ᵗʰ and "Büro Gehlen"

Büro Gehlen was an intelligence apparatus inherited from the
Bundeswehr of World War II.[47] Maj. Gen. Reinhardt Gehlen,
former head of German military intelligence on the Eastern Front,
thoughtfully brought his complete files with him when he
surrendered to the American Army. Former 6910ᵗʰ Security Group
Russian linguist Paul Garrett worked covertly with Gen. Gehlen's
group during the early 1950's. In 2002, he reminisced about his
6910ᵗʰ "covert analysis work."

Completing a 12-month Russian course (R-12-23) at the Army
Language School in Monterey just before Christmas 1951,
Garrett's class received intercept training at Brooks AFB. In April
1952, he reported to the 6910ᵗʰ Security Group where he became a
traffic analyst. He moved with the 6910ᵗʰ to Landsberg in 1953.
Here's Paul's recollection of 6910ᵗʰ collaborative efforts with
"Büro Gehlen."

*My time in USAFSS was spent initially in T/A [traffic
analysis], with responsibility first for the East German
sector (RABS203), then the USSR, and finally in a rather
catchall operation called "R&D" [Research and*

Development]. The latter gave me a free rein to do whatever in the way of intelligence gathering on the Soviet AOB [air order of battle] and capability. During the time I was in T/A and working on East Germany, I had occasion to liaise closely with Büro Gehlen, the sub rosa, unofficial precursor to the West German Bundesnachrichtendienst [BND—Foreign Intelligence Service].

As you will recall, the post WW II East and West German governments were not allowed a Bundeswehr [armed forces], Luftwaffe or Bundesnachrichtendienst for a number of years after 1945, but General Gehlen, formerly head of intelligence for the Bundeswehr in WW II, had accumulated a massive amount of data on Soviet military structure and cipher systems. Most of his information had come about in the course of interrogating thousands of the three million Soviet prisoners who had surrendered to the invading German army. He was also instrumental in forming Felhherrenost (Enemy Army East under General Vlasov) made up of volunteers from the three million POW's who had their own axe to grind with the Soviets. They, poor souls, including Vlasov, eventually came to a sticky end at the hands of their Soviet captors!

In any case, after the war when the Nürnberg investigations were underway, the sniffers came calling on Gehlen and arrested him as an accessory to sundry war crimes. The crafty and highly intelligent Gehlen, however, had taken steps to secure his future by burying trunk loads of documents related to the Soviet military. By this time the Allies had finally awakened to the Soviet threat and they not only quite happily awarded Gehlen a dispensation, but decided as well to fund him in setting up a "private" intelligence operation dubbed "Büro Gehlen" in order to circumvent the restriction on an official government intelligence agency.

In addition to having documentation of enormous value to us, he also had an extensive "sleeper" agent network throughout East Europe. It was this HUMINT network which provided us with "Q" (Quelle) validity intelligence at a time when we had so little to work with in terms of both electronic aids or background material. In fact, in 1952 we were literally sitting on orange crates in Darmstadt with only The Seaborn Report and GCHQ historical papers to fall back upon. No computers to speak of and CIA/NSA were at a stage that could best be described as "nascent."

I visited Gehlen's operations in Pulach near Munich several times and once met with a group of Jesuit priests who were being smuggled into Eastern Europe with the help of the Büro's network. The Jesuits in turn brought out defectors and sensitive information. I remember one occasion when I met a young American priest from Boston who was studying Russian at Gehlen's redoubt, preparing to go underground. It was my exposure to those Jesuits and others in the Munich area in the '50's that led to my decision to study at Georgetown.

Garrett also worked closely with GCHQ at Cheltenham in the United Kingdom, and British signals intelligence personnel traveled to Darmstadt for meetings with Garrett.

It was April 1952 in connection with one of Gehlen's projects, "Operation Dumbo," that I called on their HUMINT net to verify my suspicions that the East Germans were violating the agreement not to form military units. I noted that German traffic was being picked up on frequencies where there should have been only Russian. Also the Zerbst Soviet MiG squadron had gone off the air and off the DF scopes.

I asked Gehlen's people on the ground to report any unusual overland movement, rail or vehicular, of large containers, and sure enough there had been in recent days large containers on flat beds moving out of Zerbst. I then instructed all the RSM units to begin intensive monitoring of frequencies where our people had detected German language traffic, and stuff began pouring in.

Since both sides were aching to break the ban, it was all the Allies needed to begin arming the West Germans, of course in the name of self defense.

Outside of Germany, other work involved setting up reporting procedures to CIA/NSA at a new RSM in Tripoli, Libya, at what was Wheelus AB. That was interesting in that we ran some of the "Ferret" flights out of that base. They left Wheelus and cut through the Black Sea, Odessa, then north over the USSR following any number of routes with exit onto the Baltic/Arctic. As you well know, the objectives of the Ferret flights were two:

1) to test the Soviet air defense detection and interception capability, and 2) to verify unit ID's and locations (Soviet Air Defense Grid). We used changing dinomes and trinomes for unit ID's, all of which may have been out of vogue by the time you came along.

It was always a hair-raising occasion to hear over the loud speaker the Soviet ground controller vectoring in MiG's to intercept the target Ferret and giving fire commands. Because the controller gave grid references and compass readings to the MIG's, we knew where the Ferret was and could plot it on a huge wall map of the USSR. As dawn broke everyone breathed a sigh of relief! None of this is, of course, new to you!!

All fascinating and challenging stuff and I was briefly tempted to stay on after my four year enlistment, but decided to opt for a return to university having left after one year of Pre-Law studies to join up in July of 1950.

The Büro Gehlen ultimately became the nucleus of the West German BND—Foreign Intelligence Service. Discharged in 1954, Paul Garrett graduated from Georgetown U. His language background and continental experiences during his USAFSS tour lured him into a career in international commerce. His Russian language training helped him enormously in mastering other languages in countries where he lived—German, Portuguese, Spanish, French and Italian. Currently residing in Rome, Garrett is a partner in a small company developing software applications for mobile (wireless) technology. He also has a flat in Munich and is proud of his assignment with the 6910th Security Group in Darmstadt and Landsberg.

USAFSS in European Area—1952

At the end of 1952, USAFSS had three radio squadrons mobile in Germany (2nd, 41st and 12th), the 34th RSM in Libya, and the 10th RSM and 37th RSM in the United Kingdom. Activities of UK-based USAFSS operations and the 34th RSM operations are discussed in separate chapters. Even while the raging Korean War in the Far East siphoned off signals intelligence resources that would otherwise have been deployed in Europe in 1951-1952, the 6910th Security Group continued to grow.

USAFSS European Area Chart—31 Dec 1952	
6910th Scty Group Wiesbaden, Germany (HQ) Darmstadt, Germany (Operations) 1951-53	
2nd RSM Darmstadt, Germany Det 24, (Det 4, 2nd RSM) Berlin, Germany	41st RSM Bremerhaven, Germany
12th RSM Landsberg, Germany Det 121, (Det 1, 12th RSM) Linz, Austria Det 122, (Det 2, 12th RSM) Schleissheim, Germany	10th RSM * Chicksands, England 37th RSM * Kirknewton, Scotland 34th RSM * Wheelus AB, Libya Project Penn * Ankara, Turkey
* Addressed in later chapters.	

6910TH SG RELOCATES TO LANDSBERG

The 6910th Security Group represented HQ USAFSS wherever the command had a special intelligence interest in Europe. As the group's Sgt. Major, Sergeant Carlton was involved extensively in coordinating activities with operating locations that the group maintained in Europe in the 1951-1953 period. In 2000, Bill Carlton recalled supporting operating locations (OL's) at Darmstadt, Rhein-Main, Landsberg, Bremerhaven and Ramstein, Germany; South Ruislip, England; Paris, France; and Rabat, Morocco. Some of the OL's served as USAFSS Special Security Offices (SSO's) at major Air Force commands. In March 1953, the 6910th sent Sgt. Carlton on TDY to OL-Landsberg to coordinate the transfer of "several tons of classified documents" to Landsberg from OL-Darmstadt. The 6910th's traffic processing function was being transferred from Darmstadt to Landsberg.

Two months later (16 May 1953), as part of a relocation of the 6910th Security Group from Wiesbaden, the unit transferred 51 assigned personnel to Operating Location, 6910th SG at Landsberg—an intermediate step in moving HQ 6910th SG to Landsberg.[48] In the same special orders, the 6910th SG attached thirteen officers and airmen who were on permanent duty with USAFSS SSO, USAFE, Wiesbaden, to HQ USAFE. With these actions, HQ 6910th Security Group completed the move from Wiesbaden to Landsberg.

Going Away Party

During the 6910th's stay at Ernst Ludwig Kaserne, group morale had been sky-high, attributable in great measure to the manner in which Maj. Lammie commanded the 6910th contingent in Darmstadt. He set up "Lammie Hour" in the mess hall, making available to the troops at night free baked pies and milk. And more importantly to many, he championed the creation of an on-post club—the "Blue Note Airmens Club." Bringing in major entertainment groups from Munich, and with its bar and restaurant always open to accommodate shift workers, the Blue Note was an instant success. Off-duty U.S. servicemen from throughout the local area frequented the Blue Note. The club accumulated profits hand over fist.

Benefiting from the Blue Note's success, Ernst Ludwig Kaserne's non-appropriated morale, welfare and recreation fund was overflowing. When word filtered down the chain of command that the 6910th Security Group was leaving, the post commander let it be known that the MWR fund was a post resource—to be left in place when the 6910th departed.

Maj. Lammie's solution was to spend down the fund on amenities for his airmen before relocating to Landsberg. Then immediately before leaving Ludwig Kaserne, he honored his airmen with "one hell of a going-away party" that 6910th alumni still discuss at reunions. Former traffic analyst Jess Myers recalled the "Auf Weidersehen Party" in 2000.

> *Major Lammie had the troops fall-in on the base ramp for inspection. Then he had the first sergeant call everyone to attention and then had the group dismissed. We turned around to see the huge hangar open up with about the biggest layout we have ever seen. Food, drink, and entertainment from Munich. I know that I was surprised and enjoyed being a member of this group. Needless to say that a lot of new equipment was installed in our barracks, and a major load of sports goods were provided to our group. It was a wonderful event, and we did not forget it soon.*

Former IBM Tabulator mechanic Hugh Windsor added his comments on the party.

> *I remember that party well. What a blast. At one time, if my memory serves me well, there were guys out on the hangar floor who were "prositing" by smashing their beer steins together after a short run toward each other. This had to be stopped since the supply of steins was rapidly diminishing. What fun we feckless "Fliegers" were having.*

Moving to Landsberg with the 6910th Security Group, Maj. Lammie kept group morale high in Landsberg. Maj. Joseph Roberts became the HQ Squadron Section commander when Lammie rotated back to HQ USAFSS.

6900TH SW ACTIVATED, LANDSBERG

With the 6900th Security Wing on the horizon, the 6910th Security Group formed a Wing Development Section under Col. Philip G. Evans while still located at Wiesbaden. This section included 6910th activities destined for the wing and some new entities, including an Inspection Division under Maj. Dmitri Evdokimoff. The 6910th transferred Sgt. Carlton to the Inspection Division on 7 March 1953, and the Wing Development Section moved to Landsberg on 8 May 1953. Days later, the rest of the 6910th SG followed.

The 6900th Security Wing was activated at Landsberg on 1 August 1953 under the command of Col. Augustinus. A numbered Air Force-equivalent organization, the 6900th served as an intermediate headquarters to plan, coordinate and direct activities of USAFSS units in Europe. The 6920th Security Group, Johnson Air Base, Japan, provided the same types of support for USAFSS units in the Pacific.[49]

On 3 October 1953, the 6910th Headquarters, Landsberg, transferred in-place 42 officers and airmen, including Col. Evans and Maj. Evdokimoff, to the 6900th SW.[50] Col. Evans held the title of Wing Chief of Staff. Annette Jones Carlton became the 6900th Wing Commander's secretary. The remaining elements of the 6910th SG—essentially 6910th Operations—continued the group's analysis mission at Landsberg. Citing a "number of firsts in the Security Service record book," Bill Carlton showed his pride in the 6910th Security Group.

It was the first unit larger than a squadron, the first to command all USAFSS activities in an overseas theater, the first overseas unit with civilian personnel, the first to conduct general inspections of subordinate units and the first to host an overseas wedding of USAFSS personnel. It was a great outfit, and it did some things that couldn't be done and did them very well indeed.

Sgt. Major William Carlton and wife Annette departed the 6900th SW at Landsberg in June 1954, bound for new assignments with HQ USAFSS at Kelly AFB. In 1956, Sgt. Carlton transferred to the AF Office of Special Investigations while Annette became a mother and housewife. Promoted to Warrant Officer, Carlton

LARRY TART

returned to USAFSS in 1967, commanding the 6993rd Security Squadron—headquartered at Kelly AFB with Operations at the Medina Annex, Lackland AFB, Texas. Retiring as a CWO-4 in 1969, Bill and Annette Carlton currently reside in San Antonio.

Under the 6900th SW on the USAFSS organization chart in 1953 were the 6910th Security Group and two newly activated security groups: the 6930th SG and the 6950th SG. The 6910th Security Group org chart (1953) follows. The 6930th and 6950th Security Groups are addressed in later chapters.

6910th Scty Gp Org Chart—31 Dec 1953	
6910th Security Group Landsberg, Germany 1953-1956	
Flt A, 6910th SG Wasserkuppe, Germany 1953-1954	2nd RSM Darmstadt, Germany 1949-1955 Det D, 2nd RSM Berlin, Germany 1950-1954
41st RSM Bremerhaven, Germany 1951-1955 85th RSM (1 Kelly AFB, TX 1953-1954 Flt A, 85th RSM Sembach, Germany 1953-1954	12th RSM Landsberg, Germany 1951-1955 Det 1, 12th RSM Linz, Austria 1951-1954 Det 2, 12th RSM (2 Sembach, Germany 1953 Flt F, 12th RSM Vienna, Austria 1953-1954
(1 Activated Kelly AFB, 8 Dec '53; deployed to Sembach in Apr '54.[51]	
(2 Located earlier at Schleissheim and Kaufbeuren, Germany.	

USAFSS DETACHMENT, WASSERKUPPE

In 1953, the 6910th Security Group activated Flight A, 6910th SG at Wasserkuppe, Germany. Flt A was colocated with an air traffic control and warning unit that monitored air traffic in the southern air corridor from West Germany to Berlin. Limited available data suggest that the subordination of the detachment changed multiple times in 1954—Flight B, 2nd RSM, Flight 0, 12th RSM and finally Detachment 3, 85th RSM. When the 6910th Radio Group Mobile was activated at Sembach in September 1956, the Wasserkuppe detachment became Det 3, 6910th RGM. (The 6910th Security Group had been deactivated at Landsberg.)

Soon after USAFSS began operations at Wasserkuppe, Les Layman, a personnel clerk, traveled up the mountain to resolve some personnel issues of assigned USAFSS personnel. He discussed Wasserkuppe with the author in 2001 and 2006.

Snow was shoulder deep on the side of the road to the weather station. I drove an enclosed jeep and it was colder that the dickens. I was told that it snowed continuously from early November to early April. The building for the new site was not completed, so they were headquartered in the same building as the German weather station. The walls were extremely thin, and when classified material was discussed, they had to go outside.

A young 2d Lt. was in charge, and all the classified material, including the one time crypto pads, was in a locked briefcase attached by a small chain and handcuffed to the Lt.'s left wrist, which he said he wore 24/7. They had no safe. They did have a dedicated teletype machine hooked directly to the site at 2d RSM (Darmstadt) and were using crypto one-time pads to communicate with— which then required a thorough burning.

They also had a van that was parked on top of the hill/mountain near an unfinished building that was being built for the exclusive use of the detachment. There had been a small fire in the fireplace, which set back the work for several months. Note: A couple of the enlisted folks swore the fire was started by the Lt. who was trying to burn classified—nothing confirmed. We took action to get him a safe, and 2d RSM supply took him one within the week.

What really makes this story great is that the Lt. was recently married, and his equally young wife was with him. They were quartered in a gasthaus at the bottom of the hill/mountain. The enlisted men were quartered in the same place but were being moved to the AC&W area when sufficient room became available.

Glenn Barbour reported serving in Det 3, 6910th RGM at Wasserkuppe "with about 30 other 203xx [linguists] and about 10 ditty-boppers [Morse intercept operators]."

I was president of the "Road Hogs" Motorcycle Club on the hill, and we played hell with the 14th AC [Armored Cavalry] in Fulda. We would take a bus to town, pick up all the girls and take them to the hill for a party every first Saturday of the month. The army hated us. I sure wish I could find the other members of "HOGS" or for that matter to find out about any of the Detachment 3 crew. I ended up marrying a girl from Fulda.

A traffic analyst with Det 3, 6910th RGM, Barbour lost his security clearance and was transferred to a tactical recon squadron at Sembach.

Frank Valois, a former USAFSS Polish linguist, transferred from the 6910th RGM at Sembach to Det 3 at Wasserkuppe in October or November 1956. When the 6910th closed Det 3 in November 1957, Valois relocated back to the group at Sembach. He later served with Detachment 1, 6910th RGM in Berlin before discharge from the Air Force in late 1958.

First Echelon and Second Echelon A & R

Initially, 6910th Security Group traffic analysts performed both first echelon and second echelon analysis of traffic from the intercept sites in Europe and generated all intelligence reports. As analysts at the sites became familiar with targets and gained experience, the second echelon group delegated responsibility for some analysis and reporting to radio squadrons mobile. Per predefined instructions and criteria, RSM's issued "spot reports" to users in near-time time as significant activities unfolded. A copy of each spot report and technical details upon which the report was based were also forwarded to the second echelon group. In turn, group analysts generated follow-ups and supplementary reports as applicable. The reporting of critical information via a "critic" report followed a similar but more expeditious process.

FLIGHT F, 12TH RSM—VIENNA, AUSTRIA

In June 2006, Lawrence (Larry) Kujawa described how he participated in the activation of a new intercept site in Vienna, Austria. "Living in old wooden barracks some distance from campus," Kujawa completed a 12-month Russian course at Syracuse U. in June 1952. McCarthy's Bar with sawdust on the floor, dark beer and steamed clams was Larry's favorite hangout in Syracuse. After serving about a year in the 12th RSM in Landsberg, Germany, the squadron offered him an assignment in Austria.

In late '53, my roommate Bob Cason, I, and a few others were approached about going to Vienna. We were told that the Four-Power Treaty did not allow military personnel in Vienna, so we were given Department of the Army Civilian ID (I wish I would have kept it) and $200, and sent to the PX to buy civilian clothes—and off we went to Vienna aboard, we were told, the sealed train.

We were posted to a villa, a beautiful place, complete with dining room and bar and an Austrian staff, occupied by the CIC [Counterintelligence Corps]. They knew of my 6' 6" height before my arrival, so they had found a longer bed for me. The villa was on a hill in a residential area out at the end of the streetcar line. I can't remember the name of the street, but it was a couple miles beyond the ring and on the same street as a theater that showed Mozart operettas (the only one I think).

A colonel was in charge of the CIC detachment. Every once in a while the CIC would be sitting around with submachine guns, and attention was focused on a certain room with the inference being that they had captured someone. There was a separate flower house, and it was rumored that there was a system to waft the scent of flowers from the flower house to the dining room. Strangely, a couple of rooms were paneled with perforated steel sheets used in constructing runways. It was rumored that the Russians had previously occupied the building.

The mess was operated like an officers mess, and sometimes near the end of the month the colonel would tell us all to eat there to balance the budget. The food beat the Landsberg mess but not the local restaurants.

Initially activated as Flight F of the 12th Radio Squadron Mobile, the new unit in Vienna became Detachment 4, 12th RSM in 1954 and was redesignated Det 3, 6912th RSM in May 1955. Larry Kujawa reminisced about detachment staffing and unit operations.

I think there were about 10 AF personnel, all Russian voice. A lieutenant was in charge of the unit. I remember one other name Jim (I think) Wogsland from Minnesota. We staffed two positions 24 hours per day and after awhile were structured to work four rotating 6-hour shifts—ugh.

We were connected by teletype and one-time tape to Landsberg, I think, and it seems like we reported traffic via the TT. I wonder about the value of the takeoffs, callsigns, etc. we recorded.

It was exciting being 20 years old, attired as a civilian, living in the villa in the beautiful city, watching the Russians at the changing of the guard, and in front of the hotel they occupied, flirting with crossing out of the US Zone, etc.

I do not have it now, but there was something in my discharge paperwork that indicated I was carried on the AF books as a member of the AF band the time I was in Vienna.

Completing his enlistment in Vienna, SSgt. Larry Kujawa boarded a ship in Leghorn, Italy, sailed to America and received his discharge in January 1955. The covert intercept site that he left in Vienna was deactivated in August 1955, concurrently with the departure of the four Allied Powers that had administered Austria since the end of World War II.

USAFSS OPS AT SEMBACH

The USAFSS organization that eventually became the 6914th Radio Squadron Mobile originated at Kaufbeuren, probably early in 1953. In June 1953, Det 2, 12th RSM was compromised as being located at Kaufbeuren, Germany.[52] Four months later, the squadron referenced Det 2, 12th RSM as being located at Sembach, Germany.[53] Sixteen months later (February 1955), the 12th Radio Squadron Mobile reassigned airmen from Landsberg to Det 2, 12th RSM, Hof, Germany.[54] (Det 2, 12th RSM at Sembach had been deactivated in 1954, with the 12th RSM reusing the detachment number for its new unit at Hof.)

DET 2, 12TH RSM—KAUFBEUREN

In 1999, Charles Simpson, a traffic analyst, discussed his assignment at Kaufbeuren. The unit had a SIGINT mission with 14 to 16 intercept positions. When he arrived in July 1953, the detachment was preparing to relocate to Sembach.

In October 1953, we hooked up our mobile trailers (the ops people had to learn how to drive tractor trailers) and drove the entire detachment up the Autobahns to Sembach AB (which had just opened). We parked the trailers about 20 miles outside of Sembach (in the middle of some woods), put up the antennae, and became the first truly mobile squadron in the SS [Security Service], residing on Sembach and riding to work at the mobile site in the back of 6 x 6's.

We ate one meal during shift out of mess kits in the field. Our unit designation was changed from a detachment (forget the number) to the 6914th RSM, and we were operational under the described scenario and unit designation right up to my departure in July 1956, when I transferred to a very small (about 15 personnel) Berlin, Germany, detachment at Tempelhof.

With the arrival of the 85th RSM, Det 2, 12th RSM was deactivated.

85TH RSM ARRIVES AT SEMBACH

On 8 December 1953, Air Force Security Service activated the 85th Radio Squadron Mobile "Light," commanded by Capt. William P. Thompson at Kelly AFB.[55] The unit deployed to Sembach AB, Germany, as Flight A, 85th RSM to assume the personnel, functions and responsibilities of Det 2, 12th RSM.[56]

The 85th RSM left Kelly AFB on 17 April 1954 and, upon arrival at Sembach on 1 May, absorbed the men, equipment and functions of Flight A. The 85th RSM Headquarters and billeting were located at Sembach while its Ops compound was situated at Grünstadt. Having arrived with Det 2, 12th RSM from Kaufbeuren in 1953, Ed Robinson vividly remembers two USAFSS operations sites in the Landstuhl Air Base-Grünstadt area.

Sometime in the summer of 1953 we moved to Sembach AB, still as Det 2, 12 RSM. Our operations site was near Landstuhl AB in the woods just off the Autobahn and on the approaches to the runway at Landstuhl. Who can forget the noise from landings and takeoffs. Specially noisy were Vampire jets of the RAF that apparently used Landstuhl from time to time. You could not mistake a Vampire silhouette. We later became the 85th RSM.

The 85th reported to the 6910th Security Group at Landsberg. The 85th RSM unit designator was deactivated on 8 May 1955, replaced by the 6914th Radio Squadron Mobile. As pointed out by Robinson, it was about this time that the squadron moved its operations compound to a new area.

A new site was constructed on the top of a hill just above the village of Grünstadt am Weinstrasse. By then we were the 6914th RSM.

Our primary radio intercept coverage was of the Russian 24th Air Army in East Germany.

The 6914th RSM was replaced by the 6910th Radio Group Mobile.

6910TH RGM—SEMBACH

Activated on 1 September 1956, the 6910th Radio Group Mobile assumed the mission and resources of the 6914th. The 6910th RGM conducted intercept and first echelon analysis and reporting and assumed control of existing detachments in Berlin, Kassel, Wasserkuppe, Landshut, Hof and Wiesbaden (Camp Pieri). The 6912th RSM at Bingen also reported to the 6910th RGM, and the detachment in Linz, Austria, was deactivated in 1957. In August 1959, the 6910th RGM relocated its van-housed intercept and processing equipment from Grünstadt, colocating operations with headquarters on Sembach Air Base. The group set up its operations vans in an area next to the flight line. The 6910th moved from Sembach to Darmstadt in 1961. Chris Jones, a former 6910th Security Group Morse intercept operator-DF operator, remembers the move well.

I moved to Darmstadt from Sembach in May of 1961, I believe it was. We worked a mid, packed up our worldly treasures and drove to Darmstadt, signed in, were assigned a room, unpacked and then settled in before we worked another mid. I don't think I could do that today [August 2006].

6900TH SW RELOCATES TO FRANKFURT

During the second half of 1954, the 6900th Security Wing relocated from Landsberg AB to Frankfurt am Main, Germany— moving into the IG Farben Building. Located near the Main U.S. Army Post Exchange on WAC Circle in downtown Frankfurt, the Farben Building already housed European offices of the Army Security Agency, Naval Security Group, National Security Agency and Central Intelligence Agency. In 1956, Col. Richard P. Klocko assumed command of the 6900th SW, replacing Col. Augustinus.

Personnel assigned to the 6900th SW shared some of the finest facilities and amenities in Europe—comfortable family housing and an American high school, excellent enlisted quarters, extensive, well-stocked post exchange facilities, and the plush Terrace Club (officers) and Topper Club (NCO's). Single enlisted men of all American services lived in Army billets, a former

German apartment building on Eichenimerlandstrasse, off WAC Circle across from the Main PX.

Contributed by Bob Fortin

Army PX, WAC Circle, Frankfurt, Germany, 1959

In 2003, former A1C Robert Fortin nostalgically recalled his tour with the 6900th SW from 1958 to 1961. With Class A passes—no curfew—and seemingly unlimited, friendly Frauleins, Fortin called Frankfurt a single airman's paradise. Stark's Café and Leon's Bier Bar were popular 6900th stomping grounds by WAC Circle, and the Blue Grotto near the Bahnhof on Kaiserstrasse had the best pizza in town. The Fischerstube and Royal Bar were also favored "G.I." hangouts. As did other airmen in Germany, Fortin typically arrived in the downtown bars after 10:00 p.m. to make out with Frauleins whose Army would-be suitors had to return to quarters for an 11:00 p.m. curfew. This was a common phenomenon in Europe wherever U.S Air Force and U.S. Army forces were colocated after WW II.

The enlisted men's apartments where Fortin lived had thick ropes attached to the upper floor outside balconies. Intended as emergency fire escapes, airmen sometimes used the ropes to lower young Frauleins to the ground—the Army frowned on romantic trysts in their barracks. The military brass generally did not interfere with airmen in their quarters, except that the Army Officer of the Day sometimes knocked on their doors during a security-fire check of the apartment complex.

Kaiserstrasse, Frankfurt, Germany, 1960

Hauptbahnhof (Train Station), Frankfurt, Germany, 1960

Fortin's most memorable moment on duty in the 6900th SW dealt with the shoot down of Air Force C-130 60528 in September 1958. As the TSC Clerk in the Top Secret Control Office, Fortin vividly remembers the arrival of a Flash precedence message announcing the disappearance of the C-130 over Armenia. He immediately hand-carried the message to Col. Gordon W. Wildes.

A year later, 6900th wing commander Col. Klocko hosted a luncheon honoring Col. Wildes on his reassignment from the unit. Col. Russell L. French replaced Col. Wildes as the 6900th Director of Operations. The 6900th SW and later its successor organization, the European Security Region, controlled USAFSS activities in Europe through 1972.

At the end of 1954, the 6900th wing still had three security groups—6910th, 6930th and 6950th. With the 6930th and 6950th Security Groups covered in their separate chapters, changes within the 6910th SG during 1954 are shown in the org chart that follows.

6910th Scty Gp Org Chart—31 Dec 1954	
6910th Security Group Landsberg, Germany 1953-1956	
2nd RSM Darmstadt, Germany Det D, 2nd RSM Berlin, Germany	41st RSM Bremerhaven, Germany Det 1, 41st RSM Fassberg, Germany
12th RSM Landsberg, Germany Det 1, 12th RSM Linz, Austria Det 2, 12th RSM Hof, Germany Det 4, 12th RSM Vienna, Austria	85th RSM HQ Sembach, Germany 85th RSM OPS Grünstadt, Germany Flt A, 85th RSM Sembach, Germany Det 1, 85th RSM (1 Berlin, Germany Det 2, 85th RSM Kassel, Germany Det 3, 85th RSM (2 Wasserkuppe, Germany
(1 Flight A, 2nd RSM; Jan-Oct 1954. (2 Flight B, 2nd RSM; Jan-Oct 1954.	

SITE SURVEYS—NEW EUROPEAN USAFSS OPERATING LOCATIONS

Air Force Security Service followed a methodical process in expanding its intelligence gathering capabilities throughout the world, preceding the creation of new intercept or direction finding sites with a "hearability study" (site survey) in areas of interest. During the early 1950's, the 2nd RSM supported site studies in Europe. The scope of each survey varied from a small intercept team deploying to a potential site for a few days with a couple of intercept receivers to a detachment-size team visiting and evaluating several possible sites during an extended deployment of several weeks.

TSgt. Loreto J. (Larry) Stracqualursi, a 2nd RSM Morse intercept supervisor, served as team NCOIC during several hearability site surveys in 1954. During July and August, Sgt. Stracqualursi and his team deployed to Spain for several weeks and carried out hearability studies of several days per location at Las Figuras (Cádiz Province), Gerona, Barcelona, Majorca, Valencia, Madrid and Seville. The officer in charge of the survey team was authorized to "hire guides, taxies, mules, etc. as required in the accomplishment of the mission."[57]

Later in November-December 1954, a team that included First Lt. Walter G. McCarroll, Sgt. Stracqualursi and 37 other 2nd RSM airmen performed site surveys in France—at St. Nazaire, La Rochelle, Potier, Camp Bussac and Bordeaux.[58] Capt. Harry J. Wells (41st RSM) and Second Lt. Gerald W. Lockwood (6910th SG) also participated in the deployment. The men deployed as a self-contained detachment, traveling from Darmstadt to France in a convoy of 2nd RSM vehicles—one staff car, two 3/4-ton trucks, three deuce-and-a-half trucks and two shop vans. Spending seven weeks on the road, the team arrived back at Darmstadt just before Christmas. In 2006, Larry Stracqualursi recalled that the 6910th Security Group had conducted an earlier survey in France in 1953—possibly as part of a tentative plan, later cancelled, to move the 6910th SG to France.

A previous survey performed by the Group was accomplished in 1953 but was not very successful and more info was needed, thus a larger more detailed survey was called for.

Stracqualursi added that he had participated in numerous other hearability studies, including surveys at most of the new USAFSS sites activated in Germany during the early 1950's, "but they were mostly very small teams and for only a few weeks at most."

Greasing the Skids for Site Surveys

Col. Philip G. Evans, 6900th Security Wing Chief of Staff, was personally involved in wing-level surveys in advance of the on-site hearability studies by USAFSS intercept teams. Gordon Wicklund, an enlisted member of the initial cadre that stood up the 6900th SW at Landsberg, provided documentation on advance site surveys that occurred in 1954 and 1955. Wicklund, who was the 6900th Chief of Staff's chief clerk, relocated to Frankfurt with the wing in 1954 and participated in the advance surveys.

Unlike the multiday hearability surveys carried out by an intercept team, the advance 6900th visits involved single-day VIP-level courtesy calls on senior officials in the areas to be visited by the 2nd RSM intercept teams. The 6900th survey team traveled aboard the wing's C-47 aircraft based at Rhein-Main and crewed by a 6900th aircrew (pilot, copilot, crew chief and radio operator). The advance team consisted of Col. Evans, a USAFSS intelligence officer and SSgt. Wicklund. The OIC of the survey team was authorized to "hire guides, taxies, mules, etc. as required in the accomplishment of the mission."

The wing survey team departed Rhein-Main on 5 July 1954 on ten days of temporary duty with planned stops in Chateauroux, France, and Madrid, Zaragoza, Barcelona, Valencia, Cartegena and Seville, Spain.[59] Eight months later (24 April 1955), the survey team returned to Madrid and Seville for a follow-up survey.[60] The next wing survey trip on 6 June 1955 covered stops in the Middle East and West Asia: Rome and Naples, Italy; Tripoli, Libya; Cairo, Egypt; Beirut, Lebanon; Dhahran, Saudi Arabia; Karachi, Pakistan; Baghdad, Iraq; Adana, Ankara and Istanbul, Turkey; Athens and Iraklion, Greece. During the 24-day TDY, the team also made side stops at Lahore, Quetta, Rawalpindi, and Peshawar, Pakistan.[61]

While major emphasis on this trip was exploring areas for an intercept site in Pakistan, Col. Evans also paid visits to existing USAFSS units in Libya, Turkey and Greece (Crete). Working for the 6900th Chief of Staff and participating in the site surveys had its rewards. Wicklund rose from the rank of A2C in October 1953 to SSgt. in April 1955 and was awarded two Air Force Commendation Medals during his 6900th SW assignment. And never in his wildest dreams did he think about visiting so many of the world's "garden spots" when he enlisted in the Air Force in 1951.

USAFSS Europe at a Glance—December 1954

With the 6900th Security Wing relocating to Frankfurt, USAFSS Headquarters continued its expansion activities in the European area in 1954. The most significant USAFSS squadron-level changes in Europe included the relocation of the 85th RSM to Germany and the activation of 34th RSM elements in Turkey and Greece (Island of Crete).

In March 1954, there was a change of command in the 2nd Radio Squadron Mobile—Lt. Col. Richard D. Small Jr. replaced Lt. Col. Van Tuil as 2nd RSM Commander. The next and most far-reaching organizational changes in USAFSS history occurred in May 1955.

69XX UNIT IDENTIFIERS—MAY 1955

In May 1955, Air Force Security Service implemented a major change in its unit designators—replacing all single-digit and double-digit unit identifiers with a numeric designator in the 69xx series. HQ USAF had directed the redesignation so that USAFSS unit designators conformed to the standard USAF four-digit designation pattern.

The 34th RSM became the 6934th RSM; 31st CSS was renamed the 6931st CSS; 2nd RSM was now the 6911th RSM, etc. (reference the table that follows). Each squadron that was assigned a new designator issued orders transferring its members in place to the new unit identifier—a paper move only. The organization charts for the period May 1955 and beyond show the new 69xx unit numbers.

USAFSS Europe Designators—31 Dec 1955 *

Location	Pre-1955 Unit	1955 Unit	Remarks
Frankfurt, Ger.	6900th Scty Wg	6900th Scty Wg	
Landsberg, Ger.	6901st Spec Comm Gp	6901st Spec Comm Gp	Landsberg, 1955
Landsberg, Ger.	6905th Comm Sq	6905th Comm Sq	
Landsberg, Ger.	6910th Scty Gp	6910th Scty Gp	
Darmstadt, Ger.	2nd RSM	6911th RSM	
Landsberg, Ger.	12th RSM	6912th RSM	Bingen, 1955
Landsberg, Ger.	None	Det 1, 6912th RSM	July 1955
Linz, Austria	OL-1, 12th RSM	OL-1, 6912th RSM	
Hof, Germany	Det 2, 12th RSM	Det 2, 6912th RSM	Activated, 1954
Vienna, Austria	Det 4, 12th RSM	Det 3, 6912th RSM	Closed, Aug '55.
Bremerhaven, Ger.	41st RSM	6913th RSM	
Fassberg, Ger.	Det 1, 41st RSM	Det 1, 6913th RSM	To Schleswig
Schleswig, Ger.	Det 2, 41st RSM	Det 2, 6913th RSM	Open Sept '55
Sembach, Ger.	85th RSM HQ	6914th RSM HQ	Billeting,
Grünstadt, Ger.	85th RSM Ops	6914th RSM	Operations
Berlin, Ger.	Det 1, 85th RSM	Det 1, 6914th RSM	
Kassel, Ger.	Det 2, 85th RSM	Det 2, 6914th RSM	
Wasserkuppe, Ger.	Det 3, 85th RSM	Det 3, 6914th RSM	
Brooks AFB, TX	6950th Scty Gp	6950th Scty Gp	
Chicksands, Eng.	10th RSM	6951st RSM	
Kirknewton, Scot.	37th RSM	6952nd RSM	
Wheelus AB, Libya	6930th Scty Gp	6930th Scty Gp	
Wheelus AB, Libya	34th RSM	6934th RSM	
Ankara, Turkey	Det 1, 34th RSM	6933rd RSM	TUSLOG 3
Trabzon, Turkey	OL-2, Det 1, 34th RSM	Det 1, 6933rd RSM	TUSLOG Det 3-1
Samsun, Turkey	OL-1, Det 1, 34th RSM	Det 2, 6933rd RSM	TUSLOG Det 3-2
Sile, Turkey	none	Det 3, 6933rd RSM	TUSLOG Det 3-3
Diyarbakir, Turkey	Det 3, 34th RSM	Det 4, 6933rd RSM	TUSLOG Det 8
Iraklion, Crete	Det 2, 34th RSM	6938th RSM	
Chicksands, Eng.	6906th Scty Flt	6906th Scty Flt	COMSEC
Frankfurt, Ger.	31st Comm Scty Sq	6931st CSS	COMSEC
Burtonwood, Eng.	Det 1, 31st CSS	Det 1, 6931st CSS	COMSEC
Bushy Park, Eng.	Det 2, 31st CSS	Det 2, 6931st CSS	COMSEC
Camp Pieri, Ger.	Det 3, 31st CSS	Det 3, 6931st CSS	COMSEC
Wheelus AB, Libya	Det 4, 31st CSS	Det 4, 6931st CSS	COMSEC
* 69xx designators also implemented in Far East & Alaska, May '55.			

6910TH OPERATIONS—LANDSBERG

Relocating to Landsberg, the second echelon processing element of the 6910th Security Group continued analyzing and reporting traffic intercepted by the group's subordinate squadrons—the 6911th, 6912th, 6913th and 6914th RSM's. After completing traffic analysis school at Brooks AFB, Ray M. Thompson reported for duty with the 6910th at Landsberg in May 1953, arriving about the same time that the group's Operations Division arrived from Darmstadt. Thompson worked in the civilian air section headed by First Lt. Hector Quintanilla Jr.

A Mexican Christmas in Bavaria

Lt. Quintanilla invited the single airmen in his section to join him and his family for a home-cooked meal at Christmas 1954—not the traditional Christmas dinner; mind you, but "A Mexican Christmas in Bavaria." Reminiscing over the Christmas holidays in 1998, Ray Thompson penned a tribute to Lt. Quintanilla and his wife Eleanor.[62]

> *I remember it like it was last Christmas, but it was really—Christmas 1954. A bunch of very non-military college-age kids were serving in the United States Air Force Security Service (USAFSS). Our unit was the 6910th Security Group, based at a former German air base just outside the beautiful little Bavarian town of Landsberg am/Lech. Our daily jobs were part of an Air Force intelligence mission and highly classified. Although far from home at Christmas, most of us privately gave thanks that we were not in Korea; we knew we had a plum assignment in Bavaria. We spent our spare time chasing frauleins, drinking German beer, snapping our German cameras, traveling throughout Western Europe and dreaming about getting out at the end of our 4-year enlistment. . . . .*
>
> *Yeah, we were kind of a smart-aleck bunch of kids. Our CO was 1st Lt. Hector Quintanilla Jr. Hector was college educated (PhD. in Physics) and understood and tolerated our non-military ways. Hector's other claim to fame was his beautiful wife Eleanor, which brings me back to my Christmas story.*

The invitation to a Christmas dinner at the home of Hector and Eleanor came as a real surprise. As enlisted troops, we only admired Eleanor from afar, which was the norm for military life. To be invited to their home for a meal, especially at Christmas, was something special! The real surprise was the meal that was served was Mexican! You see, all of us had developed a taste for Mexican food during our stint in San Antonio. We had now become connoisseurs of German food and drink, we didn't expect to taste Mexican again until we ZI'd (went home)! However, as a wonderful treat, Eleanor sent home for enough Mexican fix'ins to feed Hector's entire T/A (traffic analysis) section.

Concluding his trip down memory lane, Thompson vividly remembered the Quintanilla children, "The kids were the other part of the celebration that made it memorable." In 1995, with the help of other former 6910th traffic analysts, he launched a campaign to find Hector Quintanilla.

After returning to civilian life many of us saw Hector's name in the news from time to time because he was tapped to head "Project Blue Book," the official Air Force program at Wright-Patterson AFB that investigated UFO sightings. You can still see these investigations from time to time on the Discovery Channel.

Sadly, they learned that retired Col. Hector Quintanilla had passed away in 1998, but his son Gene was carrying on the military tradition. During the late 1990's, Col. Eugene H. Quintanilla was Commander, 17th Support Group, Goodfellow AFB, Texas—where thousands of airmen and officers began their Air Force Security Service careers.

Landsberg Under the Hammer

Hugh Windsor, a former member of the 6910th Security Group, told a story in 2000 about an innovator with an idea that he sold to management as a replacement for burn detail.

Back in the good old days at Landsberg AB we had to dispose of classified trash by burning it. The section I was assigned to, Machine Accounting I think the Air Force referred to it as, had a large quantity of IBM tabulating cards to burn.

Every couple of weeks "Burn Day" came around. Operating personnel reported to work in fatigues and assembled in the back room. Once there, all settled in for a killer day. Each and every tab card had to be crumpled before being tossed in a bag for destruction. The cards were prime paper stock, heavy and resistive to crumpling by the nature of their original use. We spent all morning and some part of the afternoon crumpling cards, bagging them and stapling the bags shut before transport to the incinerator. Labor intensive to be sure and of course, we weren't processing anyone's intercepts during this time.

Up in the front office some brass hat swooned and had a brainstorm—6910th could improve mission response capability if we could just keep the guys in their regular function instead of crumpling cards. The outcome of this inspiration was the acquisition and installation of a large hammer mill to be used to reduce cards to shreds so small no one could possibly reconstruct them.

The shredded cards would be collected and sold to "denazified German contractors" who would turn them into paper sludge from which they could make cardboard. A kind of early recycling exercise. HQ USAFSS approved the destruction scheme so all stops were pulled out.

The hammer mill weighed a couple tons and eventually got installed on the first floor of a room adjacent to the Tab Shop. A hole had been cut in the concrete floor so that the shredded card stock could exit the mill directly into the bagging facility beneath it. It was a very neat installation.

A hammer mill is used often for grinding grain for livestock feed. This one had a heavy shaft running horizontally through the length of the unit. Pinned longitudinally to the shaft were three rows of steel bars, each shaped like a hammer. The hammers were loosely pinned to the shaft so they could swing freely. The bottom of the bore in which the hammer shaft spun was a screen through which the paper shreds were forced and from whence they wafted down into the bagger apparatus. The top of the bore was a large hopper into which the tab cards were to be deposited.

Came the first day of operation. All 6910th brass gathered for the launching. Also in attendance were some bird colonels from ASA Frankfurt. They intended to do the same thing up there. Well to the rear was me, myself, the faceless IBM Tabulating Equipment Repairman [83170].

With a low rumbling whoosh the mighty mill began to turn. In a minute or so its hammers extended from the shaft by the rotational inertia and the stage was set for action. Some selected honorary threw in the first card, which promptly vanished. The mill was well and successfully launched. A new day for tab card destruction had arisen. All about in the room was a sense of excitement as palpable as that present on a later day when they shot John Glenn off the earth.

More cards were tossed into the maw of the monster shredder. The brass were ecstatic and thoughts of drinks and stories at the Officers Club pulsed in many of their imaginations. Surely this would break the Commies and end the war in Korea. The possibility of early release from service was also possible.

Eventually one of the bird colonels from ASA said, "Let's see how this baby does in production mode." He hefted a good four-inch block of tab cards and pitched them into the hopper.

The block of tab cards remained intact and hit the hammers with much the same affect as a same sized block of iron. Loud smashing noises came from the mill. One hammer broke from the shaft, flew up out of the hopper piercing the ceiling tile and imbedding itself in the concrete of the floor above.

After the mill was shut down the Ground Safety guy came charging up from the cellar to see what had happened upstairs. He was a first john and a brave one at that. Once *things quieted down he said he would not permit operation of the hammer mill. Never, never.*

The basement of Ops was in a zero visibility condition because of card dust in just the short time the mighty mill had run. He explained that card dust, like grain dust or coal dust was a powerful explosive mixture fully capable of totally removing 6910th Operations and its staff from the face of the planet.

That was the end of the mighty hammer mill. The officers retired to the Officers Club for libations and war stories. Depression settled in amongst the tab shop staff. And finally an order was posted on the "bull board" reinstating the old burn day routine. We had come full circle.

Responding in 2006 to a request for permission to use his anecdote in the 6910th unit history, Hugh Windsor responded, "The incident is yours to use. It was one of those magic moments of managerial exuberance, wasn't it?"

NEW USAFSS REPORTING RESPONSIBILITIES

In March 1954, HQ USAFSS proposed an expansion of processing activities at the squadron level and direct reporting by USAFSS to using commands. The plan envisioned consolidating USAFSS second echelon analysis and reporting in the field. To test proposed concepts, in June 1954 HQ USAFSS deployed processing teams to Europe and the Far East. The 6901st Special Communications Center in Europe (Germany) and 6902nd SCC in the Pacific (Japan) initiated point of analysis and reporting on a test basis.[63] During the tests, USAFSS intercept units forwarded copies of intercepted traffic to their respective SCC's, which did the analysis and reporting. The objective was direct and timely reporting in response to requirements from supported military commands.

6901ST SCG DEPLOYS TO LANDSBERG

"The point of intercept analysis and reporting concept" won approval in August 1954 and USAFSS redesignated the units 6901st and 6902nd Special Communications Groups. Subsequently,

USAFSS deployed the 6901st Special Communications Group to Landsberg, Germany, on 1 October 1955 to conduct the command's second echelon analysis and reporting mission in Europe. Concurrently, USAFSS stood up the 6905th Communications Squadron at Landsberg to provide comms support for the 6901st SCG. The transfer of the 6902nd Special Communications Group from Kelly AFB to Shiroi, Japan, the same year served a similar second echelon analysis and reporting function in the Far East.

6910th T/A Mission Assumed by 6901st SCG

With the 6901st SCG acquiring the USAFSS analysis and reporting mission in Europe, in the fall of 1955 the 6910th Security Group transferred associated officer and enlisted traffic analysts in place to the new special comms group. Commenting on morale following consolidation of the European T/A mission in the 6901st Special Comm Group, Duane Russell, who had relocated with the 6910th to Landsberg, called the new organization "one big, happy family."

We became the 6901st and moved into processing big time, especially driven by the designs of one Col. Phil Evans.

Scaled back to its squadron management functions, the 6910th Security Group remained at Landsberg into 1956 when the group was deactivated.

USAFSS Europe—Cold War Impacts (1955)

On 9 and 14 May 1955 respectively, the Federal Republic of Germany regained its sovereignty and was admitted as a member of the North Atlantic Treaty Organization. Countering West Germany's admission to NATO, the Soviet Union and the Bloc of East European nations signed the Warsaw Pact Agreement on 14 May 1955. The occupation of West Germany by the U.S., Britain and France officially ended with these actions.

Break out the Civvies

During the Allied Occupation following World War II, occupying forces were required to wear a military uniform at all times—no civvies either on or off duty. The uniform rule ended with the signing of status of forces agreements in 1955, but civilian clothes were a scarce commodity in Europe for months afterwards. Ed Robinson, a former 6914th RSM airman, recently reminisced about the first civilian suit that found its way into the squadron in 1955.

Very few of us had civvies. When Tony Baciewicz and John Coronna transferred back to Sembach from Berlin, one of them brought back a civilian suit. It had to be the world's ugliest suit. It was a grey herring bone tweed, double breasted job that supposedly was stolen in Berlin from a comatose kraut. (My money is on Baciewicz for the theft.) It had enormous cuffs on the trousers. The good thing about the "suit" was that it fit everybody and anybody.

Whenever someone went on leave, the suit went with him. The "suit" traveled all over Europe. When I left Sembach in 1956, the "suit" was still there. What stories it could tell if it could only talk.

Anthony (Tony) Baciewicz corrected Robinson regarding how he acquired the suit.

The suit referred to by Ed Robinson was mine and was one classy suit. It was not stolen from a comatose kraut but was given to me by my girlfriend in Berlin. It was originally owned by her husband who was a MSgt. in the SS in Poland. After the war he escaped to Australia. More likely Argentina than Australia, but that's what she told me.

Ironically, the lifting of the ban on civvies produced some petty, often illogical rules on the wear of both the uniform and civilian clothes. The wearing of class B uniforms (fatigues or other work uniforms without a tie), athletic clothing and Levis in civilian establishments (off-post stores, restaurants, bars, etc.) was forbidden. In addition, some commanders would not permit the wear of Levis in on-base theaters and clubs. In contrast, today's Air Force uniform of the day is the camouflage BDU (battle-dress uniform)—modern-day fatigues.

Landsberg AB Returned to German Control

U.S. Air Force units—including all USAFSS organizations—evacuated Landsberg Air Base in the 1955-56 period, returning the base to German control for use as a West German Air Force pilot training base. The 6912th Radio Squadron Mobile became the first USAFSS unit to leave Landsberg in the summer of 1955.

6912th RSM Relocates to Bingen am Rhein

For the 6912th RSM's new home, the Air Force could not have selected a more scenic and enjoyable locale than Bingen am Rhein, a small town at the confluence of the Rhein and Nahe Rivers.

Contributed by Gayle Stelter

6912th RSM, Bingen, Germany, circa 1956

Sitting at the southern entrance to Germany's premium wine country in the Rheinland-Pfalz State, Bingen is 15 km from Wiesbaden (USAFE HQ in the 1950's-60's) and 30 km from Frankfurt. Just across the Rhein from Bingen lies Rüdesheim—arguably Deutschland's wine capital and a world-famous tourist Mecca.

The 6912th RSM relocated to Bingen in June-July 1955, leaving behind on an interim basis a newly created Detachment 1, 6912th RSM at Landsberg Air Base. Plans for the move were well underway when SSgt. Paul Morgan arrived in the squadron on 15 June.[64] Assigned as the chief clerk in Operations, his full-time job over the next few weeks involved transporting squadron property to the unit's new facilities in the Bingen area. Reporting to the motor pool where he obtained a military drivers license for, among other vehicles, the deuce-and-a-half (6 x 6) truck, Morgan participated in the convoys between Landsberg and Bingen that supported the 6912th relocation—altogether five or six trips.

With a jeep leading the way, a convoy (approximately fifteen trucks loaded mostly with furniture) completed the day-long first trip to Bingen in late June and returned to Landsberg the following day with no difficulties. With more trucks and H-1 vans, some of the convoys extended over a couple of miles along the autobahn enroute to Bingen. Lt. Leslie, squadron personnel officer, served as convoy commander. Morgan was involved in the only accident incurred during the move. He broke his right thumb while connecting his tractor to a trailer (H-1 van).

DET 1, 6912TH RSM—LANDSBERG AND LANDSHUT

Relocation of the 6912th Radio Squadron Mobile to Bingen necessitated reorganization of the squadron's detached units. The 6912th RSM deactivated Det 1, 6912th RSM at Linz, Austria, concurrently activating Det 1, 6912th RSM at Landsberg—probably in July 1955. In turn, the squadron's unit in Linz, Austria, became Operating Location 1 (OL-1) of Det 1, 6912th RSM. Detachment 1 of the 6912th represented the squadron in USAFSS matters at Landsberg until the following year when the 6912th permanently moved its Det 1 from Landsberg to Landshut, Germany.

Humbert D. Kincaid was a member of an advance party that deployed to Landshut in the spring of 1956 to set up the Det 1, 6912th RSM operations site. The advance party spent "a few months" at Landshut—preparing for the transfer of the unit mission—before Kincaid returned to Landsberg to "help bring H-1 vans over when we were ready to set up Ops."

In July 1956, Detachment 1, 6912th RSM traveled in convoys (primarily 6 x 6 trucks and tractor-towed H-1 vans) transporting the detachment's equipment and personnel from Landsberg to Landshut. Fifty-seven airmen and one officer (Capt. Edward E. Frisa, who was the Det 1 commander) made the move between 14 and 19 July.[65]

According to Gene Vogelgesang, a Det 1 Morse operator who made the move to Landshut, the detachment commander and first sergeant, Capt. Frisa and MSgt. Marvin Schultz, were top-notch leaders, well respected by the men in the unit.

Det 1, 6912th RSM activated its operations initially adjacent to an Air Force radar unit on a hill east of Landshut, while colocating its headquarters and barracks with the U.S. Army on Pinder Kaserne, Landshut. The detachment made its mark in the signals intelligence world in October 1956, when voice intercept operators on Dog Trick detected the first SIGINT reflections of Soviet reaction to an expanding revolt against Communist rule in Hungary. Later, the unit moved its operations into the attic area of the barracks on the Kaserne.

Last 6912th Airmen at Landsberg

After graduating from a 12-month Serbo-Croatian class at the Army Language School, Monterey, Gordon Crocker joined the 6912th RSM in Landsberg in July 1954. When the 6912th relocated to Bingen in 1955, Crocker remained behind in Landsberg with other airmen in Det 1, 6912th RSM. A year later, when Det 1, 6912th RSM moved from Landsberg to Landshut, Gordon Crocker and Ray Haertel, a Hungarian linguist, had only days remaining on their enlistments, so the squadron transferred them to the 6905th Comm Squadron. They continued their voice intercept mission in an H-1 van for about a month, leaving Landsberg on 1 August 1956 for discharge from the Air Force. The departure of Crocker and Haertel ended 6912th and USAFSS intercept operations at Landsberg.

Det 1, 6912th/Landshut Becomes Det 4, 6910th RGM

By September 1957, Det 1, 6912th RSM at Landshut had evolved into a near-squadron-size detachment. On 1 October 1957, Det 1, 6912th personnel (two officers and 79 airmen, including Morse intercept operators and voice intercept operators trained in Hungarian, Czechoslovakian, Romanian, Russian and Serbo-Croatian) transferred in place to Det 4, 6910th Radio Group Mobile—the 6910th RGM was at Sembach.[66] Detachment 4 continued intercept operations at Landshut until 1959, when the unit's intercept mission was transferred to other USAFSS sites in

Germany and Det 4, 6910th RGM was deactivated. The 6910th RGM retained a direction finding capability at Landshut, designating the DF site Operating Location 1, 6910th RGM. Undergoing a couple of unit designator changes, the 6910th maintained a DF site at Landshut into 1964.[67]

Bingen—6912th HQ and Billeting

The 6912th Radio Squadron Mobile moved into a small, former *Schutzstaffel* (Nazi SS) post (La Marne Kaserne) on the west bank of the Rhein River in northwest Bingen. Situated on a rectangular shaped strip of riverbank, the Kaserne was bounded on the north by the Rhein, on the west by the Nahe River, and on the south by Bingen's main street (Mainzer Strasse) and sets of railroad tracks. A wrought iron fence separated downtown Bingen from the Kaserne, with the *Stadthalle* (Town Hall) located just to the right of the fence. A French occupation force was the Kaserne's last occupant before the arrival of the 6912th RSM.

Contributed by Gayle Stelter

6912th RSM, Bingen am Rhein, Germany, 1956

The 6912th airmen lived in open-bay quarters in a large four-story barracks fronting on the Rhein to the left of the *Stadthalle*. The barracks also housed a small library, BX and laundry/dry cleaning pick up point in the basement. An Airmens Club open to all ranks around the clock sat immediately to the left of the barracks, and the Bingen-Rüdesheim Ferry Landing was only a five-minute walk in the opposite direction. Or an airman could walk downtown beyond the *Stadthalle* to most of Bingen's restaurants and wine cellars in ten to fifteen minutes. Likewise, on-post support facilities and recreational amenities were within minutes of the airmen's quarters. Decisions, decisions! All-in-all, La Marne Kaserne was a very compact facility, the size of six to eight football fields—and right in the heart of Bingen.

Contributed by Gayle Stelter

6912th RSM Airmens Club, Bingen am Rhein, circa 1956

Richard Leary, a former 6912th Morse intercept operator who arrived in Bingen in November 1955, discussed his Bingen tour in an email exchange in June 2006. Leary had an excellent view of the Rhein from the fourth-floor barracks area that he shared with a dozen or so other airmen.

> *The unit was sorta fenced off from the town, but right inside it. No problem "walking" to the nearest gasthaus. Then there was always the ferry to Rüdesheim across the river.*

Paul Likus, who served in the 6912th, discussed "Bingen then and now" in an email exchange in June 2006. In 1957, he and fellow airmen often chatted with tourists as their boats tied up at a dock just outside their barracks. Returning to Bingen with his wife of 44 years in 1992, Likus noted that his former barracks and other buildings no longer existed.

We had our barracks building right on the river next to the town hall. Also inside the fenced compound was a small snack bar, our mess hall and administrative buildings. Our motor pool/theater was located about 200 yards down the railroad tracks toward the Nahe River. Located on the Rhein River in the same vicinity we had a really nice Airmens, NCO and Officers Club [all-ranks club].

The entire site had been razed and now was home to a modern hotel complex where the Likus' stayed while revisiting Bingen. Likus continued reminiscing.

During the summer months, after work a lot of us crossed the Rhein to party in Rüdesheim, the Rhein wine capital. It was always full of tourists and a lot of American girls. They had a swimming pool where we spent a great deal of time, but the main attraction was the Drosselgasse, a very narrow street that probably has fifteen wine taverns along its length. It was only about 300 yards long.

(A narrow alley, the Drosselgasse is the most famous street in Rüdesheim. Many of the Drosselgasse's wine gardens have live music.)

Author's Collection

There was always a lot of drinking and dancing going on. The places closed about midnight, but the last ferry boat to go back to Bingen was earlier, so a lot of nights the boat which was parked on that side of the river was full of G.I.'s sleeping on the benches. The operator always left a window open for us to get inside.

As a matter of fact, my wife and I went over to Rüdesheim for the evening while we were there, and we rode on the exact same boat—the Miss Binger. It brought back some sweet memories.

During their return trip to Bingen, Likus did not visit the site of the former 6912th operations compound. He recalls the site being located about a 40-minute ride from Bingen, but can't remember the name of the town—only that "it was located on top of a giant hill and was surrounded by barbed wire."

Bingen/Dromersheim—6912th Operations

The 6912th operations compound was in Dromersheim—on a hill overlooking the Nahe Valley about 16 kilometers from Bingen.[68] Built on the side of a steep hill, the site was rather cramped and difficult to reach via a winding road. With vineyards covering the hillside, the site's perimeter fence was just above the top row of grape vines.

Maneuvering tractor-trailer rigs through the narrow, twisting streets of Dromersheim and negotiating a narrow, winding lane to 6912th Operations called for professional driving to get the tractor and H-1 van rigs, and even the deuce-and-a-half trucks, into the area. The operations facility included a large concrete block building, Morse and voice intercept positions housed in H-1 vans and power generators. Additionally, according to Likus there was a small PX and mess hall (snack bar) at the operations site.

The vans were backed up to and opened into the block building so that unit operations personnel could move from one van to another without exposure to the elements, a morale booster since the Rhein River froze over at Bingen during severe winters. Otis Maxwell (6912th veteran 1955-58) walked across the Rhein by Bingen when it froze over in 1955. Former 6912th RSM traffic analyst James F. (Jim) Kimmett provided his recollections of the Dromersheim operations facility to the author in 2006.

My first assignment out of T/A tech school at March AFB was to the 6912th RSM at Bingen am Rhein in November 1957. And I helped close it down in the spring of '59. The 12th had as I recall 20 or 25 Morse racks in either four or five H-1 vans backed up to the square concrete ops building on the Dromersheim site. We also had either ten or fifteen voice positions, probably ten.

As I recall—when you entered the ops building by a right rear door, immediately across the hall was the comm center. The first van on the right was electronic maintenance, then there were three or four Morse vans. The front of the building had three vans, two of which were analysis and reporting vans. Down the left side were four or five more vans with one being XXX [unidentified target] analysis and two radiotelephone [R/T voice], and maybe one more Morse or R/T.

The center of the building had the OIC's desk—a captain with dark hair, horned rim glasses and a voice that could singe paint. Nate Goode's desk and the air defense shop were also in that area. All the vans had [side] doors, but they were to be used only in an emergency, and they were alarmed. There were some of us who spent several days on site grabbing a nap when possible during the comm changes. Great folks, great times.

Kimmett was in awe of Chief Warrant Officer Nathan Goode whom he regarded as Air Force Security Service's "Mr. Traffic Analyst."

We all took the T/A exam created by WO Nate Goode before he would let us take our 5- and 7-level [specialty upgrade] exams. If you could pass Nate's exam, the USAFSS exam was a snap.

According to Kimmett, CWO Goode had been a radio operator on B-17's during World War II and ended the war in a POW camp. Captured after bailing out of a crippled bomber, Goode was incarcerated in Stalag 17b, a special German prisoner of war camp for Allied Air Corps NCO's in Austria. Goode, a well respected officer, was a flight commander in the 6986th RGM, Wakkanai, Japan, during the author's tour with the 6986th in 1962-63.

Hazardous Duty—Driving To/From Work

Traveling the zigzagging roads to work was a real challenge. The motor pool provided a combination of military vehicles— Volkswagen buses, larger passenger buses and deuce-and-a-half (6 x 6) trucks—to carry airmen from Bingen to the operations compound. Most 6912th veterans have special recollections of trips to and from work. With some heat and a relatively comfortable seat, Paul Likus considered himself lucky to have been a 6 x 6 driver, while his comrades bounced around sitting on wooden benches under a canvas tarp in the back of the truck. Henry Miller-Jones, another 6912th Bingen veteran, jokes about taking windowsills off local houses at 06.45 a.m. while navigating a 6 x 6 through the twisty, hilly roads of Dromersheim and other villages enroute to Operations. Cobblestone streets and other perilous driving conditions notwithstanding, no serious accidents are known to have occurred on the Bingen-to-Dromersheim grand prix circuit.

6912TH RSM—BINGEN CLOSEOUT

The 6912th Radio Squadron Mobile continued signals intelligence operations at Bingen-Dromersheim through 30 June 1959, when the 6900th Security Wing deactivated its unit in Bingen. The shutdown of 6912th RSM operations in Bingen was part of a reorganization of Air Force Security Service activities in Europe. To reduce overhead operating costs while giving up little if any mission effectiveness, Air Force Security Service spread the resources and SIGINT mission from its Bingen squadron among other USAFSS units in Germany.

Former 6912th traffic analyst and presently retired National Security Agency SIGINT professional James Kimmett transferred to the 6910th Radio Group Mobile at Sembach in the weeks leading up to the squadron shutdown in Bingen. He remembers that many of the squadron's linguists relocated to Berlin, while most of the Morse intercept operators joined USAFSS units at Sembach and Darmstadt. He also recalls that some of the H-1 intercept vans moved to Sembach, with others probably ending up at Darmstadt.

A U.S. Army outfit occupied La Marne Kaserne when Kimmett visited Bingen in 1974. Later while touring the Rhein area again in the early 1980's, he noted that a German Wehrmacht unit was using the former 6912th operations compound at Dromersheim.

6912TH RSM ACTIVATED IN BERLIN

On 1 July 1959, the 6900th SW reactivated the 6912th Radio Squadron Mobile at Berlin Tempelhof Central Airport. This was not a direct transfer of the 6912th RSM from Bingen to Berlin. Rather, the new 6912th assumed responsibility for the existing resources and mission of Tempelhof-based Detachment 1, 6910th Radio Squadron Mobile, and Det 1, 6910th RGM was deactivated.

Air Force SIGINT Units in Berlin

For the next three decades, the 6912th Radio Squadron Mobile (and its Berlin-based successor units) were at the forefront of signals intelligence collection in Europe. The Air Force maintained 6912th HQ and billets at Tempelhof Airport throughout its stay in Berlin while moving its SIGINT operations to newly constructed facilities within the city.

Summary—Air Force SIGINT Operations in Berlin

Intercept operators and analysts stood watch in Berlin from the start of the Korean War through the collapse of the Soviet Union four decades later. Those highly dedicated signals intelligence professionals served in silence behind the Iron Curtain, and their contributions to the disintegration of Communism in Eastern Europe remain sealed and unavailable to the public. They witnessed the building of the Berlin Wall dividing the city in 1961 and the tearing down of the Wall in 1989. The payoff was the end of the Cold War.

In July 1950, the first Air Force Security Service signals intelligence facility in Berlin consisted of a voice intercept receiver and a borrowed radar scope housed in a broom closet of the partially bombed-out Tempelhof control tower building. Forty-two years later, the Air Force Intelligence Command's 690th Electronic Security Group turned out the lights on Air Force SIGINT activities in Berlin.

On 19 September 1991, a formal retreat and closure ceremony was conducted at Berlin's Marienfelde, Germany, site, and keys to the site were turned over to the host air base group commander. The formal closure of Marienfelde came after 26 years of existence as one of the premier operations of the Command. HQ 690th ESG inactivated at Tempelhof Central Airport, Germany, effective 1 July 1992.[69]

That broom closet operation from 1950 evolved during the Cold War into two sophisticated SIGINT collection complexes—690th ESG Marienfelde Operations and a British station shared by US and UK personnel at Teufelsberg (Devil's Mountain).

American and British Intelligence created their two SIGINT facilities in West Berlin upon vestiges of destruction from the Second World War—atop two artificial hills created from mounds of rubble and garbage from the latter stages of the war. USAFSS built its intercept site on a reclaimed trash dump in the southern Berlin district of Marienfelde. At the highest elevation in the American Sector, the site overlooked a long stretch of the infamous Berlin Wall and provided outstanding reception of line-of-sight signals. Constructed on a similar rubble heap in the British Sector—at the highest elevation in West Berlin—the Teufelsberg field station provided unobstructed reception of signals from all directions.

Contributed by Kenneth Pearsall
Tempelhof Flughafen, Berlin, Germany, 1950

The U.S. Army Intelligence and Security Command had the lead in American SIGINT operations at T-berg. However, a sizeable contingent of linguists from the Air Force unit at Tempelhof shared intercept, transcription and analysis duties with INSCOM specialists at Teufelsberg. We next address the Air Force Security Service unit that served at Hof, Germany, from the mid-1950's to 1971.

The chart on the next page lists the officers who commanded the Berlin contingent of Air Force Security Service (and successor commands), along with identifying unit designators.[70]

USAFSS Unit Commanders—Berlin
July 1950-July 1992

Rank and Name	Dates	Unit Designator/Remarks
Lt. Kenneth F. Pearsall	Jul 1950-Aug 1953	Det D, 2nd RSM (Jul 1950-Jan 1954)
Lt. Clarence W. Blanford	Aug 1953-Apr 1954	Det D, 2nd RSM
Capt. Arthur Folkerts	Apr 1954-Dec 1955	Flt A, 2nd RSM (1 Jan 1954); Det 1, 85th RSM (1 Oct 1954)
Capt. Sherman Fort	Dec 1955-Aug 1958	Det 1, 6914th RSM (8 May 1955); Det 1, 6910th RGM (1 Sept 1956)
Capt. Sidney Bennett	Sept 1958-Jun 1959	Det 1, 6910th RGM
Maj. Woodrow W. Gentry	1 Jul '59-15 Jun '60	6912th RSM (1 Jul 1959)
Maj. Hugh E. McCall	16 Jun '60-2 Jun '63	6912th RSM
Lt. Col. Carl L. Cook Jr.	3 Jun '63-13 Jun '66	6912th Security Sqdn (1 Jul 1963)
Lt. Col. Robert F. Stark	14 Jun '66-17 Apr '69	6912th Security Squadron
Lt. Col. Stanley K. Moe	18 Apr '69-25 May '70	6912th Security Squadron
Lt. Col. Richard G. Webb	26 May '70-25 Jun '74	6912th Security Squadron
Col. John P. Joyce	26 Jun '74-31 Jul '75	6912th Security Squadron
Lt. Col. Robert R. Williams	1 Aug '75-21 Sept '75	6912th Security Squadron
Col. Jesse R. Owen Jr.	22 Sept '75-25 Mar '76	6912th Security Squadron
Col. William T. Ballard	26 Mar '76-19 Apr '79	6912th Security Squadron
Col. Lewis M. Chapman	20 Apr '79-31 Jul '80	6912th ESG (1 Aug 1979); USAFSS became Electronic Scty Command
Col. Alton L. Elliott	1 Aug '80-31 May '82	6912th Electronic Security Group
Col. Charles L. Bishop	1 Jun '82-31 May '83	6912th Electronic Security Group
Col. Jerome M. Wucher	1 Jun '83-5 Jul '85	6912th Electronic Security Group
Col. Jay J. Jaynes	6 Jul '85-7 Feb '88	6912th Electronic Security Group
Col. Ben C. Hardaway Jr.	8 Feb '88-Jun 1991	690th Electronic Security Wing (15 Jul 1988)
Col. Robert A. Leech	Jun 1991-19 Sept '91	690th ESG (11 Jun 1991; deactivated 1 Jul 1992).

USAFSS SIGINT OPS—HOF, GERMANY

No official Air Force histories of USAFSS SIGINT operations at Hof Air Station are available to the author; however, limited documentation and anecdotal evidence exist on the early USAFSS years at the station. Former USAFSS airmen from the 12th Radio Squadron Mobile recall commencing operations at Hof in November 1954.

When Jack "Ace" Lyckberg, a former teletype and crypto maintenance technician, arrived at Landsberg AB, Germany, in August 1953, the 12th RSM loaned him out to the colocated 6910th Security Group to work in the group's communications center. Early in 1954, Lyckberg began working in the 12th RSM's comm center, and by summer he was hearing talk about a new 12th RSM detachment to be established at Hof, West Germany.[71]

Hof—Military History

Located adjacent to Czechoslovakia on the Saale River in the northeast corner of Bavaria, Hof became a German Security Service intelligence-gathering post in early 1938. Operating from Schmidtlar Kaserne on Kulmbacherstrasse, the Nazis collected political intelligence on the Czech border districts (Sudetenland) during the months leading to the occupation of Czechoslovakia in the fall of 1938. Later in 1942, Schmidtlar Kaserne served as a Wehrmacht (army) training base—preparing troops for the Front.

Various U.S. Occupation Forces used the military facility— renamed Hof Kaserne—immediately following World War II. Army veteran William Okerlund served with the occupation forces at Hof soon after Germany capitulated in May 1945. Okerlund discussed his Hof activities in an internet exchange in 2006.

Served in European Theater with 90th Division. Stormed the beach at Le Harve, France the day the war ended—8 May 1945—in a convoy of 5,000 men. Guess the Germans heard we were coming, so they quit. Served in army of occupation in Hof for eleven months after war ended. Went as a rifleman [Corporal] but ended up as a clerk in Hof.

Hof Kaserne became home to the 603rd Aircraft Control and Warning Squadron in May 1948 and was formally renamed Kingsley Barracks in June 1949—honoring Army Air Corps WW II Medal of Honor recipient Second Lt. David R. Kingsley.[72] During the Cold War, the U.S. Army's 2nd and 3rd Armored Cavalry Regiments used Hof as a border outpost for reconnaissance companies that patrolled the East German and Czech borders.

USAF Photo

Being at the end of the logistics supply chain and with severe harsh winters, Hof offered few amenities for military personnel. Rotating its patrol companies through Hof on monthly tours of duty, the cavalry regiments at Nurnberg had little concern for the comfort of those permanently assigned to Hof. A small PX sold cigarettes and toilet articles. The closest PX of any size was 70 miles away at Grafenwohr—itself a remote Army training facility—and the nearest military hospital and dental clinic was at Nurnberg, 110 miles from Hof. Adding to its remoteness, Kingsley Barracks had very few recreational facilities during the 1950's.

By 1954 when a USAFSS team arrived at Kingsley, the 603rd had relocated, leaving behind at Hof a subordinate radar unit (Detachment 1, 603rd AC&WS).[73] In early 1954, TSgt. Loreto Stracqualursi and a deployed 2nd Radio Squadron Mobile intercept team set up operations at Hof to conduct a "hearability" site survey. Finding a lucrative enemy voice and Morse intercept environment, the 6900th Security Wing directed the 12th RSM to activate an intercept detachment at Hof.

To provide a required teletype communications link between Hof and Landsberg, the U.S. Army Signal Corps contracted with the German Bundespost to install a dedicated landline on Kingsley Barracks. With the landline in place, in the fall of 1954 the 12th RSM made final plans to colocate a detachment of the squadron with the AC&W unit and Army patrol companies at Hof.

Early USAFSS Operations at Hof

A1C Lyckberg and A2C Bratcher received the task of carrying a teletype machine to Hof and establishing communications with the 12th RSM at Landsberg.[74] In mid-November 1954, a Detachment

2, 12th RSM advance party—MSgt. Albert R. Drummond and SSgt. Lyons—proceeded from Landsberg to Hof. They made final arrangements with the host Army unit at Kingsley for quarters and mess facilities for the USAFSS team members that followed. Sgt. Drummond served as Det 2's first commander.

Initially, the Army provided the USAFSS airmen billeting on the far side of Kingsley. About mid-1955, Det 2, 12th RSM moved into the second and third floors of a barracks near the Kaserne's front gate; the AC&W detachment occupied the first floor of the barracks.

On Monday of Thanksgiving week, Lyckberg and Bratcher drove a 6 x 6 (deuce-and-a-half) truck loaded with teletype equipment and supplies from Landsberg to Hof, arriving in the evening. They set up and checked out the Hof-Landsberg TTY circuit on Tuesday and drove back to Landsberg on Thanksgiving Eve. Between Thanksgiving and Christmas 1954, the main group of Det 2, 12th RSM personnel arrived at Hof in a convoy of squadron trucks and H-1 vans carrying intercept equipment and supplies to establish the detachment.

Roughing it at Hof

The facility where Det 2, 12th RSM set up operations in December 1954 was decidedly dismal. To quote Lyckberg, "The area was just an open field, no hardtop, no security fence or security lights, no guard shack." They set up operations in H-1 vans in the open field. The ground was frozen when they arrived, but many concluded later that they preferred the freezing cold to the foot-deep mud and mire encountered during the spring thaw in 1955.

Improvising was essential to survival. A 100-watt light bulb—inside a tin can to protect it from the elements—hung over each van door for security lights. And with no guard shack, air police guards walked a beat or sat in the cab of a vehicle parked near the operations vans. When a Det 2 air policeman was unavailable, operations or maintenance personnel had to fill in as security guards. Initially, there was no phone system between Operations and the detachment headquarters; a courier had to carry messages between Ops and the orderly room. A couple of field phones soon rectified that situation.

Solving a Power Dilemma

Lacking access to commercial power, reliable electrical power was a major problem during the first winter in Hof. Two PE-95 gasoline-powered generators operating one at a time did not produce adequate power to run the intercept gear plus electric heaters in the vans—the men had to wear heavy coats and gloves at work. Later, a 60-kilowatt diesel provided adequate electrical power, but under extreme cold, the diesel fuel thickened to the consistency of Karo syrup. The fuel pump could not suck the thick fuel into the engine, and the generator shut down. The airmen solved the fuel dilemma by keeping a replacement drum of diesel fuel in addition to the drum being used in front of the diesel generator's radiator where warm air from the radiator kept the fuel warm. The power problem was further resolved during the summer of 1955 with the arrival of two 100 KW Buda diesel generators that were housed in a newly-built building where diesel fuel could be kept adequately warm and flowing even during the harshest Hof winters.

Spring of 1955 Brings Improvements

The spring of 1955 brought other relief when a German contractor constructed a blacktop asphalt pad for the operations area, installed a security fence and blacktopped the road from Operations to the orderly room and billets. In addition, over the summer of '55, Hof's USAFSS detachment used self-help, limited funding and ingenuity to expand and further improve Det 2's operations compound. On the newly blacktopped operations pad, the men built a large room with openings on one side into which they backed their four H-1 vans. The back doors of the vans opened into the room, permitting airmen within Operations to go from one van to another without going outside. The new room connecting the vans within Operations also provided additional critically needed workspace. Adding to the improvements, they built a guard shack at the entrance to the compound and illuminated the fenced compound area with 500-watt security floodlights.

Summer of 1955—Continued Expansion and Improvements

While little is known about early USAFSS operations at Hof, many changes affecting Security Service units at Hof and Landsberg occurred during the summer of 1955. First Lt. William D. Litchfield assumed command of Det 2, 12th RSM about the time the detachment was redesignated Detachment 2, 6912th RSM (May 1955). Meanwhile, Det 2's enlarged operations compound allowed the 6912th to expand the mission and increase USAFSS staffing at Hof. Although unsure of the date, Airman Lyckberg recalls that the 6912th deployed a direction finding system to Hof in 1955. Housed in an HO-17 hut on a 6 x 6 truck and powered by a cable laid to Det 2's operations compound, the DF site operated in the field between Det 2 Operations and the AC&W radar site.

Detachment morale was sky-high under Lt. Litchfield's command—he gained his men's respect and loyalty by defending their welfare in dealing with an unsympathetic host Army commander. Further, he turned a blind eye to his airmen's beer cooler in the barracks and did not harass the men with frequent inspections and the like. Illustrating Litchfield's philosophy on punishment for minor infractions, Lyckberg recalled that when the Army Military Police cited Litchfield for a traffic violation, he told the MP's to send the ticket to the Commander, Detachment 2, 6912th Radio Squadron Mobile. The Army MP's did not realize that Litchfield was the Det 2 commander. And when a Det 2 member got a traffic citation, he'd typically caution the defendant without further punishment.

Beer Breaks—An Old German Custom

The bevy of German construction workers involved in facility upgrades on Hof Kaserne brought with them what the American airmen considered strange but enviable work habits. Instead of coffee or tea breaks, the Germans enjoyed morning and afternoon beer breaks.

Those of us who have lived in Germany will remember with fondness the beer wagons that delivered cases of "snap-caps" weekly—right to our apartment door. Leave your case of empty snappies outside your door and the beer deliveryman replaced the "empties" with freshly brewed beer, bottled at the local brewery.

The airmen in Detachment 2, 12th RSM negotiated an even better arrangement with a local Brewmeister. The brewery furnished a beer cooler, installed it in the Detachment 2 day room and kept it stocked with beer. Using an honor system, each airman in the barracks kept track of the beers he'd drunk during the month. On paydays, they'd step up to the pay table, receive their pay, move to the next table and pay their monthly beer bill. Somewhat astounded, the Brewmeister said he delivered more beer to Detachment 2's barracks that he delivered to many Gasthauses.

In 2006, Nathan (Nate) Cameron Britt, a long-time friend of the author, discussed Hof and confirmed the existence of Det 2's day room beer service.[75]

Hof was terribly cold and snowy. Even the locals called it "Little Siberia." There was indeed a stocked refrigerator in the day room. Everyone's name was on a sheet of paper attached to the refrigerator. You made a mark by your name when you had a beer. We settled up on payday. This honor system seemed to work. I never heard any complaints. I don't remember how the refrigerator was stocked.

Speaking of payday, our pay envelopes were brought by truck from Bingen. More often than not the truck was delayed by snow and ice and was days late in arriving. The arrival of the pay truck was usually a joyful occasion.

A retired Air Force Security Service linguist/voice intercept operator, Nate Britt arrived at Hof Air Station soon after graduating from Czechoslovakian language training at Cornell University. The airmen in Britt's Czech class sailed from the Brooklyn Navy Yard aboard the USS Taylor to Bremerhaven, Germany, in September 1955. With orders assigning them to Landsberg, they were diverted to Bingen upon debarking in Bremerhaven. Soon after arriving in Bingen, the 6912th RSM sent the new Czech linguists by train to Hof.

Hof's Night Life and Bars

A "down-home Tarheel country boy," Nate Britt had never left his home state prior to enlisting in the Air Force. He thought he had died and gone to Heaven when he arrived in Germany.

Growing up on a farm in a "dry" county in eastern North Carolina, Nate Britt found Hof a downright "pleasant assignment."

> *There were two establishments of note frequented by the G.I.'s in Hof at this time—the Schönblick and the Theresienstein. The Schönblick was right outside the gate. It was the typical German Gasthaus, not particularly high class or clean, a working man's place if you will, handy for drinking beer. The Theresienstein was my favorite nightclub in all of Germany. It was a converted castle on a hill on the edge of Hof very near the five-K zone [five kilometers from the Czech border]. Not cheap nor sordid, it had a good band and plenty of young ladies looking for a good time.*

Retired USAFSS MSgt. Lonnie Henderson, another Hof veteran and long-time friend of the author, recently recalled that Hof was home to seven breweries, and even though he can not remember the brewery names, a couple of local bars easily came to mind.

> *The "Schönblick" was across the street from the front gate of Kingsley. It was a hangout, but the main hangout was downtown at the Erika Bar, more commonly known as Jake's.*

Lonnie served as a Russian linguist at Hof from 1961-64 and 1965-68. He, Nathan Britt and the author later served together as airborne voice intercept operators with the USAFSS flying unit at Rhein-Main and other locations.

Hof's Infamous Army Chow

Nathan Britt and other former Det 2, 12th RSM airmen agree unanimously when rating the Army mess hall at Hof—it served "lousy food." According to Britt, the cooks dished out lots of powdered stuff (eggs and milk). Fresh milk was seldom available, and C Rations were the norm about three meals per week. Britt remembered going to the mess hall once for midnight chow after working a swingshift, only to find the mess hall closed. The night cook reportedly had gotten drunk in a downtown Gasthaus and failed to report for duty that night. The food in the snack bar was fair, but the lower four grades were issued meal cards in lieu of separate rations pay. Besides, with the snack bar located across the parade ground from the barracks, the Schönblick served lots of schnitzels and 'wursts to airmen, especially during the days immediately after payday.

USAF Photo

Hof Air Station-Kingsley Barracks, 1965

New Mess Sgt.—Improved Chow Hall Food

To share the food preparation workload, the 6912th RSM agreed to assign two Air Force cooks to detached duty in the Army mess hall at Hof. The two airmen worked for the Army Mess Sergeant.

One of the airmen—A1C William Bryant—was a good cook and when he was on duty, "it was okay to eat in the dining hall." Promoted to staff sergeant, Bill Bryant became the Mess Sergeant, and dining hall food improved markedly. No one asked or cared how SSgt. Bryant managed to produce such tasty fare in an Army mess hall. Eventually, the military court-martialed Bryant and demoted him to A1C. In turn, an Army cook resumed Mess Sergeant duties. Back to typical, tasteless Army mess hall dining! Reportedly with no personal gain for himself, Airman Bryant had been trading mess hall C-Rations on the black market for more palatable German food to feed the troops in the mess hall.

Hof—NCO Club and Liquor Rations

In late summer 1956—while Bill Bryant was still Hof's Mess Sgt.—he led an effort that established an NCO Club at Kingsley Barracks and managed the club as a secondary job. The Hof NCO Club was a satellite club operation of the Bingen NCO Club. Bryant hired "Ziege," a former WW II Wehrmacht paratrooper, as the head bartender, and the club was an immediate success.

Low-cost, tax-free liquor and cigarettes for American military forces overseas were rationed to minimize black market sales to foreign nationals. Military units issued rationing cards to assigned personnel and authorized adult dependents. The rationing card form (folded twice to billfold size) authorized the bearer of the card to purchase one carton of cigarettes (or a box of cigars) and one bottle of liquor weekly—with liquor rations restricted to "of-age" (21 yrs or older) NCO's, officers, married personnel and dependents. Issuing officials were supposed to remove liquor rations from cards issued to those not authorized to purchase hard liquor (lower grade enlisted personnel living in barracks).

The 6912th at Bingen provided ration cards to Det 2 at Hof, and, for a while, the detachment issued cards authorizing both liquor and tobacco purchases to all personnel regardless of age or rank. The only problem was that there was no Class VI Store (liquor store) on post at Hof. As a "G.I. workaround"—the Hof NCO Club manager could be coaxed into loaning a fellow airman a bottle of booze, to be replaced by a like item after a purchasing trip to the Class VI Store at Grafenwohr or Nurnberg.

Det 2, 12th RSM Operations

Detachment 2 had a small but well-organized Operations section when A2C Britt arrived at Hof in the fall of 1955. With approximately eight to ten intercept positions, Russian was the primary language of interest. The voice section had two Czech intercept positions, and Britt's trick chief (shift supervisor) was a three-striper (A1C). The detachment intercepted both VHF and HF voice traffic, and Britt was fascinated with one of their VHF intercept antennas. Homemade, the antenna essentially consisted of an oversized soup can—open at one end and attached to a pole within the compound—with a lead-in cable coupled to the receiver. Simplicity at its best, but it worked remarkably well!

Airman Nathan Britt's stay at Kingsley Barracks, Hof, Germany, was brief. In the spring of 1956, Britt, Robert Berry and Robert Barrow—all Czech linguists—transferred to Detachment 1, 6911th Radio Squadron Mobile, the new USAFSS airborne reconnaissance unit at Rhein-Main Air Base, Germany.

Banished to Hof

Kingsley Kaserne was a bit of a letdown for A2C William Little when he reported in to Det 2, 6912th RSM the day after Christmas in 1955.[76] Arriving in Landsberg the previous March, Bill Little was now a seasoned veteran—he had served on temporary duty with Det 1, Linz, Austria, and moved with the 6912th RSM from Landsberg to Bingen, Germany, in June 1955. Bingen proved to be Little's nemesis. Much in the manner that errant German civil servants were reputedly transferred to Hof for misdeeds, the 6912th banished Airman Little to Hof.

As Little tells the story, he and some comrades got in a brawl with some French sailors in the "Greasy Spoon," a riverfront establishment in Bingen. "We kicked some ass and went on about our business," said Little. However, the next day, the French commander in the former French Zone of Occupation complained to Col. Ed Allen, 6912th commander, and Airman Little was the only suspect among U.S. airmen identified in a line-up.

With the French CO demanding that Little be punished, the 6912th first sergeant beckoned Little to the orderly room and said, "Pack your bags and clear the squadron; you are being reassigned to Det 2 at Hof." The first sergeant directed Bill Little to find A1C Collins, squadron supply clerk, and travel with him to Hof the day after Christmas.

"It was snowing like hell," and after seven hours on the road with no heat in their deuce-and-a-half truck, frostbite was about to set in when Collins and Little drove into Kingsley Barracks around 9:00 p.m. Issued bed linen and shown where he would be bunking, the next thing Bill Little saw was Airman David Muirhead coming through the door holding out a beer for Bill. This place wasn't too bad after all.

Det 2, 6912th RSM, December 1955

Discussing USAFSS staffing at Hof, Little estimated that there were approximately 75 men in Detachment 2, 6912th RSM when he arrived in December 1955, broken down as follows:

- One orderly room clerk
- One supply specialist
- One motor pool technician
- Four air policemen
- Two crypto operators
- One crypto maintenance technician
- Two cooks
- Two radio maintenance technicians
- One Operations NCOIC
- One officer (detachment commander)
- Remainder were linguists (voice intercept operators) and Morse intercept operators.

An RCA technical representative (Mr. Batson) also had a work van in the operations compound.

Additional personnel arrived in the spring and summer of 1956, including Lt. Reis, who became Detachment 2, 6912th RSM's first operations officer. Assigned to Det 2 for only a brief spell, Lt. Reis was replaced by Lt. Melvin G. Goodweather. William Litchfield was promoted to captain in April 1957 and rotated to the United States, at which time Lt. Goodweather assumed command of Det 2, 6912th RSM. Redesignated as Det 5, 6910th Radio Group Mobile later in 1957, the unit became the 6915th RSM on 1 July 1959.

Four years later (1 July 1963), as a further restructuring the 6915th RSM became the 6915th Security Squadron. Taking control of Kingsley Kaserne, USAFE renamed the facility Hof Air Station under the command of the 6915th commander. Also in the early 1960's, the 6915th gained a medical staff—doctors and medics—to care for its personnel and dependents. During the late 1960's, the 6915th detached linguist intercept teams to the ASA intercept site at Rimbach-Eckstein, Germany, on the Czech border 210 km south of Hof.

USAFE assumed control of Hof Air Station from the 6915th Security Group in 1971, later transferring the facility to West German Luftwaffe control. Having gone full circle, the former Hof AS is now General Hüttner Kaserne, home to a Luftwaffe unit.

USAF Photo

6915th Scty Group Ops, Hof Germany, mid-1960's

6915TH HERITAGE

USAFSS maintained signals intelligence intercept operations at Hof for 16 years. The unit designator changed aperiodically as the command modified its force structure in Europe. The lineage of the unit follows.

Lineage of USAFSS Unit at Hof	
Unit Designator	Action/Comments
Det 2, 12th RSM	Arrived at Hof in late 1954
Det 2, 6912th RSM	Det 2, 12th RSM redesignated 8 May 1955
Det 5, 6910th RGM	Resubordinated to 6910th RGM in 1957
6915th RSM	Replaced Det 5, 6910th RGM 1 July 1959
6915th Scty Squadron	Redesignated 1 July 1963
6915th Security Group	Redesignated September 1964
OL-BB, 6910th SG	6915th SG deactivated 1 July 1971
OL-BB, 6910th SG	Mission to Rimbach-Eckstein 1 Oct 1971

USAFSS Europe at a Glance—December 1955

The year 1955 ended with the 6900th Security Wing still commanding three security groups (see org chart below). In addition, the wing activated the 6901st Spec Comm Group and the 6905th Comm Squadron at Landsberg.

6900 SW Org Chart—31 Dec 1955	
6900th Security Wing Frankfurt, Germany	
6901st Spec Comm Gp Landsberg, Germany 6905th Comm Sq Landsberg, Germany	6910th Scty Gp Landsberg, Germany
6930th Scty Gp * Wheelus AB, Libya	6950th Scty Gp * Brooks AFB, Texas
* 6930th and 6950th Security Groups are addressed in later chapters.	

As shown in the 6910th org chart that follows, organization changes within the group in 1955 included the activation of a DF site at Schleswig and the relocation of the 6912th Radio Squadron Mobile from Landsberg to Bingen.

6900 SW Org Chart—31 Dec 1955	
6900th Security Wing Frankfurt, Germany	
6911th RSM Darmstadt, Germany	6913th RSM Bremerhaven, Germany Det 1, 6913th RSM Fassberg, Germany Det 2, 6913th RSM Schleswig, Germany
6912th RSM Bingen, Germany Det 1, 6912th RSM Bingen, Germany OL-1, Det 1, 6912th RSM Linz, Austria Det 2, 6912th RSM Hof, Germany	6914th RSM HQ Sembach, Germany 6914th RSM OPS Grünstadt, Germany Det 1, 6914th RSM Berlin, Germany Det 2, 6914th RSM Kassel, Germany Det 3, 6914th RSM Wasserkuppe, Germany

In 1956, USAFSS moved its European second echelon processing group, evacuating Landsberg Air Base, which had served as a primary USAFSS facility in Europe for the previous five years.

DET 1, 6901ST SCG—CHICKSANDS

At some point (probably September) in 1956, the 6901st Special Communications Group at Landsberg activated Detachment 1, 6901st SCG at RAF Chicksands. Traffic analysts assigned to the 6950th Security Group who had been performing second echelon analysis at Chicksands transferred into Det 1, 6901st SCG and related context... relocated to Zweibrücken in late 1956. Detachment 1 of the 6901st was subsequently deactivated.

6901ST SCG—ZWEIBRÜCKEN

With a commitment to return Landsberg to West German control, the 6901st Special Communications Group and its support element, the 6905th Comm Squadron, relocated to Kreuzberg Kaserne (aka Turenne Kaserne),[77] Zweibrücken, West Germany, on 1 November 1956. Eleven months later, the 6905th Comm Squadron was deactivated.

Zweibrücken ("Two Bridges") is located near the French border on the Schwarzbach River in Rheinland-Pfalz, the state that borders France, Saarland, Luxembourg and Belgium. The Nazis had built Kreuzberg Kaserne on the area's tallest hill (1,121 ft) in the outskirts of Zweibrücken in 1940. USAFSS airmen based at Kreuzberg Kaserne loved being within easy traveling distance to many great cities in Europe—Paris (227 miles), Luxembourg or Frankfurt (85 miles) and Munich (205 miles). They also fell in love with the Park Bräu Brewery in Zweibrücken, but climbing the hill back to the Kaserne after a night in the local gasthauses was a real challenge. Alexander Ames, a Russian linguist at Zweibrücken from 1959 to 1962, is proud of having mastered that steep climb during his tour in the 6901st.

Going back uphill my first year always required rest stops; by the time I left, I could make it all the way full speed without stopping. Great exercise! Ushi's Bar at the bottom of the hill was interesting.

In olden days a cross ("Kreuz") stood on the hill ("Berg"), giving the hill the name "mountain with a cross." Hence the Kaserne's name.

"Sunny Zwei"

Locals and outsiders alike had a field day carping about Zweibrücken's weather, and "Sunny Zwei" was an aberration from reality in the 1960's. Jon Gwinn found the weather, the Kaserne and the dense military population in the area somewhat displeasing when he arrived in 1961. So did David Larson, who was even more dispirited upon arrival in 1963.

What I got was the closest to a deep depression that I ever want to be. The place called Kreuzberg Kaserne was anything but picturesque, anything but poster-like. More like scenes reminiscent of a concentration camp. Barbed wire. Drab colors on the buildings. Rain. Mist. Drizzle. Sleet at appropriate times.

Gwinn reminisced about Zweibrücken in 2006.

I arrived in "Sunny Zwei" [Zweibrücken has very few sunny days per year] in November 1961, following Basic Russian at Indiana University and ALK-20331 at Goodbuddy [voice intercept training at Goodfellow AFB, Texas]. It was my first operational USAFSS assignment.

Graduating number seven in a class of 107 students at language school, Jon got to choose his follow-on assignment from available options.

The top seven students picked Zweibrücken because of its location in proximity to London, Berlin, Paris, etc. None of us had any clue what a rotten assignment it really was.

The weather was rotten most of the time. In the spring of 1962, the sun came out one morning and there was a picture of the sun on the front page of the local German, Zweibrücken newspaper. The headline read, "Don't be alarmed. A farmer here saw the same thing several years ago. It's just the sun."

Accommodations on Kreuzberg Kaserne added to Gwinn's disappointment. Many of the open bays housed as many as twenty-four airmen, and the mess hall food was lousy.

Zweibrücken was a U.S. Army "sub-post." The main post was in Pirmasens. The barracks were large, three-story rectangular steel & concrete buildings. We lived in open bays with double (upper/lower) bunk beds and foot lockers.

The barracks were rather depressing. The Army mess served K-rations five days per week and C-rations two days per week. The most edible thing in the mess hall was their SOS [creamed beef on toast]. I thought the SOS was terrific, but perhaps that is because all the other food was so bad.

Gwinn also felt that there were "too damned many" troops in the area.

Zweibrücken was a small "military" town. There was the U.S. Army sub-post, a German Army camp next door, a French Army post and a large, Canadian Air Force Base—far too many "G.I.'s" for such a small town.

The job wasn't really the greatest either because we were always processing "old stuff." Not nearly as exciting as a live mission.

Jon Gwinn found few reasons to like his assignment in the 6901st.

6901st Mission

Being a second echelon processing center, the 6901st Special Communications Group processed traffic—communications intelligence and electronic intelligence—collected by other organizations; it had no intercept capability of its own. Subordinate to the 6900th Security Wing, the 6901st was tasked to provide technical support to the command's radio squadrons mobile and detachments in Europe. The group also monitored and provided advisory warning for airborne recon missions in Europe. To deliver technical support around the clock, the 6901st operated a surveillance and warning center. The intercept units forwarded a copy of intercepted messages to the '01st (aka the "Oh-Worst"), where analysts analyzed traffic and generated reports and technical feedback as applicable. In addition, a 6901st voice transcription section transcribed backlogged tapes from USAFSS sites that recorded more intercepted messages than they could process and tapes recorded by collaborating foreign entities. A separate section processed and exploited ELINT data.

OPSCOMM

In the early 1960's, the 6900th Scty Wing created a secure operations communication network linking 6901st Operations to all USAFSS units in Europe and to the National Security Agency. An OPSCOMM terminal at each site communicated with a teletype terminal in the 6901st OPSCOMM area. In addition, a 6901st OPSCOMM operator could manually connect (patch) any site's OPSCOMM link to another unit—providing secure operational communications between two or more sites. USAFSS implemented a similar OPSCOMM capability amongst its units in the Far East in 1962.

The OPSCOMM became indispensable to SIGINT operations; however, USAFSS did not provide additional manpower to field sites to man the OPSCOMM terminals. Each unit had to take its OPSCOMM operators "out of hide," typically using lower ranking linguists and traffic analysts on each shift to staff the OPSCOMM terminals. As a "newbie," (new airman) (aka a "Jeep"), Dave Larson began his USAFSS career as an OPSCOMM operator. He reflected on OPSCOMM duties on a 6901st alumni association website that he maintains.[78]

The work at the 6901st Special Communications Group was jerky. At first, while waiting for a specific Russian language assignment, I worked in the teletype communications section. There were perhaps ten or twelve teletype machines on either side of a narrow isle. Yellow perforated tape wound through them as bells sounded and messages were sent. Football scores seemed everywhere.

Long reports were ripped off, separated into the different colors of paper, and put into bins for who knows what purpose, at who knows when. Carbon paper was shoved into burn bags making our hands black.

Six-Ply Fanfold Paper

The colored paper was six-ply fanfold paper—six different colored layers of paper and five carbon paper inserts, packaged as a continuous stack of perforated sheets folded accordion-style into a box from which the sheets fed into a typewriter or teletype printer. (Intercept sites used the same type paper to produce six-ply copies of intercepted voice and Morse messages.) Removing the carbons yielded a transcript, report or other document in six different-colored copies (blue, green, goldenrod, pink, yellow and white). Typically, RSM's filed the white (# 6) copy as the station copy; other copies were distributed to the 6901st, NSA, other

RSM's, etc. The 6901st received the goldenrod colored copy of transcripts and Morse messages from all RSM's in Europe.

Memories of President Kennedy Assassination

It felt good to get away from the clattering noises of the OPSCOMM teletype machines. While on break, Larson had just walked into the Kreuzberg Kaserne theater to take in a movie when he learned that President Kennedy had been shot. He rushed back to work.

All hell broke loose that night. Shortledge was the airman in charge. He was the first guy I ever saw that had pink eyes. And he was good at his job. We all worked ourselves silly for weeks after that, fearing other events that might be linked to the assassination.

Rescued from the OPSCOMM job when MSgt. David Cambridge recruited him for an analysis job, David Larson spend his remaining USAFSS career performing airborne reconnaissance-related traffic analysis. Completing his enlistment, he left Zweibrücken and the Air Force in January 1965.

Surveillance and Warning Centers

In 2006, Dave Cambridge provided the author an overview of the surveillance and warning center, the operations nerve center within USAFSS operational units.

The S&WC was the heart of the European reporting system. We had OPSCOMM's with every S&W in Europe as well as the NSA. Most reporting came through the 6901st S&WC. However, the hot stuff, Critic, Spots, etc. went from the individual intercept unit and then the 6901st would take care of the wrap-up reporting. All of the OPSCOMM's were located in the S&WC.

COMA—Analysis Division

The analysis division (COMA) was divided into sections responsible for the various air problems—COMA-1 (Civair), COMA-2 (Tacair), COMA-3 (LRA), COMA-4 (Air Defense), COMA-5 (Missiles), et al. The S&WC and OPSCOMM were in COMA-4 (Air Defense Division).

COMA 41F—Airborne Recon Support

When traffic analyst SSgt. David Cambridge arrived in Zweibrücken in January 1961, Air Force Capt. Bernard (Ben) Ardisana (officer in charge of COMA 4) designated him the NCOIC of COMA 41F.[79] Second Lt. Ernest (Ernie) Short was the COMA 4 assistant OIC. (Ardisana, Short and Cambridge played major roles in the evolution of USAFSS in the 1960's and 1970's.)

Located in a compartmented area by the surveillance and warning center, COMA-41F kept track of and monitored the progress of airborne recon missions. Dave Cambridge provided an overview of the COMA-41 mission.

During the flight following of a PARPRO [peacetime aerial reconnaissance program]activity we used the S&WC OPSCOMM's. We were located adjacent to the S&WC. The individual units would send us the tracking data. We would consolidate it and issue the 15 minute reports to the SAC Reconnaissance Center (SRC) in accordance with existing TECHINS [Technical Instructions].

When Cambridge came aboard, COMA 41F was a small airborne reconnaissance flight following and advisory support project in the European Theater. He transformed the fledgling European airborne recon support program into "White Wolf"—a national recon support program that the National Security Agency implemented in the mid-1960's. Cambridge continued his discussion on White Wolf.

After Zwei I was assigned to A33 at NSA with the specific task of moving COMA 41F from Zwei to NSA. NSA had decided to centralize the White Wolf and Reconnaissance Reporting programs at Ft. Meade. Until then they were decentralized to the European, Pacific and Alaskan theaters. They were just forming the NSOC [National SIGINT Operations Center], and we were an adjunct to that.

I brought back several of the people who worked for me at Zwei and wrote TECHINS 4032 which detailed how the SIGINT Community would report on PARPRO activities. I left NSA in May 1967 and was assigned to the 6921ˢᵗ SW at Misawa AB, Japan.

In 1968, David Cambridge traded in his enlisted stripes for second lieutenant gold bars, completing Officer Training School and joining Air Force Security Service's large pool of "mustang" officers.

Meteoric Rise—Then a Mustang

Only one percent of Air Force basic trainees met requirements on qualification tests for USAFSS skills,[80] and the command always had the highest enlisted to officer ratio of any command—93 percent in USAFSS vs. 70 percent for the rest of the Air Force in 1976.[81] On a related issue, almost half of the USAFSS officers in 1979 were ex-USAFSS enlisted members—OTS-trained and commissioned mustangs.[82] Thus, it was a routine event when Cambridge became a second lieutenant in the U.S. Air Force, except that he received chief master sergeant's pay in his last enlisted pay check.

David Cambridge holds the distinction of having held every rank from airman basic to chief master sergeant and second lieutenant to captain. Arriving in Zweibrücken as a staff sergeant, he left three years later as a master sergeant. And in near record time, he received promotions to senior master sergeant and chief master sergeant, although he never wore his Chief's stripes. Being promoted on 1 December 1968 and receiving his commission twenty days later, the Air Force paid Dave Cambridge Chief's pay for twenty days in 1968.

Many contemporaries questioned his decision when he continued to OTS after learning that he was on the Chief's promotion list in 1967.

I caught a lot of flack from the Senior NCO's that I associated with over giving up E-9 to be a brown bar. My motivation was simple. I loved the Air Force and what I was doing. Staying an E-9 would have limited the kinds of jobs I could expect to hold. As an officer they were available to me.

As a 2ⁿᵈ Lt., I was Commander, OL-1, 6988ᵗʰ Security Squadron (a hotbed location after the Pueblo incident).

And as you know, I was later Ops officer of a unit that was the hottest in the Command, the 6916th in Athens, during very dynamic times—the dictatorship overthrow, the Greek/Turk potential hostilities, the Arab/Israeli war, the attempted Libyan shoot down of our C-130 in the Central Med and the subsequent Operation Flashback.

Having retired as a captain in 1979 after several choice officer assignments, Cambridge is very happy that he traded his Chief's stripes for those gold officer bars in 1968. The author served with Dave Cambridge in Athens where he was the 6916th Security Squadron Ops Officer from 1972-1974. A great USAFSS officer and friend!

SUPP—Support/Processing Division

The Support Division had multiple processing sections. The processing sections included an ELINT processing section (office symbol unknown), a voice transcription section (SUPP-11) and a cryptanalytic section (SUPP-2).

SUPP-11 (Voice Transcription Section)

With open-bay barracks and inedible Army mess hall food already weighing on his mind, Jon Gwinn found little solace at work, at least in the beginning. His first job in USAFSS was as a transcriber in the 6901st voice transcription section.

SUPP-11 was the organizational designator. We transcribed backlog from other sites (including the 6916th RSM) and also processed tapes from 2nd and 3rd party locations, some covert. Alexander Ames was my first supervisor. About the only thing he said to me for the first several weeks was, "Beep, beep—God damned jeep."... He was actually a pretty good guy, and we became friends after a while.

The voice transcribers at the 6916th RSM and other RSM's that were forwarding backlogged tapes to SUPP-11 would not have been surprised that Jon Gwinn and other transcribers at Zweibrücken found the traffic that they were processing tedious and boring. The field sites transcribed the "good stuff" in-house and passed off the routine traffic to the "Oh-Worst."

Where's my Goldenrod

While most 6901st operations personnel were USAFSS officers and airmen, some were GS-rated civilian analysts and linguists, including a few male and female NSA specialists. Gwinn is fond of a story involving a female NSA analyst. She had a daily routine: arrive for work at 8:00 a.m. sharp, retrieve the goldenrod copy of transcripts from her in-basket, then shuffle papers all day at her desk. She knew that linguists in SUPP-11 transcribed the traffic she analyzed. So finding her in-basket empty when she arrived at work, she marched into SUPP-11 and said, "I didn't get my goldenrod this morning." The entire office—all male transcribers—guffawed as she blushed and retreated to her office.

"It's 6901st Time"

The one salvation for single airmen at Zweibrücken was their Class A Pass permitting them to go and come as they pleased. In fact, they could rent an apartment off post at their own expense, and no one asked questions as long as they met all duty commitments. In contrast, the U.S. Army treated its soldiers like juveniles. Jon Gwinn elaborated.

The Army guys had "bed check" at 11:00 p.m. five nights per week and at midnight on Friday and Saturday nights. The Air Force guys had no such thing. In the bars downtown, it was common for some soldier to ask his buddy about the time and some airman would answer, "It's 6901st time," meaning time for you guys to go to bed check and for us to take your girls home. That often started a bar fight.

Gwinn made the most of his off-duty time and loved their shift schedule that provided three-day breaks a couple of times per month.

We usually traveled to other points in Germany over the three-day break. One popular activity was to just drive from village to village and stop at every gasthaus and sample the local brews and collect the coasters.

Having grown up in West Virginia, Gwinn loves hiking and spent lots of time hiking the French countryside, the old Maginot Line bunkers around Zweibrücken and the Black Forest by

Stuttgart. Of course, weather often affected his off-duty activities, and after a year in the 6901st, he volunteered to transfer to TUSLOG 3-2, Samsun, Turkey, where the sun truly shined. A decade later, Jon Gwinn and the author served together as USAFSS airborne voice intercept operators flying reconnaissance missions from Athens, Greece.

"This Tape is Classified"

According to Alexander Ames, security was very lax in the 6901st—at least in the voice transcription section where airmen occasionally filched 7.5 " magnetic tapes for personal use. Strictly a "no-no" in USAFSS.

I recall returning the VW bus to the motor pool one night. We were able to clearly hear the conversations (and Russian tapes) from the SUPP-11 workspace because the windows were open. Those were considered very sensitive. But once in a while, the guys would borrow some tape to record music on. Once sitting in the barracks, we put a tape on to listen, and out of the speakers came: "The Classification of this tape is TOP SECRET CODEWORD, repeat ... " and many dove towards the off button!

Though not mentioned by Alex Ames, that tape most likely found its way back into the tape cabinet in SUPP-11. Volunteering for a USAFSS "2-T" program under which airmen in certain career fields could receive a promotion for accepting a consecutive overseas tour, SSgt. Alexander Ames transferred to Wakkanai, Japan, in 1962.

6901ST DEACTIVATION

The 6901st Special Communications Group operated under the control of the 6900th Security Wing from its arrival in Europe on 1 October 1955 until the 6900th wing was deactivated on 1 October 1961. From that point through March 1968, the 6901st commander reported directly to HQ USAFSS. By the end of the first decade of 6901st SCG operations in Europe, the U.S. Defense Department was looking at ways to reduce intelligence gathering budgets while NSA was consolidating many of the military's second echelon analysis and reporting functions at Agency headquarters, Fort Meade, Maryland. Decisions were made to close the 6901st

operations at Zweibrücken. With its mission absorbed by other organizations, primarily other USAFSS units and NSA, the 6901st SCG was deactivated on 31 March 1968.

6901st Detachments

During its stay at Zweibrücken, the 6901st Spec Comm Group detached teams to a few field stations in England and Germany for extended periods.[83]

6901st SCG Detachments		
6901st Special Communications Group Zweibrücken, Germany 1956-1968		
Detachment	Location	Period
Det 1	Chicksands, England	1 Feb 1956-1 Dec 1956
Det 1	Baumholder, Germany	1 Jul 1961-2 Feb 1962
Det 1	Rothwesten, Germany	2 Feb 1962-1 July 1962
Det 1	Munich, Germany	21 Jan 1963-1 Jan 1966
Det 2	Frankfurt, Germany	1 Aug-1963-1 Jul 1964
Det 2	Frankfurt, Germany	1 Jul 1965-1 Jan 1966

6911TH RGM

On 1 September 1956, the 6911th Radio Squadron Mobile at Darmstadt became the 6911th Radio Group Mobile with responsibility for two subordinate units—6913th RSM in Bremerhaven and Detachment 1, 6911th RGM at Rhein-Main AB, Germany. We address the Rhein-Main based recon unit in a separate chapter and the 6913th has already been discussed.

Aaron "Ron" Kriegel and Kirk Stokes, two Morse intercept operators who served in the 6911th in the late 1950's, loved their group CO's approach to monthly Commander's Call. Answering a Kriegel query regarding Darmstadt's jewel of beer, "Zum Golden Anker" in 2006, Kirk Stokes responded affirmatively.

Ron, I fondly remember Anker Bräu. We used to have Commander's Call at the brewery after the last day watch. Five marks for all the bier you could drink during the time that the flight commander was there. Often led to trips to Frankfurt afterwards. Kirk

Unlike in today's American military, monthly "beer calls" were sanctioned functions in many USAFSS field units in the 1950's, '60's and '70's. Stokes and Kriegel transferred to Detachment 1, 6911th RGM at Rhein-Main in 1958 and 1959, respectively.

6900th SW Organization—Late 1950's

Following the reorganization in 1956, 6900th Security Wing Commander Col. Richard P. Klocko commanded the four radio groups mobile, plus the 6901st Spec Comm Group. The 6937th Communications Group was activated in 1958 and also reported to the 6900th wing. The 6900th SW org chart for the years 1956 through 1958 follows.

6900th SW Org Chart—Jan 1956-Dec 1958	
6900th Security Wing Frankfurt, Germany 1954-1961	
6910th RGM HQ Sembach, Germany 1956-61	6911th RGM Darmstadt, Germany 1956-61
6910th RGM Ops Grünstadt, Germany 1956-59 (1	
6930th RGM (2 Wheelus AB, Libya 1956-1957	6901st SCG Zweibrücken, Germany 1956-1968
6950th RGM (2 Chicksands, England 1956-63	6905th Comm Sq Zweibrücken, Germany 1956-57
6937th Comm Gp (2 Peshawar, Pakistan 1958-1970	
(1 6910th RGM Ops moved to Sembach in 1959. (2 Unit addressed in later chapter.	

Elevating the intercept squadrons at Sembach/Grünstadt (6910th) and Darmstadt (6911th) to group-level sites was in line with expanding and realigning the USAFSS mission in Europe.

Germany-based RGM Org Chart 1 Jan 1956-31 Dec 1958	
6900th Security Wing Frankfurt, Germany 1954-1961	
6910th RGM HQ Sembach, Germany 1956-1961 6910th RGM OPS (1 Grünstadt, Germany 1956-1959	6911th RGM Darmstadt, Germany 1956-1961
Det 1, 6910th RGM Berlin, Germany 1956-1 July 1959 Det 2, 6910th RGM Kassel, Germany 1956-1957 Det 3, 6910th RGM Wasserkuppe, Germany 1956-1957 Det 4, 6910th RGM Landshut, Germany Oct 1957-1 July 1959 Det 5, 6910th RGM Hof, Germany 1957-1 July 1959 Det 6, 6910th RGM Camp Pieri, Germany Oct 1957-1963 6912th RSM (2 Bingen, Germany 1955-30 June 1959 Det 1, 6912th RSM (3 Landshut, Germany 1956-Oct 1957 OL-1, Det 1, 6912th RSM Linz, Austria 1955-1957 Det 2, 6912th RSM Hof, Germany 1955-Oct 1957 Det 3, 6912th RSM Camp Pieri, Germany 1956-Oct 57	Det 1, 6911th RGM (4 Rhein-Main, Germany 1956-1 July 1959 6913th RSM Bremerhaven, Germany 1955-1963 Det 1, 6913th RSM Fassberg, Germany 1955-1956 Det 2, 6913th RSM Schleswig, Germany 1955-1967
(1 6910th Operations relocated to Sembach in 1959. (2 Deactivated on 30 June 1959. (3 Activated at Landsberg; moved to Landshut July 1956. (4 Det 1, 6900th SW on 1 July 1959, FTV, Vol IV, Airborne Recon.	

USAFSS European Activities—1959

Significant organizational changes in 1959 included deactivation of the RSM at Bingen am Rhein, elevation of the 6910th intercept detachments in Berlin and Hof to radio squadrons mobile and re-subordination of the 6911th detachment at Rhein-Main. The new unit designators are reflected in the org chart that follows.

Germany-based USAFSS Org Chart 1 Jan 1959-31 Dec 1961	
6900th Security Wing Frankfurt, Germany 1954-1961	
6901st Spec Comm Gp (1 Zweibrücken, Germany 1956-1968	
6910th RGM Sembach, Germany 1956-1961	6911th RGM Darmstadt, Germany 1956-1961
OL-1, 6910th RGM Landshut, Germany 1 July 1959-1961	6916th RSM (2 Rhein-Main, Germany 1 June 1960-1 July 1963
Det 6, 6910th RGM Camp Pieri, Germany Oct 1957-1963	Det 1, 6916th RSM Adana AB, Turkey 1 June 1960-1 July 1963
6912th RSM Berlin, Germany 1 July 1959-1 July 1963	6913th RSM Bremerhaven, Germany May 1955-1 July 1963
6915th RSM Hof, Germany 1 July 1959-1 July 1963	Det 2, 6913th RSM Schleswig, Germany May 1955-1 July 1963
(1 6901st SCG controlled reporting in Europe, but other units reported administratively to 6900th SW. (2 6916th RSM was Det 1, 6900th SW (1 July 1959-1 Jan 1960); discussed in FTV, Vol IV, Airborne Reconnaissance.	

6910TH RGM REPLACES 6911TH RGM

On 15 May 1961, the 6910th RGM relocated from Sembach to Darmstadt. Robert Corey, a former 6910th Morse intercept operator, discussed the move in 1999.

> We moved into a brand new building from an old wooden place at Sembach. I was on Dog trick, and the new commander (Dorothy) [last name forgotten] had brought her dog, a small cocker spaniel (female). At that time we had lost our great guard dog, a German Shepherd, and one of the AP's [air policemen] was going to get a replacement. Well, he came back with a small terrier mix, and guess what, he made friends with the Captain's dog and almost every shift, we had to throw water on both of them.
>
> Those were the early days. In fact, at Sembach we had trailers for a while. They were nice to work in—hot! hot!. We moved to Darmstadt and found a nice air-conditioned building with all of the bells and whistles. We were the first ones in the new building, and it was at the time that was most active.
>
> We had the Cuban Missile crisis and the Berlin Wall. The antennae field where we had our beer bust opened up and revealed a nice set of NIKES (not the ones you wear), and all of the dependents were given IBM tracking cards. I was on duty that day, and I could not leave until I was relieved. In the morning coming to work the Army had all sorts of weapons out; all I had was my headsets!!!

With the arrival of the 6910th RGM at Darmstadt, the 6911th RGM was deactivated, with its resources integrated into the 6910th. As depicted in the org chart below, the 6901st Special Comm Group reported directly to Headquarters USAFSS. The 6910th RGM and its subordinate units had a dual chain of command. Technically, they answered to the 6901st SCG while being under administrative command of the European Security Region.

ESR Org Chart—Germany-based Units 1 Oct 1961-30 Jun 1963
European Security Region (1 Frankfurt, Germany 1 Oct 1961-June 1972 6901st Spec Comm Gp (2 Zweibrücken, Germany 1956-1968
Darmstadt, Germany 6910th RGM (3 1961-1963
Det 1, 6910th RGM Landshut, Germany 1961-1963 Det 6, 6910th RGM (4 Camp Pieri, Germany 1957-1963 6912th RSM Berlin, Germany 1959-1963 6915th RSM Hof, Germany 1959-1963 6916th RSM Rhein-Main, Germany 1960-1963 Det 1, 6916th RSM Adana AB, Turkey 1960-1963 6913th RSM Bremerhaven, Germany 1955-1963 Det 2, 6913th RSM Schleswig, Germany 1955-1963
(1 Replaced 6900th Security Wing on 1 October 1961. (2 Reported to HQ USAFSS effective 1 October 1961; other units reported to European Security Region. (3 Relocated from Sembach to Darmstadt on 15 May 1961; replaced by 6910th Security Wing. (4 Replaced by Det 2, 6910th Scty Wing.

Operational Wing Concept

By 1963, Air Force Security Service strength approached 30,000 Air Force and civilian personnel—time to reorganize to accommodate the growth. The next major USAFSS organizational change in Europe occurred on 1 July 1963 "in response to the Air Force problem of how to reduce or eliminate intermediate echelons and separate units." The USAFSS answer was to initiate the "Operational Wing Concept."[84]

Under this concept, the mission unit was discontinued and a support squadron was organized. The functions of the mission unit were absorbed into the wing structure. The concept was implemented in Europe late in 1963 and in the Pacific in 1964.[85]

ESR Ops Wing Concept—1 Jul 1963-1967		
European Security Region (1 Frankfurt, Germany 1961-1972 6900th Support Group Frankfurt, Germany 1963-1972 6901st Spec Comm Gp (2 Zweibrücken, Germany 1956-1968		
6910th Scty Wg Darmstadt, Ger. 1963-1970 6910th Supt Sq 1963	6950th Scty Wg (3 Chicksands, Eng. 1963-1967 6950th Supt Sq 1963	6933rd Scty Wg (3 Karamursel, Turkey 1963-1970 6933rd Supt Sq 1963
6917th Scty Gp (3 San Vito, Italy 1963-1979	6930th Scty Gp (3 Iraklion, Crete 1963-1973	6937th Comm Gp (3 Peshawar, Pakistan 1958-1970
(1 The security wings reported to the European Security Region. (2 6901st SCG reported to HQ USAFSS. (3 Unit addressed in later chapter.		

The operational wing concept apparently only applied to the larger radio groups mobile. By 1963, the European Security Region had five radio groups mobile: 6910th, 6950th, 6933rd, 6917th and 6930th RGM's. ESR deactivated three of the five—6910th,

6950th and 6933rd RGM's and reactivated them as security wings, along with subordinate support squadrons. Being smaller units, the 6930th and 6917th RGM's were deactivated and reactivated as the 6930th Security Group and 6917th Security Group, respectively, without attached support squadrons. The 6937th Comm Group also remained unchanged.

Concurrently, USAFSS radio squadrons mobile became security squadrons on 1 July 1963. The 6910th Security Wing org chart that follows depicts the wing's newly designated security squadrons. Two of the squadrons—6915th SS and 6913th SS became security groups in 1964.

ESR Germany-based Org Chart 1 Jul 1963-1967 (1	
European Security Region Frankfurt, Germany 1961-1972 6901st Spec Comm Gp (2 Zweibrücken, Germany 1956-1968	
Darmstadt, Germany 6910th Security Wing with 6910th Supt Sq and 6911th Scty Sq (M) 1963-1970	
Det 1, 6910th SW Landshut, Germany 1963-1964	Det 2, 6910th SW (3 Camp Pieri, Germany 1963-1969
6912th Scty Sq Berlin, Germany 1963-1979	6915th Scty Sq (4 Hof, Germany 1963-1 Sept 1964
6916th Scty Sq Rhein-Main, Germany 1963-1973	6913th Scty Sq (5 Bremerhaven, Germany 1963-1 Oct 1964
Det 1, 6916th Scty Sq Adana AB, Turkey 1963-Jan 1967	Det 1, 6913th Scty Sq Schleswig, Germany 1963-1964

(1   Radio squadrons mobile became security squadrons 1 July 1963.
(2   Reported to HQ USAFSS, OL-1, ESR also at Zweibrücken.
(3   Det 2, 6910th SW became OL-3, ESR in 1969.
(4   Became the 6915th Security Group on 1 September 1964.
(5   Became the 6913th Security Group on 1 October 1964.

6911TH SECURITY SQUADRON (M)

USAFSS activated the 6911th Security Squadron (Mobile) at Darmstadt on 1 July 1963 as one of three new emergency reaction units—the other two being the 6926th SS (M) in the Philippines and the 6948th SS (M) at Goodfellow AFB.[86] The squadron reported to the colocated 6910th Security Wing. The rich heritage of the 6911th organization lived on. No doubt, some of the vans and intercept equipment that had previously belonged to the 6911th RGM that had been deactivated two years earlier ended up in the new 6911th Security Squadron (Mobile) inventory.

The 6911th SS (M) was housed in H-1 vans and S-141 "Little John" huts with auxiliary wheels (mobilizers). The squadron maintained readiness to be airlifted anywhere in Europe for contingency operations with a 48-hour notice. Most of the mobile intercept equipment had been in the 6910th Security Wing inventory since USAFSS created its contingency operations capability in 1956.

Minimally staffed in garrison, the CONOP (operations concept) for the 6911th SS (M) called for other USAFSS units in Europe to provide appropriate staffing: linguists, Morse operators, traffic analysts and maintenance technicians during 6911th deployments. The 6911th Security Squadron (M) maintained operational proficiency by participating in field training exercises.

6911th Scty Sqdn (M)—Rhein-Main

The 6911th Security Squadron (M) moved from Cambrai-Fritsch Kaserne, Darmstadt, to Rhein-Main Air Base on 1 June 1972. In an email message in 2004, maintenance technician Joe McPherson described how he finagled an assignment to the 6911th SS (M) to avoid being transferred to a less desirable overseas destination.

I was stationed at Kelly for USAFSS depot maintenance, then found I was frozen for overseas orders. I beat feet to CBPO [consolidated base personnel office] and picked the 6911th at Rhein-Main AB. There we had a compound with all the huts and maintenance trailers. There were only 37 of us, and we just went from hut to hut pulling the PMI's [preventive maintenance inspections] and keeping all the equipment ready to go.

When we received orders, they brought the operators in from England. We deployed for two-to-three weeks and worked East German and Russian radio traffic. We also used a U-2 to fly the borders and relay signals down to us. This was named Operation Top Hat.

Joe McPherson left the 6911th SS (M) in 1975 when the squadron was in the process of permanently leaving Rhein-Main. A change in leadership at USAFE Headquarters resulted in a redirection of the 6911th Security Squadron (M) mission.

Early in 1974, General John Vogt, Commander in Chief, United States Air Forces in Europe (CINCUSAFE), based on his experience with intelligence support during the Vietnam War, established a requirement for timely intelligence support. Headquarters USAF decided USAFSS could best provide this support through its 6911th Security Squadron (M) which would become a direct support unit.

But first the unit had to undergo a significant expansion of personnel, equipment, and real estate and be moved from Rhein-Main, Germany, to Hahn Air Base, Germany.[87]

6911th Scty Sqdn (M)—Hahn AB

On 1 July 1975, the 6911th Security Squadron (M) relocated from Rhein-Main to Hahn Air Base, approximately 75 miles west of Frankfurt. Hahn is located in one of Germany's best known wine regions—in the Rheinland-Pfalz state of western Germany in the small Hunsrück mountain range that is bounded by the river valleys of the Mosel, Nahe and Rhein Rivers. Hahn Air Base—now Frankfurt-Hahn Airport—is within 60 miles of four other former American air bases in Germany: Zweibrücken, Sembach, Bitburg, and Rhein-Main, plus Ramstein, which continues to be a U.S. air base.

Using the equipment and vans from Rhein-Main, the 6911th set up operations in an old hangar on the Hahn AB flight line and began an expansion of its capabilities as the unit accepted a new mission.

That happened on 25 July 1975 when it was converted to a direct support unit (DSU) immediately responsive to requests from European consumers, mainly USAFE, for intelligence support of a primarily tactical nature.[88]

To deaden the constant noise of F-4 Phantom fighters belonging to the 50th Tactical Fighter Wing, squadron personnel worked within tents inside the hangar. One of the 6911th contingency missions involved providing threat analysis and other tactical intelligence to the 50th TFW. The squadron also supported exercises throughout Germany. In 1977, Danny Martinez III from the 6931st Security Group on Crete supported the 6911th during a NATO Reforger Exercise.

I was an operator in one of the vans. Our mission was COMSEC. We finally made our way to a hill in Kempton, West Germany. There, we set up our unit. Most of the participating operators were from other SS units throughout Europe.

Housed in H-1 vans, the ground-based mobile SIGINT system was only the beginning of direct support capabilities that USAFSS made available to the USAFE commander. Plans were also underway to activate a new fixed intercept site at Hahn AB and assign a mobile airborne system (Comfy Levi) with the 6911th Security Squadron (M).

COMFY LEVI—CONTINGENCY SYSTEM

The Comfy Levi platform proved itself as a highly flexible contingency airborne SIGINT collection system during the Vietnam war. Developed for USAFSS under Project Comfy Echo[89] in the mid-1960's, the intercept system consisted of the same types of intercept and recording equipment installed in the command's "Rivet Victor" C-130 airborne COMINT reconnaissance platforms. However, whereas intercept equipment was permanently installed in the Rivet Victor ACRP, Comfy Echo's receivers, recorders, demodulators, etc. were housed in mobile S-141 shelters that rolled onto and were operated aboard standard C-130 transport aircraft. Typically, two shelters formed one Comfy Echo system aboard a C-130.

USAF Photo

Inside View, S-141 Intercept Hut

No longer required in Southeast Asia, USAFSS returned the two Comfy Echo portable airborne SIGINT systems to a contractor repair depot in Greenville, Texas, about 1974. The U.S. government loaned one of the shelters to the Israeli government, and it is rumored that this system supported Israeli commandos during their highly successful hostage rescue mission at Entebbe Airport, Uganda, in July 1976. Under new project name Comfy Levi,[90] USAFSS allocated the remaining shelters to the 6948th Security Squadron (M) at Kelly AFB in 1975 for contingency airborne intercept support.

As an emergency reaction unit, the 6948th used its Comfy Levi shelters for airborne operator training, including providing support to Air Force participants in the annual Red Flag training exercises at Nellis AFB, Nevada. In 2006, a former USAFSS airborne intercept operator-linguist, retired SMSgt. Daniel Hagy, discussed Comfy Levi, 6948th and 6911th Security Squadron (M) operations.[91]

We flew Levi in stateside exercises starting at least in 1975. And for a system with no DF [direction finding], we usually helped the side we supported win the day. Even had a few real SAR [search and rescue] missions thrown in. We had one successful SAR as we flew out of Norton AFB—even made the Los Angeles Times. An aircraft with two Air Force pilots and their wives had been missing for like 20 hours. As we took off one morning, we picked up an ELT [emergency locator transmitter], and with the help of the front-end's use of the TACAN antenna, found the downed aircraft. All four people aboard were recovered alive. (I still have that newspaper clipping somewhere.)

Dan Hagy was assigned to Operating Location EA (OL-EA), 6948th Security Squadron (M) at Offutt AFB, Nebraska, while flying Comfy Levi missions in the United States. Dual qualified in German and Russian, he was a certified airborne mission supervisor, airborne analyst and airborne intercept operator on Comfy Levi and other recon platforms at Offutt. Sgt. Hagy had been alerted for a ground assignment in Berlin when he learned that the 6911th at Hahn Air Base would soon be tasked to fly Comfy Levi missions.

AMS Needed for 6911th

The decision in 1976 to assign a Comfy Levi system to the U.S. Air Forces, Europe as a tactical SIGINT direct support resource created a slot in the 6911th manning document for an airborne mission supervisor. Chief Master Sergeant Terrence Almeter, HQ USAFSS/DOR, immediately began a search for an AMS to fill the slot and was contacted by Hagy. Chief Almeter intervened with CMSgt. Woodrow Hobbs in HQ USAFSS/Personnel, and TSgt. Hagy became the first AMS in the 6911th Security Squadron (Mobile).

COMFY LEVI SUPPORT TO USAFE

Carried aboard conventional C-130 transport aircraft, the Comfy Levi airborne mobile SIGINT system filled a major USAFE direct support contingency mission. "Creek Storm"[92] was the USAFE designator applied to Comfy Levi missions in Europe. Many challenges lay ahead for Sgt. Hagy at Hahn Air Base before the first Comfy Levi mission was flown in Europe in 1977.

When I got to Hahn as a brand new TSgt., I found that operations was in a tent in a hangar on the flight line. The unit was an "emergency reaction unit" and trained with real world signals in preparation for deployment. The operators sat in H-1 vans positioned in the hangar, with analysts and S&W [surveillance and warning] in other H-1 vans. Periodically, they would deploy in convoy and set up operations in the field. Our briefing area was in a tent that was used by the commander, Lt. Col. Tom Ozgo. Maj. John Fretz was the DO [operations officer]; CMSgt. Sam Radoman was the Ops superintendent.

Airborne Mission vs. Ground Site Mentality

Dan Hagy reported for duty in the 6911th at Hahn Air Base in April 1977. He quickly learned that activating an airborne SIGINT direct support operation manned by enlisted crew members—especially within a heretofore ground site-oriented USAFSS unit—would be a lengthy, drawn-out process.

Some of the major obstacles I faced were things such as changing an HF ground-site mentality about crew rest, Stan/Eval [standardization and evaluation] rather than ground unit type training and PROCERT [proficiency certification], obtaining flight gear and getting life support established on a fighter base (didn't understand why enlisted guys needed to fly).

Logistic support improved markedly when the USAFE commander ordered the start-up of Comfy Levi missions and directed related C-130 and logistics squadrons at Rhein-Main and Hahn Air Bases to support the Comfy Levi/Creek Storm mission.

Things changed when a real world situation arose and CINC USAFE wanted to deploy his new toy. Col. Ozgo, Maj. Fretz and I went to Ramstein to tell "the man" what it would take to get Levi in the air. By the time we returned to Hahn, the base was in full alert, and we received anything we needed and deployed that evening. Billy Griffin, Bill Wetterer, Rick Dodson, Bill Watters, and a host of other guys arrived from the US to provide support and assist with training. Dave Blazel came TDY in the early summer of 1977 and blessed me as the first AMS in the unit. I took it from there.

Totally in charge of the airborne mission and responsible for aircrew member welfare in many areas, AMS Hagy often pushed the Article 15 (non-judicial punishment) envelope with heated arguments about billeting, crew rest requirements, training, etc.

For one deployment against a possible real world threat, they wanted to billet us in tents at Rhein-Main. I said that if there were real beds available that met our needs, that's where the crews would sleep. If it culminated in war, we would sleep anywhere we could lay our heads (under the wings, at our racks, or whatever), but until then.... There were some rather spirited exchanges between me and the DO [operations officer], and I was guilty of raising my voice to emphasize a point here or there. The DO knew where my heart was, so I didn't get court martialed or an Article 15.

Comfy Levi Configuration in Europe

The Comfy Levi system had matured somewhat and offered more flexibility with regard to possible deployment configurations since its earliest use as Comfy Echo in Vietnam. Hagy described hardware configurations and the mission equipment in Europe.

The Levi system was designed with 6-position shelters. The original configuration design could be one shelter (Shelter 1 had AMS, airborne analyst, and 3-4 other positions) with a maintenance pallet, or two shelters with maintenance pallet, or three shelters with a maintenance "wedge" on the ramp. Our system at Hahn was two shelters with maintenance.

Comfy Levi Maintenance in Europe

The airborne maintenance technicians assigned to keep the Levi mission-ready had years of experience maintaining SIGINT systems aboard other USAFSS airborne platforms. Dan Hagy has nothing but praise for the 6911th AMT's.

We were fortunate to have a fantastic team of AMT's at Hahn. Their ingenuity and initiative enabled us to overcome countless technical obstacles. For example, the average loading time to get the Levi onto a C-130 and have it mission ready was 8-hours plus. And that was if they had a K-loader with the Levi shelter on it, ready to load. The guys cut that time at least in half, using heavy duty forklifts and coordinated teamwork.

In addition to anchoring two shelters in the aircraft, the AMT's had to replace the standard rear side (paratroop) doors and forward overhead hatch on the C-130 with special Levi doors and a hatch containing intercept antennas.

6911th Comfy Levi Crews

The 6911th Comfy Levi missions were manned by linguists (primarily Russian, German and Polish), Morse intercept operators and airborne maintenance technicians (AMT's). Reginald Wood, one of the Russian intercept operators, was well known for his height and long arms—he could change tapes on a tape recorder mounted in the top position of his Levi equipment rack without standing up. In addition to Hagy, airborne mission supervisors included Dean Hansen and Ron Doranski, whom Hagy had certified on Comfy Levi. Hagy and David Acre also shared ground mission supervisor duties within the Transportable Ground Intercept Facility (TGIF) with Skip DeRousse.

Comfy Levi/Creek Storm Operations

Most USAFE Comfy Levi/Creek Storm missions staged out of Hahn Air Base as described by Dan Hagy.

We established a routine of flying five missions (using MAC [Military Airlift Command] "rent a plane" and later PANG [Pennsylvania Air National Guard] assets) per month in response to theater tasking from USAFE (as well as USAREUR [U.S. Army Europe], EUCOM [European Command], DIA [Defense Intelligence Agency], and anyone else that wanted to chip in). This was necessary to develop a trained cadre of operators that could support "drop of the hat" reaction to any deployments the CINC required.

Due to the costs associated with hiring a plane, our Comfy Levi flights usually took place toward the end of the month with five flights, then five more at the beginning of the next month. We staged out of Hahn, but due to the frequent adverse weather, we ended up recovering at Rhein-Main. (Hahn Air Base was renowned for having the absolute worst flying weather in the entire theater.) I was later able to justify using Mildenhall as an alternate base because of the 6988th [Electronic Security Squadron] being there with appropriate [cryptologic] storage facilities.

6911th Aircrew Traditions

Like other USAFSS airborne reconnaissance units, the 6911th developed its own practices and celebrations. Hagy talked about some 6911th rituals.

We devised a few traditions of our own—when an individual achieved a fully qualified position (Category III/IV), he was likely to be doused by the AMT's sneaking through the back of the briefing tent with the large water can (ice and all). When we had a long series of tiring flights, I wanted to bring in beer (delivered to my house by the beer man) for the crew. The DO was adamant—"NO! No alcohol in a secure area!" Col. Ozgo asked me if there would be any evidence the next day. As soon as I replied, he requested that no one be permitted to over-indulge.

Allowing aircrew members to relax with a brew or two at post-mission debriefings was a tradition in most USAFSS airborne squadrons.

"BERLIN FOR LUNCH BUNCH"

The "Berlin for Lunch" reconnaissance missions in the air corridors between West Germany and Berlin were strictly a USAFE endeavor for years until the 6911th Security Squadron (M) was asked to provide some COMINT intercept operators in 1977. Based at Wiesbaden Air Base, USAFE's 7405th Support Squadron conducted photo and electronic intelligence recon missions throughout Europe and the Middle East for two decades.[93] Except for an RB-26 used on some missions during the early years, the squadron used a mix of cargo aircraft outfitted with hidden sensors. With cameras and infrared sensors hidden under the cargo floor in the bottom of the aircraft, the crews operated covertly under the guise of logistics support—transporting cargo and passengers. Eventually, a four-position ELINT intercept suite was added. With no intelligence gathering antennas in evidence externally, the 7405th aircraft appeared to be standard cargo planes to an observer on the ground. USAFE identified 7405th flights as "Creek Fury" missions.

From the early 1950's, one of the squadron's primary missions involved patrolling the three 20-mile-wide air corridors leading from West Germany to Berlin and the 40-mile radius surrounding the city as part of a project called "Rain Drop." While in flight, SIGINT collection antennas were extended and external panels that hid the cameras and infrared sensors were opened, with filming proceeding and intercept operators recording signals of interest. After flying meandering routes within a corridor, the crew retracted antennas and closed all camera lens panel doors before landing at Tempelhof Airport. Sometimes, the Rain Drop missions circled within the 40-mile radius control zone around Berlin for "crew proficiency training." Retired Air Force Lt. Col. Vance Mitchell, who flew missions in the air corridors for six years, discussed the missions in a magazine article in 2000.[94]

> *The spectacle of transport aircraft landing at Berlin Tempelhof Airport, the crew, sometimes numbering upward of 15 having lunch and then returning to West Germany with no effort to either on-load or off-load passengers or cargo, strained the logistics cover story beyond any credibility.*

Crew members who flew the corridor missions proudly called themselves the "Berlin for Lunch Bunch." Renamed the 7405th Operations Squadron, in 1975 the unit relocated to Rhein-Main Air Base where it operated three C-130E recon aircraft. In 1977, USAFE HQ requested the 6911th to participate in the Berlin air corridor recon missions.

6911th Support—"Berlin for Lunch" Missions

As the 6911th Security Squadron (M)'s point of contact for airborne direct support to USAFE, Dan Hagy coordinated the use of voice intercept operators aboard 7405th Creek Fury missions.

Here, he reminisces about 6911th support for "Berlin for Lunch" corridor missions.

In late 1977, Ron Doranski and I were asked to start flying support on one of the corridor birds and direct the onboard sensors (Ravens [Electronic Warfare Officers-ELINT intercept operators]—several we had flown with on Combat Sent). When things were slow, we started asking other sensor operators if they were interested in near-real-time events. As we started feeding them info, they had more successful missions.

Seeing a situation wherein a Comfy Levi shelter could significantly enhance the USAFE Creek Fury missions, Sgt. Hagy drafted a message containing a suggestion for submission to HQ USAFE through the 6911th operations officer and HQ USAFSS. The 6911th ops officer was not supportive of the suggestion, prompting Sgt. Hagy to bring the proposal to Col. Allen J. Montecino Jr., who had recently taken command of the squadron.

He asked me what my problem was, then asked to review my message, scratched through the cite that was on it and made it CC [6911th Commander]. He signed it and said "Looks good! Send it!" The proposal was pushed through the HQ and subsequently approved by USAFE. We couldn't hang any antennas on the aircraft, but AMT ingenuity and skill found other sources for our receivers: one end of the long wire that isn't used, "borrowing" the TACAN antennas, replacing the forward escape hatch in flight, etc. They strapped it together, and we went flying (1979-1980, as I recall).

Taking place during a major exercise event, the test was a phenomenal success when we steered the platform to events that were obscured by weather. Based on our input, the pilot pushed the lower edge of the envelope, and the mission take exceeded expectations. It ended up being a very long day.

I participated in reconfiguration of a smaller, unused shelter (with 3 equipment racks) into a mission system for our operators. We had two positions with a jump seat in the middle, with a FLIR [forward looking infrared] screen in the middle rack. That was successful, and a second shelter was procured/installed in the third aircraft as it rotated through Ontario [Lockheed Depot Maintenance Facility in California].

On 1 August 1979, the 6911th Security Squadron (Mobile) was renamed the 6911th Electronic Security Group concurrent with U.S. Air Force Security Service becoming the Electronic Security Command. The 6911th ESG continued providing SIGINT direct support to the Headquarters, U.S. Air Forces Europe.

COMFY LEVI LEAVES EUROPE

The following year brought an end to Comfy Levi operations in Europe. The actual date of the final Levi mission is not recorded, but was "sometime in 1980" according to Daniel Hagy. Factors contributing to the demise of Comfy Levi operations in Europe included the high costs of maintaining an airborne contingency SIGINT cadre in a "ready to go" state. At the same time, the Transportable Ground Intercept Facility (TGIF) that was coming online at Hahn Air Base with its high flying U-2 platform was perceived as covering USAFE's targets of interest adequately, although it lacked the flexibility of the Comfy Levi system. ESC continued supporting 7405th Creek Fury missions throughout the Cold War, but the 6911th flying operations terminated in 1982.

6911TH FLYING OPS TO LINDSEY AS

Daniel Hagy continued supporting TGIF and the 7405th Creek Fury missions until February 1982 when Col. Michael Christy, 6910th Electronic Security Wing Commander, hand-picked him to set up Detachment 1, 6910th ESW at Lindsey Air Station, Wiesbaden. At that point, all of the 6911th airborne reconnaissance operations moved to Lindsey AS. The 7405th Operations Squadron flew its last Berlin Corridor mission on 29 September 1990.[95]

COMPASS EARS/S&WC

Another major component of 6911th Operations at Hahn Air Base was the Surveillance and Warning Central (S&WC) developed under the Compass EARS (Emergency Airborne Reaction System) program. Equipped with graphics display terminals, the S&WC provided USAFSS (aka ESC) traffic analysts with the capability to merge radar tracks from friendly radars and SIGINT-derived radar tracking and deliver intelligence to tactical users in real time. Built by General Dynamics, Fort Worth, Texas, Rome Air Development Center delivered the first production model S&WC to the 6911th Security Squadron at Hahn Air Base in 1978.[96] Former USAFSS traffic analyst, James (Jim) Riley Jr. discussed the S&WC in 2006.

> *As a young SSgt., I was selected to be one of the initial group of 202's [traffic analysts] to man the Compass EARS (Emergency Airborne Reaction System—later designated the Surveillance and Warning Central) that was built by General Dynamics at the Ft. Worth plant. I received my training in 1979 there at GD plant under the tutelage of TSgt. (later Chief) Des D'Orange and MSgt. Mike Phillips.*

> *The S&WC basically took SIGINT from a wide variety of sources and declassified it to a straight Secret level to be shared freely with all NATO partners. The data was shared via a TADIL-B (Tactical Digital Information Link) and also sent to the Compass Jade system.*

The S&WC became the focal point of tactical data analysis and direct support within the squadron. Compass Jade, another radar track manipulation system delivered to the 6911th ESS in 1982, is discussed later.

6911TH OPERATIONS—METRO TANGO

While 6911th operations proceeded within the hangar on the Hahn Air Base flight line, plans were underway to transform a former missile facility north of Hahn AB into a new USAFSS state of the art tactical SIGINT direct support facility. The heart of the new facility was to be the Transportable Ground Intercept Facility (TGIF). An annex of Hahn AB, the TGIF site had been named "Metro Tango" (M/T) during its days as a Missile Training facility.

6911th ESS, Metro Tango, Hahn AB, Germany, circa 1991

TGIF Overview

TGIF was the ground component of a real-time remoted SIGINT intercept system. COMINT operators at intercept positions in the TGIF shelter at the ground site controlled receivers aboard a U-2R or TR-1 [improved U-2] aircraft by means of an encrypted data link between the ground facility and the aircraft. ELINT operators in a "Senior Ruby" van at M/T also used receivers aboard a TR-1 to collect electronic intelligence. The initial COMINT receiver package aboard a U-2 flying recon missions for the 6911th was "Senior Book." Later, the COMINT and ELINT receiver packages aboard a TR-1 aircraft supporting the TGIF at Metro Tango were "Senior Spear" and "Senior Ruby" receiver subsystems, respectively.[97] TGIF was also known as the RTASS (Remote Tactical SIGINT System).

TGIF missions were patterned after USAFSS airborne SIGINT reconnaissance missions—primary difference being that the TGIF crew members were "chairborne" on the ground vs. airborne operators on aerial recon missions. An NCO ground mission supervisor controlled TGIF missions much in the same manner that an enlisted airborne mission supervisor controlled SIGINT missions aboard airborne SIGINT reconnaissance platforms.

TGIF—Metro Tango

Master Sergeant Seguin L. (Skip) DeRousse was one of the first TGIF ground mission supervisors at Metro Tango. The M/T facility was still under construction, and 6911th operations still was housed in tents inside the hangar at Hahn when Skip DeRousse arrived in August 1979. He discussed Metro Tango and TGIF in July 2006.[98]

We had huts, vans and tents pitched inside this hangar and that was everything except for the operator van, which was parked out by the link van due to cable lengths.

About Christmas, we began the move to Metro Tango, an old Army missile repair facility located about 5-10 miles north of Hahn. We finally had a real orderly room/commander's office and a real building for offices. Operations, except for the S&W [Surveillance and Warning] Center was still in vans, but at least we were inside a building. Getting from Ops to the S&WC and other operations offices was still out in the weather. We had the new TGIF shelter, about eight 8'x10' or 8'x12' shelters all hooked together.

We also got the Senior Ruby van, which was a 45 ft van on wheels. (We had several other vans sitting around with various things in them.) Senior Ruby was a fully automated ELINT system run by NCO's, no officers whatsoever. TGIF was hooked to it electrically, so we could see what they had, but not vice versa. They also reported automatically. It had been in Europe once before for testing purposes.

Although USAFSS had fielded real-time remotely operated SIGINT collections systems at other locations, the TGIF was a new prototype that established a baseline for upgrading existing command SIGINT systems. As explained by Skip DeRousse, TGIF evolved from the USAFSS automated COMINT collection package aboard the upgraded Rivet Joint airborne SIGINT reconnaissance platform.

The TGIF started life at Greenville, Texas, as the ground training system for RJ Block II or III, not sure which one. E.-Systems, Greenville, sold it via E-Systems, Falls

Church, to the Air Force a second time. Then Falls Church spent a lot of money making it into a remoted system. The system was powered by HP 1000 computers with 10 MB removable hard disks—about a dozen computers, and if any one of them, including the airborne system, hiccupped, they all had to be restarted in sequence, about 30-60 minutes to get back in operation.

6911th Ops Chief of Computer Systems

The new operations officer, Maj. John T. Novak, designated MSgt. DeRousse the Chief, 6911th Operations Computer Systems. Himself a mustang officer with years of experience as a Russian linguist in both USAFSS ground site and airborne operations, Maj. Novak could not have picked better leadership to implement TGIF in the 6911th ESG. Although Skip DeRousse possessed no engineering or software/programming background, he had years of experience as an airborne and ground analyst and voice intercept operator (Russian, French and Vietnamese), including a tour in another remoting intercept unit. Innovative and savvy in SIGINT direct support related matters, DeRousse was a highly motivated self-starter, eager to provide USAFSS personnel with the best possible tools to perform their mission.

TGIF OT&E

In January we started OT&E, Operational Testing and Evaluation, and did that for about three months. Ruby worked fine, an occasional problem but not many. TGIF was horrible; we were lucky if we only had to restart everything twice a mission. Contractors everywhere and every time you turned around, some damn VIP's visiting. There wasn't room in there to swing a dead cat—between trainees and contractors and when you added VIP's, it was ungodly.

The TGIF search system sucked, as well as the response time. We had Air Staff wienies all over us during the mission and for debriefs. New software loads every week or so. When we finally finished OT&E, Air Staff wanted some recommendations. Gee, did they get some!

Post-OT&E Cleanup

By the end of testing and evaluation, all concerned parties recognized the importance of having operations personnel involved in system development. Skip DeRousse explained.

First off, we told them that they should never let a bunch of non-SS [non-Security Service] officers design/build a system by themselves. Get a senior NCO into the program office. The response? Which one of you wants to go? Dean [Hansen] was closest to rotation, so he volunteered for Dayton. The next item was comms; I designed my requirements on the back of an envelope—full up computerized switches so that we did not have to unplug cannon plugs every time TGIF went down.

In the initial configuration, operations personnel had to physically disconnect TGIF from the Senior Ruby van during the dreaded computer reboots. Sgt. DeRousse wanted computer redundancy with automated switchover to eliminate time-wasting restarts. He also wanted automated signal switching to accommodate automated receipt of multiple data streams— elimination of manual switching and torn-tape relay was a must! As the 6911th's computer guy, DeRousse and a cleared contractor engineer specified the functions for an RTASS interface module (RIM).

By that time, I was Chief of Computer Systems for Operations (as far as I know, the first unit with this office). It was a captain slot, but we had me; as a matter of fact, I was the whole office.

The only programmer the contractor had to write the software for the RIM was a young uncleared female software engineer. Sgt. DeRousse set aside a van within the operations compound for the engineer's work space.

We made her an office in one of the 45-ft vans and put a combo padlock on the outside of it when she was in there. She would write code, then we locked her up and tested it, cleaned all of the classified out, went and let her out and told her what it did... six months we went like that before we got it working right. We forgot her one day, and she almost wet her pants waiting for us to let her out.

744

Sgt. DeRousse and wife Niecie threw a Christmas party for the engineers. It had been a long improvement process, but TGIF shaped up as a tactical SIGINT direct support system. It was about this time that DeRousse decided to become more knowledgeable about computers.

Somewhere in there I bought myself an Atari [computer] and started teaching myself programming so that I could talk to the contractors. They didn't understand operations, and ops didn't understand computers.

Working with the support contractors, the 6911th kept improving TGIF—primarily with software upgrades. Finally, the squadron got its first peek at the radar picture by hooking into a TADIL-B (tactical digital information link) net depicting radar coverage of West Germany and the East European border areas.

Compass Jade

The 6911th capabilities were further enhanced in 1982 with delivery of Compass Jade to Metro Tango. Jade was a radar track correlation system developed to use SIGINT inputs to complement friendly radar tracking. To no one's surprise, the 6911th designated MSgt. DeRousse as System Test Director for Compass Jade when the system arrived at M/T.

This was our first real connection to the real outside world. It hooked us directly into the radar net via Ramstein. We had a TADIL-B data link running down there, and from them we got the entire radar picture of Germany.

So, who was the officer in charge of Compass Jade during DeRousse's assignment at Metro Tango?

The officer who was technically in charge of Jade was some young captain; I think I pinned his railroad tracks on for him. Some bright young kid named Koziol... chuckle!

Maj. Gen. John C. Koziol assumed command of the Air Intelligence Agency during the summer of 2005. The combination of Compass Jade and an expanded RIM capable of handling 32 circuits permitted TGIF to receive tracking data via TADIL comms with AWACS and Rivet Joint, and SIGINT and NATO ground radar sources.

We could ID tracks, put activity on them, etc. We were also hooked via secure voice UHF to AWACS, who couldn't see our data directly because they only had an uncleared TADIL-A capability. They were NATO at the time.

A prototype, Compass Jade testing was scheduled to end 30 September 1982, but the 17th Air Force commander declared the system operational on 1 October with the 6911th directed to continue staffing and operating the Jade system. Each added capability brought an influx of new visitors. To the 6911th staff, it seemed that Metro Tango had been added to the "must do" list of stops for American VIP's touring military facilities in Europe.

Impressing VIP's

Skip DeRousse took the briefing of high-level officers in stride, never letting a briefing interfere with mission performance.

When I was running a mission, I had OPSCOMM, voice to Augsburg, voice to TGIF, Ruby and the S&WC and voice to AWACS and RJ. I was one busy SOB. One day this Admiral showed up (Deputy DIRNSA). I was up to my ears in alligators, so I pulled off one earphone and said, "I'm awfully busy sir; Julie, brief the Admiral." She was a two-striper and had never seen an admiral. I kept an ear on her, and she did good. He said, "Thanks," and went away happy!

On another occasion, DeRousse drew praise for his analytic prowess and knowledge of enemy air operations.

One day we were talking with AWACS and a PENREP [Soviet bomber overflight of East European air space warranting a "penetration report"] came wandering through. I idented it the minute it hit the screen (number, type, nationality and mission). Turned out there was a bunch of NATO generals getting a demo flight, and we impressed the hell out of them.

Area Specialists and Exercises

The 6911th sent Sgt. DeRousse and Jim Moore, another squadron NCO, to Ramstein for what they perceived to be a familiarization flight aboard a European area AWACS mission. The AWACS mission commander saw their presence differently.

When we got off the ground, they asked what frequency we wanted. Seems we were supposed to be the first area specialists with them; trouble was nobody told us that. Anyway, they gave us a console and we played with tracks for the mission. A lot of the stuff we could ID just from flight patterns, etc.

Thus began further 6911th expansion into direct support to USAFE operations. During exercises the unit also interfaced with the USAFE Airborne Battlefield Command and Control Center (ABCCC) C-130 aircraft. Skip DeRousse mused about supporting both Red and Blue forces during one exercise.

We played both sides of the exercise, so one day we had some A-10's who were going to hit a bunch of tanks. (Oh yeah, Lt. Sperry and some other [6911th] officer were given a console on the ABCCC and were our contacts.) They had control of Coronet Solo (a jammer). We had no way to warn the tanks, so we decided the next best thing was to jam the A-10's... Took the Director of the Airborne Battle Staff several days before he figured out the back end of the aircraft was directing the jamming against the front end of the aircraft... Once he settled down, he decided it was good training.

Simulating Metro Tango—Support to WPC

The Warrior Preparation Center evolved as a war-gaming center at Einsiedlerhof Air Station near Ramstein Air Base, Germany, in 1983. MSgt. DeRousse led the 6911th team that helped develop the concept and provided the SIGINT input to start up the WPC, a computer simulation center focusing initially on air defense and electronic warfare.

During the spring of '83, I was sent to Ramstein and told to report to Col. Moody Suter. Had never heard of him; found out much later that he was the guy who founded Red

Flag. [Red Flag is an advanced aerial combat training exercise hosted at Nellis AFB, Nevada.] The building at Nellis is now named for him and has a small display about him. Anyway, Capt. Snake Clark (another aggressor force guy) took me in to meet him. Here is this colonel, sitting there with his feet on the desk, tie pulled loose, sleeves rolled up, a coffee cup in one hand and a cigarette in the other. He said, "Glad to meet you, son. We're gonna kick ass. What do you need to simulate Metro Tango here?"

I thought about it for a few minutes and told him what I thought we needed. He hollered at this CMSgt. and said, "You get that, Chief?" He said, "Yes sir, it will be on the truck in a couple of hours." Turned out we were setting up an exercise center for a demonstration for CSAF [Air Force Chief of Staff]. It eventually became the Warrior Preparation Center near Ramstein.

I called down 3-4 kids from M/T, and we set up a little S&W Center, one position emulating Senior Ruby. (I got movies shot of a Ruby console during a mission... Suter could work miracles.) One position was set up to emulate TGIF, and I even had a real tape of activity that I could turn on when a demo was going on.

There were Army and Air Force setups as well as a COIC [Combat Operations Intelligence Center] area. I reported to them via a remoted printer, like we were sending messages.

I had all of my kids get jump boots and dickies, and the first rehearsal, we showed up dressed like that. The colonel went ballistic! Stood us up in front of everyone and said "I want everyone to look like that tomorrow!" Most of the officers didn't even own fatigues, much less jump boots.

He even had Russian weapons—a T-54 tank, a ZSU-4 AAA gun, and all kinds of stuff in the compound. We briefed 21 stars in three days, ending up with the CSAF. When we finished the demo, Moody was sitting there chatting with him and telling him how we simulated a lot of stuff. He said to me, "Skip, tell him how you really get a TACREP [tactical report] from M/T to COIC!" I said I send it to the States via England and they send it back!

The briefing to CSAF Gen. Charles A. Gabriel was well received, and today the Warrior Preparation Center is a joint service operation that "enables commanders to effectively conduct air, land and sea campaigns anytime, day or night, and never spill a drop of blood."[99] A plaque by the entrance to the WPC names MSgt. Seguin L. DeRousse as one of the center's founders.

Sgt. DeRousse departed Metro Tango in August 1983, replacing Dean Hansen in the Compass Bright (U-2 platform intelligence gathering systems) office of the Aeronautical Systems Division at Wright-Patterson AFB, Ohio. Hansen had played a major role in the implementation of TGIF at M/T. DeRousse returned to Metro Tango on temporary duty to deliver TGIF II, which expanded TGIF at M/T from 10 to 24 COMINT operator positions. By that time according to DeRousse, plans were underway to relocate Metro Tango's SIGINT direct support capabilities to hardened underground facilities, but the Cold War ended before that move could be effected.

Plans were made to bury M/T, and they were actually starting construction on it when I brought TGIF II out for delivery in late '83; never got finished as far as I know. The [Berlin] Wall came down first.

Gen. Gabriel had interrupted DeRousse's briefing at the Warrior Preparation Center months earlier to comment on hardened facilities to better protect 6911th Operations.

One of the comments the CSAF made was in the middle of my briefing. He turned to his staff and said "We gotta get that place buried! Excuse me, Sgt., please continue."

Wüscheim Underground Facility

The area that was selected to become a hardened new home for the 6911th Electronic Security Squadron[100] was a former American missile site on Wüscheim Mountain in the Hunsrück some 20 to 25 miles northeast of Metro Tango. Wüscheim had been a U.S. Air Force Matador and Mace ground-launched cruise missile site during the 1960's and a U.S. Army Nike surface-to-air missile site during the 1970's. Around 1980, the governments of the United States and West Germany developed a plan to create a massive bunker on Wüscheim to house a combined U.S. Air Force

Electronic Security Command/German Foreign Intelligence Service underground operation. The site was to be used for remoted SIGINT intercept activities from both a USAF TR-1 aircraft and a small German air force reconnaissance plane.

The 6911th ESS maintained a small operation on Wüscheim in the late 1980's, but the end of the Cold War, among other factors, resulted in the termination of the development of the Wüscheim underground bunker. By the mid-1980's, the top of Wüscheim had been opened up and work had started on the bunker; however, as work progressed it became apparent to all concerned that its survivability was in doubt because they couldn't get the whole operation in the bunker.[101] When the Berlin Wall came down on 9 November 1989, all construction on the Wüscheim bunker ceased. In 2003, a former 6911th airman who had recently visited the Hahn area reported in an email that the Wüscheim site is unoccupied.

Wüscheim is a ghost town guarded by a guy in a Winnebago and a big dog, but he will let you drive a trip down memory lane if you ask a/o [and/or] bring beer.[102]

Bottled Exclusively for 6911th SS

The 6911th Security Squadron was the only Air Force Security Service unit to have had its own labeled wine. Located within an hour of dozens of wineries along the Mosel, Nahe and Rhein Rivers, 6911th personnel had their choice of the most exquisite white wines in the universe at rock-bottom prices, and many 6911th troops became wine connoisseurs. Wine tastings up and down the rivers were a favorite pastime for many squadron airmen.

David Morgan, a dual-qualified German-Russian linguist, fell in love with the wines at "Zum Eulenturm Weinkellerei" (Owl's Tower Winery) when he arrived in the 6911th in 1978. Located in the village of Briedel am Mosel 25 km from Metro Tango, Zum Eulenturm is one of hundreds of small wineries in Germany's wine region. Dave Morgan developed a special bond with the Zum Eulenturm proprietors and their outstanding wines. Speaking no English, owners Hans-Otto and Marie Louise Stölben were a thirty-ish couple whose wine cellar had been in the Stölben family since 1525. Amazed at Morgan's German, including a Hunsrück country accent that matched theirs, Hans-Otto and Marie adopted Dave Morgan as their dark-haired American hero.

Contributed by Jim Kimmett

Mosel River viewed from Cochem Castle, June 1989

Given the camaraderie—and liberal amounts of the best wines in the Stölben Keller—Morgan and fellow Russian linguist Bill Brooks spent their off-duty hours assisting Herr Stölben during the grape harvesting seasons. In the fall of 1980 when Herr Stölben suffered a back sprain, Dave lugged all of the Stölben grapes from steep hillside vineyards down to a loading area and across the river to the Zum Eulenturm; the winery was on the west bank of the river while most of the family vineyards were on the east bank.

As a shift worker, Dave had lots of free hours during the day and often accompanied coworkers to the winery and served as their translator and advisor during tastings. The word spread within the squadron, and one day Col. Montecino, 6911th commander, asked Morgan to go with him to Briedel. The colonel was so impressed with the wines that he asked SSgt. Morgan to investigate the possibility of having the Zum Eulenturm package a special lot of wine expressly for the squadron. Dave helped Hans-Otto and Marie select varieties and vintages that would most likely appeal to American palates and accompanied Col. Montecino and a couple of other 6911th wine aficionado wannabes during a tasting.

Col. Montecino placed an initial order for 1,200 bottles. The Stölbens were astonished; their best German customers did not place such a large order. Dave Morgan prepared the wording for a special bottle label that read, "Bottled exclusively for the 6911th SS." The wine was available for sale by the case (10 bottles) in the 6911th squadron orderly room, with profits going to the unit morale fund. Sales were brisk from the start; hardly any of the constant stream of visitors to the unit left empty handed. New tastings and additional orders followed.

Return to Briedel

In 1984, as DoD contractors conducting engineering analysis on an Air Force contract, David Morgan and the author spent a few days interviewing TGIF operators and gathering operational data in 6911th Operations at Metro Tango. Rough duty, but someone had to do it! It was a nostalgic trip for Dave Morgan and German friends in the Hunsrück. Free drinks and Prosts wherever we went, and a true homecoming at the Zum Eulenturm Winery.

Planning to surprise the Stölbens, we visited the winery unannounced. Herr Stölben was away for the day, but Marie Louise was every bit the hostess that Dave had described and more. Although normally closed on Mondays, she opened the tasting room exclusively for us and joined in with the tasting. After sampling the varieties available for purchase, Marie brought out a bottle of 1948 vintage reserve Riesling Spätlase and a 1949er Silberner Preis-winning Riesling Kabinett "Qualitätswein mit Prädikat"—private stock, not for sale. What an afternoon! No sales discussions, just a sincere invitation to return the next day when Herr Stölben would be available.

Finishing our work early at the 6911th the following day, we drove to the Zum Eulenturm after lunch, and Herr Stölben had set aside his afternoon for our visit. Although not as generous with the special reserve labels as Marie Louise, Hans-Otto insured that his American guests did not leave thirsty or hungry. Sampling several vintages, including some that Morgan had helped produce in 1979 and 1980, Dave and I purchased one case each of mixed varieties and vintages. Nothing like a three-hour wine and cheese lunch to end our visit to the Hunsrück. Using a leather belt wrapped around the case to form a handle, we hand-carried our wine aboard our aircraft for the trip home to Pennsylvania.

6911TH ESS DEACTIVATED

On another trip to Europe during the summer of 1994, I made a side trip to Briedel, specifically to call on the Stölbens at the Zum Eulenturm. Some of their most avid customers—6911th Electronic Security Squadron members—had left Germany the previous year. The 6911th ESS was deactivated in April 1993. Today, with Frankfurt-Hahn Airport (formerly Hahn Air Base) serving as a hub for several smaller European airlines, the former 6911th dormitories at Metro Tango have been converted to office space.

Author's Collection

Hans-Otto, Marie Louise and Larry Tart, 2 July 1994

6911TH SCTY SQDN (M) HERITAGE

The heritage of the 6911th Security Squadron (Mobile) that stood up at Darmstadt in 1963 spans six decades. Activated as the 139th Signal Radio Intelligence Company by the Army Air Corps at MacDill Field, Florida, in 1942, the unit arrived in France as the 2nd Radio Squadron Mobile in April 1945. It served in the Allied Occupation Force after World War II and began its tenure as a USAFSS unit as the 2nd RSM in 1949. Designated the 6911th Radio Squadron Mobile in 1955, the squadron served USAFSS (and its successor commands) in Europe longer than any other USAFSS organization.

The chart that follows depicts overall 6911th lineage.

Lineage of 6911th Scty Sq (Mobile)	
Unit Designator	Action/Comments
139th Signal Radio Intel Co. (Aviation)	Activated at MacDill Field, FL, 14 Feb 1942
2nd AAF RSM (Germany)	Redesignated 16 Mar 1944
2nd AAF RSM (G)	Relocated to Camp Pinedale, CA, Aug 1944
2nd AAF RSM (G)	Deactivated at Camp Pinedale, March 1945
2nd AAF RSM (G)	Reactivated at Vittel, France, 14 Apr 1945
2nd AAF RSM (G)	Relocated to Heidelberg, Ger., 24 Apr 1945
2nd AAF RSM (G)	Moved to Bad Kissingen, Ger., 31 May 1945
2nd AAF RSM (G)	Reassigned to 9th AF, USAFE, 1 July 1945
2nd AAF RSM (G)	Relocated to Bad Vilbel, Ger., 16 Jan 1946
2nd AAF RSM	Reassigned to Army Sec Agency, 1 Feb 1946
2nd AAF RSM	To Herzo Base, Herzogenaurach, early 1947
2nd RSM	Transferred to USAFSS, 1 Feb 1949
2nd RSM	To Ludwig Kaserne, Darmstadt, 27 Feb 1949
2nd RSM	To Cambrai-Fritsch Kaserne, early 1953
6911th RSM	Redesignated 6911th RSM, 8 May 1955
6911th RGM	Redesignated 6911th RGM, 1 Sept 1956
6911th RGM	Deactivated, 15 May 1961
6911th Scty Sq (Mobile)	Activated at Darmstadt, 1 July 1963
6911th SS (M)	Relocated to Rhein-Main AB, 1 Jun 1972
6911th SS (M)	Relocated to Hahn AB, 1 July 1975
6911th Electronic Scty Gp	Redesignated 6911th ESG, 1 Aug 1979
6911th ESG	Reassigned to Elec Scty, Europe, 30 Sept 1980
6911th Electronic Scty Sq	Redesignated, 1 Jul 1981; under 6910th ESW
6911th ESS	Reassigned to Elec Scty, Europe, 1 Jan 1985
6911th ESS	Reassigned to 6910th ESW, 1 Sept 1987
6911th ESS	Reassigned to 691st Elec Scty Wg, 15 Jul 1988
6911th ESS	Reassigned to 26th Intel Wing, 1 Oct 1991
6911th ESS	Deactivated, 1 Apr 1993
402nd Intel Squadron	Activated at Bad Aibling, 1 Oct 1993
402nd IS	Deactivated, Aug '00; became Det 2, 26th IOG
Det 2, 26th Info Ops Gp	Deactivated 30 September 2004.

6910th SW Operations—1968-1970

Following the deactivation of Detachment 1, 6950th Security Group in Bremerhaven in March 1968, the 6910th Security Wing enjoyed fairly stable operations for the next two years; see the organization chart that follows.

ESR Germany-based Org Chart—1968-1970	
European Security Region Frankfurt, Germany 1961-1972	
6910th Security Wing Darmstadt, Germany 1963-1970	
Det 2, 6910th Scty Wing Camp Pieri, Germany 1963-1969	6911th Scty Sq (ERU) (1 Darmstadt, Germany Jul 1963-31 May 1972
6915th Scty Gp Hof, Germany 1964-1971	6912th Scty Sq Berlin, Germany 1963-1979
6916th Scty Sq (2 Rhein-Main, Germany 1963-1973	Det 1, 6950th Scty Gp (3 Bremerhaven, Germany 1967-1968
(1 6911th Security Squadron (Emergency Reaction Unit) (2 6916th Security Squadron discussed in FTV, Vol IV, Airborne Recon. (3 USAFSS unit in Bremerhaven was deactivated in 1968.	

Operational Wing Concept Discontinued

Commencing in 1970, the operational wing concept fell "by the wayside as USAFSS reorganized its subordinate unit posture to strengthen the role of the Regions."[103] The USAFSS overseas wings were redesignated as groups and their subordinate units placed under the direct control of the European Security Region in Europe and the Pacific Security Region in the Far East. The ESR org chart for USAFSS units in Germany for the period 1970-1972 follows.

ESR Germany-based Org Chart—1970-1972	
European Security Region Frankfurt, Germany 1961-1972	
6910th Scty Gp Darmstadt, Germany 1970-1972	6911th Scty Sq (ERU) Darmstadt, Germany 1963-1972
OL-AA, 6910th Scty Gp Rimbach-Eckstein, Germany <u>1971-1972</u> OL-BB, 6910th Scty Gp Hof, Germany <u>1971-1971</u> OL-CC, 6910th Scty Gp Augsburg, Germany <u>1971-1972</u> OL-JH, 6910th Scty Gp (1 Darmstadt, Germany 1972-1972	
6912th Scty Sq Berlin, Germany 1963-1979	6915th Scty Gp Hof, Germany 1964-1971
6916th Scty Sq (2 Rhein-Main, Germany 1963-1973	OL-F1, 6970th Supt Gp Bad Aibling, Germany 1971-1975
(1 Interim unit during 6910th SG move from Darmstadt to Augsburg. (2 6916th Scty Sqdn discussed in FTV, Vol IV, Airborne Recon.	

In 1971-1972, the 6910th Security Group activated several operating locations (OL's) in conjunction with the relocation of organizations within Germany. In addition, the 6970th Support Group, Fort Meade, Maryland, deployed a team of intercept operators and analysts (OL-F1, 6970th SG) to Bad Aibling, Germany, in 1971. The 6910th OL's (OL-AA, OL-BB, OL-CC and OL-JH) are addressed after Air Force operations at Bad Aibling.

AF CRYPTOLOGIC OPS—BAD AIBLING

Air Force Security Service activities at Field Station Bad Aibling, Germany, was a fairly well-kept secret, even within the

American cryptologic community. Located in Bavaria, Bad Aibling airfield had been home to Luftwaffe Messerschmitts during World War II. U.S. SIGINT operations commenced there in 1952 when the Army Security Agency (aka Intelligence and Security Command) opened FS Bad Aibling in a hangar at the airfield. The station was a conventional ASA ground HF intercept site for two decades prior to the installation of a dome-covered satellite dish antenna outside the hangar.

In 1971, the 6970th Support Group—USAFSS entity supporting the National Security Agency—detached a small team (OL-F1, 6970th SS) to Bad Aibling as part of a joint service team.[104] As a national program, the team's mission was managed from the United States with only minimal interaction with other intercept sites in Europe that were managed by one of the service cryptologic organizations (USAFSS, INSCOM or the NSG.)

Management of the Air Force contingent at Bad Aibling shifted over the years. OL-F1, 6970th became Detachment 72, 6950th Security Group in 1976, OL-FT, Det 1, HQ USAFSS in 1978 and the 6915th Electronic Security Squadron probably in 1979. On 1 October 1991, the 6915th was deactivated, replaced by the 402nd Intelligence Squadron. Finally in 2000, the 402nd was inactivated, with Detachment 2, 26th Information Operations Group assuming its responsibilities at Bad Aibling. Det 2, 26th IOG was deactivated 30 September 2004 when the United States returned the station to the German government.

In an online exposé published before the station closed, a research group speculated on the Bad Aibling operational mission.

Bad Aibling is a ground station for the interception of civil and military satellite communications traffic operated by the NSA. About 1,000 personnel are on the staff at the Bad Aibling Regional SIGINT Operations Center in Germany, which conducts satellite communications interception activities and is also a downlink station for geostationary SIGINT satellites, like the CANYON program or the MAGNUM/ORION system. Operational responsibility of the ground station was transferred to the ARMY Intelligence and Security Command in 1995, but there is also influence from the Air Force's 402nd Intelligence

LARRY TART

Squadron. Till the end of the Cold War the main target was the Soviet Union.[105]

The last 402nd squadron commander, Lt. Col. Paul Gifford, told the author in 2005 that the squadron was deactivated around May 2000, soon after he transferred to Fort Meade. Maj. Walter Gagajewski was the Det 2, 26th IOG commander in 2000.

EUROPEAN SCTY REGION DEACTIVATED

As part of a reorganization of U.S. intelligence agencies and activities, USAFSS deactivated both the European Security Region (30 June 1972) and the Pacific Security Region (31 December 1972.) Eliminating the intermediate headquarters between USAFSS and its field units, the command's overseas units reported directly to HQ USAFSS.[106] The organization chart that follows shows USAFSS units in Germany at the end of 1973.

ESR Germany-based Org Chart—1973	
HQ USAFSS Kelly AFB, Texas 1953-1979	
6900th Scty Sq Frankfurt, Germany 1972-1973	OL-AB, HQ USAFSS, HQ USAFE/Ramstein AB, Ger.
6910th Scty Gp Augsburg, Germany 1972-1974	
Det 1, 6910th SG Rimbach-Eckstein, Germany 1973-1974	6911th Scty Sq (M) Rhein-Main, Germany Jun 1972-Jun 1975
6912th Scty Sq Berlin, Germany 1963-1979	OL-F1, 6970th Supt Gp Bad Aibling, Germany 1971-1975

6900TH SECURITY SQUADRON

USAFSS activated the 6900th Security Squadron at Frankfurt, Germany, in 1972. The squadron had a COMSEC mission in direct support of U.S. Air Forces Europe and U.S. European Command. The 6900th SS moved to RAF Chicksands in 1973 and conducted operations at Chicksands through 1975.

6910TH SCTY GP RELOCATES TO AUGSBURG

On 10 June 1972,[107] the 6910th Security Group completed its move from Darmstadt to Augsburg, Bavaria—approximately 70 Km northwest of Munich. The relocation began in 1971 with activation of OL-CC, 6910th SG in Augsburg. Col. John L. Kelly II, commander of the 6910th, set up his group headquarters and billeting at Sheridan Kaserne, one of five U.S. Army posts in Augsburg; the other four were: Gablingen Kaserne, Flak Kaserne, the Quartermaster Supply Center and Reese Barracks. All of the posts were former WW II Bundeswehr camps. The 6910th headquarters was colocated at Sheridan Kaserne with a 63rd Armored Regiment tank battalion. Army Security Agency and Naval Security Group field units also had their headquarters and billets at Sheridan.

Field Station Augsburg

Field Station Augsburg, which ASA activated on Gablingen Kaserne north of Augsburg in 1970, became home to 6910th Operations. ASA, USAFSS and NSG worked side-by-side at FSA, sharing the Army's AN/FLR-9 antenna system that become operational in 1970. In 2006, the author discussed 6910th Augsburg operations with former commander Col. Kelly, who retired from USAFSS in 1975.

Intel Command Standards vs. Conscription Army Practices

During a pre-move site survey trip to Sheridan Kaserne and Field Station Augsburg in the fall of 1971, Col. Kelly observed a drastic difference between regular Army standards and those of the three services' intelligence commands. Army support commands, even at

Darmstadt but more pronounced at Augsburg, had different (lower) standards with regard to morale-building activities such as comfortable living quarters and recreational facilities. Kelly found working with ASA and NSG to be pleasant; the three intelligence commands had an appreciation for each other's mission and worked cooperatively. On the other hand, with conscription still the Army's primary manpower source, Army support commanders painted life on military facilities with an olive drab brush.

ASA Field Station Augsburg, Germany, circa early 1970's

RHIP and Interservice Friction

Rank has its privileges in the military, but it can also affect interservice relationships in joint service scenarios. Sheridan Kaserne had one general officer house, and since Col. Kelly was the ranking officer on post, the housing officer assigned those quarters to Kelly and his family. That rankled the post commandant, an Army O-6, and it was not unusual for the commandant's boss, an Army 2-star general, to sit in on interservice meetings between Col. Kelly and Army support organizations on Sheridan. Nonetheless, Kelly did not kowtow to Army dictates that he perceived as detrimental to the Air Force mission or the welfare of 6910th officers and airmen.

In fending off what he considered unnecessary or counterproductive Army policies that would impact his airmen, Col. Kelly developed a reputation within Army support elements at Sheridan as not being a team player. So what, 6910th airmen appreciated the manner in which their colonel stood up for them, and morale was excellent. In 2006, former MSgt. John Stapchuk, a 6910th mission supervisor who relocated with the Group from Darmstadt to Augsburg, recalled an incident that curried favor with the single 6910th airmen.

> *I remember that Col. Kelly had gone down there to look the place over prior to the move. When he came back he was adamant that "none of my troops will live in those conditions," meaning of course the barracks. They were fixed up quickly and well, before we moved the troops into them. The tankers [tank battalion draftees] on the other hand were not that fortunate. Some of the barracks they were in were really, really bad.*

6910th Transportation Issues

Col. Kelly won several battles with Army motor pools, beginning at Darmstadt during the move to Augsburg. The motor pool provided transportation for 6910th equipment and furniture, and the belongings of single airmen to Augsburg, but lower ranking airmen who were not authorized transportation for their families and furniture got no sympathy from the Army. Having brought their families to Germany at their personal expense, the government had no obligation to assist with their move, and the transportation officer would not bend rules one iota. By scheduling shipments in a manner in which excess space "magically" happened to be available on Army trucks, the 6910th managed to include private property of the lower ranking married airmen, and the Army officials were none the wiser.

The 6910th had its own small fleet of vehicles—a few buses, a couple of small trucks and a staff car—all painted Air Force blue. The post transportation officer at Sheridan objected to the Air Force having its own "motor pool." He tried to have the 6910th vehicles transferred to the Army motor pool, where the Army would paint them olive drab and sign them out to the 6910th on a per trip basis. Col. Kelly politely told the transportation officer to pound sand—the 6910th needed its own vehicles to transport shift workers to/from work at the Field Station and meet other Air Force needs. Going a step farther, he made the group's buses available for off-duty travel. Trick workers, church groups, athletic teams, et al could check out a bus for day tours or overnight trips—the only stipulation being that personnel show up for duty at their next scheduled shift.

The Keller

One of the greatest Air Force morale boosters in Augsburg—and a real point of friction between Col. Kelly and local Army brass—was the *Keller*, an Air Force bar and recreation center that the 6910th created on Sheridan Kaserne. The post facilities officer assigned an abandoned Army mess hall to Col. Kelly as a USAFSS administered property. The 6910th converted the former mess hall into Air Force administrative offices, and with self-help and unit morale funds, transformed the building's basement into a German-style *Bierstube* that was appropriately named the *Keller*.

The *Keller* was an immediate success, especially with unmarried 6910th airmen who lived in barracks at Sheridan. As with all USAFSS intercept units throughout the world, approximately 80 percent of the 6910th personnel were "trick" workers. Split into four flights called tricks, the trick workers worked a 24/7 schedule on eight-hour day, swing and midshifts. One trick was always on break, but unlike "day weenies" (those who worked a Monday-Friday dayshift), the trick worker schedule included weekends and holidays: three swings, 24 hours off; three mids, 24 hrs off; three days, 72 hrs off; then repeat schedule.

The *Keller* provided an on-post facility where airmen could relax during off-duty hours. The trick getting off a swingshift at midnight had a place to unwind after eight grueling hours of monitoring enemy communications. Those finishing a midshift at 8 a.m. could sip a beer or two (or several) before retiring, and morning "roll call" after the last midshift of a work cycle was a tradition throughout Air Force Security Service. In addition, the trick that had worked days—and day weenies after duty hours—found the *Keller* a convenient location to share war stories. As explained by former Morse intercept operator Lenny Mingroni, Col. Kelly endeared himself to assigned trick workers with his generosity.

I remember folks like Col. John Kelly who used to every now and then "buy the rounds" for the shift coming off [and] going on break at the Air Force "Keller," where I can still remember paying about 20 cents for "Greenies" (aka Heineken!.)

To the utter consternation of the Kaserne commandant, the *Keller* operated around the clock, serving local beer on tap, plus bottled Heineken, a few American brands and sodas. In addition, the *Keller* served Field Station Augsburg's own private-label Thorbräu bottled beer.

The 6910th group also created a beer garden next door where off-duty airmen could enjoy picnics. For recreation, there was a dart board, a foosball table and a poker game in a back room of the *Keller*. There were weekly dart matches between Air Force teams and Naval Security Group teams—NSG had its own version of the *Keller*, larger than the *Keller* but not as lively.

The post commandant considered it sacrilegious and illegal that airmen had beer available at breakfast time on his Kaserne and asked Col. Kelly to remove the beer from what he deemed to be a day room. Kelly's response, "My airmen are shift workers, they eat breakfast at midnight, and have a few beers after work at 8:00 a.m." Over the commandant's objections, the *Keller* not only survived, but was the most popular facility on post.

Tri-Service Patrols

The Army did have disciplinary problems within its tank battalion on Sheridan Kaserne and support units at other Kasernes around Augsburg. To ameliorate the situation, the Augsburg area Army commander decided to initiate tri-service courtesy patrols of local off-post bars and clubs frequented by G.I.'s. The area commander issued a letter to all tenant organizations announcing the start-up of the tri-service patrol program and directing tenant commanders to detail assigned officers and senior NCO's to patrol duty on a rotating basis. Col. Kelly declined to have his 6910th leaders participate, pointing out that Air Force Security Service personnel for the most part refrained from getting into trouble, and it was not an Air Force responsibility to monitor and control the off-duty conduct of errant Army soldiers. Such actions by the senior officer on Sheridan Kaserne did little to promote harmonious Army-Air Force relations.

The Problem Solver

The acrimonious relationship between Col. Kelly and the Army support command community in Augsburg was more serious that Kelly realized. Unbeknownst to him, Army brass undoubtedly complained directly to Kelly's boss—Maj. Gen. Carl W. Stapleton, USAFSS Commander. Details are sketchy, but someone in Europe apparently discussed 6910th-Army support relations with the USAFSS commander when he visited Augsburg in 1972. While concerned about the Army-Air Force rift, Gen. Stapleton took no overt actions. He was satisfied with Col. Kelly's overall performance. However, he did initiate covert actions that came to the author's attention during discussions with retired USAFSS Lt. Col. Waldemar (Wally) P. Scherer.

Having been an ASA Chinese interpreter-translator in the mid-1950's, Wally Scherer received his commission through the Air Force ROTC program in 1961 and became a USAFSS intelligence officer. In part due to his ASA background, Gen. Stapleton assigned Capt. Scherer as commander of Detachment 4, 6922nd Security Group, Ramasun Station, outside Udorn, Thailand, in 1971. Being an ASA station, it was like old-home week for Scherer, and Det 4 had an outstanding rapport with ASA's 7th Radio Research Field Station personnel at Ramasun.

Thus, Capt. Scherer's name came to mind when Gen. Stapleton returned from his tour of USAFSS sites in Europe in late 1972. Having purchased a home in San Antonio and just settled into a three-year assignment at USAFSS Headquarters, Wally Scherer was on leave in early 1973 when Gen. Stapleton called his office in USAFSS/DOM. The call caused quite a tizzy in headquarters because no one knew why the general was looking for Capt. Scherer. Scherer's boss called him at home. Sweaty and wearing a two-day beard, Wally was working in his yard.

Appreciating that The General does not call a captain to shoot the bull, Wally Scherer wracked his brain while showering and driving to work to report to Gen. Stapleton. Col. James H. (Herb) Macia Jr., USAFSS Chief of Staff, ushered Capt. Scherer into Gen. Stapleton's office, excused himself, and closed the door. Gen. Stapleton got right to the point, "Wally, how are you?" "I want you to go to Germany for me." "Well, yes, sir. I can pack a bag and get airline reservations immediately. A TDY trip is no problem at all."

Gen. Stapleton cut Scherer off and said something to the effect that we need more than that. "We have problems in Augsburg— the place is a mess—our people don't know how to get along with the Army." "Wally, I want you to go PCS over there and straighten the place out."

Confused, Capt. Scherer stuttered, "But, sir; you have an O-6 in charge at Augsburg." "I am not sure what my mission is to be."

Stapleton responded, "You are an experienced mustang officer; you'll figure it out after you arrive at Augsburg." "When can you leave?"

"Well, sir; we just settled on our new house here in San Antonio." "I'll need to sell that; I can probably leave in about 30 days." "Thirty days you have if you really need it; see how many of those days you can give me back!"

Promoted to major while enroute to Germany, everyone at Augsburg was confused about his assignment when he signed in at the 6910th Security Group. Maj. Carl Clair was the operations officer, filling the only O-4 slot in Operations. Maj. Scherer became the 6910th assistant operations officer anyway. It was like old-home week again at Field Station Augsburg—Wally Scherer had served on Okinawa with many of the ASA old timers when he was an ASA Spec-5 Chinese linguist. Relations were excellent between the 6910th and Field Station Augsburg officers.

Eventually, Col. Kelly moved Maj. Clair to headquarters as his deputy commander, and Maj. Scherer became 6910th operations officer. There were no operational problems to fix, and Wally Scherer never discussed with Col. Kelly how the decision had been made to assign him to the 6910th. Nor did he discuss Augsburg again with Gen. Stapleton, who had retired by the time Scherer arrived in Germany.

Midway through his 6910th assignment, USAFSS curtailed Maj. Scherer's Augsburg assignment and reassigned him as Air Force Special Security Officer at USAFE Headquarters/Ramstein. He's still puzzled as to how Gen. Stapleton expected him to fix the "mess" at Augsburg.

6910TH SG/AUGSBURG DEACTIVATED

As part of a major reorganization in 1974,[108] USAFSS deactivated the 6910th Security Group on 30 June. Personnel with sufficient time for a follow-on assignment were reassigned to other USAFSS units in Europe. Bob Blackmon was reassigned to the 6917th Security Group in Italy.

Only spent about 6 months with the unit prior to it closing, I worked at the Keller as a bartender and remember several good card games in the back room. The beer was great and I killed lots of brain cells but enjoyed the short time I spent there. I went to sunny San Vito when the unit closed.

Lenny Mingroni provides a good summary regarding the dispersal of 6910th personnel when the group was deactivated.

After the Air Force unit closed operations, I can say for the Baker Flight people: some retired, rotated stateside, off to Turkey, off to Crete, off to England, off to Italy.

A well placed source told the author that a factor in ceasing 6910th activities at Augsburg was that Gen. Galligan was tired of fighting the local Army support command bureaucracy. With the deactivation of the 6910th Security Group, two of its subordinate units in Germany, 6912th and 6913th Security Squadrons, reported directly to USAFSS Headquarters. The 6911th Security Squadron (M) reported to newly activated 6955th Security Group in Texas. The USAFSS org chart for Germany-based units at the end of 1974 follows.

USAFSS Germany-based Org Chart—1974	
HQ USAFSS Kelly AFB, Texas 1953-1979	
	OL-AB, HQ USAFSS, HQ USAFE/Ramstein AB, Ger.
6911th Scty Sq (M) * Rhein-Main, Germany Jun 1972-Jun 1975	6912th Scty Sq Berlin, Germany 1963-1979
6913th Scty Sq Rimbach-Eckstein, Germany 1974-1975	OL-F1, 6970th Supt Gp Bad Aibling, Germany 1971-1975
* Resubordinated to 6955th Scty Group, Kelly AFB, TX, 1 July 1974.	

USAFSS AT ASA BORDER SITES

Though few details are available, during the 1970's USAFSS had German and Russian linguists assigned to ASA sites along the border between East and West Germany at Gross Gusborn, Wobeck, Mount Meissner and Rimbach-Eckstein, West Germany. Among others, Daniel Hagy and William Lewis served at Gross Gusborn by Dannenberg on the Elbe River—by the entrance to the Northern Air Corridor to Berlin. Dennis Bateman, Charles Carrick and Bobby Ray Newton were stationed with ASA Detachment K at Wobeck (Central Air Corridor). No significant details are available regarding USAFSS operations at a Mount Meissner site, which was located east of Kassel by the Southern Air Corridor to Berlin. The larger of the USAFSS Germany-based operations was farther south along the West German-Czech border at Rimbach-Eckstein.

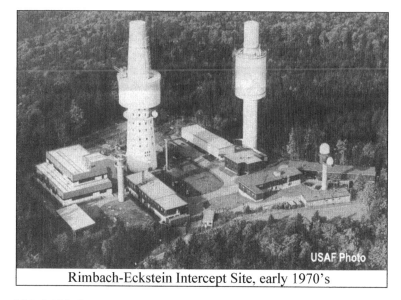

Rimbach-Eckstein Intercept Site, early 1970's

USAFSS—RIMBACH-ECKSTEIN, GERMANY

Situated in eastern Bavaria three miles from the Czech Republic, Mount Eckstein—at 3,520 feet the taller of two peaks on Hoher Bogen Mountain—has a commanding view to the east. On summer nights, from Eckstein one can see the lights of Pilsen and Prague, but winters can be severe, with temperatures of minus 25 degrees F., blizzard conditions (60-70 MPH winds) and 6-8 feet of snow. During winter months, sunlight is rare, with fog and clouds day and night. Rimbach, the closest village with access to the Eckstein site, lies three miles west of the mountain.

Commencing in 1958, the ASA deployed a team to Eckstein on temporary duty each summer to cover annual Soviet-Czech maneuvers along the border. Finally, ASA Field Station Herzo Base, Herzogenaurach, opened a permanent border site, "Detachment K," at Eckstein in the mid-1960's.[109] The Eckstein unit became Detachment N in March 1972 when Field Station Augsburg assumed responsibility for the Rimbach-Eckstein operation from Herzo Base. Retired USAFSS Czechoslovakian linguist Loran Unger discussed Rimbach-Eckstein operations in 2006.

In early 1968, I was a SSgt. (E-5) assigned to the 6915ᵗʰ Security Group, United States Air Force Security Service

(USAFSS) located in Hof, Germany. A team of airmen was being assembled by MSgt. John T. Kamensky to be sent TDY for the summer to a site on Mt. Hoher Bogen outside of the small town of Rimbach, Germany. Mount Hoher Bogen overlooks the Czechoslovak border. This team would be colocated with and supported by a much larger Army contingent out of the U.S. Army Security Agency base at Herzogenaurach, Germany. When I heard of this unit, I lobbied my good friend, John Kamensky, to be included in the mission. So in May, when most of the snow had melted off the mountain, we set off for Rimbach.

Our Air Team consisted of seven people. There were three shifts of two airmen each to man the day and swingshifts while one shift was on break, plus an NCOIC (me.) The Air Force did not work mids at this site. The Army provided us with what is known as a 292 [intercept] van, mounted on the back of a two-and-a-half-ton truck. The Army also provided us with security and communications support. A Captain Phil McGowan commanded the Army and SSgt. (E-6) John Campbell was the Army NCOIC.

The site was rather primitive, with an outhouse for sanitary facilities, concertina wire and cover music for security. The views from Mount Hoher Bogen are some of the most beautiful and breathtaking in Bavaria, indeed in the world. The Army brought drinking water up the hill in a two-wheeled tank trailer, which they called a "water buffalo."

The site was located about a half mile from the Schönblick, which is a local "Gasthaus" (German Pub) popular with hiking tourists. The Army ran a field telephone wire to the Schönblick from the site and lunch orders were called in to the kindly landlady, Frau Wartner, for pick up. I should add that the site was also near a German air force site and tower, which was manned by our German and French counterparts.

The road up the mountainside to the site consisted mostly of a steep one-lane nineteen percent grade with uphill traffic leaving on the hour and downhill traffic on the half hour. The hours of the Army and Air Force shift changes did not coincide, so the Air Force had an ancient camo-colored four-door Dodge Power Wagon for transportation. There was always a question whether it would make it up the steep grade.

As it happens, an Army MP ran into this vehicle with a deuce-and-a-half truck and totaled it. The Air Force then gave us a relatively new Air Force-blue Power Wagon. We were housed in hotels and pensions in Rimbach area and received per diem to cover our food expenses.

The Army had operated this site in the summer for quite a few years. The Air Force also had operated a small air team for at least two years prior to 1968. The Air Team NCOIC in 1967 was TSgt. Joe Gerard, and much of the team came from the 6910th Security Group out of Darmstadt, Germany. I believe Joe got married in 1967 after his summer TDY, so the NCOIC job became available for me in 1968.

In August 1968, Warsaw Pact forces invaded Czechoslovakia to stem the "Prague Spring" reforms of Aleksandr Dubcek. Because of the invasion and the ensuing uncertainties, the U.S. military decided to make the installation permanent. The Army increased the number of personnel many times over, but the Air Force contingent remained at seven airmen. The Hoher Bogen site was too small for the increased new operations, so a new site was selected on another ridge, Mount Eckstein, about a mile from Hoher Bogen.

They installed a "Quonset" style building with two pot-bellied stoves for heat. They also had an indoor latrine with an electric stool to incinerate the solid waste. Luckily, this latrine was on the Army end of the building because at least once a week some prankster would plug up the vent pipe and the entire end of the building would be flooded with malodorous fumes.

I rotated to the States in December 1970 and was assigned to Ft. Meade, Maryland. From there I attended advanced Czech language training at the Defense Language Institute, Presidio of Monterey, California. Then I was sent back to Rimbach, Germany, in June 1972.

6910th Detached Operations—Rimbach

When Loran Unger left Germany in 1970, the 6915th Security Group at Hof managed detached USAFSS personnel at Rimbach. When Unger returned in 1972, he was assigned to OL-JA, 6910th Security Group (Operating Location JA) at Rimbach.

I was the flight commander of Charlie Flight until the unit at Mount Eckstein closed down and moved to Augsburg, Germany, in early 1976. In my 22 years in the Air Force, my two tours in the Rimbach area were far and away the most enjoyable.

6913th SS Reactivated at Rimbach-Eckstein

In the fall of 1971, the 6910th Security Group activated OL-AA, 6910th SG at Rimbach-Eckstein to assume the USAFSS mission formerly performed by airmen from the 6915th SS at Hof Air Station. OL-AA and the colocated ASA unit had their headquarters in the village of Rimbach, while their jointly operated intercept site sat atop Mount Eckstein.

OL-AA became OL-JA, 6910th Security Group in 1972—when the 6910th relocated to Augsburg. Reportedly, OL-JA numbered approximately 65 personnel in 1973.[110] OL-JA was redesignated Det 1, 6910th Security Group in 1973, commanded by Maj. Harold J. Businger. The following year when the 6910th SG was deactivated, Det 1, 6910th became the 6913th Security Squadron with Maj. John T. Lewis as its first commander.

In 1971, the joint Eckstein operations compound consisted of one large Quonset hut and a few H-1 vans. The following year, the vans were grouped around the Quonset hut, and a roof and hallway structure enclosed the work area. Operations personnel could move from one office to another without going outside. Former 6913th Russian linguist Pat Mower, who served at both Rimbach-Eckstein and Augsburg, discussed Eckstein operations and the move to Augsburg in 2006.

Ops at Rimbach was in the Quonset hut. A very small place with five racks along one wall, the search rack at a right angle on the back wall of the hut, a door, then the analysts' desk, then two MOD 28's for OPSCOMM use, then the Czech analyst desk. The Russian analyst desk was right in the middle of the floor between the walls. (It got really cold sitting there, I can tell you!)

According to Mower, the ASA also had some non-Morse (printer) intercept positions and analyst desks in vans outside the Quonset hut. Although in close quarters, the ASA and USAFSS teams operated independently against their separate targets.

Lacking running water on the mountain, "The Hill," as the Ops site was called, was indeed a primitive facility. Water for coffee and hand washing had to be hauled to the site, and the "comfort facilities" were not very comfortable. There was a single, two-hole outhouse and a standup "p*** tube" in a three-sided phone booth-like structure. Ironically, ASA built a small 8-10 person barracks and added a 10,000 gallon water storage tank, septic system and flush toilets at Eckstein towards the end when intercept operations on the mountain was being transferred to Augsburg.

Modernization came to Eckstein in 1974 when ASA transformed the SIGINT site into a La Faire Vite remotely operated facility. Using a new microwave tower for remote control of antennas, operators located 265 km away at Field Station Augsburg performed the intercept mission previously conducted at Eckstein. During a switchover in 1976 while debugging the La Faire Vite system, both old and new operations occurred at the site. Ultimately, Eckstein became an antenna site maintained by maintenance technicians who doubled as security guards.

Getting to Rimbach

Travel to Rimbach, Germany, from Crete was a multifaceted odyssey for SSgt. Mower. Accepting a consecutive overseas tour from Crete, Mower took a car ferry from Crete to Patras, southern Greece, and drove to Piraeus by Athens. From Piraeus he caught an overnight ferry to Bari, Italy, then traveled north through Italy and Austria to Germany. His sponsor at Rimbach, MSgt. Joseph Gerard, provided explicit driving directions for reaching

Rimbach—including specific instructions to go no closer than one kilometer to the German-Czech border.

Just drive north on the Autobahn till you hit Regensburg, Then turn right (east), follow the big road to Furth-Im-Wald, and turn south on the last road before the border. When you get to Rimbach, look for the church. As you pull up across the street from it, that is the "Café Hoher Bogen," and our unofficial NCO Club. The "Pension Silberbauer" is the location for the orderly rooms of both the Army and Air Force.

SSgt. Pat Mower was among the last USAFSS operations personnel to relocate from Rimbach to Augsburg. Jim Brendell led the way in activating the 6913th at Augsburg.

6913TH TRANSFER TO AUGSBURG

Former USAFSS Russian linguist James B. (Jim) Brendell was the first 6913th member assigned to Field Station Augsburg. In 2006, he discussed his assignment at Rimbach and Augsburg.

I left the 6990th [Security Squadron] in March 1974 and was assigned to Det 1, 6910th SG at Rimbach/Mt. Eckstein. After processing thru the '10th at Augsburg, my family was assigned quarters in Regensburg, while I was assigned to Det 1 as a flight commander. Not long afterwards, I was designated the Project Manager for La Faire Vite, and in March/April 1975, I was PCS'd to Field Station Augsburg to establish OL-DA, 6913th SS. Not only was I the first Air Force guy back to FSA, I was the only one for two months.

At FSA I worked with the Army Special Projects Office tasked with planning the integration of the USAFSS mission into FSA. In May or June 1975, I had one CZ [Czech] linguist transferred from Rimbach to OL-DA, as well as one RU [Russian] from Wobeck. All personnel who had been selected for assignment by USAFSS to Rimbach had their orders changed, and by Jul 1975 they were beginning to "show up" at Augsburg. I believe the Rimbach mission was closed down in Jul 1976; OL-DA then became the 6913th SS.

Jim Brendell called his assignments to Rimbach and Augsburg "one of the most unusual experiences of my Air Force career." Retiring from the Air Force in 1980 while assigned at the National Security Agency, he worked for NSA as a civilian for 16 years.

OL-DA, 6913th SS—Augsburg

Retired USAFSS CMSgt. Robert W. Womack was assigned to Operating Location DA, 6913th Security Squadron at Sheridan Kaserne to oversee the move of the 6913th from Rimbach-Eckstein to Augsburg. He discussed the move via email in 2006.

In July 1975, I was assigned directly to Augsburg, Germany, as Superintendent of a detachment of the 6913th. A SMSgt. then, my job there was to take care of operational and logistical matters necessary to facilitate the move of the 6913th from Rimbach/Mt. Eckstein to Augsburg. At the time, I was the senior Air Force member in the Augsburg Military Community. As such I had the dubious pleasure of attending a lot of community meetings with Army colonels and command sergeants major. Fun? I reckon!

With no operating budget, it was beg and borrow (wasn't authorized to steal) from the Army and Navy. Had a great crew helping me. MSgt. James Brendell (now retired) spearheaded issues relative to Operations with Field Station Augsburg. TSgt. Walter Kanavel handled most of the details relative to supplies, equipment, etc. He spoke both German and Spanish and grew up near Detroit with lots of "Bros," so he was in good shape for talking to Army supply folks where most of the civilians were German and a large percentage of the Army troops were Hispanics and Blacks.

He was highly effective in getting them to loan us beds, desks, wardrobes, etc. Plus, they provided vehicles and personnel to help us move it from wherever it was to the NSGA building. Note here that Walt was not a Bro. Also note that there was no base, post or station at Rimbach/Mt. Eckstein. The troops lived in private homes so we needed everything associated with life in the barracks.

To make a long story shorter, the NSG Augsburg contingency had their own building on Sheridan Kaserne, which was about twice as much as they needed for administrative and billeting space. They had already agreed to share the building with the 6913ᵗʰ, so all my troops and I had to do was borrow furniture to set up rooms for the troops and offices for the commander, first sergeant, personnel, etc. All of the Army units in the community let us have enough stuff to do that.

When the 6913ᵗʰ personnel arrived from Rimbach, they had a place to call home. Thanks to Sgt. Brendell, start up of 6913ᵗʰ operations at Field Station Augsburg also went well. Completing his three-year assignment in 1978, Chief Womack returned in 1981, again as squadron operations superintendent. Concluding, he said, "Gotta say I enjoyed every minute of it."

TURNING OUT LIGHTS AT ECKSTEIN

Richard Prokopchuk, a former Czech linguist, joined the USAFSS unit at Rimbach in April 1974 and helped the 6913ᵗʰ turn out the lights in Eckstein operations.

Shutdown came in 1976. We completed it in two waves. The two flights moved first and got the operation up and running. For a period of time there was dual coverage as they compared what the Eckstein site got against what Augsburg was getting via the remote link from that huge array they built at Eckstein. I think it was a month or so later that the remaining two flights migrated.[111]

Pat Mower recalls that the "day ladies and HQ guys" moved to Augsburg with the first group. The 6913ᵗʰ SS closed out intercept activities at Eckstein in mid-1976. The relocation was *deja vu* all over again for USAFSS—new 6913ᵗʰ headquarters was at Sheridan Kaserne, while the squadron moved its operations to Field Station Augsburg.

6913ᵗʰ HQ and Barracks—Sheridan Kaserne

Relocating from Rimbach as part of an advanced party in late 1975, Maj. John J. Reid, squadron commander, set up new 6913ᵗʰ headquarters in a barracks that the unit shared with the Naval

Security Group detachment at Sheridan Kaserne, Augsburg. Roger Smith, former 6913th Russian linguist, lived in the barracks on Sheridan Kaserne for about a month until his wife and kids joined him in on-post family housing.

> *I arrived in Augsburg in July '79. The Sheridan operation was a four story building. The commander's office, first shirt, orderly room and some other support functions plus the NSG billeting was on the first floor. The 2nd and 3rd floors were rooms for single unaccompanied field station troops—all 208's [Air Force linguists]. The top floor was the recreation area and the MARS station at one end of the building. This building was just inside the rear gate to Sheridan Kaserne. Similar buildings nearby housed the US Army field station troops. A sports area (grassy field) separated these billets from an Army armored unit.[112]*

The Naval Security Group detachment also had its orderly room in the lower bay of the barracks, and some called the recreation area on the top deck the NSG *"Pub."* Serving in 6913th operations at Field Station Augsburg (Gablingen Kaserne) as the Chief of Stan/Eval for two years, Roger Smith transferred to Electronic Security Europe (ESE) at Ramstein in February 1982.

The Pub

Operated as a Naval recreational activity, the Navy and Air Force shared the NSG *Pub* which operated on a 24/7 schedule. As explained by former Major (now retired Colonel) Anthony Jensen, who replaced Maj. Reid as 6913th commander in August 1978, the local NSG commander justified beer sales in the *Pub* under a loosely interpreted naval regulation allowing a captain to have alcohol aboard his ship. Perhaps somewhat more subdued than the 6910th *Keller* from the 1972-74 era, the *Pub* was nonetheless a class act. The 6913th held Christmas parties and other special events in the *Pub*, and according to Tony Jensen, it was quite a sight to see the Löwenbräu truck parked outside the barracks while the beer man hauled case after case of the golden suds to the *Pub* on the top deck.

Army Support—Air Force Relations

Relations between the Augsburg Army support units and the Air Force had improved markedly after the 6910th Security Group departed two years earlier. For one thing, the 6913th commander did not outrank the post commandant. In addition, the 6913th was a much smaller organization. The org chart that follows shows the USAFSS Germany-based units for the period January 1975 through 31 July 1979.

USAFSS Germany-based Org Chart January 1975-31 July 1979	
HQ USAFSS Kelly AFB, Texas 1953-1979	
	OL-AB, HQ USAFSS, HQ USAFE/Ramstein AB, Ger.
6911th Scty Sq (M) Hahn AB, Germany 1 Jul '75-31 Jul '79	6912th Scty Sq Berlin, Germany 1975-31 Jul '79
6913th Scty Sq Augsburg, Germany 1975-31 Jul '79	Det 72, 6950th SG Bad Aibling, Germany 1975-1978

This constitutes the Air Force Security Service units that existed in Germany in 1979 when USAFSS was deactivated. To personnel assigned to those units, it was business as usual on 1 August 1979 as their units reported to the new Electronic Security Command. While this book's main emphasis is USAFSS history, it also addresses the history of the successor commands to USAFSS, but in significantly less detail than the USAFSS history. The organization chart that follows shows the Electronic Security Command units located in Germany in 1979.

ESC Germany-based Org Chart—1979	
HQ Electronic Security Command Kelly AFB, Texas 1 Aug 1979-30 Sept 1991	
	ESC HQ Liaison HQ USAFE/Ramstein AB, Ger.
6911th ESG Hahn AB, Germany 1 Aug '79-30 Jun '81	6912th ESG Berlin, Germany 1 Jul '79-15 Jul '88
6913th ESS Augsburg, Germany 1 Aug '79-13 Mar '91	6915th ESS Bad Aibling, Germany 1 Aug '79-30 Sept '93

DET 4, 6911TH ESG—AUGSBURG

By 1979, the Air Force Security Service (and successor Electronic Security Command) had become concerned about having too many SIGINT direct support resources bedded down at Hahn Air Base. With the TGIF about to come on-line at Metro Tango, ESC directed the 6911th Electronic Security Group to find a new home for its ground-based contingency resources. With favorable site survey results in the Augsburg area, the 6911th ESG gained approval to detach its ground-based mobile direct support systems to Flak Kaserne.

These were the "emergency reaction" resources that had formed the nucleus of the squadron when the unit arrived at Hahn AB in 1975. In the spring of 1980, the 6911th activated Detachment 4, 6911th ESG at Flak Kaserne.[113] Jim Riley Jr. made a permanent change of station to Det 4 at Flak in August 1980 and helped integrate an S&W Central terminal into Detachment 4's Comfy Shield mobile system. The org chart for Germany-based ESC units on 31 December 1980 follows.

ESC Germany-based Org Chart—1980	
HQ Electronic Security Command Kelly AFB, Texas 1 Aug 1979-30 Sept 1991	
Electronic Security Europe (ESE) Ramstein, Germany 1 Oct 1980-30 Sept 1986	

6911th ESG Hahn AB, Germany 1 Aug '79-30 Jun '81	6912th ESG Berlin, Germany 1 Jul '79-15 Jul '88
Det 4, 6911th ESG (1 Augsburg, Germany Spring '80-June '81	

6913th ESS (2 Augsburg, Germany 1 Aug '79-13 Mar '91	6915th ESS Bad Aibling, Germany 1 Aug '79-30 Sept '93
(1 Det 4, 6911th ESG merged with 6913th ESS about June 1981.	
(2 6913th ESS reported to 6911th ESG after Det 4, 6911th & 6913th merged.	

Effective 1 July 1981, the 6911th Electronic Security Group was demoted to a squadron-level unit, becoming the 6911th Electronic Security Squadron.

ESE/RAMSTEIN ACTIVATED

On 1 October 1980, Maj. Gen. Larson, ESC commander, activated Electronic Security Europe (ESE) at Ramstein Air Base, with Col. Gary W. O'Shaughnessy as ESE's first commander. The Germany-based ESC units that had previously reported to HQ ESC now reported to Col. O'Shaughnessy.

6913th ESS Relocated to Flak Kaserne

Even before Det 4, 6911th ESG arrived in Augsburg, Electronic Security Command managers began investigating the consolidation of Det 4 and the 6913th ESS into a single squadron to reduce overhead costs. Flak Kaserne had adequate facilities to accommodate both ESC units. In June 1981, Maj. Jensen relocated the 6913th headquarters and billeting from Sheridan to Flak Kaserne—colocating the 6913th with Det 4 of the 6911th.

6913th and Det 4, 6911th Merged

Concurrent with the move of the 6913th to Flak Kaserne, Det 4, 6911th was deactivated. The 6913th absorbed the detachment's resources, creating two separate missions for the squadron. It continued fixed operations at Field Station Augsburg (Gablingen Kaserne), while the unit's newly acquired mobile section staged its operations from Flak Kaserne. According to Roger Smith (Chief of Stan/Eval), mobile operations was housed in two buildings within a fenced compound that also provided space for its S-141 shelters. Mobile ops had an antenna field in a parking lot across from the barracks that became the command section for the 6913th and billets for its troops.

Mobilizers for the S-141 huts, deuce-and-a-half trucks, wreckers and other deployment equipment were parked elsewhere on Flak and generally used only during deployments. The mobile ops huts included an S&W Central/Comfy Shield system, a TSC-57 comms hut and two-three intercept shelters, plus a couple of huts for field analysis/office space. The airmen assigned to mobile operations deployed often, training for contingency operations in the field and participating in exercises.

Comfy Shield S-141 Huts Under Camouflage Canopy

6913TH ESS DEACTIVATED

The 6913th Electronic Security Squadron continued its operations at Gablingen Kaserne for another decade, closing down in 1991.

On 13 March 1991, the command ended over 17 years of operations at Augsburg, Germany, with the inactivation of the 6913th ESS. During its history, the unit provided rapid radio relay, secure communications and command, control and communications countermeasures support to U.S. and allied forces.[114]

6910TH ESW—LINDSEY AS, GERMANY

On 1 July 1981, HQ ESC activated the 6910th Electronic Security Wing at Lindsey AS, Germany, "to perform in-theater planning with USAFE and other service staffs on ESC's C3CM [command, control and communications countermeasures] and tactical intelligence support missions. This included performing peacetime, exercise, contingency and wartime planning for intelligence and C3CM programs/projects."[115] Col. Michael T. Christy, wing commander, and CMSgt. Richard H. Gantzler, senior enlisted advisor, were the first men assigned to the 6910th ESW. Dick Gantzler discussed the activation of the 6910th ESW in 2006.

Colonel Mike Christy was the original commander of the reconstituted 6910th ESW. Mike and I were both in place for the activation. Unfortunately, Mike was not physically there at Lindsey Air Station in Wiesbaden when we had the activation ceremony. He was on emergency leave in Arizona because his mother died. Maj. Gen. Doyle Larson presided at the activation ceremony. By the way, my wife Mary Jane prepared the documents that Larson signed activating the wing. She had some calligraphy skills that Mike wanted to use.

We started on a shoestring. We didn't have furniture or supplies or any accounts set up. In a way it was very much like getting Det 1 of the 6916th up and running in Athens in '68. Luckily, Mike had great connections at NSA, and he had them ship us a bunch of furniture (desks, chairs, *tables, etc). One of our LG [logistics] troops had come to us from a covert organization in the area. He managed to get us ten four-drawer Diebold safes.*

The 6910th ESW was located in a former barracks, and Col. Christy turned the whole 2nd floor—including a latrine and shower—into a special compartmented information facility. Gantzler commented that their SCIF was the only one he was aware of in the command that had a shower—handy for use after jogging over the lunch hour. During his tenure in the 6910th, the wing commanded the 6911th at Hahn, 6913th at Augsburg, 6918th at Sembach and the 6952nd at RAF Alconbury, England. Departing the 6910th ESW during the summer of 1983, Chief Gantzler next served as the senior enlisted advisor to Maj. Gen. James Pfaulz, commander of the Air Force Intelligence Service at Fort Belvoir, Virginia. He retired from the Air Force in 1985. Col. Christy's next tour was at HQ USAF.

Limited data suggest that the 6910th ESW was replaced by the 691st Electronic Security Wing, Lindsey Air Station, on 15 July 1988.[116] Thirty-eight months later (1 October 1991), the 691st ESW appears to have become a detachment of the 26th Intelligence Wing. Located at Ramstein Air Base, the 26th IW was deactivated on 1 June 1993—replaced by the 26th Intelligence Group.[117]

6952ND ESS—RAF ALCONBURY

Although located in the UK, the 6952nd Electronic Security Squadron, RAF Alconbury, came under Col. Christy's 6910th chain of command, in part because the unit supported remoting SIGINT operations to the 6911th ESS at Metro Tango.

The 6952nd ESS, which provided maintenance support for the TR-1 aircraft, was activated at RAF Alconbury, United Kingdom, and assigned to the 6910 ESW, effective 1 January 1982, to ensure all ESC critical support requirements would be in place prior to the Strategic Air Command's TR-1 bed-down at Alconbury in early 1983.[118]

The first TR-1 airframe was deployed to RAF Alconbury, United Kingdom, on 10 February 1983, and the 6952nd ESS entered the era of providing direct support to intelligence operations in Europe. Concurrent with the arrival of the TR-1, U-2R operations in the Central European theater ceased, and ESC U-2R maintenance personnel assigned to the 6988ᵗʰ ESS at RAF Mildenhall, United Kingdom, were transferred to the 6952ⁿᵈ ESS.[119]

TR-1 missions in the European Theater from Alconbury reportedly continued into 1991. The final disposition of the 6952ⁿᵈ Electronic Security Squadron is unknown.

6918ᵀᴴ ESS—SEMBACH AB/GRÜNSTADT

The Electronic Security Command activated the 6918ᵗʰ Electronic Security Squadron at Sembach Air Base/Grünstadt, replacing a detachment of the 6911ᵗʰ Security Squadron at the facility, probably on 1 August 1979. Richard Prokopchuk served with USAFSS/ESC at Sembach from October 1978 to 1982. He said that the unit was OL-HB, 6911ᵗʰ Security Squadron when he arrived. An unofficial USAFSS unit list[120] shows OL-AX, HQ USAFSS at Sembach in 1973. Apparently redesignated OL-HB, 6911ᵗʰ SS in 1975, then Detachment 3, 6911ᵗʰ SS in the first half of 1979, the unit became the 6918ᵗʰ ESS, most likely on 1 August 1979.

6918ᵗʰ ESS Guardrail Support

The 6918ᵗʰ ESS and its predecessor unit at Sembach/Grünstadt was an Air Force direct support unit that operated ground-based intercept positions of the Army Security Agency's Guardrail RU-21 (Beechcraft Super King Air) SIGINT Collection platform. The author was serving in the 6916ᵗʰ Security Squadron at Rhein-Main in 1971 when ASA commenced operational testing of the Guardrail system. The 6916ᵗʰ SS sent MSgt. Gary Hizer and two intercept operators on extended temporary duty to Grünstadt to assist the Army in checking out Guardrail—the beginning of what became 6918ᵗʰ ESS operations at Sembach/Grünstadt in 1979. Rick Prokopchuk, a ground mission supervisor on Guardrail missions, has fond memories of Guardrail operations.

ESC covered exactly half of the voice mission. Army took ground targets and data signals, and we took Air and Air Defense of all types, but mostly tactical air. We manned four positions and one GMS on every mission. We covered the Czech-German border and the German-German borders on different days. One bird would fly essentially north-south, several hundred miles from the second bird, which usually flew east-west.

This enhanced DF capabilities significantly. Usually we flew three two-bird missions a week. The RU-21's were heavily laden with pods of all kinds and various blade and internal antennas. Pilots were mostly captains and warrants stationed with the 330th ASA Company (Forward) in Kaiserslautern. Birds were bedded down at Ramstein. (Often more bedded than MR [mission ready].)

I recall issuing the PMFR [post mission flight report] for one mission where my statement was, "Mission RTB [return to base] at +30 min due to aircraft mission gear door departure from the aircraft in flight." The Army did not appreciate that.

We ALSO had a mobile tactical mission. Operations was three tractor trailers arrayed side by side with a tunnel connecting all three in the center part of the trailer. These and the downlink antennas were packed up and trucked to another location in the event of either an anticipated incoming strike or need to back off or approach the FEBA [forward edge of battle area].

We did much in the red/blue field exercises, alternately supporting one side or the other depending on the phase of the exercise. I recall one mission very well, a Red field commander was on the radio to his troops for about 20 minutes telling his folks they had to be very careful, as the other side had an airborne collection platform with very [effective] DF capability. By the time he was halfway through his info, we had located him within about 100 meters squared, issued the tactical report, and he was a casualty of war within an hour or so. I believe he was also reprimanded for compromise of platform capability.

Lastly, little known fact, we were directly involved with the US General Dozier kidnapping in Italy. We flew a three bird relay mission. One bird tethered at shorter range to the IPF (the integrated processing facility or vans), one over the Alps and one over northern Italy. The third bird was temporarily deployed to Aviano, I believe.

FREEDOM THROUGH VIGILANCE, VOLUME II

Prokopchuk refused on security grounds to discuss the search for Gen. Dozier, stating only that the Guardrail team had been heavily involved. The Italian leftist "Red Brigade" terrorist group kidnapped U.S. Army Brig. Gen. James L. Dozier from his apartment in Verona, Italy, in December 1981. An Italian anti-terrorist special team rescued an unharmed Dozier 42 days later from an apartment in Padua, Italy.

Dick Gantzler recalls that the 6918th was one of four squadrons that reported to the 6910th ESW. Ironically, the 6912th ESS in Berlin (and perhaps the 6915th ESS in Bad Aibling) reported to Electronic Security Europe at Ramstein. The organization chart that follows depicts the Germany-based Electronic Security Command units during the period 1981-1986.

ESC Germany-based Org Chart 1 July 1981-30 September 1986	
HQ Electronic Security Command Kelly AFB, Texas 1 Aug 1979-30 Sept 1991	
Electronic Security Europe (ESE) Ramstein, Germany 1 Oct 1980-30 Sept 1986	
6912th ESG Berlin, Germany 1 Jul '79-14 Jul '88	6915th ESS Bad Aibling, Germany 1 Aug '79-30 Sept '93 (1
6910th ESW Lindsey AS, Germany 1 Jul '81-14 Jul '88	
6911th ESS Hahn AB, Germany 1 Jul '81-1 Apr '93	6913th ESS Augsburg, Germany 1 Aug '79-13 Mar '91
6918th ESS Sembach, Germany 1 Aug '79-30 Sept '86	6952nd ESS (2 Alconbury, England 1 Jan 1982-early 1990's
(1 Replaced by 402nd IS. (2 Although based in the UK, 6952nd ESS reported to 6910th ESW.	

ESC Tactical Assets Consolidated in 6914th ESS

Having served as the 6910th ESW "desk manager" for the 6914th Electronic Security Squadron in the mid-1980's, former USAFSS/ESC COMSEC traffic analyst Carl Traub reminisced about the evolution of that squadron in an email in 2003. His recollection that the 6914th ESS comprised mobile elements of the former 6911th ESS and the 6918th ESS is corroborated by Air Intelligence Agency history.[121]

> *In 1984, the ESC Commander, Major General John B. Marks, directed a concerted staff effort to investigate various strategies which would serve to re-posture and/or realign the command's tactical assets to better support exercise and wartime tasking. An outgrowth of this tasking was a proposal to consolidate the mobile ESC assets located at the 6913th ESS, Flak Kaserne, Augsburg, Germany, with those of the 6918th ESS, Sembach AB, Germany, at the Mehlingen Annex of Sembach Air Base.*
>
> *On 15 April 1985, ESC/CC formally proposed this initiative to USAFE/CV who accepted and approved it on 19 July 1985. This combined unit was to be called the 6914th ESS. On 1 October 1986, the 6918th ESS vacated its Sembach AB location and set up at Mehlingen Annex and was renamed the 6914th ESS. The move of the 6913th ESS (Mobile) from Augsburg to Mehlingen Annex was slated for April 1987.*

With the transfer of 6913th mobile resources from Augsburg to Sembach/Mehlingen, the 6914th ESS became the only mobile ESS in Europe. The 6911th ESS had transferred all its mobile ground contingency resources to the 6913th/Augsburg in 1979-1980. Final disposition of the 6914th ESS is unknown.

6919TH ESS ACTIVATED AT SEMBACH AB

To support Compass Call airborne electronic warfare operations, the Electronic Security Command embedded EW system operators (primarily linguists/voice intercept operators) in a Tactical Air Command electronic combat squadron in Arizona in the early 1980's. When the Air Force directed the activation of a new Compass Call squadron in Germany in 1986, HQ Electronic Security Command created a new electronic security squadron rather than embed its ESC personnel in a newly activated USAFE electronic combat squadron.

On 28 March 1986, Major General Martin approved 6919th ESS as the designator for the new ESC Compass Call squadron, and on the same day USAFE transferred 109 manpower billets to ESC effective 1 October 1986. USAFE agreed to provide ESC all facilities and equipment required to support the USAFE Compass Call mission.[122]

On 1 October 1986, ESC's European Electronic Security Division activated the 6919th Electronic Security Squadron at Sembach Air Base under the command of Lt. Col. Ron Duncan. Flying aboard USAFE EC-130H Compass Call aircraft, 6919th aircrews provided the USAFE commander with electronic warfare support. Alan Daugherty, a Russian linguist who served with the 6911th at Metro Tango and Det 1, 6910th ESW, Lindsey Air Station, talked about Compass Call operations in 2006.

Mission was jamming enemy communications, but [Compass Call missions] were mainly accredited with fratricide when they were too close to the RJ [Rivet Joint] or Comfy Levi. The mainly linguist crew was overseen by a mission commander. Their main weapon was brute force jamming that effectively blocked any intercept of the target. Blew the hell out of Gen. Larson's proscribed theories as to how targets should be handled— monitor/exploit, spoof, jam, or destroy.

Retired USAFSS/ESC CMSgt. James (Jimmy) Mayer discussed the genesis of the 6919th and Compass Call activities in 2006. As described by Chief Mayer, Compass Call EC-130 operations originated at Davis-Monthan AFB, Arizona, with Electronic Security Command SIGINT aircrew members assigned directly to the Air Force using command.

The flying unit that we linguists were assigned to was the 41st ECS (Electronic Combat Squadron) under TAC (Tactical Air Command). I got there in 1982. Believe the unit was officially brought on board in 1981. Jim Dillingham [a former ESC special signals intercept operator] was the Ops superintendent, and a Col. Bernard (first name escapes me) was the commander.

Detachment 2, 67th Intelligence Group (ESC) provided our training, order of battle, etc. The Det 2 guys flew with us and were qualified on the aircraft. Ed Truelson was one of Det 2's commanders. Bob Lambert and Charlie McCranie were a couple of the first linguists assigned to the 41st.

The 67th IG was colocated with HQ ESC at Kelly AFB, Texas. The transfer of Air Force cryptologic aircrews to the Tactical Air Command constituted a first for ESC. Previously, cryptologic aircrew members had flown on aircraft belonging to other commands but had remained assigned to USAFSS or ESC.

41ST ECS AND 43RD ECS

While assigned to the 41st ECS, the aircrews learned electronic warfare techniques and gained experience during joint forces exercises and training flights. Then in 1990, the 41st deployed to Riyadh, Saudi Arabia, and supported combat operations during the Persian Gulf War (Desert Storm). The 6919th sent a few operators (Arabic linguists) to Saudi Arabia to assist the 41st ECS in the war.

USAF Photo

EC-130 Compass Call Aircraft over West Germany, 1986

When the Air Force transferred Compass Call EC-130H aircraft and aircrews to Sembach in 1986, the "back-enders" (SIGINT crews) were reassigned to the newly activated 6919th ESS. The EC-130's, front-end crews and support personnel were assigned to a newly activated 43rd Electronic Combat Squadron. The Electronic Security Command carried out a major reorganization, aligning most of its field units under operational wings in 1988.

Shown in the organization chart below are ESC's Germany-based ESC units subsequent to the reorganization.

ESC Germany-based Org Chart 1 Oct 1986-30 Sept 1991
HQ Electronic Security Command Kelly AFB, Texas 1 Aug 1979-30 Sept 1991
European Electronic Security Division (EESD) Ramstein, Germany 1 Oct 1986-30 Sept '91

690th ESG Berlin, Germany 11 Jun '91-1 Jul '92	6915th ESS Bad Aibling, Germany 1 Aug '79-30 Sept '93

691st ESW (1 Lindsey AS, Germany 15 Jul '88-30 Sept '91

6911th ESS Hahn AB, Germany 1 Jul 81-1 Apr 93	6913th ESS Augsburg, Germany 1 Aug 79-13 Mar 91

6914th ESS Sembach, Germany, Mehlingen Annex 1 Oct 86-(1991)	6919th ESS Sembach, Germany 1 Oct 86-21 May 91

6952nd ESS (2 Alconbury, England 1 Jan 82-early 1990's	
(1 ESC reorganized most of its units under operational wings in 1988. (2 Although based in the UK, 6952nd ESS reported to 691st ESW.	

Arriving at Sembach in 1989, Jimmy Mayer served as 6919th operations superintendent. In January 1991, the 6919th deployed with three Compass Call aircraft to Incirlik AB, Turkey. Commencing with the outbreak of the bombing campaign, during Desert Storm combined 43rd ECS/6919th Compass Call aircrews conducted EC missions abeam northern Iraq.

The Turkish government had denied the U.S. Air Force permission to deploy EC-130 aircraft to Incirlik earlier. A brief history of Sembach Air Base provides a synopsis of Compass Call operations at the base without any mention of the 6919th ESS.

> *Sembach gained an electronic combat mission when the 65th Air Division and the subordinate 66th Electronic Combat Wing stood up on 1 June 1985. The 43rd ECS activated under the 66th ESW on 1 October 1986 with EC-130H Compass Call aircraft for which a high-security facility and special maintenance hangars were built in the eastern dispersal loop. Following the withdrawal of their aircraft after Desert Storm, the 43rd ECS inactivated on 31 July 1991.[123]*

Following its departure from Germany, the 43rd Electronic Combat Squadron was reactivated at Davis-Monthan, with many of the linguists who had served with the 6919th being transferred to the 43rd ECS in Arizona.

6919TH ESS DEACTIVATED

Electronic Security Command history addresses the shutdown of the 6919th Electronic Security Squadron.

> *On 25 April 1991, the 6919th ESS flew its last operational mission, closing out another chapter in the proud history of ESC airborne operations. The 6919th ESS was inactivated on 21 May 1991 at Sembach AB, Germany.[124]*

The same month, Jimmy Mayer transferred to the 6988th Electronic Security Squadron at RAF Mildenhall, England.

GERMANY-BASED AFIC UNITS

On 1 October 1991, HQ Air Force activated the Air Force Intelligence Command at Kelly AFB and deactivated the Electronic Security Command.[125] The fall of the Berlin Wall had expedited the drawdown of ESC squadrons in Germany. The organization chart that follows shows Cold War-era Germany-based units that AFIC inherited from ESC.

AFIC Germany-based Org Chart 1 Oct 1991-30 Sept 1993	
HQ Air Force Intelligence Command Kelly AFB, Texas 1 Oct 1991-30 Sept 1993	
26th Intelligence Wing * Ramstein, Germany 1 Oct 1991-30 Jun 1994	
690th ESG Berlin, Germany 11 Jun '91-1 Jul '92	6911th ESS Hahn AB, Germany 1 Jul '81-1 Apr '93
6914th ESS Sembach, Germany, Mehlingen Annex 1 Oct 86-(1991)	6915th ESS Bad Aibling, Germany 1 Aug '79-30 Sept '93
* Replaced EESD as senior Air Force cryptologic unit in Europe.	

AFIC existed a mere two years—a period of transition from a Cold War-era major air command to a smaller field operating agency. The 26th Intelligence Wing/Ramstein AB was activated on 1 October 1991, replacing the European Electronic Security Division that was deactivated. With the dissolution of the Soviet Union, three of AFIC's four Germany-based Cold War-era intercept units (6911th and 6914th ESS, plus the 690th ESG) no longer had viable missions and were deactivated. The 690th ESG turned out the lights at its facility in Berlin on 1 July 1992, the 6911th ceased operations at Hahn on 1 April 1993, and the 6914th departed Sembach probably in 1991.

The fourth site, 6915th ESS/Bad Aibling, tuned its overhead satellite receivers to new mission assignments and continued serving the U.S. cryptologic community. Ironically, the 6915th ESS was the only Cold War-era Air Force SIGINT intercept unit to continue operating in Germany beyond 1993. A brief history of Germany-based Air Intelligence Agency units follows.

GERMANY-BASED AIA UNITS—1993

With Air Intelligence Agency replacing Air Force Intelligence Command on 1 October 1993, the remainder of this chapter addresses the history of AIA support to USAFE operations in Europe.[126].

26TH IG/RAMSTEIN

When Air Intelligence Agency stood up in 1993, its senior authority in Europe was the 26th Intelligence Group, Ramstein Air Base, Germany. Replacing the 26th Intelligence Wing that was deactivated on 30 June 1993,[127] the 26th IG controlled six squadrons in Europe and by the mid-1990's was embedding AIA specialists in the USAFE organizations that the 26th supported.

An article in the Air Intelligence Agency *Spokesman* magazine in 1999 does an excellent job of showing how airmen of the 26th IG and USAFE worked as a warfighting team. It lays out the mission of the 26th IG and the role that the group's personnel played in Allied operations against Serbia and while monitoring for violations of the northern "no-fly zone" of Iraq during 1998 and 1999. Early in the article, the writer cited changes in Air Force cryptologic forces in Europe since the end of the Cold War.

In addition to several name changes to the organization itself, the number of personnel has been reduced by about 4000, and the number of major units has been reduced from ten to the current 26th IG structure, comprising six squadrons, three detachments and five operating locations. These reductions occurred as part of the overall European drawdown. Even though the numbers have drastically changed, the impact of AIA forces remains key as they provide critical products, data and services to their European warfighting partners.

There are 900 members assigned to the 26th IG and over 90 percent are dedicated enlisted experts. This highly-trained force is comprised of nearly 50 Air Force Specialty Codes, including 14 languages.

The units are located in seven countries, with activities and operations throughout 25 countries. The group's six *squadrons and locations are: 26th Intel Support Squadron,* *colocated with the group headquarters, Ramstein Air* *Base, Germany; 402nd IS, Bad Aibling Station, Germany;* *426th IS, Vogelweh, Germany; 451st IS, Royal Air Force* *Menwith Hill, United Kingdom; 485th IS, Mainz-Kastel* *Station, Germany; and 488th IS, RAF Mildenhall, United* *Kingdom.*

Close Integration With Warfighters

As expressed by group commander Col. Gary Selin, the 26th IG was especially proud of the extent to which its forces were integrated into European theater commands—a trait that held true with other AIA forces in other theaters.

We perform our mission by totally integrating with our *European warfighting partners. Everyone in the group has* *worked extremely hard to become an integral part of the* *team they work with day-to-day. The results are readily* *apparent and our people directly contributed to the* *success of the [Kosovo] air war.*

The professional team members of the group do not wait *until the shooting starts to become involved. The very* *nature of the mission means they are involved in the* *planning and spin-up as well as the actual shooting. In* *fact, members of the group were involved in these kind of* *activities for over a year before the air war over the* *former Republic of Yugoslavia began 24 March 1999.*

Using the Kosovo air war and no-fly zone air patrols as a backdrop, the author of the *Spokesman* article highlighted the role of 26th IG elements in integrated operations.

26TH INTEL SUPT SQUADRON

Working as an integral part of a USAFE team, the 26th Intelligence Support Squadron began planning for intervention in Kosovo in March 1998.

26th ISS operations personnel started working in the 32nd *Air Intelligence Squadron alongside the USAFE* *Operations and Intelligence personnel developing target* *folders and intelligence, surveillance and reconnaissance requirements for the air campaign.*

USAFE targeteers and 26th ISS/DOI [operations intelligence] analysts developed critical command and control nodes and other targets. Experienced aircrew personnel from the 26th ISS and the 488th IS worked with USAFE reconnaissance planners to develop requirements for ISR support and aircrew augmentation.

The team completed initial plans by the end of March, but into the summer, 26th IG personnel participated almost daily in refining the plans. The pace slackened by July, with occasional "ramp-ups" throughout the next eight months.

Of course, air campaign planning was not the only task on the horizon. Since Desert Storm ended, Iraq was continually testing limits of the no-fly zone restrictions, prompting preparation for the deployment of Rivet Joint RC-135 aircraft to Incirlik AB, Turkey, to support Operation Northern Watch (ONW). The 26th ISS provided crucial augmentation of communications and logistics to support Rivet Joint operations from Incirlik.

This was the first time in the last nine years the Rivet Joint had deployed to a non-fixed, forward-deployed location. To help the 488th IS accomplish their mission, several 26th ISS communications experts deployed to Turkey and developed robust classified and unclassified communication networks in less than three weeks. . . . .

The 26th ISS logisticians worked around the clock with EUCOM, AIA and the 488th IS to deploy RC-135 maintenance shelters critical to the logistics requirements of RJ assets in theater.

The 488th IS flew 25 RJ missions and issued over 90 imminent threat warning calls to allied airmen at ONW before their aircrews and support personnel were recalled from Turkey to Mildenhall to participate in Allied Force. It was quite an accomplishment moving the most complicated "recce" platform in the business on such short notice, while still providing threat-warning services to strikes at a moment's notice in multiple theaters.

The 488th Intelligence Squadron operations officer, Capt. John Proctor, credited the 26th ISS technicians as being the "catalysts" to the success of the Northern Watch deployment.

These outstanding airmen improved the communications capability of the ONW Intelligence Directorate, brought a real-time air picture to the desk of the 39th Operations Group commander and provided hands-on training for 39th Communications Squadron personnel–all in 20 days.

During the opening days of the Kosovo air war, 26th ISS personnel provided crucial augmentation to the USAFE Intelligence Operations Center.

Their integration into headquarters USAFE resulted in all-source intelligence fusion for situational awareness, near-real-time threat warning, force protection, collection management and ISR planning/scheduling.

The hard work immediately paid off as one of the group's youngest airmen, A1C Heather Duvall, jumped into the fray to brief the USAFE commander, Gen. John Jumper, in a blow-by-blow account of nightly flight activity.

This was the first of many contributions made by the integrated team. The team's dedication throughout the crisis contributed to direct kills of radar and SAM systems, the passage of mission-critical data to Compass Call, efficient planning and selection of C4I [command, control, communications, computer and intelligence] targets, and up-to-the-minute situational awareness for commanders and national decision makers.

As explained by 26th ISS commander Lt. Col. Felipe Alonso, the 26th made significant contributions to the air war by bringing critical skill sets to the fight that would not have otherwise been available to USAFE.

426TH IS/OPSEC AND TECH EXPLOITATION

By the mid-1990's, communications security monitoring gave way to full-fledged multinode Electronic Security Systems Assessment (ESSA) operations—monitoring radio traffic, phone calls, email, fax and other computer traffic.[128] The 426th

Intelligence Squadron provided operations security and communications security monitoring, plus technical exploitation of enemy systems during the campaign.

> *Long before bombs dropped on Belgrade, the men and women of Electronic Systems Security Assessment Central-Europe, 426th IS, Vogelweh, Germany, were busy participating in EUCOM [European Command] operations.*
>
> *Last fall as the theater prepared to grapple with the latest Kosovo crisis, ESSAC-EUR went to work monitoring telephone calls, emails, and faxes to assess the types and amounts of planning information available to adversaries. They were key to providing operational security to all theater combatants.*
>
> *Augmented by individuals deployed from various AIA units in the CONUS and Pacific, the 426th IS stepped up its information protect role. Electronic Systems Security Assessment teams immediately deployed to three locations in-theater and shifted the in-house monitoring of HQ USAFE already being performed for ONW.*
>
> *Realizing events might quickly overwhelm the capabilities of ESSAC-EUR, adjustments were made to handle the huge manpower and dollar demands. Software written by SSgt. Thomas Forward and hardware innovations by TSgt. John King and SSgt. Anthony Mesenbrink permitted a fully-automated system of call packaging and transfer via secure means to ESSAC-EUR.*

Using the newly created message transfer capabilities, the forward-deployed teams sent hundreds of calls back to the 426th in near-real time for processing, analysis and reporting. The 692nd Intelligence Support Squadron (later 352nd Information Operations Squadron) and the 68th Intelligence Squadron operated ESSAC-PAC and ESSAC-CON, respectively.

> *Upon re-evaluation of EUCOM and USAFE OPSEC needs, four more locations were added to the 426th ESSAC tasking. Despite system improvements, ESSAC-EUR again was reaching its limits. With assistance from the 26th ISS and 488th IS, the 426th pioneered a worldwide networked*

defensive information operations capability. By May, data from several monitoring locations was being sent to ESSAC-PAC at Hickam AFB, Hawaii, and ESSAC-CON, Brooks AFB, Texas, for processing and analysis while ESSAC-EUR continued to process three sites and performed collection management and centralized reporting. By the end of the air war, ESSAC-EUR and its sister units had collected and analyzed over 300,000 telephone calls, 150,000 emails, and 2,000 faxes. . . . . ESSA products and services were available to the warfighter on time, on target, on demand.

According to 426th IS commander Lt. Col. Robert Piacine, the decision to execute major combat operations literally hinged on the nature of their products and recommendations. And 426th Intelligence Squadron contributions were not limited to ESSA activities.

The 426th Science and Technology branch was instrumental in providing technical expertise for the operation. When two MiG-29 fighters were shot down during the opening days of the Kosovo air war, two S&TI [scientific & technical intelligence] engineers deployed to the wreckage area to assess the aircraft, weapons loads, and equipment condition, all for the purpose of determining the readiness status of the Serbian air force.

Later, six engineers, including the group commander's executive officer, were deployed to Bosnia to assist during inspections of military equipment held in Bosnian cantonment sites. These inspections were conducted to ensure Bosnian Serbs were not manufacturing equipment or subassemblies and spare parts for transfer to Serbian forces in and around Kosovo.

To facilitate future short-notice requirements, the S&T section established a Scientific and Technical Intelligence Liaison Officer position on the SFOR CJ2 [NATO-led Stabilization Force in Bosnia Combined Joint Intelligence and Security] staff, able to provide immediate assistance to SFOR, as well as coordinate the deployment of more robust teams as needed.

"The S&TI teams did a superb job keeping our warfighters apprised of the Yugoslav threat—their analysis of the MiG-29 shoot downs, for example, prevented technological surprise and contributed directly to the determination of the aircraft's intentions," said Piacine.

Summing up his squadron's success, Col. Piacine commended his troops for devising a new concept on the fly and succeeding beyond expectations.

I'm extremely proud of the major operational role played by the 426th IS during Operation Allied Force. Our offensive counter-information, defensive counter-information, and information in war personnel were in the middle of the fight from beginning to end.

488TH IS—OPERATION ALLIED FORCE

Highly visible during operations in Kosovo, the 488th Intelligence Squadron provided 26th Intelligence Group contributions in the air.

The primary job of the 488th IS was to protect aircrews and act as a communications platform. One of the most important jobs the Rivet Joint did was to assist in combat search and rescue efforts. Because of their altitude, robust communications suite, and endurance, the RJ crews played a vital part in both the F-117 and F-16 operations [search for downed F-117 and F-16 crewmen].

At the peak, the 488th IS had four jets and six separate crews on station, providing the perfect blend to accomplish the mission. This was a team effort with linguists from different languages and areas of responsibilities participating in this operation.

Squadron members flew over 100 RJ missions (averaging two missions per day), provided 1,000 hours of on-watch time, issued 53 threat calls and provided direct targeting information for Operation Allied Force. During Allied Force, the 488th IS had over 30 augmentees, including airborne linguists, analysts, and communications experts, at different times involved in unit operations.

AIA commander Maj. Gen. John R. Baker hailed the aircrews for their "contributions" and for "proving invaluable to the success of this important operation." Baker also noted their "performance is a testimony to the dedication, devotion to duty, and selfless sacrifices of world-class airmen."

Lt. Col. James Poss, 488th IS commander, spoke effusively about his aircrews.

I couldn't have been more proud of my troops—especially my linguists and airborne maintenance technicians. This was an air war we did right—Able Flight was spot-on with their training and analysis of the Serbs, our LG folks handled double our normal maintenance load, plus juggling three different RJ baselines at once, and my SC folks did some of the fastest circuit and computer upgrades I've seen.

"It really showed the advantages of forward-based forces tightly integrated with USAFE and NATO. We wouldn't have done nearly as well if we had to deploy in from the states and fight this one from a "cold start," said Poss.

The 402nd, 451st and 485th Intelligence Squadrons played a less conspicuous, but certainly no less significant role during the air war.

402ND IS SUPPORT TO KOSOVO AIR WAR

Operating as part of a joint service team at Bad Aibling, the 402nd Intelligence Squadron responded to both national level and theater intelligence requirements.

Squadron personnel at the 402nd IS produced about 500 tailored, commander-driven, national- and tactical-level product reports during Operation Allied Force.

They provided critical force protection and indications and warning intelligence to deployed U.S., multinational, and NATO forces. As part of a joint service reporting cell, squadron members worked more than 2,500 man-hours accomplishing around-the-clock reporting mission and 1,100 man-hours maintaining the Senior Watch Officer and Senior Intelligence Analyst positions, leading national-mission collection assets for tactical customers and commanders.

Himself a former voice intercept operator, Lt. Col. Paul Gifford, 402nd IS commander, had hands-on experience in high-intensity tactical SIGINT direct support operations. As a Korean linguist, he flew reconnaissance missions against North Korea during the U.S.S. Pueblo incident in 1968. He had also flown recon missions for three years over the Adriatic Sea as a Serbo-Croatian voice intercept operator, and served on extended temporary duty with Rivet Joint crews in Saudi Arabia. Lurking in the background at Bad Aibling, he entrusted his NCO's to get the job done, and they didn't disappoint the "boss." Comments for the *Spokesman* article expressed his pride in 402nd support to Operation Allied Force.

I was deeply impressed with how our personnel used state-of-the-art technologies to gain and exploit a broad spectrum of information previously not available, then worked with theater planners to focus this effort to fit the overall battle plan.

451ST IS SUPPORT TO KOSOVO AIR WAR

Like the 402nd IS, the 451st Intelligence Squadron in England supported Operation Allied Force as part of a joint service team.

Participation by the 451st IS, part of a multiservice team on Menwith Hill Station, was diverse with broad-sweeping impact. Their contributions led to the successful evacuation of thousands of Americans and foreign nationals threatened by coups or civil unrest. They provided national- and tactical-level commanders with timely intelligence on threat systems and capabilities used by an array of high-priority threat nations.

Squadron members issued time-sensitive reports that provided a clear and accurate picture to warfighters. These airmen brought their USAF mindset and experience to the forefront of a multiservice, multinational operations workforce to ensure NATO fliers and mission planners received the right information at the right time to conduct their missions as accurately and safely as possible.

The 451st commander was Lt. Col. Rich Osgood. He was proud of the manner in which the 451st refocused its normal day-to-day national mission "to meet immediate, critical theater needs."

485TH IS SUPPORT TO KOSOVO AIR WAR

Colocated and teaming with the European Technical Center at Mainz-Kastel, Germany, the 485th Intelligence Squadron quietly established itself as a vital player in the air war.

On any given day, 485th IS technicians were deployed to Cryptologic Service Groups throughout the theater installing, maintaining or upgrading secure communications equipment. They worked hard to ensure vital data was getting through the vast network of communications systems, with the heart of it all centered at the European Technical Center.

Commenting that the public would never know about his squadron's role in the fight, Maj. Joseph Shannahan repeatedly received thanks and kudos for the job "our troops were doing." He took great pride, knowing that their actions had positively impacted the outcome of the air war.

26th IG and Operation Joint Guardian

At the end of the air war, the focus of the 26th Intelligence Group shifted to assisting with Operation Joint Guardian—a follow-on NATO effort to facilitate a lasting peace in the Balkans. The 26th team (and its successor unit) remains active in Kosovo on a peace monitoring mission to this day. Meanwhile, during Operation Joint Guardian the U.S. Army announced plans to deactivate Field Station Bad Aibling.

RETURN TO DARMSTADT

The American exit from Bad Aibling followed earlier cost-cutting steps taken by the Department of Defense in 1998 when INSCOM relocated its 66th Military Intelligence Group from Field Station Augsburg to Darmstadt. While most INSCOM resources moved from Augsburg to Darmstadt, some of the 66th MI Group had transferred to Bad Aibling. The U.S. military bade farewell to Augsburg.[129] The departure from Bad Aibling station marked the end of U.S. SIGINT operations in Bavaria. The *Stars and Stripes* newspaper (European edition) addressed the move in October 2003.[130]

> **GRIESHEIM, Germany**—*Some of the U.S. Army intelligence assets currently in southern Germany's Bad Aibling will move north to Darmstadt.*
>
> *About 150 soldiers from the 66th Military Intelligence Group will head to Darmstadt by next summer, according to Capt. George Hammar, a spokesman for the group. The Bad Aibling base, about 20 miles north of the Austrian border, is scheduled to close on 30 Sept. 2004. . . . .*
>
> *The Army announced in May 2001 that Bad Aibling would close by September 2002. The planned closing was postponed after the terror attacks of 11 September 2001. But the work to relocate to Darmstadt went ahead as planned. A 2,500-foot expansion of the unit's Dagger Complex in Darmstadt was completed. Office space at the Nathan Hale Depot has been renovated.*
>
> *Hammar said the 66th MIG's move was not related to the upcoming installation of satellite systems at the nearby August-Euler Airfield in Griesheim. "The radars have nothing to do with the group or INSCOM," Hammer said, referring to the U.S. Army Intelligence and Security Command. "That is specifically a Navy asset."*
>
> *U.S. Naval Forces Europe, in London, issued a statement Monday saying the satellite equipment is being moved from Bad Aibling to Darmstadt because of the closing of Bad Aibling. The equipment serves various commands, according to the statement, and should be relocated by next summer.*

While the residents of Rosenheim, the village by Bad Aibling, mourned the economic loss of the Americans leaving their area, the local Griesheim villagers staged a protest against their new neighbors. As addressed in the *Stars and Stripes*, arrival of the huge dome-covered antennas caused an uproar among local residents in March 2004.[131]

A controversial U.S. Navy communications relay—a transmitter and four green globes housing satellite receivers—arrived last week at an airfield bordering a town that fears the site may be radioactive or engaged in illegal espionage.

The military has assured the town that its "Icebox" project is both safe for neighbors and serves a noble purpose. Many local residents, though, remain skeptics. "The people are very angry and they are anxious," said Griesheim Mayor Norbert Leber.

Believing the project to be part of the *Echelon* electronic eavesdropping system, local Griesheim residents wanted the effort moved to a more rural area. The brouhaha started in 2003 when the military announced it would move "a relay" from Bad Aibling to August-Euler Airfield, and the city of Darmstadt approved the plan without consulting Griesheim. Deutsche Telekom studied the equipment and found it safe—there are no known health concerns.

The *Stars and Stripes* pointed out that the joint communications center at Menwith Hill in England has historically grappled with similar protests. With the Army pointing out that the U.S. Navy, Europe, London, runs the operation, the Navy in London did not return phone calls. Local protests have subsided, and low-key "Navy communications relay" operations proceeded at Griesheim.

It is no coincidence that this new field station is known as "Local Training Area 6910 (Dagger Complex)."[132] In 1951, the U.S. Air Force Security Service built the operations building currently used by the 66th MI Gp, and the 6910th Security Group and subordinate USAFSS units called the Griesheim facility home from 1951-1972.

With Detachment 1, 693rd ISR Group currently sharing the U.S. Navy facility at August-Euler Airfield, Griesheim, the Air Force ISR Agency (current successor to USAFSS) has returned to Security Service's 2nd Radio Squadron Mobile's roots in Darmstadt.

CHAPTER FIVE

USAFSS OPERATIONS
—SOUTHERN EUROPE AND MIDDLE EAST

During 1949 and 1950, the United States Air Force Security Service devoted most of its efforts to establishing intercept sites covering communist targets in Eastern Europe and the Far East. A major area with inadequate coverage was the Crimea and southern Russia, and USAFSS worked feverishly on issues related to the deployment of radio squadrons mobile in North Africa, Turkey and Greece. By the late 1950's, this expanded coverage included the activation of Security Service units in Pakistan and Italy.

Brooks AFB, Texas, was abuzz activating, staffing and equipping new RSM's, including squadrons that ultimately deployed SIGINT collection capabilities to Libya and Turkey in 1951. In addition to shortages of trained operations personnel and intercept receivers, USAFSS had few options with regard to suitable locations for intercept sites on the southern periphery of the Soviet Union.

34TH RSM ACTIVATED—APRIL 1951

Wheelus Air Base, Libya, got the nod to host Security Service's 34th Radio Squadron Mobile. The U.S. Air Force controlled Wheelus, and the USAF host unit at Wheelus had adequate logistics resources in place to support a USAFSS RSM. A hearability test by a USAFSS team at the base confirmed excellent reception of signals emanating from Russia.

Located outside of Tripoli (Libya's capital), Wheelus Air Base was situated on the Mediterranean coast of North Africa. A former Italian airfield that the British Eighth Army captured in 1943, Wheelus was a U.S. Air Force Strategic Air Command forward operating location for SAC B-50's, B-36's, KC-97's and KC-29's during the 1950's and 60's.

USAFE tactical aircrews from England and Germany also frequented the base for gunnery and bombing training at a nearby range. After Muammar Gaddafi came to power in a military coup in 1969, the USAF handed over the base to the Libyan government in June 1970, and the Libyans renamed the base Uqba bin Nafi Airfield.

Contributed by Richard Kisling

Richard D Kisling, Tripoli, 1951, USAFSS CMSgt./Senior Enlisted Advisor (1969-71) and CMSAF (1971-1973)

Headquarters USAFSS activated the 34th Radio Squadron Mobile under the command of Maj. James O. Netherland at Brooks AFB, Texas, on 27 April 1951.[133] Later in the year, the 34th RSM relocated to Wheelus. The command formed the nucleus of the squadron at Brooks and filled in the unit's manpower requirements with new recruits and by drawing on personnel assigned to the 2nd RSM and 12th RSM in Germany. In 1955, the 34th RSM was redesignated the 6934th Radio Squadron Mobile. Under a series of unit designator changes, USAFSS operations continued at Wheelus for a decade.

In a VFW Magazine article in 1998, William H. Brown, who served in the 6934th RSM in 1955-56, commented that the squadron "copied most everything out of Russia, all the way to the Vladivostok submarine pens in the Sea of Japan."[134] Brown also stated that he had observed Russians at a distance "with field glasses watching all flights taking off and landing" at Wheelus.

The Tripoli, Libya, area is known for its severe weather. Surrounded by 1,000 miles of desert on three sides, Wheelus experienced temperatures of 110-120 degrees during sandstorms, as Brown recalls. One of the truly remote facilities for which USAFSS was well known over the years!

EARLY USAFSS OPS IN TURKEY

The shroud of secrecy surrounding USAFSS operations in Turkey was comparable to that involved in Detachment D, 2nd RSM intercept activities in Berlin during the early 1950's. Turkey's alliance with the West after World War II had been precipitated by Soviet threats against Turkey, and a tenuous East-West détente ruled against the official stationing of U.S. intelligence gathering forces in Turkey. Instead, USAFSS intercept operators and analysts served incognito in Turkey, officially assigned as "logistics specialists" assisting in the modernization of the Turkish air force. The first USAFSS contingent in Turkey was assigned to the Joint American Military Mission for Aid to Turkey-U.S. Air Force Group (JAMMAT-USAFG) in Ankara in 1951.

The USAFSS team that arrived in 1951 consisted of Morse intercept operators, ELINT intercept operators, Russian linguists, analysts, radio maintenance technicians and a couple of teletype communicators. Initially, the USAFSS-Ankara intercept station included three Morse and one voice intercept positions. The airmen established the first USAFSS intercept station within the JAMMAT-USAFG facilities. Assigned to JAMMAT for support, the USAFSS-Ankara team reported operationally to the 6910th Security Group in Germany.

Retired Air Force Senior Master Sergeant George Barthel was among the first USAFSS cadre assigned to the JAMMAT-USAFG. He arrived in Ankara in October 1951 as a SSgt. after completing traffic analysis school at Brooks AFB, Texas. Maj. William Dacko and Capt. Carl Asmussen were the commander and communications officer, respectively. A few other USAFSS men were already in place in Ankara when Barthel arrived. In addition to their intercept mission, the USAFSS-Ankara team was heavily involved in establishing detachments at Samsun and Trabzon—small Turkish cities on the Turkish coast on the Black Sea.

First USAFSS Units in Turkey

The first officially acknowledged USAFSS unit in Turkey appears to have been Detachment 1, 75th Radio Squadron Mobile. This unit began operations as Project Penn in the JAMMAT area in Ankara in September 1951.[135] (Det 1, 75th RSM operated covertly in Turkey, and no other details on the detachment are available prior to 1951.) Another USAFSS unit associated with Ankara (in 1953) was Detachment 1, 14th RSM. George Barthel received orders assigning him to Det 1, 14th RSM on 1 May 1953—he remembers being assigned only to the JAMMAT prior to being assigned to Det 1, 14th RSM at Ankara. The following month (20 June 1953), George was reassigned in place to Det 1, 75th RSM. He rotated from Ankara to HQ USAFSS, Kelly AFB, in November 1953. A Detachment 1, 75th RSM Personnel Action Memorandum dated 23 September 1953 listed the rank, name and job title of most, if not the entire, Det 1 staff—a total of 99 assigned Air Force personnel. Key personnel on that PAM are listed below.

Det 1, 75th RSM Key Personnel—1953			
Rank	Name	Title	Remarks
Maj.	Dacko, William	Commander	
Capt.	Asmussen, Carl B.	Comm Officer	
1st Lt.	Smith, Conrad H.	Adjutant	
MSgt.	Langenkamp, Arthur B.	NCOIC, Admin Section	Plus 3 admin spec
MSgt.	Coleman, Albert W.	NCOIC, Comm Center	Plus 4 crypto ops
TSgt.	Bohn, Frank L.	NCOIC, Technical Svcs	Plus 4 radio maint.
A1C	Davis, George J.	Supply Specialist	
MSgt.	Fedyshyn, Stanley N.	NCOIC, R/T Russian lg	Plus 25 Russian lg
MSgt.	Palagi, Roland	NCOIC, Intercept Ctrl	Plus 51 Morse ops
TSgt.	Barthel, George G. E.	NCOIC, Traffic Analysis	Plus 3 Analysts

Both the 75th RSM and 14th RSM were activated at Brooks AFB in 1951—the 14th RSM in October and the 75th on an unknown date. The 8th RSM assisted in the activation of the 14th at Brooks, providing housing for 14th personnel when the squadron stood up.[136] The 14th RSM was reportedly training at Brooks for intercept duty on Cyprus, but the relocation to Cyprus did not materialize.[137] The 14th RSM most likely provided the resources used to activate an intercept site on Crete, and Det 1, 75th RSM replaced Project Penn as the USAFSS identifier in Ankara.

Former USAFSS ELINT intercept operator (SSgt.) Bill McFall discussed the Ankara intercept facility in 2006.[138] He arrived in Ankara after a circuitous route (Darmstadt and Landsberg, Germany) in early August 1953. Three weeks later (26 August), he was a member of a six-man team that activated the USAFSS intercept site at Trabzon.

My tour in Trabzon was a part of JAMMAT (Joint American Military Mission for Aid to Turkey). The 75th and later the 34th RSM's were attached to and stationed in the basement of the JAMMAT building. There was a PX in the basement, and next to that, an iron door (with sliding peep hole) that allowed entrance into squadron Operations. Major Dacko ran all of the field teams from there. Samsun and Trabzon were the only ones during my days there.

Arriving in Trabzon in deuce-and-a-half trucks, the airmen lived in apartments in Trabzon and received $9.00 per day per diem in lieu of rations. They established the USAFSS intercept site on a summit outside Trabzon.

When we set up the installation in a picnic area on top of Boztepe near a mosque above Trabzon, we set up two 6 x 6 van body trucks (one blue with many antennas and the other a GRC-26 RDF van) and a few Jamesways [huts], along with some dishes, some cones and some wire antennas on the edge and top of the mountain. We had two diesel generators that ran 24 hours a day seven days a week.

The original team was a First Lieutenant Pietre and six noncoms—TSgt. Johnson, SSgt. Roe, SSgt. McFall, A1C Howard, A1C Sheets and A1C Fontaine. We were soon joined by another dozen enlisted men and six months later, another first lieutenant. The original crew was sent to school at Keesler AFB as Special Training Airman Radar Observers. Some of us were instructors at the Keesler electronics school and some were radar repairmen from other bases.

*At the time we left for overseas (Landsberg, Germany), the
project was so classified no one could be told where we
were going other than some APO number. To this day I
have never seen anything that releases us from what we
saw and did there. Our families didn't know where we
were for a long time.*

The succession of changes in the identifier for USAFSS
operations in Turkey during Bill McFall's tour of duty added to
the confusion. From the time he disembarked a troopship in
Bremerhaven, Germany, his military assignment orders reveal the
circuitous route to Trabzon, plus the tumultuous evolution of
USAFSS unit identifiers in Turkey in 1953-54.

McFall's Military Orders		
Date	Assignment	Remarks
29 Jun '53	6910th Security Group/Darmstadt	Interim stop
10 Jul '53	6910th SG HQ/Landsberg AB	Interim stop
6 Aug '53	Det 5, JAMMAT, APO 206A	Ankara, Turkey
26 Aug '53	Trabzon, Turkey	Arrived to set up intercept site
21 Sept '53	Det 1, 75th RSM, APO 206A	Designator change only
8 Feb '54	Team B, Flight A, 34th RSM, APO 206A	Trabzon had its own identifier *
* Trabzon site also was known as OL-2, Flight A, 34th RSM in Feb '54		

Having helped set up the USAFSS SIGINT site at Trabzon,
SSgt. McFall flew out of a newly created local dirt airstrip in June
1954.

*I left Trabzon on the first plane to use the then newly
completed gravel airfield in Trabzon. It was a C-47 and
Turks came for miles to see such a large airplane.
Fontaine, Roe, Dougherty, Elliott and I all were
discharged at Camp Kilmer, NJ, on 3 July 1954. I might
add that Sheets, Fontaine, Dougherty and Roe are all
dead. I miss them.*

George Barthel's transfer from JAMMAT to Det 1, 14th RSM and ultimately to Det 1, 75th RSM was related to a reorganization of U.S. forces in Turkey.[139] U.S. Air Forces Europe assumed responsibility for logistic support for all U.S. forces in Turkey, resulting in JAMMAT being replaced by "The United States Logistic Group" (TUSLOG); see Appendix H. By 1955, each U.S. military unit and civilian component in Turkey had its own TUSLOG detachment number. USAFSS-Ankara was TUSLOG Detachment 3.

6930TH SCTY GP ACTIVATED IN 1953

Det 1, 75th RSM was last accounted for in 1953, the year that USAFSS activated the 6930th Security Group at Wheelus AB, Libya. The designator change for Trabzon (OL-2, Flight A, 34th RSM) sometime in 1953 suggests that Det 1, 75th RSM became Flight A, 34th RSM by early 1954. With the activation of the 6930th Security Group at Wheelus Air Base, Libya, the USAFSS entities in Libya and Turkey reported to the 6930th SG, and the 6930th reported to the 6900th Security Wing; see tables below.

USAFSS in Libya, Turkey and Crete 1953-1955		
6900th Security Wing (1 Frankfurt, Germany 1954-1961		
6930th Security Group Wheelus Air Base, Libya 1953-1955		
34th Radio Squadron Mobile Wheelus AB, Libya 1951-1955		
Flt A, 34th RSM (2 Ankara, Turkey (Feb1954) Det 1, 34th RSM 1954-1955	Det 2, 34th RSM Iraklion, Crete (Greece) 1954-1955	Det 3, 34th RSM Diyarbakir, Turkey 1955
(1 Moved from Landsberg, Germany, to Frankfurt in 1954. (2 Flt A, 34th RSM became Det 1, 34th RSM in 1954.		

USAFSS in Turkey—1953-1955	
Flight A, 34th Radio Squadron Mobile (1 Ankara, Turkey (Feb 1954) Detachment 1, 34th RSM 1954-1955	
OL-1, Flt A, 34th RSM Samsun, Turkey (Feb 1954) OL-1, Det 1, 34th RSM 1954-1955	OL-2, Flt A, 34th RSM (2 Trabzon, Turkey (Feb 1954) OL-2, Det 1, 34th RSM 1954-1955
(1 Replaced Det 1, 75th RSM in '53 and became Det 1, 34th RSM in '54.	
(2 Used Ankara's designator (Det 1, 75th RSM, APO 206A) previously.	

With the advent of the 6930th SG, the 34th RSM initiated actions to deploy detachments to Turkey and Crete.[140] By 1955, the 34th RSM operated detached units at Ankara, Samsun, Trabzon and Diyarbakir, Turkey, plus Iraklion, Crete. On or about 7 May 1955, the 34th Radio Squadron Mobile became the 6934th Radio Squadron Mobile. Concurrently, Det 1, 34th RSM and Det 2, 34th RSM became 6933rd RSM and 6938th RSM, respectively.

USAFSS in Libya, Turkey and Greece—1955-56

In 1955 and 1956, the 6930th Security Group at Wheelus controlled three subordinate squadrons: 6933rd RSM/Ankara, 6934th RSM/Wheelus and 6938th RSM/Iraklion; see chart below. The 6933rd RSM had detachments at Trabzon, Samsun, Sile and Diyarbakir, Turkey.

USAFSS Libya, Turkey, Greece 1955-1956		
6930th Security Group Wheelus Air Base, Libya 1955-1956		
TUSLOG Det 3 6933rd RSM Ankara, Turkey 1955-56	6934th RSM Wheelus AB, Libya 1955-56	6938th RSM Iraklion, Crete 1955-56

USAFSS in Turkey—1955-1956	
6933rd RSM (TUSLOG Det 3) Ankara, Turkey 1955-1956	
TUSLOG Det 3-1 Det 1, 6933rd RSM Trabzon, Turkey 1955-56	TUSLOG Det 3-2 Det 2, 6933rd RSM Samsun, Turkey 1955-56
TUSLOG Det 3-3 Det 3, 6933rd RSM Sile, Turkey 1955-56	TUSLOG Det 8 Det 4, 6933rd RSM Diyarbakir, Turkey 1955-56

USAFSS designators of the Turkey-based units were restricted information; each unit's TUSLOG number—not the USAFSS designator—was used in official correspondence. The USAFSS resources on Europe's southern flank continued to grow.

RGM'S IN LIBYA AND TURKEY

As part of a major realignment on 1 September 1956 in which USAFSS deactivated its security groups—replacing them with radio groups mobile—the 6930th Security Group became the 6930th Radio Group Mobile. At the same time, the 6900th Security Wing activated the 6933rd RGM at Ankara.

USAFSS Libya, Turkey, Greece 1956-1958	
6900th Scty Wing Frankfurt, Germany 1954-1961	
6930th RGM Wheelus Air Base, Tripoli, Libya 1956-1958	TUSLOG Det 3 6933rd RGM Ankara, Turkey * 1956-1958
6938th RSM Iraklion, Crete 1956-1958	
* TUSLOG Det 3 moved from Ankara to Karamursel about June 1957.	

USAFSS in Turkey—1956-1958	
TUSLOG Det 3 6933rd RGM Ankara, Turkey * 1956-1958	
TUSLOG Det 3-1 Det 1, 6933rd RGM Trabzon, Turkey 1956-1958	TUSLOG Det 3-2 Det 2, 6933rd RGM Samsun, Turkey 1956-1958
TUSLOG Det 3-3 Det 3, 6933rd RGM Sile, Turkey 1956-1958	TUSLOG Det 8 Det 4, 6933rd RGM Diyarbakir, Turkey 1956-1957
* TUSLOG Det 3 moved from Ankara to Karamursel about June 1957.	

USAFSS Realignment to Cover Middle East

The Suez War of 1956 brought about a realignment of intelligence gathering resources on Russia's southern flank. With five USAFSS intercept stations in Turkey monitoring Soviet targets by 1957, some of the intercept positions in Libya and Crete could now be redirected at non-Soviet targets. A plan was also underway to relocate the 6933rd Radio Group Mobile from Ankara to a new intercept facility at Karamursel, Turkey. At the same time, United States coverage of targets in the Middle East was lacking. In the end, as a cost reduction move USAFSS planners decided to phase down operations in Libya while simultaneously building up the intercept site at Iraklion, Crete, to devote more monitoring resources against targets in the Middle East.

Build-up on Crete—Drawdown in Libya

On 1 April 1958, the 6930th Radio Group Mobile relocated to Iraklion Air Station from Wheelus AB, Libya, while the 6938th Radio Squadron Mobile moved from Crete to Libya.[141] This was a "paper" transfer of unit designators only—a transfer of the group management function to Crete, but minimal resultant movement of personnel or resources between the two locations. The chart below shows the USAFSS units in Libya and on Crete in 1958.

USAFSS Libya and Greece—1958
6900th Scty Wing Frankfurt, Germany 1954-1961
6930th RGM Iraklion, Crete 1958-1963
6938th RSM Wheelus AB, Libya 1958-1960

The transfer of the 6930th RGM from Wheelus Air Base to Crete marked the beginning of the end for American SIGINT operations in Libya. The 6938th RSM continued its intercept mission at Wheelus for two years in a phase-down mode, with a reduction in personnel through attrition and the transfer of some men to other USAFSS units. When intercept operations ended at Wheelus in 1960, the 6938th RSM was deactivated.

6933RD RGM TO KARAMURSEL

The 6933rd Radio Group Mobile relocated to Karamursel Air Station, Turkey, during the summer of 1957. Although new to its American residents, Karamursel was anything but new when the first USAFSS and Naval Security Group personnel arrived.

WELCOME TO KARAMURSEL COMMON DEFENSE INSTALLATION!

Your tour here will be one filled with pleasant experiences both in your daily contact with fellow workers and in your recreational and educational activities.[142]

The pamphlet welcoming new personnel to the Karamursel, Turkey, "Mainsite" in 1970 had little in common with the facility that welcomed the 6933rd Radio Group Mobile to Karamursel in 1957. Relocation of the 6933rd RGM to Karamursel involved consolidation of U.S. second echelon SIGINT operations outside the confines of Ankara where the 6933rd had outgrown its facilities. When USAFSS and NSG arrived in mid-1957, Karamursel was just a wide spot in the road—a gravel and dirt road. Years later, the former World War II air base was known as the Karamursel Common Defense Installation (Karamursel CDI).

A brief geography lesson helps one visualize initial U.S. intelligence operations at Karamursel. With modern-day Turkey traditionally orienting itself toward Europe, most Americans think of Turkey as a European country; however, 97 percent of Turkey's land mass lies in Asia. The small European part of Turkey—about the size of the state of New Hampshire—is separated from Asian Turkey by the Bosphorus Straits, Sea of Marmara and the Dardanelles that link the Black and Mediterranean Seas.

Straddling the Bosphorus, Istanbul is the world's only metropolis that sits on two continents. It is Turkey's largest city and one of the largest in Europe. Karamursel is located on the Asian side (southern shore) of the Sea of Marmara some 37 miles southeast of Istanbul. Yalova also lies on the south shores of the Marmara about 17 miles west of Karamursel.

Karamursel—the Early Years

In 1957 when the 6933rd RGM transferred from Ankara, there was no military family housing at Karamursel. In fact, Quonset huts and tents on base housed the newly arrived enlisted troops. Senior NCO's and officers who were authorized to bring their families to Turkey rented housing on the economy in Yalova and Kadikoy. A USAFSS community sprung up in Kadikoy, which is an extension of Old Istanbul on the Asian side of the Bosphorus.

The unpaved road from Yalova to Karamursel was a relatively easy commute, but living in Kadikoy, with duty in Karamursel, posed some real challenges. There was no BX or commissary at Karamursel, and shopping at the Air Force exchange and commissary in Istanbul involved a trip by private car and a ferry ride across the Sea of Marmara. Likewise, dependent children living in Kadikoy journeyed to school in Istanbul by school bus and ferry—they lived in Asia and went to school in Europe. Meanwhile, the fathers of those children and others who lived in Kadikoy and worked at Karamursel drove their cars several miles to a parking area along the coast and caught a ride on a converted fishing boat across the sea to the base. It was a two-and-a-half hour commute to work, and the alternative was to drive around the eastern shore, adding 40-plus minutes in each direction.

Karamursel—Mudsite

In 1957 when USAFSS and the NSG arrived at Karamursel, the men commenced SIGINT operations in recently acquired USAFSS H-1 vans surrounded by a barbed-wire fence. The operations buildings were still under construction as were other Karamursel facilities. As the detachments at Trabzon, Samsun and Diyarbakir grew and became full-fledged radio squadrons mobile, Karamursel Air Station acquired the nickname, "Mainsite." In the fall of 1957 when the rainy season arrived, "Mudsite" became a more appropriate moniker.

An NSG communications technician who reported to TUSLOG 28 (NSG designator at Karamursel) on 1 August 1957 probably helped create the "Mudsite" legend. He found Karamursel living conditions somewhat primitive when he arrived.

Of course, you had to buy your meals from the construction company in a civilian chow hall, and the only drinking water we had was in large tanks parked outside the barracks, which didn't even have beds. Things got better within the week, the chow hall went over to the Air Force, and the food wasn't too bad. And we slowly got beds to sleep in and a few lockers for our clothes.

Things did improve quickly and shortly the place became very livable—until it started to get cold and the rains started, and Mainsite became Mudsite. The only place you can stand in mud to your knees while dust blows in your eyes.[143]

Rain seldom fell from May to November, but during the rainy season (December to April) the land area became a sea of mud.

Mudsite to Mainsite

Mudsite of 1957 became an authentic Mainsite as construction changed Karamursel's skyline with new office buildings, dormitories and other support and mission structures—plus paved streets. Over a three-year period, Karamursel matured into a facility equal to many top-notch bases in the United States. Even the dirt lane to Yalova was paved. With all the improvements came an expanded SIGINT mission and the arrival of more military and dependent personnel.

In February 1961, Karamursel went "stateside" with the opening of a 26-room school on base for grades one through eight. The school expanded in 1962 and 1968 to include the ninth and tenth grades. (Junior and senior high school students attended a boarding school in Ankara.) Family housing followed the arrival of on-base schools with the opening of a modern 100-unit housing development on Karamursel in June 1961. A 100-unit trailer park was added in 1964, and 200 more new homes were completed in 1967. The Air Force assigned single female airmen to Karamursel in 1967 for the first time.

Contributed by Rich Pointer

Base Chapel, Karamursel Air Base, Turkey, 1963

The U.S. European Exchange Service provided a centrally located modern shopping center on base to support assigned military personnel and their families. Other on-base amenities included: an NCO club, Airmens Club, Officers Mess, air-conditioned theater, Class VI liquor store, service club, gymnasium, hobby center, nursery, education center, commissary, laundromat and a large beach facility. Many USAFSS veterans considered the Karamursel Common Defense Installation their best in a series of long overseas tours.

Odyssey to Karamursel

Retired USAFSS MSgt. William Burkhart and eleven classmates, who had completed Russian language and voice intercept training before shipment to Turkey, were the nucleus of the voice intercept section that opened at Karamursel in late 1957. The odyssey that took Bill Burkhart to Karamursel boggled his mind.

After they completed a Russian course at Syracuse University in October 1956, USAFSS sent the airmen to Suitland, Maryland (National Security Agency), Fort Devens, Massachusetts (Army Security Agency), and Fort Meade, Maryland (NSA), for voice intercept training. Finally in September 1957, the group reported to Charleston AFB, South Carolina, for a flight to what they perceived to be their overseas destination—Turkey.

We went first to Tripoli, Libya, where we remained for four days without explanation (red-lined) [awaiting further direction]. We did a lot of sightseeing and stuff like that. We were housed in an old building at the far end of a forgotten runway near the engine test area (which they did night and day). We had bunk beds, and I slept on the top bed of one of the sets.

When we got to Karamursel, about 15 days after arrival I saw some of the guys, and they asked me if I had gotten my medication yet. I asked what for, and they told me that all eleven of them had "crabs." Well, I went to the infirmary, got checked out and was given a clean bill of health. I didn't get them! So far as we can determine, they came from that building we slept in while in Tripoli.

Prior to 1957, USAFSS airmen destined for Turkey had been routed via the 6930th Security Group, Wheelus AB, Libya—perhaps explaining why Burkhart and his comrades had been inadvertently sent to Tripoli. In the turmoil resulting from recent reorganizations, the USAFSS headquarters section at Wheelus Air Base booked Burkhart and gang on a military flight to Rome, Italy, where they spent four more days "without explanation."

We did a lot of sightseeing there, too. I had my first store-bought shampoo, shave and manicure. Cost me $3! It was also the first and last time that a hair dryer was used to *dry my hair. About a week after that all the hair on my head broke off!*

From Rome we were sent to Ankara, Turkey (the supposed location of our unit of assignment), only to discover that the unit had moved several days before in the middle of the night, and no one knew exactly where it had gone. I'm not sure, but I believe the delays were caused by Air Force or USAFSS trying to find out what had been done with TUSLOG Det 3. (Back then, everything was top secret and the right hand did not tell the left hand anything!)

After four days in Ankara, we were told to go to Istanbul. A liaison officer at the TUSLOG building there told us that our unit was located near a village called Karamursel on the Marmara Sea not far from Istanbul, near a port city called Yalova.

Bill Burkhart and his traveling companions took the ferry across the Marmara to Yalova and caught an Air Force bus to Karamursel—ten months after graduating from language school at Syracuse University.

Burkhart—Introduction to Mudsite

Burkhart was unimpressed with the facilities when he stepped off the bus at his first operational destination.

I remember the day we arrived in early September 1957— rainy and muddy. There were no paved streets on the site, only one long sidewalk which ran from near the main gate to the chow hall at the far end of the dirt street from the main gate. There were some permanent and semi-permanent buildings already, but very few. Fortunately for us, one of those structures was the barracks where we were to be housed.

Across "main mud street" from the barracks was a command (portable) building and several other portable structures facing the barracks area (BX, clinic, etc.) At the end of the long sidewalk, on the barracks side was a chow hall. At the end of the "main mud street" facing back toward the main gate was a structure lovingly referred to as the NCO/Airmens Club. It was a place where you could get your head and insides as messy as the mud on the site!

I stepped off the bus into ankle deep mud. Not too bad if you did not have on spit-shined shoes and blues...which I did!! Anyway, we sloshed through the mud to the orderly room (which was in the first of the two barracks that had been completed). We signed in and got room assignments. The next day they took us to operations.

6933RD RGM OPERATIONS

The operations complex consisted of four portable trailers (H-1 vans) arranged two to a side facing each other.

Between the vans were sections of portable runway (metal strips about 2x6' with holes throughout) [PSP—pierced steel planking]. As I recall one van was the comm center, one analysis and the other two were intercept stations (voice and Morse). We had to go from van to van to collect the various pieces of information we needed to complete reports, etc. You cannot imagine the frenzy when something important was going on!

When it was raining (which it nearly always was), you can only imagine the mess, too. If you forgot and stepped down onto the portable runway piece the wrong way, your end would go down and the other end would come up. As you moved forward, the far end would fall down and "splash." You got a mud bath!! It was not unusual to hear foul language being uttered softly and loudly, depending upon how much mud sloshed upon the speaking victim. That's why we called it "Mudsite."

USAFSS built a new operations building farther inland at the end of an old World War II landing strip.

The taxiways, parking ramps and runways splayed out from the main part of the base and were used as storage areas for equipment, supplies, etc.—beginning not far from the chow hall. It took about 15 minutes to walk from the "base" to Operations when it was finally completed in early 1958.

As I recall, more barracks and other permanent structures were erected and were in service when the operations building was completed. By that time, we had several hundred men on station and had a "real" intercept operation going. They also installed a "new, circular" antenna which provided greater capability than what we had enjoyed before. The antenna field and what was to become base housing in the 1960's (located on part of the old runway system) was overgrown with weeds and grasses when the operations building was completed.

In the mid-1960's, USAFSS installed an AN/FLR-9 HF circular "Elephant Cage" antenna at Karamursel, bringing the station up to par with the command's other major HF ground sites in Europe, Alaska and the Far East.

Water Reclamation

Given all the rain during his first few months on station, Burkhart was surprised that Karamursel had a water reclamation station—located near the fenced operations compound.

The water reclamation plant for the "base" took sewer water and turned it back into drinking water. Keep in mind this was in early September 1957. The plant was something of a novelty and a new innovation. The problem was when it rained hard, which it did nearly every day, the water in the system got muddy and was impossible to use for anything except gritty showers. As I recall they got that problem fixed about mid-1958, but not before I was the proud owner of about fifty t-shirts and pairs of shorts—you couldn't wash them [clean], had to buy new ones.

The muddy water at Karamursel during his first enlistment failed to sour Bill Burkhart on the Air Force. Completing his tour at Karamursel in 1959, he reenlisted and served 20 years in Security Service, including a one year remote tour at Sinop, Turkey (1973-74).

The chart below shows the USAFSS units in Turkey during the 1958 to 1962 period.

USAFSS Turkey—1958-1962		
6900th Scty Wing (1 Frankfurt, Germany 1954-1961 European Security Region 1961-1972		
TUSLOG Det 3 6933rd RGM (2 Karamursel, Turkey 1957-1962		
TUSLOG Det 3-1 6939th RSM Trabzon, Turkey 1958-1963		TUSLOG Det 3-2 6932nd RSM Samsun, Turkey 1958-1963
TUSLOG Det 3-3 Det 3, 6933rd RGM Sile, Turkey 1956-1958	TUSLOG Det 8 6935th RSM Diyarbakir, Turkey 1957-1963	OL-2, 6933rd RGM (3 Adana, Turkey
(1 Became ESR in 1961. (2 Moved from Ankara to Karamursel about June 1957. (3 Addressed in FTV, Vol IV, Airborne Recon.		

Relocation of the 6933rd RGM to Karamursel caused considerable confusion for newly arriving personnel. Many became aware of the move only upon reporting for duty at Ankara as specified in their transfer orders. MSgt. Deacon Ray Allor flew out of Charleston AFB, South Carolina, bound for his new assignment in the 6933rd RGM on 4 July 1957. Flying to Turkey via the Azores and Wheelus Air Base, Sgt. Allor had been traveling a week when he arrived in Ankara. He had to wait a couple of days for transportation to Karamursel.

I was finally able to catch a ride with the "mail" truck headed to Karamursel. The Turkish roads in those days were anything but paved highways. The trip in the back of the truck was hot, dusty, bumpy, etc., and although Karamursel was just a wide spot in the road, it was a happy sight after that trip.[144]

SILE, TURKEY—ELINT INTERCEPT SITE

The USAFSS unit at Sile, a few miles east of Istanbul on the Black Sea coast, had an ELINT mission. Ed McClelland, a USAFSS special signals operator at TUSLOG Det 3-3 in 1955, called Sile the "best USAFSS duty assignment in the world." He later served as a contractor with General Electric at Samsun and Diyarbakir during the 1955-1958 period. The 6933rd RGM deactivated its unit at Sile (Det 3, 6933rd RGM) in 1958.

DIYARBAKIR—ELINT/TELINT SITE

USAFSS had an ELINT/TELINT (Electronic Intelligence and Telemetry Intelligence) mission at Diyarbakir Air Station in southeast Turkey from 1955 to 1963. With several other USAFSS bases worldwide, on 1 July 1958 the command assumed the base-support function at Diyarbakir. General Electric installed an AN/FPS-17 space surveillance tracking radar for the Air Force at Diyarbakir in 1957-58. With antennae oriented toward the Soviet Union, the radar could track missiles during flight.[145]

In 1970, Diyarbakir AS became Pirinclik Air Station, named after the small village 30 kilometers west of Diyarbakir where the station is located. A very small base where personnel lived in one dorm, had one club for social life, and could not go off base at night, Diyarbakir/Pirinclik was so remote that an occasional trip to Incirlik Air Base was a special treat.[146] USAFSS turned over operations at Diyarbakir to a contractor (General Electric) team about 1963, probably under control of the Air Defense Command. As a result of base and force realignment actions, the 21st Space Wing, Air Force Space Command, Peterson AFB, Colorado, returned the installation to host nation control in the fall of 1997.

The 41-year-old American-Turkish Pirinclik Base near Diyarbakir, known as NATO's frontier post for monitoring the former Soviet Union and the Middle East, completely closed on 30 September 1997. This return was the result of the general drawdown of US bases in Europe and improvement in space surveillance technology. The base near the southeastern city of Diyarbakir housed sensitive electronic intelligence-gathering systems that kept an ear on the Middle East, Caucasus and Russia.[147]

6933RD SECURITY WING ACTIVATED

In 1962, the 6933rd Radio Group Mobile became the 6933rd Security Wing, while the 6933rd Support Group stood up concurrently at Karamursel. The charts that follow depict USAFSS units in Turkey, Crete, Pakistan and Italy during the 1963 to 1970 period.

USAFSS Turkey, Crete, Pakistan and Italy—1963-1970	
European Security Region Frankfurt, Germany 1961-1972	
TUSLOG Det 3 6933rd Security Wing Karamursel, Turkey 1962-1970	
6933rd Support Group Karamursel, Turkey 1962-1969	6931st Scty Group Iraklion, Crete 1963-1974
6937th Comm Group Peshawar, Pakistan 1958-1970	6917th Security Group San Vito, Italy 1963-1978

USAFSS Turkey—1963-1970		
TUSLOG Det 3 6933rd Security Wing Karamursel, Turkey 1962-1970		
TUSLOG Det 3-1 6939th Scty Sq Trabzon, Turkey 1963-1970	TUSLOG Det 3-2 6932nd Scty Sq (1 Samsun, Turkey 1963-1964 6932nd Scty Group 1964-1970	TUSLOG Det ? OL-8, 6970th Supt Gp Ankara, Turkey (2 1968-1970
(1 Became 6932nd Security Group in '64. (2 Small 6970th Support Group team supporting NSA ops in Ankara.		

Reorganizations in 1963 and 1964

The 6931st, 6937th and 6917th groups reported to the 6933rd Security Wing. (The 6937th and 6917th groups are addressed later.) The 6939th and 6932nd RSM's became the 6939th and 6932nd Security Squadrons on 1 July 1963. A year later, the 6932nd was redesignated the 6932nd Security Group—at which point the 6939th Security Squadron reported to the new 6932nd group.

USAFSS—SAMSUN AND TRABZON

Fearing the Soviet Union on its northern flank, Turkey became a strong ally of the United States after World War II, culminating in Turkey's joining the NATO alliance along with Greece in February 1952. Helping contain communism as a NATO member and in response to massive amounts of American economic and military aid, Turkey permitted the U.S. government to create new SIGINT monitoring sites on its northern coast.

USAFSS had HF Morse and HF voice intercept capabilities at its Ankara site, but with new Soviet MiG's capable of VHF voice communications, the command was desperate to begin monitoring VHF communications emanating from southern Russia. Site surveys at Samsun and Trabzon, located on the Black Sea coast south of the Soviet Crimea, confirmed the capability to intercept VHF air-to-ground Russian communications from both locations. Details on the startup of intercept activities at Samsun and Trabzon are sketchy.

According to George Barthel, his unit deployed a small intercept team to Samsun first and later sent a similar-sized team to Trabzon—all occurring before he departed Ankara in November 1953. While assigned to Flight A, 34th Radio Squadron Mobile in Ankara, Sgt. Carson King, a maintenance technician, traveled to Samsun and Trabzon in 1954 to install teletype-crypto equipment.

USAFSS Lineage—Samsun and Trabzon

The chart on the next page shows the lineage of the USAFSS units at Samsun and Trabzon as those units evolved during the 1950's and 1960's.

USAFSS Units—Samsun and Trabzon	
Samsun Lineage	Trabzon Lineage
OL-1, Flt A, 34th RSM 1953-1954	OL-2, Flt A, 34th RSM 1953-1954
OL-1, Det 1, 34th RSM 1954-1955	OL-2, Det 1, 34th RSM 1954-1955
Det 2, 6933rd RSM 1955-1956	Det 1, 6933rd RSM 1955-1956
Det 2, 6933rd RGM 1957-1958	Det 1, 6933rd RGM 1957-1958
6932nd RSM 1958-1963	6939th RSM 1958-1963
6932nd Scty Sq 1963-1964	6939th Scty Sq * 1963-1970
6932nd Scty Gp * 1964-1970	
* 6939th Security Squadron reported to the 6932nd Security Group.	

6932nd Scty Group, Samsun, Turkey, 1964

In the late 1960's, demands on the U.S. defense budget and manpower by the Vietnam War forced a reconsideration of military priorities in other parts of the world. Between 1967 and 1970, the number of Americans in Turkey dropped from 24,000 to 15,000. As part of this reduction, the American SIGINT mission in Turkey as well as other parts of the world was revamped/downsized.

The 6932nd Security Group and 6939th Security Squadron were deactivated in late 1970, and the Samsun and Trabzon intercept sites were turned over to Turkish control. The Army Security Agency and Naval Security Group operated a joint facility at Sinop, a small city on the Boztepe cape and peninsula—the most northern edge of the Turkish side of the Black Sea coast.

SIGINT Mission in Turkey

Air Force Security Service began operations in Turkey in 1951 with an HF Morse and voice intercept mission directed against Soviet targets. The mission expanded in 1953 to include VHF voice and limited HF Morse and voice intercept at Samsun and Trabzon. Later, electronic and telemetry signals associated with Soviet missile testing at the Kapustin Yar Missile Test Range (east of Volgograd and northwest of the Caspian Sea) became primary targets for USAFSS-staffed intercept sites in Turkey.

Karamursel, with its vast array of HF antennas, had primarily an HF Morse and voice intercept mission although, it had a couple of VHF voice intercept positions with limited effectiveness due to distance from targets of interest. Karamursel's voice intercept operators (and other USAFSS Russian linguists around the world) monitored Yuri Gagarin's flight into space on 12 April 1961. Karamursel also monitored the doomed flight of Vladimir Komarov as Soviet premier Aleksei Kosygin tried to console him shortly before he perished while deorbiting from a space flight six years later (24 April 1967).[148]

In addition to its primary VHF voice and ELINT/TELINT missions that were performed in separate facilities, Samsun had limited HF voice and Morse capabilities—the latter being essentially direction finding. USAFSS special signals operators (294 specialty code) and contractor (General Electric) engineers and maintenance technicians staffed the Samsun ELINT/TELINT operation. Trabzon's mission was pretty much the same as Samsun's except that Trabzon covered targets farther to the east.

John David Radomski, who served tours at Karamursel, Samsun and Trabzon during the 1960's, provided the author an anecdote in 2007 about a Turkish national who dropped into Operations at Samsun—literally—in 1962.

I was working the day some Turk contractors were fixing the Ops roof (We piped loud music into the open space of the ceiling to cover the sounds of ops) when one of the Turks fell through and landed on a Morse position! No one was mortally injured, but the look on the Turk's face (let alone the Morse guy's face) was one of absolute awe. He had not a clue of what was going on!

Coverage of the Samsun and Trabzon missions transferred to Sinop, an Army Security Agency field site, as USAFSS downsized its forces in Turkey in 1970. Some airmen who were nearing completion of their overseas tours returned to America early. In December 1970, USAFSS reassigned others with time remaining for a follow-on overseas assignment to Sinop. Like Samsun and Trabzon, Sinop is on the Turkish Black Sea Coast—halfway between the former Soviet border (Georgia) in the east and Istanbul in the west.

USAFSS—Sinop

The Army Security Agency activated Field Station Sinop—aka TUSLOG Det 4 and Diogenes Field Station—at Sinop, Turkey, in the mid-1950's.

The Diogenes Station was a three hundred-acre facility located two miles west of Sinop at the end of a peninsula. It had huge white radar domes and microwave antennas situated on a bleak seven hundred-foot hill and clearly visible from the sea and air.[149]

The station mission involved the monitoring of Soviet activity in the Black Sea area as well as Soviet missile testing activity. A major aspect of monitoring missile testing involved the interception of electronic emanations and telemetry connected with Soviet missile and space rocket launches from the Kapustin Yar and Tyuratam launch sites.[150]

Air Force Security Service activated the 6934th Security Squadron (TUSLOG Det 204) in existing ASA facilities at Sinop during the second half of 1970 as part of a joint service (ASA-NSG-USAFSS) SIGINT team. The 6934th SS remained at Sinop until 1977 when the unit was deactivated.

6933RD SG REPLACES 6933RD SW

The reduction of USAFSS forces in Turkey in 1970 resulted in the 6933rd Security Wing being downgraded to the 6933rd Security Group. The chart below depicts USAFSS units in Turkey from 1970 to 1977.

USAFSS Turkey—1970-1977	
TUSLOG Det 3 6933rd Security Group Karamursel, Turkey 1970-1977	
TUSLOG Det 94-1 6933rd Security Sq Karamursel, Turkey 1974-1977	TUSLOG Det 204 6934th Security Sq Sinop, Turkey 1970-1977
TUSLOG Det 94-2 6933rd Air Base Sq Karamursel, Turkey 1974-1977	TUSLOG Det ? OL-8, 6970th Supt Gp * Ankara, Turkey 1968-1970 OL-IW, 6970th Supt Gp 1970-1971 OL-FH, 6970th Supt Gp 1971-1975
* Small 6970th Support Group team supporting NSA ops in Ankara.	

The last two years in Turkey (1975-1977) were nerve-racking for American intelligence personnel and their families—and totally non-productive.

Turks Gain Access to U.S. SIGINT Sites

The United States operated intelligence gathering sites on Turkish soil at the pleasure of the Turkish government under a series of bilateral agreements until 3 July 1969, when the two nations signed a Defense Cooperation Agreement incorporating related terms. Whereas earlier bilateral provisions placed American cryptologic areas off-limits to Turkish nationals, the rules changed under the DCA. Designated Turkish personnel could now enter all work areas in Turkey with the exception of U.S. communications centers that remained off-limits. Hence, intercept sites were sanitized of sensitive cryptologic materials, which the cryptologic units kept in the comm centers.

Operations Suspended at U.S. Sites in Turkey

Intelligence monitoring at U.S. sites in Turkey ended abruptly on 25 July 1975, when the host Turkish government terminated the 1969 agreement on joint defense facilities and stopped operations at all facilities except Incirlik, which is a NATO base. Turkey declared the DCA null and void after the U.S. Congress imposed an arms embargo on Turkey. The Congress acted on 5 February 1975 in response to Turkish military intervention in Cyprus the previous July. The American sites affected by Turkey's suspension order included: Pirinclik (Diyarbakir), Belbasi near Ankara, Karatas near Incirlik, Karamursel and Sinop. USAFSS personnel at Karamursel and Sinop—and airmen and civilians representing other commands painted lots of rocks, played sports and cards for hours on end, and drank lots of beer over the next two to three years.

Marking Time at Karamursel and Sinop

Retired USAFSS Major George Logan had only recently arrived at Karamursel when operations was suspended. He reminisced in an email exchange in 2004.

I got there something like 8 June '75—we closed Ops about 3 weeks later—and then we spent a year and a half as a TDY squadron. Left something like 7 December of 1977.

It was a difficult assignment for everyone. Logan was thankful that his family had not yet joined him; they remained in the United States for the duration.

The closure was a most interesting experience—and maybe "interesting" is a misnomer. My remembrance is that we got something like a week to close Ops—although it may have been only a couple of days. I do remember closing the doors to Ops and then having to go back a week or so later and put padlocks on the doors.

So during the 18 months that I was there (with Ops closed) everything remained in place. The elephant cage and the round house and the Ops buildings were all intact—but closed. I do remember that we went into the Ops area on several occasions to assess the status of the equipment. It was all intact, but leaks in the roof had put positions in jeopardy. The other interesting thing we found was trails of snakes (which had probably come up from the ducts in the floor) running thru the dust on the floor.

Beyond that, it was a fully functioning base. The support squadron still had a base to keep running. Everything on the base was up and running, and although we had to consolidate some activities (the clubs), everything remained open.

One of the memories that stays with me is going out on Saturday afternoon and immediately becoming aware that all baseball diamonds (and I believe there were something like nine fields) had teams (of every age) playing on them, with spectators watching them.

According to Logan, the voice intercept mission had already transferred to other sites (probably Sinop). USAFSS used the unemployed operations personnel at Karamursel as a labor pool to satisfy shortages at other locations.

It became a hard tour for folks when Ops closed. Didn't take long for Headquarters to realize that there were better than 600 folks they could tap to go other places. So we had folks scattered from North Overshoe to Bum **** (yah that place). Very hard on the first term airmen who had paid for their wives to come over.

What did we do ???? Well within a week—maybe a week and a half, all the paint and plywood was gone. During that week, you dared not stand still—everything that didn't move got a coat of paint. A number of folks helped out in the support squadron, tees on the golf course were rebuilt—and other things on the base "honey-do" list were done. But as folks went on the road and began to DEROS [finish their tours], the base took on a very empty look. In fact in the fall of '76, walking around the base could be scary 'cause you might not see another soul.

The fortunate part was that there were very good people there who went to the wall for other folks—made things a whole lot easier. But my experience was that USAFSS folks could always be counted upon to do that.

After Congress lifted the aid embargo on 26 September 1978, Turkey responded by authorizing the reopening of the closed bases and facilities. The Army Security Agency and Naval Security Group resumed intelligence monitoring activities at Sinop, but Air

Force Security Service had long since written ground-based operations in Turkey out of its operations plan. The command dismantled the FLR-9 Elephant Cage antenna at Karamursel in 1977 and formally deactivated its intercept units at Sinop and Karamursel in late 1977.

USAFSS—CRETE (1954-1993)

The U.S. Air Force Security Service and its successor commands (Electronic Security Command and Air Force Intelligence Command) conducted SIGINT operations at Iraklion Air Station, Crete, continuously for 39 years; see chart below.

USAFSS (Iraklion, Crete)—1954-1993
6900th Security Wing (1 Frankfurt, Germany _1954-1961_ European Security Region (1 Frankfurt, Germany _1961-1972_ USAFSS/ESC/AFIC (1 Kelly AFB, Texas _1972-1993_
Det 2, 34th RSM (2 Iraklion, Crete _1954-1955_ 6938th Radio Squadron Mobile (2 _1955-1958_ 6930th Radio Group Mobile (2 _1958-1963_ 6931st Security Group (2 _1963-1978_

6931st Security Squadron (2 Iraklion, Crete 1974-1979	6931st Air Base Squadron Iraklion, Crete 1974-1978

6931st Electronic Security Squadron (2 Iraklion, Crete 1979-1993
(1 Became ESR in 1961; control passed to USAFSS/ESC/AFIC in 1972. (2 Lineage from Det 2, 34th RSM (1954) forward.

USAFSS Crete—Early Years

Although details are unavailable, a Security Service team undoubtedly carried out a site survey on the Greek Island of Crete with positive "hearability" results before the 34th RSM detached an intercept team to the island in October 1954.[151] The newly activated station was located about 10 miles east of the city of Iraklion in the village of Gournes (north central section of Crete). USAFE activated the facility as Iraklion Air Station on 5 October 1954 and supported USAFSS operations from the start.[152] Living accommodations were quite primitive—Dallas huts (square open-bay structures with thin, single-thickness plywood walls) and a communal latrine.

Iraklion Air Station, Isle of Crete, Greece

Multistory barracks that were built in the late 1950's were a welcome relief for the single airmen who lived on station. So were the amenities that evolved on base—Airmens, NCO and Officers Clubs, movie theater, bowling alley, beach, library, Class VI liquor store, Armed Forces radio and TV station, hobby shop and Service Club—plus standard support activities: dining hall, dispensary, BX, commissary, laundry, family housing, school and post office. In effect, Iraklion Air Station was a small self-contained American city, and that was good! Although Crete is Greece's largest island, it is remotely situated 100 miles south of the mainland—12-hour ferry ride from Athens in the old days—and had a rural, laid-back economy with few restaurants and entertainment venues of interest to Americans.

Iraklion AS Deactivated in 1993

The USAFSS mission changed over the years, from monitoring Soviet communications initially to including Middle East targets in later decades. During its stay on Crete, the 6931st Security Group (and successor units) were awarded eight Air Force Outstanding Unit Awards.[153] The U.S. Air Force deactivated the 6931st Electronic Security Squadron on 30 September 1993 and handed control of Iraklion Air Station to the Greek government.

USAFSS—PAKISTAN

In 1946, the Russians established a missile test range at Kapustin Yar northwest of the Caspian Sea, using captured technology and scientific support from defeated Germany. A team of Russian and German scientists launched the first rocket (one of eleven captured V-2 rockets) from the range on 18 October 1947. British RAF overflights of that area confirmed missile range activity in August 1953. The Soviet Union also exploded its first atomic bomb at Semipalatinsk (Kazakhstan) in 1949 and built the Tyuratam missile test center (also in Kazakhstan) in 1955. Tyuratam became the Baikonur Cosmodrome from which Yuri Gagarin was launched into space in 1961.

Photographs from the RAF mission to Kapustin Yar and keen interest in the atomic testing in Kazakhstan emphasized a need for a ground-based signals collection capability in this area. Fortunately, the power brokers in Pakistan—Governor-General (later President) Iskander Ali Mirza and Defense Minister Muhammad Ayub Khan were graduates of Britain's Royal Military Academy at Sandhurst. They authorized the U.S. Air Force Security Service to set up a signal monitoring station in newly independent Pakistan.

USAFSS/Pakistan—Site Survey 1955

As discussed in Chapter Four, Col. Philip Evans (6900th Security Wing Chief of Staff) and a small USAFSS team visited the Pakistani leadership in Karachi in June 1955—the first USAFSS personnel to set foot in Pakistan. About 19 August 1955, a USAFSS team (four officers and 29 enlisted) traveled to West Pakistan to conduct a site survey.[154] Loreto (Larry) Stracqualursi discussed the Pakistani expedition in 2006.

Site Survey Team in Pakistan, June 1955

We surveyed Peshawar, Lahore, Rawalpindi and Abbottabad (near the China/Russia border). We at 6911th configured all the equipment/vans and all the details concerning this survey, but most of the operators came from Tripoli to save time and money. I was the NCOIC and received the Commendation Medal from HQ USAFSS for this mission. The Pakistani Survey was designated as station 530X [USA-530X] of the 6900th Security Wing.

Lt. Col. Carl E. Dolk, 6910th Security Group, headed the site survey team, and Captain William B. Taft, 6911th Radio Squadron Mobile, served as operations officer. Capt. John H. Napier III and First Lt. Gerald W. Lockwood, 6900th Security Wing, represented the wing on the mission and served as couriers—hand-carrying intercepted data back to group headquarters at Darmstadt.

The team consisted of CW [Morse], voice operators, analysts, radio maintenance, motor pool/generator maintenance and antenna specialists, etc. All the equipment, including the vans, generators and motor vehicles, was assembled at Darmstadt and flown to Pakistan from Rhein-Main, via Tripoli and other places [Dhahran, Saudi Arabia] enroute.

Four National Security Agency civilians also participated in the survey, and the intercept environment was even more lucrative than anticipated.

Enclosed are the orders for the Pakistan survey with amendments. You will notice that we were extended from 75 to 95 days, and the prime reason for the extension was [that] the coverage of certain cases was considered to be very interesting/important, and HQ needed additional coverage.

Each site surveyed was selected based upon the technical merits of each area; however, some of the selected sites could not be used because they were vulnerable to attack and raids from local tribes (very common at that point in time). Pakistani army officers, together with the Air Force air attaché from the American Embassy, were always present and provided guidance and advice concerning vulnerability of each site during the selection process. Each selected site, was guarded/protected 24 hours daily by the Pakistani army.

In a trade-off comparing pros and cons, a wheat field a few miles outside Peshawar was selected for the new USAFSS facility that became Peshawar Air Station.

Peshawar—Geography and Climate

Located at the eastern end of the Khyber Pass near the Pakistan-Afghanistan border, Peshawar is a south-central Asian frontier city on the historic Silk Road. The city is the provincial capital of Pakistan's Northwest Frontier Province, and as such, was (is) the commercial, economic, political and cultural capital of the Pakistani frontier. The winter season in Peshawar runs from about mid-November through March, and summer months are May to September. Temperatures range from 77 °F nights to 104 °F days in summer, and 39 °F nights and 65 F °days during the winter. The average rainfall is about 16 inches annually with low humidity. Airmen who served at Peshawar tend to remember the least comfortable summer weather. To Richard Arnold, a Peshawar American Forces Radio and Television broadcaster during 1969, the weather was like a broken record.

I remember the same weather report for weeks at a time,
Clear today; highs—upper 90's, lows—lower 90's.

Sipping a brew around the pool was a favorite summer pastime.

USAFSS—Pakistan (1958-1970)

NSA would have loved to activate an intercept site immediately at Peshawar—only 150 miles from the Soviet border—but diplomacy and infrastructure development dragged on for two and one half years. Creating essential facilities was the main impediment. In July 1958, the 6911th Radio Group Mobile activated the 6937th Security Flight at Rhein-Main Air Base, Germany, and designated Capt. Luther A. Tarbox the flight's commander. The 6937th Security Flight was not an operational unit at Rhein-Main; rather, it served as a focal point for a small cadre of personnel and equipment destined for Peshawar. Under Project Sandbox, Capt. Tarbox was charged with marshalling the intercept equipment at Rhein-Main for shipment to Pakistan.

He arranged to airlift the 6937th SF personnel and equipment—some 20 planeloads, including mobile intercept positions in H-1 vans—to Peshawar during the summer of 1958. Gathering and shipping the airmen and materials was a secondary task for Capt. Tarbox; he remained in Germany.

Peshawar Airport—Temporary Operations

 USAFSS Colonel Ethyl Branham activated the "Communications Flight, Provisional" in Peshawar in April 1958, setting up headquarters downtown in the Oberoi Dean Hotel. The unit underwent three name changes during startup and kept a detachment in Karachi for five years.[155]

6937th Comm Group, Peshawar, Pakistan

- April 1958   Communications Flight, Provisional
- 1958   6937th Security Flight, Provisional
- 1958   6937th Communications Flight
- 1958-70   6937th Communications Group
- 1960-61   OL-2, 6937th Comm Group, Karachi
- 1961-65   Detachment 2, 6937th Comm Group, Karachi.

For several months in 1958, arriving Air Force personnel lived in the Dean Hotel while construction of barracks and other infrastructure proceeded on the air station. When the intercept vans arrived, the unit commenced intercept operations in a temporary fenced compound at Peshawar Airport. Former radio maintenance technician Jack Karp, who arrived in late 1958, lived in the hotel a week before moving into a newly built brick barracks on base.

Activating Peshawar Air Station

There appears to have been no formal "ribbon-cutting" to open Peshawar Air Station. Construction of essential facilities—barracks and dining hall, together with water and sanitation system, and power generation and distribution took top priority. Bradley Spencer, a 6937th ELINT intercept operator (Dec 1958-Dec 1959), dates the opening of the station's first barracks as January 1959.

> *When our small group, about four or five, arrived, we stayed at Oberoi Dean's for a month; brick barracks were under construction. We flew from Karachi to Peshawar on a Pak AF British Bristol—what a ride! I have B&W photos of the water tower while under construction, barracks construction, friends, etc.*

Fred Blair estimated in an email that there were 75 people on site when he arrived in April 1959. There was an outdoor movie, but "no BX, no club, no bowling alley." There was lots of improvising during those early days,—such as bringing your own chair to watch reruns and second rate films under the stars. A mini BX did offer bare essentials. Two of the first amenities that most remember were sports fields and the bowling alley—15 cents a line and five cents to rent shoes. With few recreational activities to occupy off-duty time, Peshawar was a remote assignment, a 12-month unaccompanied tour.

Operations Moved to Air Station

Although details on the move from Peshawar Airport are unavailable, Col. Branham most likely relocated the H-1 vans housing operations to Peshawar Air Station in early 1959 in

LARRY TART

conjunction with the airmen moving into barracks at the base. Construction of the Ops building dragged on into 1960.

Retired Capt. Walter Rosenstrom served 21 months at Peshawar AS (Nov 1960 to Jun 1962) as an enlisted Russian linguist—a voice intercept operator and transcriber. All the shift workers shared a couple of barracks that existed when he arrived. Around February or March 1961 when additional barracks were ready for occupancy, the four tricks (shifts) and the day workers split up, and each trick had its own barracks.

The operational mission was conducted in vans adjacent to the operations building construction site. Walter "Rosie" Rosenstrom has vivid memories of spinning dials on R-390 receivers in the H-1 vans initially, then in the new operations building.

We worked in the vans when I first arrived. I recall going to work in shorts, T-shirts, and shower clogs because of the heat. R/T [radiotelephone-voice section] had one van for intercept and one for T'ing [transcription]...R/T manned 6 positions plus about 3 transcription racks. Also had a posit with the huge AMPEX recorders monitoring Kabul to Moscow and other phone calls. Some of us got rudimentarily familiar with Pushtu and Persian.

Carlos Washburn, another 6937th Russian linguist (April '60-April '61), recalls that the voice intercept section moved into the new operations building by October-November 1960. A transcriber when Rosenstrom arrived in the unit, Carlos estimates unit strength at about 125 airmen when he arrived.

PAS was my first tour. The vans we worked out of were adjacent to the new Ops building as construction was underway. Worked in the vans in shorts with huge fans keeping us cool. Hottern hell!

Really enjoyed being a transcriber. Remember teaching Charlie Bishop how to transcribe. Later he became a second lieutenant, then Command IG when he inspected my unit where I was commander in Alaska. He ended up as a general. I finally retired in '85...from A2C to Lt. Col., and it all started at the 6937th.

840

Walter Rosenstrom, Carlos Washburn, Charles Bishop and Richard Oliver, who served together at Peshawar, are typical of many airmen who launched distinctive Air Force careers in the 6937th Comm Group. Many of his USAFSS/ESC contemporaries later served under now retired Brigadier Gen. Charles L. Bishop during one of his command assignments:

- 1979-1980 6993rd Electronic Security Squadron/Medina Annex
- 1982-1983 6912th Electronic Security Group/Berlin
- 1983-1984 HQ Electronic Security Pacific/Hickam AFB.

Washburn recalls that operations functions moved from the vans into the Ops building piecemeal as various parts of the new building were accepted from the contractor.

I think the day weenies, analysts and reporters moved into part of the new building first, then the rest of the rack people last.

The ELINT/TELINT section was the first intercept function to move into the new building. The entrance door to the ELINT/TELINT section was right behind the transcription section. Rosie Rosenstrom performed a special monitor mission in the ELINT/TELINT section during the launch of the first Soviet cosmonaut in August 1961.

During the Soviet's first manned launch, I sat a rack back there trying to find voice in the 300-400MHz range when the position was right. Those guys were the 294's of the day, but it seems like the AFSC was different. Interesting room...totally dark and a lot of scopes, green.

The original air force specialty code 303x0—ELINT (ECM) intercept operators—later became 294x0's. At its heyday in 1968, the 6937th Comm Group had an operations staff numbering 800— primarily Morse, non-Morse, voice and ELINT/TELINT intercept operators. An additional 500 support personnel provided essential services. Total air station population also included a few hundred dependent wives and children of assigned airmen and officers.

6937ᵗʰ Comm Group, Peshawar, Pakistan, 1969

HF Mission—FLR-9 Antenna not Delivered

The 6937ᵗʰ Comm Group had an HF mission—Morse, non-Morse (printer) and voice, plus ELINT and Telemetry associated with Soviet missile testing and nuclear testing. Sylvania Electronic Systems (then GTE Systems) was under contract to install a FLR-9 circular antenna at Peshawar, but that antenna was diverted to an intercept station in Thailand due to the tenuous situation in Pakistan in the later years of Peshawar Air Station.

Peshawar—Memories

With the recreational facilities that had evolved by the time Walter Rosenstrom arrived in November 1960, Peshawar Air Station became more tolerable.

The club (all ranks) was open when I got there, as was the bowling alley. The pool opened in mid-'61 and was used a lot. Also, they opened a separate NCO Club while I was there as well as base housing.

A gymnasium, expanded BX and commissary followed, and by the time Rosenstrom left in June 1962, some officers and senior NCO's were serving accompanied tours with their families. With the families came a dependent school (grades K through 7); older students attended boarding school in Turkey. The air station even had its own nine-hole golf course. With the more livable conditions, Peshawar became a 15-month unaccompanied tour—24 months for personnel accompanied by their families. The base had its hardships, and everyone departed with indelible memories—some good and others not so good.

Pleasant memories included: cheeseburgers grilled by the pool, ten cent beer at the club, the yellow flag flying by the consolidated mail room when mail was received and lots of intramural sports. Weather was memorable—some liked the hot, dry summers; others, who found the heat unbearable, were thankful for air conditioning in most on-base facilities. Carlos Washburn's recollections are typical.

Learned how to play Hearts, Bridge, Pinochle and how to drink. Watched movies outside sitting in our own chairs—drinking beer and eating hamburgers. Some climbed the water tower for kicks. Played a lot of softball, lifted weights and...worked.

Some of the less pleasant memories relate to powdered eggs and powdered milk, dust storms and the smell of dried camel dung burning at mealtime. Cobras scurrying across the road leading to operations also got much attention, and driving on the wrong (left) side of the road was strange. To many, the aroma that hit them when they arrived in Peshawar was (is) their most memorable experience. Fred Blair—former diesel generator repairman (1959-60)—is philosophical about his Peshawar experience.

The isolation took a lot of getting used to, but we made it. A tour to PAS had a way of seeing just how strong you were. I wouldn't want to go again but wouldn't take anything for the experience.

Charles "Chuck" MacFarlane has many unusual memories of the two tours he served at Peshawar (1959-1960 and 1963-1964). He was one of the first inexperienced Morse intercept operators to be sent directly from Morse code school/Keesler AFB to Pakistan. Previously, only experienced operators had been assigned to the 6937th Comm Group. MacFarlane was impressed that USAFSS flew his group—eight lowly A2C—to Pakistan aboard the 6900th Security Wing aircraft. They arrived in Peshawar in June 1959.

It was a unique experience as all of us were 18 or 19, and we thought we were hot stuff flying over on the USAFSS command aircraft. Spent 2 or 3 nights in a hotel in Karachi due to bad weather. I know on one of those nights I was introduced to San Miguel beer from the Philippines—I suffered the next day! We were used to drinking the 3.2 beer at the Keesler AFB Airmens Club. San Miguel was potent.

Got to Peshawar and thought I had landed in Hell. Man, was it hot. I'll never forget the 10 or so mile ride to the base on a blue goose, windows down and hot air blowing in as if you were standing in front of an oven with a fan on the inside. The base was a welcome change—new brick barracks had been built; they had a/c, and each dorm had a "bearer" (Pakistani house boy) who made your bed, cleaned your room, shined your shoes, etc. I thought I had died and gone to heaven, especially after 6 months at an ATC base.

Base facilities were limited; had a small BX (maybe 30' x 30'—I'm guessing). However, I'll never forget that besides many bare shelves, there were shelves packed with condoms and razor blades. Go figure! The movie theater was a large screen of plywood, painted white, attached to 2 telephone poles. A small brick projection booth was out in the middle of this vacant lot, and if you wanted to watch a movie at night you'd take one of your room chairs— some people had the Pak bearers buy straw/rattan chairs in Peshawar and used these—and plop it down in the field. If it rained you wore a poncho.

The mission was great; the training I received convinced me to take a consecutive overseas tour to Scotland and probably was the deciding factor in my decision to re-up. The base had a great recreation services section—tours to the Kohat gun factory, the Khyber Pass, and other places of interest locally.

Peshawar AS—Dental Clinic

MacFarlane would prefer not to have had a need for Pakistani medical (X-ray) care during his stay in Peshawar, but he did.

I had two abscessed teeth, but the dental clinic (a room in a dormitory with a dental chair and a screen to separate the waiting room with 2 chairs) didn't have X-ray equipment. There I was, a 19-year-old being driven into Peshawar in a USAF staff car to have X-rays taken. I can still smell the Pakistani X-ray tech's hands. I'm sure he was scratching his goat's ass before he shoved the X-ray film in my mouth!

U-2 Shoot Down Incident—1 May 1960

A2C MacFarlane has special memories of Gary Powers' renowned U-2 incident.

The crowning achievement of my 1st tour in Pakistan occurred on 5/1/60. I was working in a van on a swingshift, copying PVO [air defense traffic]. (At that time, the mission was getting larger and two vans— possibly three—were located outside the main ops building.) Noticed something unusual so I called my analyst (Harvey, damned if I can remember his last name, but he was an old timer for a 3-striper and knew his stuff). Harvey went nuts, had a senior op on the inside pick up my target, and then another 202 was tearing our 6-ply and comparing my copy with the senior op's (Randy Hummel).

I had picked up the first reflections of an overflight. It was Gary Powers. Within 30 minutes, the Ops bldg was a madhouse; more people in there than at Times Square on New Year's Eve. Anyway, you know the rest of the story. Harvey, Randy, and I were presented with Letters of Appreciation at the next Commander's Call. Believe Col. Spooner was the commander.

The shoot down of Francis Gary Powers' U-2 over the Soviet Union on May Day 1960 brought much unwelcome notoriety to the 6937th Comm Group. Powers departed Peshawar Airport on his fateful mission. Carlos Washburn recalled Premier Khrushchev's threats to blow Peshawar off the map.

Gary Powers was shot down while I was there. Used to see campfires of these tribes up in the foothills of the Himalayas between Peshawar and Kabul. We worried about Khrushchev lobbing a missile on us for the Powers affair. But we worried more about those tribes up in the mountains. And nobody has subjugated them yet. Tough dudes.

MacFarlane—Memories, Tour # 2

Charles MacFarlane departed Peshawar a week or so after the Russians downed Gary Powers. After serving a three-year tour at RAF Kirknewton, Scotland, he returned to Pakistan for a second tour.

Came back to Pak in '63 on the 3-D [promotion] program. Got a SSgt. stripe to return to Pakistan. Base was basically the same—bit bigger, more barracks and the crème de la crème, a swimming pool! The base chapel now served double duty; it was the base theater during the evening. The other big change was that there was now family housing. Funny story—our DF shack was behind base housing. Our Mission Supe was Bruce H. Barr—a helluva a great guy. His wife, a wonderful lady who cared for the troops, used to bake cakes and walk them out to the DF shack. Needless to say, the SP's didn't care for this, and that practice soon stopped.

I was a jeep SSgt.; however, within four months of my arrival I was a senior controller reporting on twenty-one - 1's, and believe it or not, nineteen of them were SSgt.'s assigned under the new 2-T [2-tour promotion] program.

Supervising 21 other Morse intercept operators, SSgt. MacFarlane learned quickly how to write airman performance reports (APR's). Charles MacFarlane served 32 1/2 years in USAFSS/ESC and retired as a CMSgt. in 1991.

The Coup D'état

In 2004, Joseph Zimmerer, a Peshawar veteran (July 1958-July 1959), discussed in an email an experience he will never forget.

I wonder if anyone remembers in 1958 when the Pakistani government (then in Karachi) decided on martial law? I was on duty—night before got a phone call. Pakistani telephone operator relayed a 500-group encoded message at Oberoi Dean Hotel, and I had to get to the site to have it taken care of by commanding officer. Took him to the site, etc.

Then Pakistani President Mirza declared martial law on 7 October 1958, and the army commander in chief, General Ayub Khan, staged a bloodless coup d'état three weeks later. On 17 July 1959, President Khan's government signed a lease, giving the U.S. Air Force use of Peshawar Air Station for ten years.

The Pakistani military has played an influential role in mainstream politics throughout Pakistan's history. Military presidents ruled the country from 1958–71, 1977–88 and from 1999 when Pakistani army chief of staff, General Pervez Musharraf, came to power in a coup. In 2001, Musharraf abandoned Taliban jihadists seeking refuge in Pakistan and agreed to help the West in the global war on terrorism. Musharraf resigned under pressure in August 2008, replaced by duly elected President Asif Ali Zardani the following month.

U.S.-Pakistan Relations

U.S.-Pakistani relations have been a roller coaster over the years. In the late 1950's, the Pakistani leadership made Peshawar Air Station available to the United States in exchange for a sizeable foreign aid package. Pakistan remained pro-Western and refused to curtail intelligence gathering activities at Peshawar following Gary Powers' U-2 incident in 1960, but relations chilled two years later with Pakistan growing closer to China. The Pakistani government continued its tilt to the left, and Alexei Kosygin visited Karachi in April 1968. The following month, Pakistan formally advised the United States that the ten-year lease on Peshawar Air Station would not be renewed. While firm evidence linking Kosygin's visit to the shutdown of the USAFSS base is lacking, the Soviet Union disclosed in early July 1968 that it had agreed to supply arms to Pakistan.[156] During the Soviet war in Afghanistan, 1979-1988—the Soviet Union's "Vietnam War"— Pakistan again sided with the West.

CLOSING DOWN 6937TH COMM GROUP

In October 1969, the American Embassy in Rawalpindi mailed a message announcing the closing of USA-60 ("Badaber"), USAF Communications Station, Peshawar.[157]

IN

MEMORIAM

USA-60

("Badaber")

Born:	Peshawar, July 17, 1959
Died:	Peshawar, July 17, 1969
Interred:	Peshawar, February 28, 1970

The six-page message—presented in the form of a eulogy to a recently departed loved one—paid tribute to the station and to those who had served thereon.

Now that the time has come to bury Badaber, it is ironically fitting that no effort to reconstruct its life can be made at Rawalpindi. Its early days are beyond the memory of living men in the Embassy. Its middle years have passed into the misty realms of saga. Even the final period is already encrusted with legend. And the Embassy files were destroyed several months ago during the latest of the series of troubles which have affected the deceased's beloved Pakistan. . . . .

. . . . . Well into the Twenty-first Century retired airmen sitting with their children and their children's children around the glowing barbecue pits of a thousand split levels will begin their tales: "When I first went to Badaber, back in the days when the world was young."

One may recollect that it answered to many names, accurate and inaccurate: Badaber, USA-60, Peshawar Air

Station, USAF Peshawar, "the missile site," "the U-2 base," simply "that place."

To another its charm will remain its association with the great names of history. Presidents Eisenhower, Kennedy, Johnson and Nixon were involved in its life. Chairman Khrushchev drew a red circle around it on the map. Chou En-Lai, Brezhnev and Kosygin were not insensitive to its magnetic attraction. Of lesser luminaries, Zulfikar Ali Bhutto cherished it to the end as a beloved enemy. . . . .

The tribute ended stating that the hands that built Peshawar can take great satisfaction from their achievement.

Ten years without a major local incident; billions of pieces of unique data collected; security, harmony and cooperation to the end.

The interred date reflected in the Embassy message is tenuous. Depending on the source of information, the base formally closed sometime between January and July 1970. UPI news service set the closing date as 7 January 1970.[158] Other sources have the U.S. Air Force turning Peshawar Air Station over to the Pakistani government as late as July 1970.

Peshawar AS—Final Days

Replacing Colonel Graydon K. Eubank in a formal change of command ceremony on 16 May 1969, Col. William H. Hezlep was the 6937th Comm Group's final commander. The phasedown of operations was on the home stretch when Col. Hezlep arrived. Major Joseph Tortorete "had the honor of being appointed the project officer for base closure." When Maj. Tortorete and his family arrived in July 1967, he had expected a routine two-year tour of duty as unit operations officer—closing down a large USAFSS intercept unit is anything but routine. Operations were phasing down when he departed on 22 July 1969, the day after the United States landed the first man on the moon.

I remember that [moon landing], because all the Pakistanis at the airport were beaming while offering congratulations—as if I had something to do with it.[159]

Security policeman Jim Bausch transferred from Crete to Pakistan in March 1969 to assist in the closing of the base.

I left in November '69, when the base was pretty much a ghost town. I was part of the Security Police force that was tasked to protect U.S. property and maintain the integrity of the base. I have a lot of memories of some rather hairy moments as almost every night towards the end, Pakistanis would climb over the wall and attempt to steal everything that wasn't nailed down in the old base housing. There were even attempts to breach the wall at the operations center!

Calvin Horton, a traffic analyst who had taken a consecutive overseas assignment to Peshawar from Karamursel, Turkey, in 1968, was one of the last analysts to leave in 1970.

We read in Newsweek (while still at PAS) that all of the US military were out of Pakistan. Hmmmm, they forgot about us.

Michael Peters, a Morse operator who cross-trained as a legal assistant in the later part of his Peshawar tour, processed many of the documents associated with closing the base.

I had a great time at PAS and only have good memories. I was there from late 1968 until the base closed. I cross-trained from being a "ditty bop" to legal assistant in the Staff Judge Advocate's office (Major Nero). We helped with a lot of the legalities of closing the base. Damn! That was a long time ago!

According to Peters, the U.S. Air Force officially turned the station over to the Pakistani government in July 1970.

Peshawar Air Station Today

Known by its Pakistani name, *Badaber Air Station*, the air facility that USAFSS created at Peshawar in 1958 is currently home to a Pakistani air force unit. According to a PAF flight lieutenant who was serving at Badaber in December 2004, the on-base physical plant and facilities are pretty much as left by the Americans in 1970.

I am presently serving in Pakistan Air Force and residing in Badaber. Thanks to American fellows who left a lot for us. We are still using the same infrastructure, same furniture and electricity/water system. Everything is so good that we always appreciate the efforts of those who created this station.[160]

Writing in broken English on the internet, another Pakistani veteran of Badaber chatted effusively about the base in 2004.

Well... wat can i say i used to live in PAF CAMP BADABER. Now i am in Lahore. Lived there for 8 years. love tat place... and i am impressed by you American...whaao...u just came for 10 years... and built so much stuff... to tell u the truth in Pakistan i think there are only few bowlyin alley's ...like 4 at the most... and when i tell ppl tat we have this place... in Peshawar which has bowling and a gym which converts into a basket bowl court and everything is air conditioned they get stunn'd...i love PAS...wat a wonderful place to be!

A third Pakistani airman emailing from "PAF Camp Badaber, Peshawar" found it amazing that a picture of his house is posted on a 6937th Alumni Association website. He added that "PAS is still gr8," and that people are still using air conditioners and furniture left behind by the Americans—testimonial to the ruggedness of U.S.-made products. Using G.I. ingenuity, USAFSS airmen chilled beer during the 1960's by lining up cans of beer along the grill of those same air conditioners in their barracks rooms.

6917TH RSM, SAN VITO, ITALY

In the spring of 1960, USAFSS activated the 6917th Radio Squadron Mobile at San Vito dei Normanni Air Station, a relatively small 318-acre site located some 300 miles southeast of Rome on Italy's boot heel near the port city of Brindisi. Base facilities were still under construction when the first airmen arrived. The early station pioneers lived on per diem in the Jolly Hotel near the train station in Brindisi awaiting completion of the dormitories and mess hall. Base power was provided in the early days by portable generators.

Col. John McVey was the initial commander for the base and
the 6917th RSM. Maj. Tortoriello, the squadron's first operations
officer, commenced operations with a four-flight around-the-clock
schedule in the August-September 1960 period. Initially, airmen
served on unaccompanied tours, with military families authorized
to join sponsors at San Vito in 1962.

Pre-Startup Site Survey at San Vito

In March 2006, retired Air Force Senior MSgt. Clarence Hall Jr.
discussed with the author a USAFSS site survey that occurred in
the San Vito area in January 1959. Assigned to the 6911th Radio
Group Mobile at Darmstadt, Germany, as a Morse intercept
operator, Sgt. Hall, Airman Al Thurston and several other Morse
operators conducted a hearability study a few miles from
Brindisi—presumably at the future site of San Vito dei Normanni
Air Station.[161]

Headed by a Capt. Turensky, the team flew with their intercept
equipment (housed in two H-1 vans) aboard C-130 aircraft from
Rhein-Main AB to the Brindisi civilian airport. Living in a hotel in
Brindisi (probably Jolly Hotel), the team parked their H-1 trailers
in a field outside of town, strung out some antennas, and
commenced intercept operations for about six weeks. Clarence
Hall recalls that there was quite a bit of excitement about the
success of their exploratory mission since they were able to
intercept target signals that USAFSS sites elsewhere were unable
to detect. Hall can not recall the specific dates of the site survey,
but it occurred shortly before he rotated from Germany in May
1959.

San Vito Dedication—10 April 1961

The 6917th RSM functioned inconspicuously at San Vito for
nine months before the Air Force decided to have a coming-out
party. On Monday, 10 April 1961, Maj. Gen. Millard Lewis
(USAFSS Commander) and the Hon. Italo Giulio Caiati (Italian
Undersecretary of Defense and a Brindisi native) officiated in the
on-station dedication ceremony.[162]

Attending dignitaries included Gen. Frederic H. Smith Jr.
(USAFE Commander), Italian Air Force generals, the Prefect of
Brindisi, Archbishop of Brindisi, and the mayors of San Vito,

Brindisi, Mesagne, Carovigno and Ostuni. A 6917th RSM air force formation paid tribute at the ceremony with a pomp and circumstance that reverberated through the local community for decades.

USAF Photo

Maj. Gen. Millard Lewis, USAFSS CC (1959-1962)

The official ribbon-cutting ceremony took place in the Dorm 1 parking lot at 18:00 hours, with an official banquet in the dining hall afterwards. Bruno Calo', an English-speaking Italian lawyer who began work with the station staff judge advocate's office in February 1961, served as official translator at the event.

Continuing as a U.S. Air Force employee at San Vito for 39 years, Bruno has become the station's unofficial historian. In June 2000, he wrote about the dedication ceremony, citing two important reasons that day remains burned in his memory forever: "one public, the official opening (they called it 'dedication') of San Vito dei Normanni Air Station; the other a very private one, for 10 April 1961 is the LAST day in my life when I got drunk."

Bruno had certain trepidations about mistakes in his translations of the official orators' speeches, but fear of a nightmare turned to elation when the ceremony ended with no serious blunders. At the banquet, everyone patted Bruno on the back for a "terrific" job; all of a sudden he was very popular. About 21:00 hours, the group moved to the Officers Club, just across from the dining hall. A band was playing pop music, and the bar was crowded, essentially all males since there were only four dependent wives at San Vito AS in 1961. While he was drinking moderately at the bar, several young officers kept telling Bruno that he was the hero of the day, "patting my back, offering to buy me all sort of drinks (which I found difficult to refuse.)" The drinks flowed like water, and Bruno got plastered—dead drunk.

About 3 a.m., Rodrigo Ravaioli, the club manager, woke up Bruno and asked him to leave so Rodrigo could close the club. Outside the club, as Bruno zigzagged unsteadily towards his Fiat 600 auto in the big lot in front of the 6917th compound, a couple of security policemen picked him up and plied him with strong black coffee in the dining hall. Eventually, Bruno attempted to walk to his car; he was wearing a new black tuxedo, purchased specifically for the ceremony. Between the headquarters building and compound parking lot, he staggered into a ditch along the road. He fell face-first into the ditch, but ended up flat of his back in four inches of rain water and mud.

As the icy water woke Bruno up, he stared at a sky full of stars asking himself "if I was in heaven or what." The mud had completely ruined his tuxedo, but he somehow found his car and drove to his hotel in Brindisi. The night watchman helped him to his room and poured him into bed. The time was early Tuesday morning; Bruno didn't wake up until Wednesday morning when his boss from San Vito knocked on his door, worried as to whether he was dead or alive. Embarrassed, Bruno carried his massive headache to work, promising never again to get drunk. Through four decades of work with the Air Force at San Vito, Bruno Calo' proudly kept that promise.

San Vito's "Elephant Cage"

The 6917th RSM began operations using temporary antennas installed in a vineyard behind the medical clinic, but a contract was already underway for the world's first AN/FLR-9 for the unit. In 1959, the Rome Air Development Center, Griffiss AFB, New York, contracted with Sylvania Electronic Systems to build two FLR-9 systems—one at San Vito AS, Italy and one at RAF Chicksands, England. Sylvania installed the FLR-9 at San Vito between August 1961 and May 1962; the company installed the second FLR-9 at Chicksands during 1962-63.

USAF Photo

FLR-9, 6917th ESG, Brindisi, Italy, 1984

Under a second contract, Sylvania installed additional FLR-9 systems at Misawa AB, Japan; Clark AB, Philippines; Elmendorf AFB, Alaska; and Karamursel, Turkey—the latter being installed in 1966. A discontinuation of USAFSS operations in Pakistan canceled the delivery of a planned FLR-9 in that country. Under a U.S. Army contract, two additional FLR-9 antenna systems were delivered to Augsburg, Germany, and Udorn, Thailand, in 1970.

FLR-9 Overview

Based on the Wullenweber antenna developed by the Germans in World War II, the FLR-9 was a massive circularly disposed antenna array. Each FLR-9 consisted of three rings of HF antennas. Band A (260 meter diameter outer ring) was 48 monopole elements spaced 78.4 feet apart. Band B (center ring) contained 96 sleeve monopoles spaced 37.5 feet apart, and Band C (inner ring) was made up of 48 antenna elements mounted on wooden structures in a circle. Consisting of the three concentric rings of antenna elements, the FLR-9's dimensions follow.[163]

AN/FLR-9 (Elephant Cage) Dimensions		
Item/Components	Height	Width
Required area (excluding clear zones beyond ground footprint of the circular antenna)	Tallest elements were 137.5 feet	Circle, 1,460 feet in diameter, covered 38.433 acres
Band A antenna elements (48 total, spaced 7.5 degrees apart)	105 feet	Circle, 1,198 feet diameter
Band B antenna elements (96 total; erected inside Band A, spaced 3.75 degrees apart)	35 feet	Circle, 1,116 feet diameter
Band A and B reflecting screens and supporting structure assemblies	137.5 feet (included lightening rod)	Circle, 1,075 feet diameter
Band C antenna elements (48 total; erected inside Band B, spaced 7.5 degrees apart)	68 feet with 70 feet reflecting screens	Circle, 335 feet diameter
Central Building (cylindrical structure in center of antenna array	Ceiling minimum 12 feet in center	Circular building, 90 feet diameter
Cable Tunnel of reinforced concrete (between central building and operations building); V8 1,180 feet long and V7 960 feet long. *	6.5 feet high	4 feet wide
* Extracted from technical manual for two Army Security Agency FLR-9 systems: V7 and V8; Chicksands cable tunnel appears to have been significantly longer		

Using German engineers spirited away to Russia after the war, the Soviet military deployed their own version of the Wullenweber—Soviet "Krug DF system"—during the 1950's. CMSgt. Joseph E. Rabig, Misawa AB, Japan, labeled the FLR-9 an "Elephant Cage" in response to a query by locals as to the FLR-9's purpose.[164]

*They work pretty well, don't they? You don't see any
elephants running around loose, do you?*

The name stuck! The Elephant Cage provided signal acquisition
and high-degree direction finding capabilities in the 1.5 to 30 MHz
frequency bands against signals up to 4,000 miles away. Linked
together in a network called "Iron Horse," the series of FLR-9
systems provided a worldwide DF capability.

Family Housing—San Vito AS

No military family housing existed on San Vito Air Station
when the base opened in 1960. When Bruno Calo' began his
employment at the base in February 1961, he spent his first two
months on duty as a translator helping conduct an off-base housing
survey to determine the availability of rental housing on the Italian
economy for military families. Validating the accessibility of
suitable housing, wives and children were permitted to join the
military sponsors at the base, with many families living in San
Vito, Brindisi, Carovigno, Mesagne, and Ostuni.

At the same time, the Air Force had contracted for the
construction of military family housing on base. The on-base
housing increased significantly when the U.S. Air Force
abandoned Wheelus AB, Libya. Before turning Wheelus AB over
to the Libyan government in 1970, the Air Force airlifted mobile
homes that had served as family housing in Libya to Brindisi.
Civil Engineers at San Vito AS set up the mobile homes in what
became know on base as "Officers' Row."

By the late 1980's, the 6917th ESG had 900 military family
housing units at San Vito, and family housing was still being
constructed on base when the Air Force announced the base
closure in 1992. Former ESC Capt. Kim Hagen reminisced in
2000-2001 about life on Officers' Row. She lived in the last trailer
nearest the Elephant Cage during her last tour at San Vito AS
(1992-93).

San Vito Air Base, Brindisi, Italy, circa 1980's

6917th Radio Group Mobile—1961-1963

As with other air stations where a USAFSS unit was the dominant tenant at the time, USAFSS assumed control of San Vito AS upon activating the station. The 6917th grew rapidly from the start and became the 6917th Radio Group Mobile in 1961. In 1963 as part of a command-wide unit redesignation, the 6917th RGM became the 6917th Security Group. On 1 October 1978, the 6917th SG became a tenant organization on San Vito AS, as the 7275th Air Base Group assumed responsibility for support functions on base. A similar realignment occurred at other USAFSS units/bases throughout the world.

San Vito's First WAF's

In the early 1970's, USAFSS began training female airmen—gender equality eliminated the term WAF's—in the Morse intercept, linguist and analyst career fields, with subsequent follow-on overseas assignments to San Vito, Chicksands, Karamursel and Misawa. In early 1972, the first four female airmen arrived on San Vito Air Station. A wing of Dormitory 2 was set aside for the station's "Fair Force." Later as additional female airmen arrived, Dorm 2 became an all-female billets. By the mid-1980's, a high percentage of the 6917th ESG Morse intercept operators, Russian linguists and analysts were female.

San Vito Deactivation Announced

On 9 November 1989, Bruno Calo' was sipping a glass of wine at home when a news flash reflected what amounted to the beginning of the end of the Cold War. Thousands of spirited East Berliners were demolishing the Berlin Wall. In turn, with the collapse of the Soviet Union only a matter of time, Bruno saw the handwriting on the wall that San Vito dei Normanni Air Station's days were numbered. It was all too clear in the minds of all base inhabitants (military, civilian and local nationals) that with the disappearance of the hostile East European and Soviet bloc Communist governments, the intelligence gathering unit at San Vito would have no mission. Nonetheless, new construction on San Vito proceeded as planned, and life on base continued normally for about three more years.

Col. Neil Patton, 7275th Air Base Group Commander at San Vito, announced the forthcoming base closure on 14 August 1992. In two years time, San Vito Air Station would cease to exist; at least that was the announced plan. Col. Eugene Beauvais, commander of the 6917th ESG in 1992, received the same announcement, but the Air Force Intelligence Command (successor command to the Electronic Security Command) had plans to discontinue 6917th operations significantly sooner than 1994.

6917TH ESG DEACTIVATED

In October 1992, Brig. Gen. Kenneth A. Minihan, Assistant Chief of Staff, Intelligence, U.S. Air Force, returned to San Vito as guest speaker at the last 6917th ESG Dining Out. As a lieutenant colonel and colonel, Minihan was the 6917th commander at San Vito from 1985-1987. He found it depressing to see the 6917th in a downward spiral after he'd worked so hard building up the organization during his command, including winning the Air Force Outstanding Unit Award. The Dining Out paid tribute to Col. Beauvais who had completed his tour as 6917th commander and was rotating to America.

Rather than replace Col. Beauvais with another O-6, Maj. Gen. Gary O'Shaughnessy, AFIC commander, appointed Maj. Paul Gifford, 6917th operations officer, to command the 6917th ESG during the group's phase down and close out. Both the U.S. Naval

Security Group and the 6917th ESG shut down operations at San Vito at 24:00 on 31 March 1993. A formal 6917th ESG deactivation occurred in April. Classified AFIC holdings from the 6917th ESG were transferred to the 26th Intelligence Group at Ramstein, Germany. The former 6917th ESG operations compound remained a restricted area—Special Forces personnel took over the compound for their classified operations and communications facility.

New Interim Mission for San Vito AS

In February of 1993, Special Forces units from a number of countries came to San Vito AS to provide SAR (search and rescue) and other support for ongoing activities in the Balkans. First, it was the food air drops, then it was support to war operations in Kosovo. The Special Forces aircraft operated out of the Italian Air Force base at Casale and Brindisi Airport while the troops were billeted at San Vito AS. When the 6917th moved out of the operations compound on 1 April 1993, the Joint Special Operations Task Force commander took control of the compound. His command, control and communications elements were ecstatic at finding a facility that already had secure communications, a building with solid walls, etc. They usually landed in an open field and constructed everything from scratch.

6917th Final Days at San Vito AS

Maj. Gifford departed Italy in June 1993, leaving behind a small contingent to make final disposition of equipment. That contingent departed in the late summer of 1993; the only vestige of former SIGINT equipment that remained at San Vito AS was the FLR-9 Elephant Cage system. Under contract to the U.S. Air Force, an Italian contractor finally dismantled the FLR-9 in the spring of 2002.

DET 1, 6917TH ESG

Colocated at San Vito AS, Detachment 1, 6917th ESG, was assigned administratively to the 6917th, although each had separate missions. Known on the air station as the "radome," Detachment 1 was the Comfy[165] Cloud component of Comfy Cobalt—a HQ USAF covert program with strictly enforced need-to-know access.

Det 1, 6917th ESG was activated in the early 1980's and operated a few months after the 6917th was deactivated, reporting during those final months directly to HQ European Electronic Security Division. Capt. Randy James was Det 1's last commander in late 1993.

San Vito AS Today—Solar Observatory

In 1986, the U.S. Air Force installed at San Vito AS a solar observatory—one of six global sites in the Air Force's Solar Electro-Optical Network. The sites are strategically located worldwide to ensure 24-hour sun monitoring. Reporting to the 55th Space Weather Support Squadron, Schriever AFB, Colorado, the observatory operates seven days a week year-round. The observatory's mission involves reporting real-time solar events.

A defense contractor runs the San Vito Solar Observatory. Involved in the operation of the Solar Observatory in 2006, Joseph L. Hauschild was the 6917th ESG's last link to San Vito dei Normanni Air Station. He previously served two tours with the 6917th (1977-1981 and 1983-1987) as an environmental health specialist. Except for the observatory, San Vito AS currently has the eerie appearance of a ghost town. Buildings and infrastructure are slowly crumbling away while the base remains on standby status for Balkan contingencies.

Bruno Calo''s Final Days at San Vito AS

The San Vito dei Normanni Air Station story would be incomplete without addressing Bruno Calo''s final days as a U.S. Air Force employee on the base. Even with San Vito AS being kept open to support NATO missions, the local national staffing on base had been reduced to 26 Italians, including Mr. Calo'. With the staff judge advocate's office deactivated, in August 1994 Bruno became the attorney-advisor-translator for the new 7275th Air Base Squadron (Provisional) commander.

The next five years at San Vito AS were pretty much a blur for Bruno Calo'. During that time, American military personnel served on temporary duty tours of 120 days or less at the station. Recapping the history of the air station's final months, Bruno calculates that he served fourteen commanders between September 1994 and December 1999.

Finally, Calo''s 40 years with the U.S. Air Force reached an inglorious end on 29 February 2000 when clerks from the civilian personnel office, Aviano Air Base, handed out checks to him and 24 fellow Italian workers and withdrew their San Vito AS entry passes.

The end was quite impersonal with not so much as a halfhearted "thank you." But Bruno Calo' is not resentful. While San Vito dei Normanni Air Station's chaotic fate is still to be decided, he has fond memories of many "marvelous" Americans he had the fortune to meet in the past 40 years, and he loves America as his second country.

A similar event had occurred five years earlier at RAF Chicksands, England, where an Air Intelligence Agency team discontinued SIGINT operations at the base. USAFSS airmen had commenced operations at Chicksands in 1950—rushed into operation in part by the "Berlin Blockade."

CHAPTER SIX

USAFSS OPERATIONS—UNITED KINGDOM

An attempt to drive the Western Allies from the city, the Soviet blockade of West Berlin (June 1948-May 1949), dramatically changed the dynamics of Air Force Security Service plans to expand its signals intelligence gathering capabilities. An Army-Air Force plan stipulated that USAFSS replace personnel on loan from the Army Security Agency by 30 June 1949. At the same time, the command had to build up the capabilities of the 1st and 2nd Radio Squadrons Mobile that it had inherited from ASA. Additionally, USAFSS needed urgently to deploy a radio squadron mobile in England, among other new locations.

10TH RSM ACTIVATED

Security Service activated the 10th Radio Squadron Mobile at Brooks AFB, Texas, in 1949, but little was accomplished immediately to prepare the unit for shipment to the United Kingdom. With the crisis in Berlin, beefing up the 2nd RSM's capabilities got first priority. In the spring of 1950, USAFSS Headquarters designated Major Donald Robinson the 10th RSM commander and charged him with equipping and deploying the 10th RSM to RAF Chicksands, England.

Temperatures hovered around 100 degrees F. in San Antonio as the 10th RSM came to life. Some 30 newly assigned personnel worked throughout the summer in a stifling aircraft hangar at Brooks—gathering and packaging squadron equipment and supplies in crates for shipment to their new home in England. This 10th RSM cadre would be joined in England by additional intercept operators and traffic analysts who had served and trained briefly with the 2nd RSM in Germany. In September 1950, USAFSS commander Col. Hetherington alerted Maj. Robinson for movement of the 10th RSM to England.[166]

United Kingdom and Ireland

RAF Chicksands, circa 1943

RAF Chicksands Overhead View, circa 1943

Chicksands Facilities—1950's

The author has not located official unit histories for the 10th RSM, but undoubtedly a USAFSS team conducted a site survey at RAF Chicksands prior to the deployment of the 10th RSM to the base. (William Bowers, then a USAFSS captain, told the author in 1999 that he visited Chicksands from Darmstadt during the summer of 1950.) Located 40 miles north of London, in 1950 Chicksands was a former British Y service intercept station that had lain dormant since 1946. An air station without a runway, RAF Chicksands had the following facilities when the 10th RSM arrived.

- Tech Site A—COMINT intercept facility housed in small buildings called "blocks"
- Tech Site B—communications relay facility located away from other base facilities
- Priory—former monastery north of Flit River (single officer housing)
- Nissen hut billets clustered south of the Flit River (RAF enlisted males in WW II)
- WAAF area north of Flit River (Nissen and Seco huts for enlisted females); mess hall, cinema (movie), club, former NAAFI (BX), etc. also located in WAAF area
- Communal (standalone) combination latrines and showers
- Buildings for headquarters, fire station, infirmary, motor pool, armory and supply.

Created in 1940 under wartime constraints, Chicksands facilities were spartan; however, built expressly as a COMINT intercept station, it had the essential elements to support a 10th RSM intercept mission. A small RAF detachment that occupied Nissen huts south of the Flit River operated a comms relay station at Tech Site B and served as caretaker for the entire station. When the 10th RSM arrived, the RAF ceded control of RAF Chicksands to the U.S. Air Force except the RAF area below the Flit River and Tech Site B. The former WAAF area and billets (Nissen and Seco huts) became home for 10th RSM airmen.

The drawing below provides an overview of RAF Chicksands Station during World War II. This is the station infrastructure that awaited the 10th Radio Squadron Mobile in 1950.

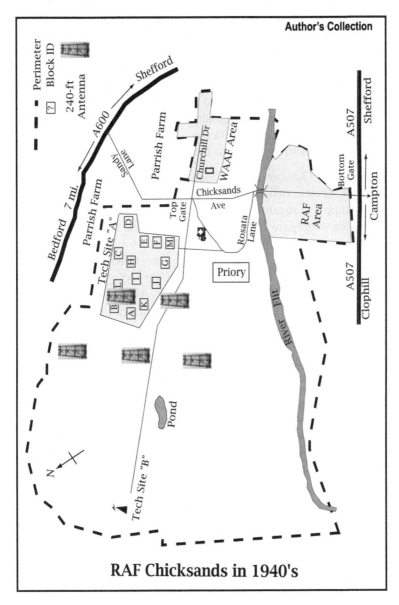

RAF Chicksands in 1940's

Getting There—1950

Major Robinson dispatched Lieutenants Edsel Wiggins and Robert Craig to Brooklyn, New York, as an advance party to coordinate movement of the 10th RSM overseas. (In 2000, Wiggins discussed activation of RAF Chicksands as an American base with the author.) Maj. Robinson and the 10th RSM cadre arrived in Brooklyn later with squadron holdings[167]—vehicles, generators, field kitchen, intercept equipment, typewriters, safes, file cabinets, limited furniture and personal belongings of assigned men. (Like other USAFSS squadrons, the 10th RSM was a self-contained "mobile" unit, outfitted to operate as a standalone unit; however, the squadron soon lost most of its mobility.)

Around 10 October 1950, Maj. Robinson sent Lt. Wiggins (technical services officer), Lt. James Parsley (supply officer), Sgt. Confer (supply sergeant) and Sgt. Hyman (mess sergeant) ahead to Chicksands to prepare the base for arrival of the main group. They flew aboard an Air Force C-54 from Westover AFB, Massachusetts, to RAF Burtonwood, an American base near Liverpool. Traveling by train from Liverpool to London, Lt. Wiggins' team checked in with U.S. 3rd Air Division at South Ruislip. The 3rd Air Division would be activating an air base squadron at RAF Chicksands to operate the base, with the 10th RSM being a tenant unit on station. However, the new air base squadron (7534th ABS) had yet to materialize, and the 10th RSM was the first American unit to arrive at Chicksands.

Lt. Wiggins' team obtained a staff car and drove to Chicksands, where he reported to the station commander, RAF Flight Lieutenant Lou Barry. The next day, Lt. Edsel Wiggins signed a hand receipt, taking control of RAF Chicksands on behalf of the U.S. government. He told the author it was an eerie feeling taking responsibility for an air station.

The Americans had two initial shocks: the unexpected cordial, warm greeting and helpful attitude of RAF personnel, and the very cold, wet, foggy, miserable weather that penetrated everything. Our mission, in a matter of three to four weeks, was to prepare livable quarters, to set up the mess hall and the shower house and to organize routes and procedures to draw rations and supplies.

Viewed from the main gate (Top Gate) at RAF Chicksands, the next two photographs depict Sandy Lane—the road leading from base towards Bedford—in 1951 and in 2000.

Contributed by George Montague

Sandy Lane from Chicksands' Top Gate, 1951

Author's Collection

Sandy Lane from Chicksands' Top Gate, July 2000

According to Wiggins, the men kept a log of when they saw the sun—it was visible for brief periods six times from mid-November

1950 through March 1951. Major Robinson and the 10th RSM cadre traveled aboard a Navy troopship—USNS General Maurice Rose—from the Brooklyn Army Terminal, arriving at Southampton in the south of England the first week of November 1950. Senior personnel included:

- Maj. Robinson   commander
- Capt. Tommy Grundy   adjutant
- Capt. Russell Verploegh   assistant operations officer
- Lt. Robert Craig   communications officer
- MSgt. Jim Adams   first sergeant

Chicksands' buildings were structurally sound, but leaky roofs and five years of neglect had taken a toll. Lt. Wiggins remembered all of the hard work he and his advance team put into efforts to have quarters and the mess hall ready for occupancy when the squadron cadre arrived from America.

> *The officers were assigned quarters with the RAF in a building that had served as a medical clinic during WW II. The airmen were quartered in WW II Nissen huts. The mess hall also had been used by the RAF during WW II. A separate building served as a shower house.*

The original mess hall was a large Nissen hut. Later, a large dining area was added at the end of the mess hut, with the kitchen part of the mess hall remaining in the Nissen building.

Contributed by Bill Gray

Chicksands Dining Hall, 1958

Wiggins explained that the advance American party received VIP treatment. He and Lt. Parsley were assigned RAF aides-de-camp.

> *As a courtesy, the officers were assigned an RAF "batman," in the British military, a soldier assigned to an officer as a servant who took care of the officer's domestic needs. Each morning before the officer awoke, his clothes were brushed and laid out, shoes were shined and a steaming cup of hot tea was in place on the night stand, but the batman was never around. It became the officer's goal to catch the batman in the room. Never did.*

The Priory and Rosata

Soon, the officers moved into a cleaned up section of the Priory, the magnificent former monastery on RAF Chicksands. With the RAF providing the American officers with stories about Priory history, the sightings and sounds of the Rosata ghost lived on.[168]

Contributed by Bill Gray

Chicksands Priory, 1958

The wind made an eerie sound. One night about 3:00 a.m., Captain Grundy heard a horrible sound coming from the fireplace chimney in his room. He finally discovered that it was a large bird fluttering down inside the chimney. No more sleep that night.

One cold, rainy, very foggy evening an RAF military policeman reported to the commander that something white was moving on the Priory lawn. Wiggins accompanied Lou Barry to the Priory in his car. Nothing was evident at the front of the building. There was talk of many possibilities, including ghosts. Several minutes elapsed. Wiggins suggested taking a flash light (torch) and walking around the building. Not a good idea. Then Wiggins suggested that Barry reposition his car so that the headlights would illuminate the area. Good idea. Several white faced cows were startled by the lights.

To this day, USAFSS Chicksands alumni often proclaim instances in which Rosata's ghost was sighted or heard. No one knows if the Rosata phenomena are authentic or merely the results of airmen reacting strangely to warm British ale!

SETTLING IN AT CHICKSANDS

Working with available furnishings—British cots, straw mattresses/pillows, bedding, and potbelly coal stoves—Lt. Wiggins' advance team had bare essentials in place when Major Robinson and 10th RSM airmen arrived. Stored in unheated Nissen huts in damp British weather for five years, the furnishings were musty and mildewed. Nonetheless, open bay Nissens were a welcome sight after being cooped up on the General Rose, plus the wait at Southampton for their vehicles and equipment to be offloaded. And convoying to Chicksands in deuce-and-a-half trucks driving on the wrong (left) side on narrow British roads was a real eye-opener for the young, mostly teenage airmen, who were away from home for the first time. Most of the airmen left England at the end of their tour with a British bride.

There were no family quarters on the base until the mid-1960's, and wives and children could not accompany their sponsor to Chicksands in the early 1950's. Married officers and NCO's were permitted to bring their families as soon as they made suitable living arrangements with a British landlord. However, with the British still recovering from the war and few support facilities— only a small BX and no commissary—on base, living on the British economy was difficult. Dan D'Apolito and his new British bride Jean traveled all the way to London to purchase groceries in an American commissary in 1952.

I remember having to go to Ruislip for the commissary when I first got married (Sept '52). We took a train to London, and underground [subway] to the base. I can still see people staring at us with growls at the big box of groceries, plus bags we were carrying full of groceries. At that time, Britain was still rationed on some items. Later trips, we took a taxi that a friend of mine drove. In '53, they reactivated a base outside Bedford—Chelveston—I think, and the trip was much closer. I left in December of '53, and Chicksands still did not have a commissary.

Contributed by Bill Gray

Chicksands Commissary, circa 1958—
built soon after the D'Apolitos departed base
(Building on right is Latrine # 414.)

Contributed by Bill Gray

RAF Chicksands Infrastructure, 1950's
Latrine # 414 left, Priory left background,
Nissen huts on right and tall antenna beyond Nissens

Contributed by Ambrose Jackson

Chicksands Priory, 1951

The 2nd RSM transferred 30 airmen, including SSgt.'s Ambrose Jackson and Murl G. Olson, from Germany to Chicksands on 5 December 1950.[169] In 2002, Jackson commented on the condition of RAF Chicksands when his group arrived from Darmstadt.

The base was a shambles, having been closed down sometime after the war. We spent nearly a month cleaning up all the buildings and making repairs before we could go into operation.

Contributed by Bill Baker

Chicksands, Part of Antenna Field, Early 1950's

Ambrose Jackson's Nissen Hut, Chicksands, 1951

Seco Huts, Chicksands, 1951

Edsel Wiggins recalled that the squadron commenced operations in Block J, using Collins 51J intercept receivers. Spiffed up, many of those World War II structures supported the USAFSS mission at Chicksands for more than two decades, although new multistory barracks replaced Nissen and Seco hut billeting during the 1960's. USAFSS also built a new operations building that replaced the intercept blocks in the early 1960's, but several original buildings are still in use at the base today.

Wiggins—Memories of Early Days

In memoirs that he shared with the author, Ed Wiggins wrote that wives of 10th RSM members arrived by ship at Southampton in early 1951, with married personnel living in rented homes on the local economy in Bedford, Luton, Shefford and other villages.

As a diversion, parties and dances were organized on the first level of the Priory for both RAF and USAF airmen. These were well received. Other events included special meals in the Airmens Mess. Sgt. Hyman put together a Thanksgiving dinner in 1950 with all the traditional fare. An old theatre building was renovated. Special services furnished first run movies and even stage plays.

Contributed by Bill Gray

Chicksands Movie Theater, circa 1957

Volunteers built an NCO/Airmens Club in one of the Nissen huts. It was very active. A few weeks later, a larger club building was designated. A small base exchange was included in the building. One popular recurring event at the Club was dances to which bus loads of girls were brought in from surrounding cities and towns.

An Officers Club was built despite the fact that there were only about five to eight officers on station. A Sgt. Beeman, the unit illustrator, helped with the design and the officers painted the inside of the building. Beeman assembled a divider that separated the open dance floor from the bar by adding pierced steel planks (PSP) on end and curving the joined pieces in an S shape, then painted the divider red. Very attractive. Parties usually involved potluck dishes prepared by the wives. One night a party was planned, which included an invitation to several local civilian dignitaries. Very bad fog set in. Every American arrived but not one British as they know when the fog is very thick parties are cancelled.

A library was organized and manned by an older British gentleman who was very knowledgeable about libraries and books. He did an excellent job and the reading traffic was routine and normal. The gentleman eventually was replaced by a very attractive lady in her late twenties. The reading traffic increased to the extent that it became hard to find a place in the library to sit and read.

The facilities described by Edsel Wiggins remained pretty much as he described for most of the 1950's. Wednesday was dance night, with English ladies bussed in from Luton and Bedford to the service club located behind the snack bar and BX at the northeast side of the base. In the course of his stay at Chicksands, Wiggins served in several roles, especially during the first six months when the 10th RSM was severely undermanned.

My role was Technical Services Officer, then later, additionally as Intercept and DF [Officer] plus such other duties as Special Services and Photo. When other officers arrived I was primarily Tech Services [Officer]. I left in August 1953.

Contributed by Paul McGee
10th RSM HQ, RAF Chicksands, late 1954

Like many other USAFSS officers over the years, Edsel Wiggins was a mustang officer who gained his commission after initially serving as an enlisted technician.

Prior to Chicksands, I was a G.I. working as an aircraft radio mechanic. When the first pilot training program started in 1947 I was accepted. After graduation I flew C-47's and C-54's with MATS until I was "volunteered" to attend communications officers school. Went to USAFSS and immediately assigned to the 10th [RSM].

After the 10th, I was OIC of the Engineering Lab at the HQ [USAFSS HQ] for a while, then assigned as a project officer in Crypto Engineering working on voice. Got the Air Force to send me to AFIT where I received my BS EE from the Univ. of Illinois. Then back to HQ where I soon became Director of Crypto Engineering for about 3 years.

Retiring as a major, Edsel Wiggins managed Apollo Space Lab experiments for NASA and served as Chief of Electrical Engineering for Learjet and Cessna Aircraft. In July 2000, Edsel returned to Chicksands as guest speaker at a 50th "Welcome Home Yanks" reunion of Americans who had served at Chicksands during the Cold War. The author met Edsel at the reunion and kept in touch until he passed away in 2004. RIP Edsel Wiggins!

10th RSM's First Linguists

A World War II Army Air Corps veteran, SSgt. Ambrose Jackson was the first Russian linguist assigned to the 10th Radio Squadron Mobile. Serving in the 327th Fighter Control Squadron (9th Air Force) supporting Allied fighter operations on the continent, Corporal Jackson's echelon landed on Omaha Beach on D-Day plus 3 and trailed behind the front through France and Belgium into Germany in 1944-1945. With the front stalled for about six months immediately before the Battle of the Bulge, Ambrose Jackson dated a Belgian lady in Verviers (near Liege). Since she and her family spoke no English, Ambrose learned French—creating a love for languages that later resulted in his volunteering to become a USAFSS Russian linguist.

Discharged in 1945, Jackson reenlisted in the Air Corps a year later and spent several months in temporary assignments because there were no openings for his air control-related specialty. Seeing an Army Security Agency bulletin seeking linguists and Morse operators, he volunteered. The earliest Russian language class was months away so he accepted an assignment to Morse code school. Subsequently, ASA assigned Sgt. Jackson as a Morse intercept operator to the 6th Detachment, 2nd Signal Service Battalion, Herzo Base, Germany, in 1948. There, he volunteered to move into a newly created non-Morse (printer) section and was promoted to SSgt. In April 1949, ASA detached Jackson to the 2nd RSM in Darmstadt, an assignment that he resisted because he loved his radioprinter job, and the 2nd RSM did not have a radioprinter mission at the time. In the end, Jackson did transfer to the Air Force (USAFSS) as a staff sergeant, assigned to the 2nd RSM.

Finally, Ambrose Jackson got the opportunity to become a linguist. Attending language school at Oberammergau in the German Alps (January-July 1950), he cross-trained as a Russian linguist. A month later, SSgt. Jackson volunteered for a reassignment to the 10th RSM at Chicksands, but the transfer was delayed on a month-to-month basis to November. Meanwhile, he was one of a handful of Russian linguists who activated a voice intercept unit in Berlin. The 2nd RSM curtailed Jackson's temporary assignment in Berlin to transfer him to England.

SSgt. Ambrose Jackson (Russian linguist) and Cpl. Donald J. Kubeck (Polish linguist) were the only linguists in the squadron when the 10th RSM operations began in England. They hand-scanned intercepted traffic live, later using the handscans to type a transcript. "We didn't have recorders in those days, and if you didn't get it the first time, you lost it." Later when they obtained a couple of tape recorders, Jackson was the intercept operator, and Kubeck, who taught himself Russian, performed transcription. (During 1961, TSgt. Kubeck was the author's supervisor in the 6913th RSM in Bremerhaven.)

10th RSM's First Traffic Analysts

Retired CMSgt. Francis Hollifield was the senior "202" (traffic analyst) among the 10th RSM cadre that commenced USAFSS operations at Chicksands. Graduating from the Army Security Agency's radio traffic analysis course at Carlisle Barracks, Pennsylvania, Pfc. Hollifield entered Security Service with the 8th RSM at Brooks AFB in April 1949. Serving in 8th RSM operations at Brooks, Cpl. Hollifield volunteered for duty with the 10th RSM and arrived at Chicksands on Groundhog Day (2 February) 1951, the ranking 202 in the squadron. Other traffic analysis pioneers with Hollifield in England included: Billy J. Calloway, John P. "Rip" Boyle, Richard Stranathan and Ernest H. Fellows.

Hollifield and Ralph "Bull" Rich, a Serbo-Croatian linguist, had become good friends while working together in the 8th RSM. Arriving together at Chicksands, Hollifield helped establish the traffic exploitation section, and with minimal need for a Serb linguist in England, Rich also became a traffic analyst. Holly, as he was known to friends, recalls that Lt. Wiggins was the traffic exploitation officer in the early days.

Bull and I were corporals, and we were still wearing the old army uniforms with blue ties, belts and hats. We received the Air Force blues just before coming to the 'Sands, and these various combinations were optional. Both Bull and I were promoted to SSgt. during the summer of 1951.

Cast into a job that lacked NCO leadership, Frank Hollifield became the squadron's traffic analysis guru and set the 10th RSM in good stead with senior Air Force officers in the UK.

During the early days we established very good relations with the General at Third Air Force. He would visit Chicksands during special operations, and Maj. Bowers and I (a SSgt.) would provide him with real-time information. Capt. Izonkirwicz was our liaison officer in Ruislip. One night we worked until about 3 in the morning with Maj. Gen. [John P.] McConnell of the 7th Air Division, Lt. Gen. [Leon W.] Johnson of 3rd Air Force, and about a dozen full birds. During the session there was a tracking grid change, and I was able to break it within a few minutes. The officers were amazed; it was no big deal, but our unit received a citation from 3rd Air Force, and I was promoted to TSgt.

After that I was called down to Ruislip for various briefings. They even credited me with saving one of our aircraft. We had an aircraft scheduled to fly a mission. I advised against it and it was cancelled. And when I was up for promotion to MSgt., I received an endorsement from Maj. Izonkirwicz mentioning the generals, which I am sure helped my promotion.

Frank Hollifield became one of Security Service's most respected analysts and NCO's, while Ralph Rich took his discharge after one enlistment and became a renowned traffic analyst as a USAFSS civil servant. Both married English brides. Francis Hollifield married wife Josie in Luton on 18 September 1951. Ralph and Jean Rich married 18 months later.

Kidnapped Bride

Best Man Francis Hollifield vividly recalls the day he and George Keesee kidnapped the bride at Ralph and Jean Richs' wedding reception.

Immediately after their wedding, some of us kidnapped Jean and took her to the train station before we were caught as we were buying a ticket for her. She thought it was very funny, but Bull didn't appreciate it.

The scene in Luton after the wedding was the talk of the town—raising a few eyebrows among the staid British townsmen. In 2007, Jean Rich, who lost Ralph to heart failure in 2003, reminisced about the wedding and the "kidnapping."

Contributed by Jean Rich

Ralph and Jean Rich Wedding, 11 April 1953

Ralph and I were married in Luton on the 11th April 1953. I lived in Luton during WW 2. We came from London and never went back.

Due to billeting shortages at Chicksands, when Ralph was promoted to SSgt. in 1951, he was allowed to move off base.

Ralph preferred Luton to Bedford, and he with his band of "Merry Men" always went there in the evenings and weekends. Their favorite watering hole was " Richard the Third" or the "The Midland." They got to know all the regulars there, including my mother and stepdad, and many of their friends. Mainly Ralph's group consisted of Rip Boyle, Bill Calloway, Bob Tipton, Holly [Francis Hollifield], Heinie Fakelman and others.

Anyway, when they were allowed to move off base, one of my mother's friends and her husband invited Ralph to live with them. One of his favorite stories was that he dated my mother before me. He used to escort the older ladies while the husbands played Bowls, which was the outside version on grass. They always played at The Conservative Clubs around the area, and he was the designated driver. My mother finally invited him to our house to supper, which was when I finally met him.

We starting going out, but back then my family was very protective, and I was not given the freedom the young people are today. In June of '52, he asked me to marry him. It took until the next April for me to get a clearance. As I said, we got married on April 11th.

It was at this point that Best Man "Holly" Hollifield and George Keesee dreamed up a great scheme to kidnap the bride.

After the reception, Ralph's friends offered to escort me to the car. I went outside, and they helped me in and took off, leaving Ralph shouting and waving his fists. They then had the problem how to get me back as by then Ralph was following with some others.

Best Man Hollifield told the author that "Bull was quite upset to say the least."

I was driving an old Chevy, and as we drove through the streets of Luton we were blowing the horn constantly. I'm surprised we never got stopped.

With Ralph Rich chasing close on their trail, Jean explained that the kidnappers finally decided to discharge their bounty in front of the Luton Town Football Club stadium.

They stopped on Dunstable Road where a soccer match had just finished, and all the men were flooding the streets. They asked me to get out and took off, leaving me standing there surrounded by all these people.

I was still holding my bouquet, in my wedding dress and veil. Being a very staid English girl, I suddenly realized that my life was going to be very different as I was surrounded by all these young full-of-fun American guys. Most of them were just getting out of their teens.

After Ralph picked me up, we all went to my mother and father's house, and I was able to calm Ralph down. As I got ready to leave, everyone from the wedding reception arrived and of course, out came the cards, and they all started playing poker. We actually missed our train to London. I remember Jack Smith offered to take me on our Honeymoon as Ralph was involved in the game!

We rented a house in Luton that had been made into two apartments. We had the top one, and Holly and Josie lived downstairs.

Their wedding vows worked to perfection, blessing Jean and Ralph with three sons. In ill health at the end, Ralph Rich hung tough to celebrate their Golden Anniversary.

Ralph's goal at the end, even though he was so ill, was to make our 50th anniversary. He told his doctor to make sure he managed that. We had a great party that our three boys and their families gave us. He died on 31st May. Very fitting as he was one of the most loyal and patriotic men I have ever seen.

Rest in Peace, Ralph Rich! The author befriended Jean and Ralph in the early 1960's in San Antonio, where Ralph owned "King's Lounge," THE unofficial USAFSS bar directly across the street from Air Force Security Service. The author bartended part-time in King's Lounge and served a Lone Star or two to many, many USAFSS pioneers who stopped by during Happy Hour (4 to 6 p.m.) for a cool brew on the way home from HQ USAFSS. It was a true pleasure observing Ralph and Jean rear their three sons: David, Chris and Tony.

King's Lounge Waitress and Bartender (Larry Tart),
August 1964

The pair of photographs below depict downtown Bedford, Bedfordshire, in 1958. While many airmen hung out in Luton and Hitchin, especially those with cars, Bedford became a favorite for those who depended on bus transportation.

High Street, Bedford, Bedfordshire, 1958

Market Square, Bedford, 1958

Getting to Chicksands—Mid-1950's

Like the Army, the U.S. Air Force transferred most of its personnel overseas on military troopships prior to the mid-1950's. While the Army used surface transportation well into the 1960's for personnel arriving in Germany, the Air Force was in the process of switching to military flights for travel to Europe when the author traveled to England in November 1956. At that time, airmen reported to Manhattan Beach Air Force Station, Brooklyn, NY. Some still had the unfortunate experience of a week to ten days on a crowded troopship, which often dropped anchor in Bremerhaven, Germany, before airmen found their way back to the UK. Others, including the author, were bussed from Brooklyn to McGuire AFB, NJ, where they boarded a C-54 or C-118 Military Air Transport System aircraft. The MATS flights refueled at Gander AFB, Newfoundland, and Shannon, Ireland, before debarking at RAF Burtonwood.

Being a country boy from North Carolina, I experienced my first train ride on a British Railways coach class trip from Liverpool (by Burtonwood) to London. Twelve of us lugged our Air Force-issue duffel bags between stations to catch a second train from St. Pancras Station, London, to Midland Station, Bedford, Bedfordshire. The ride from Bedford station to Chicksands in the back of a deuce-and-a-half truck seemed more like 20 miles than the actual 10 mile distance.

Arriving at the base after 8 p.m., we found that both the mess hall and snack bar were closed; it had been a long day! The Charge of Quarters provided each man a set of bed linen and assigned us to billets—scattering the twelve of us in multiple barracks wherever empty cots existed. Two of us ended up in the NCO barracks by the NCO Club, possibly the only barracks on the station with a toilet.

Contributed by Bill Gray

Chicksands NCO Club, circa 1957 (later Airmens Club)

Fortunately, a motor pool driver hauled our duffel bags to our barracks; otherwise, we would not have found them in the dark, snowy night. MSgt. Leggett, our first sergeant, informed us at our in-briefing the next day that Chicksands was on lockdown. The U.S. Air Force had placed Bedford off-limits, keeping Americans away from rioting British reservists who were being called to active duty to support the British and French invasion of Egypt (Suez War of 1956). With restrictions removed, we visited the Peacock Bar in Bedford Saturday night—18 years old and learning our way in the world.

Chicksands—Enlisted Quarters

After living in German-crafted, thick-walled former Nazi barracks in Berlin, Darmstadt and even the ASA barracks at Herzo Base, Germany, Ambrose Jackson was taken aback by the damp, drafty Nissen billets without latrines at Chicksands.

We lived in the Quonset [Nissen] huts (the rounded ones), and also there were a few rectangular barracks which were called "Seco huts." One large building served as washroom, shower room, and latrine for all the barracks. The roof was corrugated tin, meaning that the building had large openings at each end, which let in all the cold air. (Dec '50 and Jan-Mar '51 were plenty cold and snowy.)

Latrine # 414, RAF Chicksands, circa 1957

The barracks were heated by a coke-fired stove in each end, but if you got more than 10 feet away from the stove you froze off your whatchamaycallit.

The following winter, potbelly oil stoves and external oil tanks replaced the coke stoves. The communal bath huts—Americans called them latrines—continued to be stoked (heated) by coke.

Nissen and Quonset Huts

Airmen who served at Chicksands prior to about 1965 had a lifetime experience, living in Nissen huts, Quonset huts or Seco huts. Developed for the British military in 1916, the Nissen hut was a prefabricated structure installed on a rectangular concrete pad. Made of corrugated steel sheets bent to form an elongated building, both the Nissens and Quonsets had a semi-circular cross-section. The Nissen hut design offered three basic widths and lengths that were multiples of six feet. Most of the Nissens used for billeting at Chicksands were 16 feet wide and 30 feet long, although some located in the oak grove near the BX were the larger variant Nissen. The mess hall, cinema (theater), snack bar, base exchange, NCO Club, motor pool garage and supply buildings—all built by the RAF in the early 1940's—were large size Nissens.

Chicksands Snack Bar and BX, circa 1958

Former Snack Bar and BX, now storage, 2005

American Quonset huts derived from the Nissen design were generally larger. The most common standard size Quonset was 20' x 48', with other sizes varying up to 40' x 100'. Most aspects of life in the 10th RSM at Chicksands improved with time after the initial year of startup operations, but for personnel forced to live permanently in inadequate billeting, little could be done to ameliorate barracks life. Every airman who lived on base at

Chicksands during the 1950's can wax poetic about life in the good ole days at the 'Sands. Retired USAFSS MSgt. George Montague has an excellent recollection of Nissen Hut # 89, where he lived when he arrived at Chicksands in April 1951.

The Nissen huts had room for eight men along with footlockers, no wall lockers. There was a bar that ran end to end on both sides and that is where we hung clothes. I think there was a shelf above this but I am not sure.

The original heating was coal stoves with the British delivering a single bucket of coal to barracks daily. The kerosene tent stoves [M-41 potbelly heaters] came in late '51 or early '52.

When we arrived we had English beds and bedding, which were terrible. The mattress was straw and the blankets were so thin that they gave us 5 of them. We got U.S. beds and blankets about the same time as the tent stoves.

I lived in Hut # 89, which was just below the Officers Club and next to the mess hall. Later, when we were housed by Trick, I moved to one of the huts on the left side of the road nearer to the PX [BX]. Just across the road and to the left was the latrine.

Contributed by Bill Gray

Chicksands Officers Club, circa 1958

The author used that same latrine in 1960. A mention of bomb shelters that were dispersed throughout the barracks area and within the operations compound reminded George Montague of an incident involving an airman he only remembers as "Frenchy."

Frenchy lived with me in Hut # 89. He borrowed a sweater I had just received from my mother and went to Luton where he exchanged it for a working girl's favors. He used to sit in the club and drink sloe gin and Coke, and he is the only person I ever met who drank sloe gin.

He went to London one weekend and came back early, but he brought a working girl with him and set her up in the nearest bomb shelter to the club. He went to one of the empty huts and got a mattress or two for her and she was in business. Someone either with a moral code or who did not get any called the A.P.'s. He ended up being court-martialed.

A killjoy in every crowd! When Donald Hill arrived at the 'Sands in 1954, the 10th RSM was using Nissen huts in the RAF area south of the Flit River as overflow billeting for American airmen.

Quonset huts were the Hilton Hotels of my era. I started out in a RAF tar paper shack that the wind blew through and it was colder than a well digger's toes.

The tar shacks were located below the Priory across the creek, going down the road to the lower gate. They had coke stoves—but no coke. They had two doors and windows on the side—can't recall how many. Spent the winter of 1954 there. Not the fondest of memories as it was a cold winter. The roof leaked—we had to put our raincoats over us and in the morning everything was wet.

During his lengthy stay at Chicksands (1954-1958), Alfred W. "Bill" Gray III lived in both a Quonset hut and a smaller Nissen hut.

Larry, I lived in one of those Quonsets in Oak Grove, near the PX. It had two doors (fire regulations dictated that), windows at each end, and three pairs of windows on either side.

Contributed by Bill Gray

Bill Gray, Paul McGee and Dick Green by Snack Bar, 1956

George Montague recalls that the squadron added some Quonset huts in the vicinity of the BX circa 1952 to alleviate a billeting shortage when the unit had some personnel living in tents. The buildup of personnel in 1952 included airmen temporarily assigned to the 10th RSM at Chicksands, pending the activation of a new USAFSS squadron at Kirknewton, Scotland. Bill Gray remembers his billets in the oak grove as being a larger Quonset hut.

We had about twelve spaces for bunks in that building, but only eight in the second Quonset I lived in, right next to the theater. The latter hut did not have side windows. I feel fairly comfortable in saying there were two sizes.

The common feature was the double kerosene heaters; both the larger and the smaller huts had them, and they shared one other attribute—they usually ran out of fuel every weekend, no matter how sparingly one set the level of fire inside the burner. Since the Brit workmen had control of the kerosene trucks, and we did not, we went without heat until Monday morning.

Wayne Palmer shared time at Chicksands with Bill Gray and knew comrades who used G.I. ingenuity to restore heat when their fuel tank ran dry.

Oil was supplied via rubber hoses connected to a rack of 55-gallon drums laid on their sides and suspended above the ground by "cross buck" racks. It was not unheard of for the barracks which ran out of heat first to simply "switch hoses" with their neighbors. (This worked best when the "neighbors" were working the midnight shift.)

Bob Joyce, a former Russian linguist, has both warm and cold memories of life at Chicksands

By the winter of 1957, one of the Quonset huts across from the PX was being used as a classroom for University of Maryland classes. I took an English class there and remember that it was a bitterly cold room on a winter evening (much colder than our Seco hut down below the NCO Club). If memory serves, it was one of the smaller huts, but completely open inside with a single potbelly stove in the center.

Contributed by Bill Gray

Chicksands Education Center, circa 1960

Maybe the Brits had learned by '56-'58 how to keep the kerosene (what did they call it...paraffin?) barrels full. I don't ever remember ours running dry, and the stoves burned 24 hours a day. It sure helped to have an end bay, as I did, and you could often sleep under a single blanket.

Bill Chapman, a 10th RSM veteran, has fond memories of his hut mates, who included: John Black, Jim Daugherty, Phil Parker, Howard Meinen, Neil Steele and Larry Furness.

I lived in one of the "smaller" Quonset huts (Hut # 90) just downhill of the chow hall facing the field of play... four men to each side of the six foot divider (no door). A "cherry" stove on each side of the divider glowed cherry red half way up the pipe on cold nights...and rattled with the heat on really cold nights!

Contributed by Phil Parker

Phil Parker's Quarters in Nissen # 90, 1957

We were fifty yards from the chow hall, but (California) Howard always managed to find a construction hole to fall into when going to midnite chow with one piece fatigues over his civvies.

Only workers coming off the swingshift or heading for duty on the midshift could legally partake of the SOS [creamed beef on toast] and other scrumptious goodies dished out by the midnight chef. In reality, the cook on duty would feed anyone who showed up, as long as he was wearing a uniform. Ofttimes, a baker's dozen off-duty, inebriated shift workers rushed to their barracks after returning to base on the last bus from Bedford, put on a pair of one-piece fatigues over their civilian clothes, and showed up for midnight chow.

Phil Parker and Hut-Mates, Nissen # 90, 1957

Russian linguist Phillip Parker, who lived in Nissen Hut # 90, remembers some extra cold mornings in 1957-1958.

There were four bunks on each side of a partition. It was cold, especially when we ran out of kerosene. Woke up one morning with snow on the foot of the cot, it blew in through the cracks in the double entry door. Some fun!

Chicksands Main Street, Winter 1957

Nissen huts or Quonset huts? To most airmen they were one and the same; American military personnel tend to call all the oblong half-round buildings Quonset huts.

Seco Huts

Designed by Uni-Seco Structures, Ltd in 1942, Seco huts were prefabricated wooden frame and plywood multipurpose buildings that were somewhat more modern than Nissens. Like Nissens that had been the mainstay of temporary British military structures in earlier years, Seco design allowed the huts, which were installed on concrete slabs, to be built in varying lengths by adding extra side panels. Side panels had hinged windows that opened out, affording each occupant in a Seco hut barracks a window view.

Author's Collection

Seco Hut # 503 adjacent to BX (1950's-1960's)

More spacious than the Nissen (about 20' x 36'), a typical barracks version had four side panels (with windows) on each side. Three four-feet tall mini-walls (room dividers) on each side divided a Seco barracks into eight cubicles—only limited privacy since, except for the dividers, a Seco hut billet was one large open bay area.[170] A potbelly M-41 oil heater at each end of the hut kept occupants relatively comfortable in winter. Each "four-panel" Seco barracks housed 12 airmen (one each in the four end cubicles and two airmen in each of the other four cubicles).

Seco Hut # 503 (where author lived, 1959-60)

The Seco huts were undoubtedly more comfortable than Nissen and Quonset huts, but residents of all three types of billets had to dress and leave their hut to use the bathroom, shower or even to brush their teeth. Occupants got lots of fresh air and exercise.

To eliminate overcrowding and accommodate continuing growth, the RAF built several Seco huts at Chicksands during the 1942-1945 period. In addition to Seco units that served as WAAF billets, the RAF equipped at least one Seco with a toilet and used it as an office during the war. (USAFSS used that Seco hut as an NCO barracks.) To accommodate more WAAF in on-base billets, the RAF also built one Seco hut that facilities engineers equipped as a communal latrine with sinks, commodes and showers.

Communal Latrines

There were at least five communal latrines at Chicksands when the Americans arrived in 1950—dispersed around the billeting areas with each serving the airmen living in several huts in the immediate vicinity of the latrine. Lack of heat and cold water were standard conditions in the latrines—most of the time—during the 1950's. The cold water situation was especially acute on weekends and British holidays when the latrine furnaces were not kept adequately stoked.

During four years at Chicksands (1956-1960), the author lived in two separate Seco huts (Barracks 474 and 503) and often visited more than one latrine in search of warm water for a shower. Lack of warm water in 1957 raised the ire of one airman to the point that he complained to his congressman, who also happened to be his uncle. His complaint brought results—for a month or so. For a few weeks, the unit deputy commander, a bird colonel, inspected the latrines daily, and hot water was always available. On more than one occasion, dressed in his Air Force raincoat and shower clogs, the author drove from latrine to latrine around base searching for a warm shower—usually, but not always, finding a latrine with hot water.

Contributed by Bill Gray

Base Flagpole, RAF Chicksands, 1958

10TH RSM—EARLY OPERATIONS

Ambrose Jackson recalls that part of the delay in commencing USAFSS operations at Chicksands involved repairing/replacing antennas on the five tall wooden antenna masts, along with the replacement of cables that had corroded over the years. Cables running from individual intercept blocks to a central control block (Block "I") permitted controllers in each block to choose their antennas for monitoring various targets. USAFSS also inherited from the British Y Service a pneumatic tube system for zapping messages between some of the blocks.

According to Jackson, the Soviet 24th Air Army in East Germany was the primary target initially, but soon the squadron was copying targets in the Soviet Baltic states as well as in Russia itself. The 10th RSM commenced operations in early 1951. The 10th commander, Maj. Robinson, was promoted to lieutenant colonel in 1951 and was replaced by Col. Harry Towler at a later date. Reminiscing, Ambrose Jackson described sparse conditions in the beginning.

I believe that we started with only one CW intercept block of 15 positions, and I had a small room in one end of the building adjacent to the antenna room, where I had one SP-600 receiver, one MC-88 typewriter, a field phone, and little else. I copied, and Don Kubeck transcribed.

I remember once, when the 24th Air Army was on maneuvers in East Germany, I copied 70 pages as fast as I could write (using a type of shorthand symbols which I had learned when I was at 2nd Radio Squadron, and which was developed, I believe, by Virgil Fordham at Darmstadt). We wrote a short curved symbol indicating turns, speed increases, dives, climbs, etc. Made it possible to copy more than one could otherwise do in a given time.

Don and I both worked at the same time, and our Ops officer left it up to us to work according to how much traffic we could find over the days and evenings. The 24th Air Army happened to be on maneuvers at that time, and there was heavy activity all day and up into the nights. Don and I worked sometimes all day, knocking off at night. Then some days, we stayed off during the day and went up to the site in the evenings and worked till late at night.

A few weeks after we started, we got a new Russian linguist, Sgt. Thomas Sutton, and we began to work shift, tho not around the clock, so we began to get better coverage. I can not remember when 203's [linguists] began to arrive in numbers, but sometime later, we set up our own intercept block, "D" Block, to be exact, and that became the R/T [radiotelephone] Intercept Branch.

CMSgt. Thomas D. Sutton and the author attended the Advanced Russian course at the Defense Language Institute, Monterey, California, in 1971. (Located in the northeast corner of the intercept compound at Chicksands, D Block still exists although most of the other former intercept blocks have been torn down.) Ambrose Jackson continued reminiscing.

A TSgt. Kenneth Crawford arrived on the scene, along with a Capt. Martin Spolarich. The captain was the R/T officer, although not a linguist. Crawford was a linguist, but was Arabic-trained.

Several other linguists had joined the R/T section by this time, including Ralph "Bull" Rich who was a graduate of a twelve-month Serbo-Croatian course at Army Language School. SSgt.'s Andrew Stewart and Ambrose Jackson, and Cpl. Donald Kubeck were promoted to TSgt. and SSgt., respectively in June 1951, and with the R/T section getting top-heavy with rank, the operations officer moved TSgt. Jackson to a new block as NCOIC of a newly activated teleprinter section.

His transfer to the printer section proved to be the last time that Ambrose Jackson worked in the R/T section, as Maj. Bowers used him to fill management vacancies in various sections. For a while, he worked for Max Hawkes in the Control Section and later served as NCOIC of Traffic Exploitation.

Ferret Missions

Ambrose Jackson recalls that the 10th RSM began monitoring the progress of U.S. "ferret" reconnaissance missions along the periphery of the Soviet Union in 1951.

Every time there was a mission, everyone worked all night until the mission was over. We were all in the Control Room waiting for reports to come in, and the intercept positions were alerted to watch for unusual traffic that might indicate reactions to the flight. The operations officer, Maj. Bowers; Capt. Verploegh, the asst. Ops officer; and sometimes the commander were all present. It was a very big deal, and things did not get normal until the flight returned safely.

SSgt. Floyd L. Foltz Jr., like Ambrose Jackson a former ASA Morse operator who had arrived in England from Darmstadt with the initial group, gained experience copying traffic associated with the ferret missions. He volunteered to fly reconnaissance missions when USAFSS deployed its prototype COMINT recon platform, RB-29A 44-62290, to Europe for evaluation flights in early 1953. SSgt. Henry P. Stacewicz, a 2nd RSM Russian linguist, also participated in the RB-29 missions. Ironically, Ambrose Jackson roomed with Stacewicz in Darmstadt for a short period.

I was Henry's roommate. He had a small room on the ground floor, and I shared it with him until I shipped to England. He was a big muscular guy who liked to fight, and he and the assistant mess sergeant, SSgt. Oswald Ballantine, who was much like Henry, buddied together. Their main recreation, I think, was taking on the members of the 1st Division Army whom they met in town.

Jackson commented that Stacewicz and Ballantine kept the U.S. Military Police busy on their night patrols around Darmstadt. USAFSS was a small command—Stacewicz and the author have been friends since 1965.

William Bowers—Operations Officer

Arriving at Chicksands from Darmstadt in November 1950, Capt. William Bowers was the 10th RSM's first operations officer. Well respected by fellow officers and enlisted, he gets much of the credit for the early successes of the squadron. USAFSS promoted Bowers to major in 1951. TSgt. Ambrose Jackson established long-term working relations with Bill Bowers during their pioneering days at Chicksands.

I used to see him practically every day. He always came around visiting the various buildings and talking to people. A very popular and likeable guy! He was the man responsible for getting me immediately reassigned to the 10th RSM at the end of my first tour.

Jackson returned to the States in March 1952, but time spent back in the United States was brief.

In those days, a man could ask for immediate reassignment to his old unit, which I did. When I left

Chicksands, it was already arranged that I was coming back. On arrival in the States, I had a 30-day leave home, reported to San Antonio, and on beginning the Check-In, I told the personnel clerk that I was to be reassigned to Chicksands. He verified it, and the day after I finished clearing in, I began the clearing out process. I arrived back at Chicksands in June, '52, and resumed duties in what was then called the Intelligence Section.

Completing his second tour at Chicksands, MSgt. Jackson again worked for then Lt. Col. Bowers at HQ USAFSS in the mid-1950's. Jackson returned to Chicksands for a third and final assignment (July 1956-July 1959). Promoted to full colonel, William Bowers later served as the USAFSS inspector general. At 82 years old, retired Col. Bowers had fond memories of the early days at Chicksands when he chatted with the author in 1999. He had much respect and appreciation for 10th RSM NCO's, speaking with reverence about SSgt.'s Ralph Rich and George Keesee, TSgt. (later CWO-4) Max Hawkes and MSgt. James C. Swindell (communications NCOIC). Inducted into the Command Hall of Honor in 1988, Col. Bowers passed away in 2000.

NCO Club

Asked about clubs, Ambrose Jackson recalled that the base NCO Club began as a concession, with refreshments furnished by a local brewery. The club initially offered drinks only—no food.

A friend of mine and I went into Bedford one day and purchased a large ball of Edam Cheese, some bread, mustard, and a few other things for the club, and that was the first food the club served. This was in time for Christmas '50. We got alcoholic beverages on consignment from the brewery of Wells and Winch, Biggleswade. At that time, the brewery furnished not only the beer and ale, but also all the hard stuff.

Later when the base opened a Class VI liquor store, the NCO and Officers Clubs purchased their booze at more reasonable rates from the Class VI. For the first 2-3 years, the NCO Club was located in the large Nissen hut on the far eastern side of the base, in the building that later became the base snack bar.

During George Montague's tour in the 10th RSM (1951-52), this was the NCO Club. In the 1953-1954 period, the NCO Club moved into another large Nissen about 200 yards east of the mess hall. Finally in 1959, the base built a new NCO Club, situated between the snack bar/BX Nissen complex and the base gymnasium, and the old NCO Club became the Airmens Club. Today, the former U.S. NCO Club is the British Sergeants and Warrant Officers Mess.

Airmens Club

The Airmens Club—former NCO Club—was an immediate success when the NCO's vacated the premises for the new NCO Club in 1959. Finally, the lower four grades had their own facility where they could entertain guests. International floor shows were a common feature monthly, and live bands played on weekends. Young unaccompanied British lasses appeared often at the Top Gate and the Bottom Gate seeking an escort to take them to the Airmens Club—all foreign nationals had to be escorted while on base. The air policeman on duty at the gate always obliged by calling the club and asking if any airman wished to go to the gate and sign in a couple of nice looking unescorted females. Owning a car to pick up the ladies from the gate and drive them home when the club closed was a worthwhile investment. Life was good, even for those of us living in Nissen and Seco huts on base.

Chicksands Gymnasium

Although one of the smaller bases in the United Kingdom, Chicksands was renowned from the early 1950's for fielding outstanding base-level sports teams. Soon after moving to the base, the 10th RSM fielded a basketball team even though there was no gymnasium on station. The base team made up of players from the 10th RSM and the 7534th Air Base Squadron practiced and played their home games at RAF Cardington Camp, near Bedford. The team was phenomenally successful, winning the games played on its home court (Cardington Camp) against the American teams from larger bases in England. In fairness to their competition, the Chicksands "Chicks" had an unfair advantage—playing (and practicing) on an uneven floor installed in an old WW II hangar at Cardington Camp. The Chicks players knew the quirks of the uneven floor and played them to their advantage. In

1955, the Chicksands Chicks were the basketball champions in the USAF United Kingdom League.

WELCOME to CHICKSANDS
Home of the Chicks
1955 UK BASKETBALL CHAMPS

Contributed by Paul McGee

Chicks—United Kingdom Basketball Champs, 1955

Chicksands finally built its own gym with shiny new hardwood floors in what had been a cow pasture immediately south of the station billeting area. Col. Walter Lavelle and A2C James W. "Jim" Berry, Chicksands Chicks' star basketball center, conducted a ribbon cutting, opening the gym in 1957. After the ceremony, in the first attempt at a basket, Jim executed a perfect 3-point jump shot. Days later, the Chicks lost their first game ever on their home court—in their new gym. The basketball team did not win the United Kingdom trophy in 1957 but they remained competitive, and Jim Berry went on to star on the University of Alabama Crimson Tide teams in the early 1960's.

Legend of the Fighting Chicks

During the squadron's first two years at Chicksands, the squadron obtained enough gloves, balls and bats to equip softball and baseball teams, but acquiring football equipment for a new air base in the UK seemed an intractable problem. In 2006, Francis Hollifield shared the "Legend of the Fighting Chicks," the story of the phenomenal success of Chicksands' football team in the early years.

LARRY TART

We had our first football team in 1953. Bull Rich (now deceased) started the team and was our only coach. After receiving approval for a team, we had no equipment. A request was sent out to various teams for any excess equipment they had. The equipment we received was old and worn out. We even got a couple of helmets that were made of leather back in the days of Jim Thorp. We did obtain some money to buy uniforms.

In his memoirs, Edsel Wiggins described how the base acquired much of its football equipment. A U.S. Navy unit at Londonderry, Ireland, had excess football equipment, but no boxing equipment and not enough personnel to field a football team. On the other hand, special services at Chicksands had an oversupply of boxing equipment. Captains Wiggins and Verploegh flew a USAF C-47 from RAF Bovingdon to Londonderry to exchange boxing gear for football equipment. Hollifield described early Chicksands football activities.

Bull was our coach, and he also played tackle. To everyone's surprise we won four games. Burtonwood was the European champion that year. The following year we played them at Burtonwood, and we won 7-0 to everyone's surprise. In 1954, we won 5 games—losing to London again, to Wethersfield and tying Bentwaters. I then rotated back to the States. The 'Sands had good teams in '55 and '56, but each time losing to London. I mention this since everyone hated the London Rockets.

MSgt. Hollifield returned to Chicksands for a second tour in 1958.

Then in '57 we lost again to London. In '58, I was made assistant coach for the line. We had London beat with less than a minute to go. Then our coach made a mass substitution thinking the game was won, but London did a Hail Mary pass and won the game. Col. Lavelle fired the head coach and told me I was now the head coach. We finished the season with a defeat to Bentwaters, but a win over Burtonwood. We had great players, but we also had a player Col. Lavelle got transferred from Darmstadt that caused a lot of dissention.

906

He refused to get into shape and took over the team while on the field, ignoring any info from the coaches. I tried to cut him, but I was overruled.

When we played Bentwaters, I refused to play this problem child. The game was very close, and we had a great chance in winning. Then the colonel ordered me to play this player, and when I put him in the team fell apart. Fortunately, he left the service after the '58 season.

Hollifield was determined not to have another prima donna player if he coached the team during the 1959 season.

Col. Lavelle rotated, and we got a new commander—Col. Rice. He called me in and told me that he wanted me to coach the team. I told him I would, provided I was the only head coach and I could use whomever I wanted to play and to assist me in coaching. He agreed with me. I then asked John Polo if he would be my assistant and would coach the backs. John had played on the '57 and '58 teams and was a great fullback and linebacker. He was also a great coach, instilling determination and a never-quit attitude in the players.

We used a multiple "T" with various options. We also started every game with a series of no huddle plays, and the quarterback had the option to call a series of plays without the huddle anytime during the game. As the season progressed, we won our first three games. We then played Alconbury, who was leading us 7-6 with only a couple of minutes remaining. We ran two end sweeps, and then we scored on a fake end run with the pass option from our halfback Bill Patterson. Jim Core caught a 56 yard touchdown pass to win the game 12 to 7. You could see the confidence and determination in our team. They were in outstanding physical condition and could go the entire game without substitution if necessary.

The next game pitted the Chicksands Chicks against their nemesis, the London Rockets, who were the European champs the previous year and undefeated in the '59 season.

During practice, I had to call off the Wednesday scrimmage after halfway through. The blocking and tackling were unbelievable as you could see the determination in the team. Then on Thursday, the same determination was everywhere. Our team was ready. I was working with the line on the blocking sled. They were hitting it so hard they knocked me off, and I busted my head on one of the frames. I was dizzy and lost my memory. I was taken to the dispensary and later to the hospital at Ruislip for observation. I regained my memory and was released and returned to Chicksands the following day. I had quite a headache, but still was okay for the light practice and last minute briefing.

Then the big day came. I gave the team their pep talk. I told them I wanted them to win the game for all the members of the base that had witnessed our defeats from London and how the London spectators would yell "Here chick, chick, chick. Here chick, chick" after our defeats. Then I told them how the Illinois football team got their name "The Fighting Illini" after defeating the four horseman of Notre Dame. I told them if they would beat London I would ask Col. Rice to change our name from the Chicksands Chicks to "The Chicksands Fighting Chicks." The team yelled approval and we headed for the field.

The first half was won by London who led 7 to 0 at the half. They practically had the same team that won the European championship the year before. They also had a great punter, plus their fullback Danny Fuller quick kicked us twice, pinning us inside our 20.

During the halftime break, we changed a couple of plays. I then told Dick Ebersole, who played middle guard, and Dix Compton, who played middle linebacker on our basic 5-3-2-1 defense. I noticed that when Fuller quick kicked he would lift his right hand about a foot off the ground out of his 3-point stance. I told Dix to key off of Fuller and if he came off his 3-point stance, he was to slap Ebby on the butt, and then Ebby was to charge hard to his left and Dix would do likewise to the right of the center. They had to block the kick.

The second half began. London scored again and led 14 to 0, but then the game started to change. We started winning the battle of the trenches, and the London offense came to a halt as our offense came to life. The battle continued but we could never get the break we needed.

Then the referee signaled the four minute warning. We had London pinned back on their own 20 with 3ʳᵈ down and 12 to go. Then the break came. They went back in formation and Danny Fuller came off his 3-point stance. Dix looked over and smiled and slapped Ebby on his butt. Ebby looked over and smiled, and as he dug in. I smiled back and shook my fist at them and thought, "Now."

The ball was centered between the legs of the center and quarterback, and two freight trains came charging in, slamming both the center and quarterback backwards—with Ebby hitting Fuller low and Dix hitting him high as the ball was blocked backwards. Fuller was knocked flat on his back and was taken out of the game.

We recovered the ball on the 12 yard line, and Bill Patterson took the first handoff and went to the 4 yard line. Then Art Sheldon, our quarterback, called a "Tap Play," and he scored the touchdown. (The quarterback had the option to call a Tap Play anytime the defense was weak directly in front of the center.) The score was now 14 to 6. We used a new play we put in during the week as Art Shelton faked to Bill Patterson on a dive play on the left side. Our left end faked a block on the linebacker, then cut hard to the outside. Art pulled the ball out of Patterson's arm and threw a pass to our end who was 10 yards in the clear. The score was now 14 to 8.

We kicked off to London whom we stopped dead for 3 plays on their 20 yard line. They punted and we returned to midfield. Art split our right end out and put both halfbacks on either side of the end and about a yard back. The ball was centered and the halfbacks started straight down field then split to the outside. Our end held for a 2 count, then charged straight down field. Our line gave Art plenty of protection as our end broke open, and Art threw a 35 yard pass.

Tony Small, the defensive halfback, recognized the play and charged full speed towards our end and dove into the air and tipped the ball. The other defensive half back was running towards the ball and tripped with the ball bouncing off his shoulders, and Patterson snatched it out of the air and scored untouched. The score was now tied 14 all. We kicked the extra point and led 15 to 14.

There were still a few seconds remaining, and we kicked off with several players gang-tackling the London receiver on their own 20, and the game was over. The legend of "The Fighting Chicks" was born.

The base went wild. They were yelling and screaming with horns blowing, and several of them were dancing up and down. Most of the swingshift had refused to go to work until the game was over. The dayshift was screaming for their relief.

Richard and Pauline Ebersole had gotten married earlier that Saturday morning.

Ebby was married that day, but had the wedding moved to the morning so he could play the game. Some of our players played the entire game without substitution. There were very few substitutions. I watched the players closely, and every one of them gave his best every play. They were in excellent shape and determined to win the war. It was a war especially in the trenches. You could close your ears and hear the crash as the line blasted out as the center centered the ball.

Coach Hollifield left his wife Josie at the NCO Club with friends while he closed out matters with the team. The club was jammed with everyone yelling and screaming.

I went to the dressing room and to my surprise, Col. Rice was there. He presented me the game football. Next to the strings it had LONDON 14 and below was CHICKSANDS 15. Every one of the players and the Colonel signed the ball. My eyes were a little watery, and I thanked the colonel and the team. Then I told Col. Rice that I had told the team if they would beat London, I would ask him to rename our teams, "The Fighting Chicks." He said, "Request granted, so be it." The Fighting Chicks were now reality. Again, the team went wild.

I returned to the club to get my wife and it was next to impossible to get in the club—it was so crowded. And the noise was practically unbearable. As I elbowed my way in, I was constantly slapped and offered a drink, but I had a strict No Drinking rule, which I also honored.

The club secretary saw me and come over to shake my hand. I told him about changing our name to the Fighting Chicks. He immediately announced it over the loud speaker, and the club shook as the noise was deafening. I finally got to my wife, who was so drunk she could hardly stand. Everyone was buying her drinks and toasting the victory.

On Monday, I got a call from the club secretary, who told me the club was going to host a banquet for us at the end of the season. He said he couldn't close the club for over an hour and a half later than normal hours. And even then, he could only close the club since every drop of beer and hard liquor was sold out.

I also received a call from Dave Snow. He wanted to see me. He had drawn a sketch of the Fighting Chick to be used as our emblem. The chick was holding a shield at the end of his left wing with a sword in his hand at the end of his right wing. It was the toughest and meanest chick I had ever seen. It was tremendous. I told him to see Col. Rice and present it to him for his approval, and to tell him that I had seen it and thought it was great.

Col. Rice approved the emblem, and the rest is history. The spirit of the Fighting Chicks prevailed in all sports. All UK teams knew they had to defeat the Fighting Chicks if they were to have a chance at winning the championship.

Euphoria reigned for a week, but a pumped-up Suffolk Titans (Bentwaters-Woodbridge) team defeated the Fighting Chicks 14-5—Chicksands' only loss of the season. In turn, the Titans lost to the Wiesbaden Flyers 14-12 in the 1959 European Championship game.

Dick Ebersole's Double Duty

Imagine being involved in every defensive play during 60 minutes of high-intensity football! That was precisely Dick Ebersole's calling on 5 September 1959—four hours after his wedding. Ebby addressed his double duty in response to Hollifield's missive on the Chicksands Fighting Chicks.

Hey Holly—you sure did let the cat out of the bag for me. Supposedly, not many people knew of my "Double Duty" that wonderful day in my life. I remember when I went in front of Col. Rice to get his permission to marry a British national. He looked over the investigative paperwork of my intended spouse (Pauline) and stated that all documents before him appeared that I had made a great choice. (He was surely on target, as after almost 47 years that choice is still the Main Lady in my life.)

He then pulled out his sliding side desk tray which had the Chicksands football team schedule taped. He went to 5 September on it and looked at me and advised that he would approve my marriage plans only if I would be available to play against the London Rockets on that same date. The change to a 4-hours earlier wedding time was the only way out of my dilemma. Needless to say that day in my life has turned to be history making and one of the most wonderful days any fellow could experience. There are two very "special reasons" for that day to be so great for me. I was able to get married to my wonderful wife and become a "Fighting Chick" all on the same day. My big lifetime secret is out again. Thanks to Holly!

Francis Hollifield acknowledged that Dick Ebersole was one of the Fighting Chicks who played the entire game against the London Rockets in 1959 without a substitution.

Chicksands—Soccer

Dick Ebersole was also pretty adept with the other international football game that used a round ball—soccer. Along with the author, Ebby was a member of the Chicksands Chicks soccer team in the late 1950's. Our team competed against both USAF and RAF teams. Coming in as the runners-up in the Air Force UK league in 1958, we were very competitive against the American teams, but were in the game for the "fun" when playing RAF teams. Traveling to away games against British teams was a thrill, with RAF hosts always honoring us with parties and fetes after games. And the RAF female airmen were our greatest fans.

Chicks Soccer Team[171]—UK Runners-Up, 1958

Mental Map of Chicksands

Reminiscing with Ambrose Jackson about the locations of functions on base in the old days, the author and Jackson created a mental map of RAF Chicksands as the base existed during the 1950's. Sandy Lane connects Chicksands to A600—main highway to Bedford. Approaching the base on Sandy Lane, the olive drab block buildings in the fenced intercept compound (USA-51 Operations) were visible on the right. At the Top Gate, the U.S. Air Force fire station, a large Nissen building (garage) and motor pool parking lot sat on the right. The chapel was located on the right at the intersection inside the Top Gate, and to the right of the chapel, alongside and to the rear of the motor pool, were the administration-personnel building, 10th RSM (later 6950th RGM) HQ, the armory, mailroom and provost marshal's office. The dispensary-dental clinic and supply buildings were a bit farther from the Top Gate on the right side. (Except for the chapel, fire station and the intercept blocks, most of those structures still existed when I last visited Chicksands in 2005.)

Chicksands Motor Pool and Top Gate, 1958

A main road (currently called Chicksands Avenue) runs north to south from the Top Gate across the Flit River to the Bottom Gate, bisecting the base. The Priory (now officer quarters and club) is located a few hundred yards west of this main road, immediately north of the river. The RAF base fire station was located on the north bank of the river on a lane leading off the main road to the Priory. During the 1950's, an RAF detachment occupied Nissens south of the Flit River, between the river and the Bottom Gate, while north of the river, the 10th RSM built a bowling alley and a commissary.

Looking south onto the station from the Top Gate, the base's main street (now called Churchill Drive) turned left (east) off the main road. The Finance Office was located in a Nissen hut on the left side of Churchill Drive, and the Officers Club sat on the right side. Farther along Churchill, the base theater was in a large Nissen and to the right of the movie, was the mess hall. Another large Nissen housed the NCO Club farther east from the mess hall. Continuing east on Churchill, the Alexandre Tailor, library and Class VI liquor store were in Nissens along the left side, and a Stars & Stripes Newsstand was in another Nissen across the street.

Latrine on right, BX and Snack Bar in center, circa 1957

Former Latrine near old BX, now office space, 2005

Churchill Drive ended in a parking lot by two joined Nissens that housed the snack bar and base exchange. (Some of these functions shifted to other huts over the years.) The Special Services office was also in a Nissen on Churchill Drive. The USO Service Club was located to the rear of the snack bar. Airmen lived in Nissens on both sides of this street, and in Seco huts clustered in areas off Churchill Drive. Four Seco huts were also located adjacent to and south of the old BX building. (The author lived in the first Seco hut—# 503—by the BX in 1959-1960.)

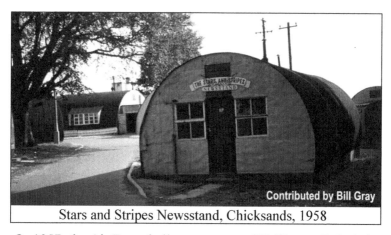

Contributed by Bill Gray

Stars and Stripes Newsstand, Chicksands, 1958

In 1957, the Air Force built a new street (Wellington Drive) that starts in front of the old BX (at Churchill Drive) and followed south, then west, paralleling the existing billeting area and ending at Chicksands Avenue—directly across the sports fields from the Priory. The gym was built along the south side of Wellington in 1957, and the new NCO Club was opened on the eastern side of the gym in 1959. This then was the Chicksands that existed in the early 1960's—before new enlisted billeting, family housing and a school were built on the base in later years.

Contributed by Bill Gray

Chicksands BX Parking Lot, 1958

10TH RSM DIRECTION FINDING

When the 10th Radio Squadron Mobile began operations in early 1951, a handful of the unit's officers and airmen had had exposure to COMINT intercept operations, and one or two may have trained on direction finding equipment in the 8th RSM in Texas. However, none had any operational experience using AN/TRD-4 DF receivers and triangulation techniques to locate enemy target transmitters. Given the squadron's miniscule knowledge of enemy order of battle and modus operandi, the 10th RSM placed a high priority on establishing a direction finding network in early 1951.

DF Station—RAF Henlow Camp

Maj. Bowers put TSgt. Murl G. Olson in charge of developing a DF capability for the unit. George Montague, a Morse intercept operator who got in on the ground floor of DF operations at Chicksands, discussed related activities in 2004.

I arrived at Chicksands in April '51, so DF would have started around June/July '51 time frame. We started out just outside the fence around Operations. This was just a learning period; we were checking out the equipment and practicing on setting up the antenna system. Just worked days, no shift work. At the time we were negotiating with the British to locate the site on their base between Shefford and Hitchin; if memory serves me, it was RAF Henlow.

The squadron set up the DF site about eight miles from Chicksands on a grassy knoll at RAF Henlow Camp, halfway between Shefford and Hitchin. Communications being rather primitive at the time, the DF site had neither radio nor landline contact with unit operations.

We had a list of callsigns and freqs that they wanted bearings on, and the rest of the time we shot bearings on any good stuff that was transmitting. When we started, all CW callsigns came out of the "Baker Book," and there was very little that was unknown in that area. I am not sure, but I believe we did have a "Slipstick" to check on which book the callsign came out of, and we had a list of which books were current.

It was at this time that half of our group along with some new guys left for Scotland. When we received the OK from the British we set up on RAF Henlow, which did not have any paved runways, only a grassy field.

Montague remembered going to the motor pool Nissen hut by the Top Gate to check out a jeep for trips to the DF site.

We had our own jeep to get back and forth. We had two-man tricks, and both of us were 292's [Morse intercept operators]. I am not sure, but I think we took our power from the RAF; I do not remember having any generators.

On the road to Hitchin, you could see the site because we had to paint the hut in a yellow and black checkerboard pattern. There was a tea shop on the right side of the road just before it went under the railroad tracks. The DF site was opposite the tea shop. We used to climb over the fence during dayshifts and get some take away.

We were limited to confidential material. We had a .45 and a few [ammo] clips at the site and always had a .45 with us on the jeep ride back and forth. At the end of the shift we brought the logs and bearings into Ops.

Airman Montague left Chicksands in 1953. Former SSgt. Elwood "Robbie" Roberts, another Morse operator, also performed DF duties at the Henlow Camp site.

When I was there in '56, there were two huts, two fuel trailers, and a maintenance shack, in which we also had food and a hot plate. There was a fence to keep the cows out and a place to park the pickup. And you guys seem to forget the view of Henlow Camp and the Hastings aircraft making practice parachute drops. We were on a small hill overlooking Henlow. It was just a short walk from the end of the village closest to the site.

There was nothing to be seen between the site and Henlow camp except cows and fields as I remember it. Maybe an occasional building.

Robbie Roberts may have worked at a different DF site, relocated from Henlow Camp. Accounts from others, who operated a DF system closer to Chicksands in the late 1950's, show that the squadron relocated its local DF site from Henlow Camp in the mid-1950's.

DF Station—Meppershall

Former A2C Robert Joyce, a Russian linguist, performed duties at a DF site near the village of Meppershall in 1956-58.

Meppershall is a couple of miles south-southeast of the Campton [Bottom] Gate, beyond the village of Campton.

A two-man team on each shift, a Morse intercept operator and a Russian linguist, worked at the site, traveling to and from the site in an Air Force Standard Vanguard pickup. Joyce recalls that volunteers from the voice section worked the DF function.

Meppershall evidently replaced the site overlooking Henlow Camp. Meppershall had a trailer (actually a box that fit on the back of a 6 x 6) with the radio and RDF equipment inside and an antenna on a relatively low tower. The equipment was lined up along one wall, leaving just enough space for two desk chairs side by side facing the equipment. The door was in the side of the trailer. No windows. No heat that I remember, though I don't remember freezing either.

USAFSS used HO-17 shelters that could be hauled on deuce-and-a-half trucks to house DF systems during the 1950's.

There was also a tent for maintenance work and cooking. The site was probably no bigger than 40' x 40' and was surrounded by a simple barbed wire fence to keep the cows out. It had a great view of the countryside. I worked with a 292 SSgt., and we also had a maintenance tech on duty during days (in addition to the herd of cows that grazed that pasture). It was a great place to work. Because we carried classified material back and forth, and the RDF site was unsecured, we were required to wear sidearms.

John Pontius, another Russian linguist, also worked at the Meppershall DF site.

Drove those pickups back and forth and had a .45 strapped on. Stopped once in Shefford to mail a letter and forgot I had the .45—got numerous looks from the Brits. Also, during the Suez Canal crisis when gas was very scarce—rationed—I was allowed, I think, 10 gallons a month. The old Nash (remember her—seats that folded down) used that much to get off base. Anyway, I used to stop periodically at the DF site to fill up the tank from the gas tank at the site. Yes, we had 203's and 292's at the site. One for each trick.

Yank Cars and Expensive Petrol

A real behemoth on British roads and resembling an upside-down bathtub on wheels, "Red" Pontius' 1950 Nash Ambassador Sedan was a hit with lasses who frequented the Peacock in Bedford. Petrol (gasoline)—imported from the Middle East at the time—was in short supply and cost one £ sterling ($2.80) per gallon, wiping out Red's biweekly check to fill his tank. The impressionable, young English ladies were partial to big "Yank" cars, and lots of young single airmen did not disappoint them.

Tony Hester from California had a neat, customized 1950 Chevy coupe; Jim Wiggins owned a spotless 1950 Ford Deluxe Tudor sedan; and Roger Thurman's '49 green 4-door Studebaker Champion was a real classic. Then, there was Bob Pitts' 1948 Chevy, and SSgt. Skip Thompson arrived in England sporting a white 1955 Buick Century convertible with a continental kit—a set of wheels that was outclassed only by First Sgt. McConnell's pink and white Packard convertible. The author's personal favorite was a 1953 Chevrolet 4-door station wagon that he sold to Bennie MacDonald when he left England. With the back seat folded down, there was room for a party in the back of that station wagon.

Soon after the Suez War of 1956, the U.S. Air Force opened gas stations on American bases in England; earlier, everyone paid regular prices for petrol at British stations. Based on engine size, airmen with privately owned vehicles were allowed to purchase at the base gas station at $.30 per gallon enough petrol for five round trips to work per week—eight gallons per month for the author, who lived on base. Rumors abound that the black market sale of American cigarettes and booze subsidized petrol costs for many airmen's cars!

USAFSS EXPANSION IN UK

In 1952, USAFSS added a second radio squadron mobile in the United Kingdom—the 37th RSM at RAF Kirknewton, Scotland. Kirknewton Aerodrome is located near the small village of Kirknewton—about 10 miles west of Edinburgh.

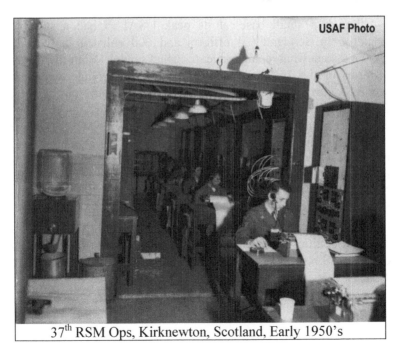

USAF Photo

37th RSM Ops, Kirknewton, Scotland, Early 1950's

An auxiliary airfield during World War II, RAF Kirknewton facilities were minuscule and more rundown compared to those at Chicksands, necessitating more time and effort to start up 37th RSM operations. Likewise, when the 37th airmen arrived, Kirknewton's billeting and working conditions were more primitive than Chicksands'; however, a couple of years of new construction at Kirknewton placed facilities at the Scottish base ahead of 10th RSM facilities in England. Bill Bowers—not the operations officer but a former traffic analyst NCO at Chicksands who later became a mustang officer—compared Kirknewton village to Shefford village by Chicksands.

The base itself was just outside of Kirknewton village, which wasn't even as big as Shefford; no traffic lights and only one pub, no fish and chips shop but a van that made the rounds of the little villages at night. The base was actually built on an old abandoned WW II airfield. The runways were still there but clearly "X'd" out so no fool tried to land in the midst of our antennae field. Our ops building was on the runway side of the small main road that bisected the base.

Although a small base, at its peak USAFSS had a sizeable squadron in Scotland (24 officers and 600 enlisted in the late 1950's—somewhat comparable to Chicksands). With the early histories of the 10th RSM and 37th RSM closely intertwined, it seems logical to discuss the two sister squadrons together. Development of USAFSS intercept squadrons in the UK proceeded in tandem with the activation of new RSM's in Europe and other areas—all limited by the availability of equipment and trained personnel. Facilities also played a major role. As a mothballed major British Y service intercept station, RAF Chicksands made it possible for Air Force Security Service to bring the 10th RSM online with relative ease. In turn, Chicksands became the springboard for launching the 37th RSM in less suitable facilities in Scotland. The next UK-associated expansion of USAFSS resources occurred not in England or Scotland, but in Texas.

6950TH SECURITY GROUP ACTIVATED

In 1953, USAFSS HQ activated the 6950th Security Group at Brooks AFB. The 10th and 37th RSM commanders reported to the new 6950th SG, which became the second echelon analysis center for its two squadrons. Remaining at Brooks until a new facility (Block M) was built at Chicksands, the 6950th Security Group relocated to Chicksands probably in 1954. On 8 May 1955, the 10th RSM and 37th RSM were redesignated the 6951st and 6952nd Radio Squadrons Mobile, respectively—part of a USAFSS-wide unit designator change. The last special order issued by the 10th RSM transferred all assigned personnel to the 6951st RSM with no change in station or duties. Nineteen officers and 589 airmen were assigned to the 10th RSM when the squadron became the 6951st RSM.[172]

6950th Scty Gp Org Chart—8 May 1955	
6950th Security Group RAF Chicksands, England 1954-1956	
6951st RSM Chicksands, England 1955-1956	6952nd RSM Kirknewton 1955-1963

Getting back to historic milestones in the evolution of the UK-based USAFSS units from 1951 forward, we next address activation of the 10th RSM's second DF site.

DF STATION—RAF EDZELL, SCOTLAND

TSgt. Olson headed a 10th RSM team that deployed to Scotland in mid-1951 to set up a second DF station while George Montague and a stay-behind team activated the local DF site at Henlow Camp. The squadron arranged through the Air Ministry to detach Olson's team at RAF Station Edzell, about 10 miles west of Montrose—a port city on Scotland's North Sea coast 90 miles north of Edinburgh and 35 miles south of Aberdeen. The DF site was located in a pasture about five miles from RAF Edzell, probably near Stracathro, Angus.

Capt. Edsel Wiggins had negotiated through the British Air Ministry to deploy an American direction finding team to Scotland. A site survey team that included Wiggins, Sgt. Olson and Captains Verplocgh and Bobo surveyed facilities at RAF Edzell and RAF Kirknewton prior to the deployment of the DF team to Edzell.

Det 1, 10th RSM Activated

Activated as Detachment 101, 10th RSM,[173] the DF team lived in RAF billeting at Edzell and commuted to the site by jeep. Situated some 450 miles apart, the two DF stations (Edzell and Henlow Camp) provided excellent base legs for location fixes against targets on the continent. Thinking back on the activation of the two sites, George Montague recalls that the Edzell DF site was up and running awhile before the site at Henlow Camp became operational.

DET 2, 10TH RSM ACTIVATED

Soon after opening its DF site at Edzell, the 10th Radio Squadron Mobile dispatched a team to activate a second detachment in Scotland. In early 1952, the squadron published orders activating Det 102, 10th RSM at Kirknewton RAF Station, outside Edinburgh. In mid-1952, the 37th Radio Squadron Mobile arrived at Kirknewton and assumed the mission and the airmen assigned to Det 2, 10th RSM.

37TH RSM—ACTIVATED

USAFSS activated the 37th Radio Squadron Mobile at Brooks AFB, Texas, in August 1951,[174] intent on outfitting the unit as soon as possible for duty in Scotland. Few details are available regarding the 37th during its stay in Texas; however, war was raging in Korea and USAFSS struggled to deploy new intercept units concurrently in Asia, Europe and North Africa. The activation and development of five other RSM's and the 6910th Security Group at Brooks in 1951, plus inadequate infrastructure at Kirknewton, delayed the shipment of the 37th RSM to Scotland until mid-1952.

A sizeable number of "earmarked" airmen were sent ahead overseas to Darmstadt, Bremerhaven, Landsberg and Chicksands where they trained and gained experience in USAFSS intercept operations in Europe. Under the plan, earmarked airmen would continue to Kirknewton when that station could accommodate them. Delay after delay occurred, and, in the end, several of the earmarked men finagled reassignments to their host squadrons overseas, leaving the 37th RSM short of much-needed field experience when the squadron finally arrived at Kirknewton.

Retired Major Joseph Tortorete began his USAFSS career at Brooks Field and was a member of the original 37th RSM cadre. Enlisting in the Air Force in late 1948, Tortorete received cryptologic training at the Navy Cryptologic School in Washington before his introduction to USAFSS as a cryptologist/traffic analyst in the 8th RSM in 1949. Promoted to staff sergeant, Tortorete transferred into the 37th RSM when the unit was activated. He married the 8th RSM commander's secretary in April 1952 and relocated with the 37th RSM cadre from Brooks AFB two months later.

37th RSM—Moved to Scotland

Joe Tortorete provided the author a copy of the Movement Order promulgating transfer of the 37th RSM to RAF Station Kirknewton.[175] Naming squadron members—six officers and 37 airmen—the order specified 10 June 1952 the readiness date at Brooks for overseas shipment. All squadron equipment, including "general and special purpose vehicles," was included in the shipment.[176] Squadron commander Major Russell L. French led his unit's move, traveling by train to the New York Port of Embarkation, Brooklyn, New York, "for further movement by water transportation." Joe Tortorete confirms the relocation date as June 1952. His new bride joined him in Scotland a few months later. Details provided by others clarify many of the issues involved in establishing USAFSS operations in Scotland.

George Montague Assigned to Edzell

Finding life in Texas boring after two years in England, George Montague reenlisted to return overseas. On his second enlistment, he served in the DF detachment in Scotland.

I left Chicksands in April '53, went to 8th Radio at Brooks and reenlisted in June for assignment in Scotland. Arrived at Kirknewton in August and met Murl Olson in October. Ended up at Edzell in late October 1953. It was detached service, not PCS. We had no mess facilities, so we drew money; am not sure if it was the same as separate rations or more because of the nonavailability. We had our own kitchen in the building the office was in, and we made a monthly trip down to Kirknewton for operational matters and also as a commissary run.

Edzell was the same as RAF Henlow, nothing higher [classified materials] than confidential. We used one time pads to transmit data between the DF site and Chicksands. I can't remember if we had weapons at Edzell, yet I remember vividly about the weapons at the 'Sands.

Montague described the DF system in use in Scotland.

When it was first set up, it was the same as what we had at the 'Sands. I believe it was called an HO-17 hut, which could sit on the back of a 6 x 6. In the beginning, it was manned the same as the 'Sands, a pair of 292's. When I arrived things had changed. Each trick had one 292 and one 203 (Russian). The equipment was taken out of the HO-17 and installed in a wood-framed squad tent which had a tent stove.

We also had a direct teletype link to Chicksands. For power we had a pair of generators. The actual site was in the middle of a large sheep pasture. We could drive directly to the site but when we left the road there was a gate, then a drive of 100 or so yards to another gate and then another drive of 200 or so yards. During rainy weather we would leave the jeep at the gate by the road and walk in to relieve those on duty.

The entire detachment was made up of the NCOIC, five 292's, five 203's, one maintenance man and one motor mechanic. Although Edzell was an active RAF base—it had some Lancaster bombers and a few other aircraft—it was not a large base. It did have a paved runway though. We had our own area where we lived, but the E-4's and above lived in the RAF sergeants' area and belonged to

926

the RAF Sergeants Mess. I was an E-3 at the time, and we lived in the USAF area where we had a kitchen and office for the NCOIC. The maintenance man and the motor mechanic also had their work places in this area. We had three 6 x 6's and two jeeps for transportation.

The airmen often drove into Aberdeen to movies and other recreation. I have never met George Montague, who retired from USAFSS in 1971—retiring down under in Australia. However, George and I had a close mutual friend, Robert P. "Frenchy" Demers. George recalled that Frenchy arrived for his first duty at the Edzell DF site in 1954.

I remember the night he arrived. We were out in the kitchen playing cards and drinking, and someone suggested we stop and have something to eat. When we did this, we all put in one food item and cooked everything in the same pot. One guy put in some eggs, another added a can of ravioli, someone added a can of Irish stew, and there were a few other things also. Frenchy came up on the monthly run and arrived in the middle of this "meal" preparation. Here he was a new guy just out of language school, and he comes in a room with a bunch of drunks cooking some ungodly concoction, and because we were nice people, we offered him a drink and part of our meal. He accepted the drink but declined the meal.

George and Frenchy were both from Massachusetts—Boston area—and they palled around after discharge from the Air Force in 1957.

Frenchy and I reenlisted together in Dec '57. I was working for Raytheon at the time. When I went home after work, there was a Christmas card from him, so I got in the car and drove down to New Bedford to see him. I had been thinking of reenlisting, I had even talked to the Navy and they said they would take me in at the same rank (E-4) as I had when I left the Air Force, but they insisted I would have to go to their radio school. I did not think much of that idea.

Frenchy was thinking the same thing, and he told me he had been talking to the Air Force recruiter in New

Bedford, and when he told me his name, I told him that I knew him from Chicksands. We went in to talk to him, and Frenchy said he wanted to go to advanced Russian, and I told him I wanted to go to southern Japan. He got on the phone and called Headquarters, and in 10 or so minutes we had what we wanted and that was that.

An excellent example of the close-knit, small USAFSS command!

A couple of weeks later Frenchy was at Kelly waiting for his clearance to be updated, and I in California getting a clothing issue and waiting for a plane to Japan. That was when Frenchy met his wife. He was making appointments for the dental clinic, and she was the one he called to make the appointments.

The author and Frenchy Demers served together during the early 1970's, working for CMSgt. Thomas H. Tennant. A USAFSS legend who served the command 33 years, Chief Tennant— "THT" to his friends—was the 37th RSM Personnel Sergeant Major when Robert P. Demers signed into the squadron in 1954. Using his incredible photographic memory, THT has filled in many peripheral holes in the history of early USAFSS COMINT operations in Scotland, England and Germany.

THT Odyssey to Kirknewton

Tom Tennant's fact-filled account of detours that he and other early USAFSS pioneers encountered enroute to RAF Kirknewton illustrates typical hurdles that USAFSS endured in fielding new squadrons in the early days of the command. Tennant resigned from a job in the finance office at McClellan AFB, California, and enlisted in the Air Force in September 1950. In the last week of basic training, Air Force officials noticed his civilian background and kept Airman Tennant at Lackland as a payroll clerk in a basic training squadron.

I hated it and fought it. I wanted to go to weather or Intel school, then overseas, not get stuck in Texas. My initial MOS was converted to a personnel AFSC, 73250, as the Air Force widened the breach with the old Army. I finally got out of Lackland by volunteering for just about every overseas levy that came up.

In 1951, Corporal Tennant applied for a "specific levy as a personnel clerk (73250) to go overseas to Germany for assignment to USAF Security Service (whatever that was)."

Got selected and reported to Camp Kilmer, NJ, on 15 Jan '52 for out-processing. Was told I was going to the 6910ᵗʰ Security Group, APO 633 (Wiesbaden), but also that I was "earmarked for the 37ᵗʰ RSM, Scotland."

Arriving in Bremerhaven on 1 February 1952 aboard the USNS M. L. Hershey, the Army herded Cpl. Tennant onto a troop train to Sonthofen, an Army replacement depot in Bavaria, where after six days, another train took him to Wiesbaden. Representatives of the 6910ᵗʰ Security Group routed him and other arriving USAFSS personnel to their next destination.

Mine was Bremerhaven in the 41ˢᵗ RSM, which reportedly had been newly located there in December, just a couple of days before Christmas. I was told I was there to work and become familiar with how things went in Europe and USAFSS, while waiting for my ultimate unit, the 37ᵗʰ RSM, to deploy overseas from Brooks AFB to Kirknewton, Scotland, sometime in June. There were a number of others there at Bremerhaven who had actually been assigned to the 37th RSM at Brooks before being sent overseas as "earmarked," including Morse ops, 202's, comm center ops, and various types of maintenance.

By 10 February 1952, Tennant was working as the payroll clerk in the 41ˢᵗ RSM. He was promoted to staff sergeant 1 June 1952. The transfer of earmarked airmen began.

About half of us (mostly operations types and maintenance) left in May to go to Kirknewton, where there was a small Det 102, 10ᵗʰ RSM in place. To the best of my ability, prior to Jul '52 all detachments of USAFSS units had the digits of the parent unit followed by a 1-up number as a designation, without hyphens or dashes. Thereafter, they dropped the digits of the parent unit, and just gave a 1-up number.

Most of the rest of us were moved later, 30 June, reporting to the 10ᵗʰ RSM at Chicksands on 1 Jul '52. Again, we were told this was strictly temporary, until the 37ᵗʰ RSM could absorb some more troops. Reportedly, the 37ᵗʰ unit, about 100 strong, had made the move in June. They had arrived in Scotland the end of June but found they had almost no barracks space, or even usable working space.

Six weeks later, on 14 Aug '52, I and a few others proceeded up to Kirknewton. It was a mess. About 90 or so arrived with the unit, picked up another 25 or so from the old Det, and picked up another 25 or so in July-August of "earmarked" personnel such as myself, from temp assignments to Chicksands, B'haven, Darmstadt and Landsberg.

Very shabby barracks for lower 4 grades, a makeshift mess hall, and a combo of huts, Quonsets, tents and vans that made up the ops compound. SSgt.'s and above all lived off base, and the E-1-E-4's lived mostly in open bay prefab type buildings, each with one or two private rooms available for the most senior troops to fight over. The Ops area also was originally in a series of these WW II vintage prefabs, but a huge H-frame Ops building was in the process of being erected at the same time. I do recall distinctly that all construction projects were agonizingly slow, mostly due to foot-dragging by the UK Ministry of Defence on-site representatives. They did have a large Quonset-type hangar that housed the motor pool and supply, but everything else was pretty ugly.

In fairly short order I gleaned a pretty good unclassified idea of how the 37ᵗʰ had evolved. Early planning in 1950 called for establishing a unit at Kirknewton as soon as they could get it done. About the same time, they planned for the establishment of the 41ˢᵗ RSM at Bremerhaven. Dets of the existing 2ⁿᵈ RSM and 10ᵗʰ RSM started limited work at the sites, while the units were activated at Brooks and an organizational structure established.

The 37ᵗʰ cadre had been formed up at Brooks sometime in the summer of '51, and the initial commander was a Capt. A. D. Clemons. Most of the cadre thought he also would be the first overseas commander, but just before deployment, Major Russell L. French came out of nowhere to be the new CC. He was a no nonsense, humorless but hardworking Ohio State grad who carried the AFSC of 3016, Communications Electronics Staff Officer. I don't believe he had much experience in SIGINT operations, but his first Ops officer Capt. William J. Dodds did, as well as other Intel experience.

I am told most of the original cadre had come over from the 8ᵗʰ RSM and included a few who had returned from tours at the 1ˢᵗ RSM or 3ʳᵈ RSM, plus a good many who had been dragged out of other commands. (We had about 10 E-6/-7's [TSgt.'s and MSgt.'s] who were carried as Morse operators, but their only past experience had been as actual ground or air radio operators, not intercept ops.)

In Tennant's opinion, the lack of experienced senior NCO's—there were very few with SIGINT experience in 1950—together with inadequate facilities at Kirknewton, "led to some obvious morale and discipline problems that they certainly didn't need." Six months after Tom Tennant arrived in Scotland as a brand new staff sergeant (personnel specialist), the first sergeant's tour was curtailed for hardship (seriously ill child), and the personnel sergeant major received a reassignment back to the States on humanitarian grounds.

That left me as the second ranking man to a rather senior SSgt. who begged off that he couldn't take the pressure of a NCOIC job, so with just over 2 1/2 years service I ended up as the personnel sergeant major in charge of a 16-man personnel shop.

Almost every single person who came into the 37ᵗʰ RSM between Aug '52 and Aug '54 used my broken Parker Quink pen to sign their travel vouchers during in-processing. Two young linguists who signed in to the outfit just a month or two before I left were Robert P. Demers and Robert H. Bergeron.

Both being married to lasses from Edinburgh, Bergeron and Tennant had a close relationship during years working together in

USAFSS. Deemed a human computer by long-time associates, Tom Tennant has a vivid recall of 37th operations even though he had no direct involvement in USAFSS operations at that point in his career. He held a top secret special access clearance and made the occasional foray into Ops on personnel matters. And reams of personnel action memorandums that he typed for airmen and officers—changes in duty titles, job classification and skill upgrades—brought Tennant a unique perspective of personnel in the unit and the jobs they performed.

The unit quickly had about 20 HF positions at work, and a staff of around ten 202's doing the A&R [analysis and reporting] work in the very compartmented system of that time. The true boss of the 202's was a 22 year old TSgt. named William R. "Sam" Barr, who was a little later to become a 23 1/2 year old MSgt. with only 5 1/2 years in service.

Second in charge was SSgt. Joseph Tortorete, who made TSgt. a year or so later. If memory serves me right, his primary AFSC actually was 20170 (cryptanalyst), but he also had a 202 awarded. Like most of the truly qualified Ops types, he spent most of his time in Operations, with little contact with the Personnel Shop, so I'm not surprised he doesn't remember me. A few months later, a security cop, then AFSC 96150, came in and was assigned to OJT [on-the-job training] as a 202, completing the conversion in a very short time. His name was Donald E. "Sam" Hodshire, who later served at least one, perhaps two, tours in Operations at Bremerhaven, so you might know him also.

37th RSM—Basketball Powerhouse

Even in its early days, the 37th Radio Squadron Mobile added to the superb USAFSS tradition of fielding outstanding basketball teams, and Scotland welcomed two 6937th RSM teams into its amateur league. In 1947, local burghers in Edinburgh had formed the East of Scotland Basketball Association and created an amateur league. The following year, the United States Olympic team beat a Scottish team in Edinburgh before winning the Olympic title in London. Then during the 1952-53 season—37th

RSM's first year in Scotland—the squadron entered two teams, Comets and Knights, in the Scottish league. Led by Earl Hamner, the Comets went through the season undefeated. They won the league title and also collected the Scottish Cup.[177] The Comets were repeat league winners in the 1953-54 season, while the Kirknewton Knights became one of the best teams in the USAF league within the United Kingdom.

Tortorete—Mustang Officer

A long, uncomfortable night as the Charge of Quarters (CQ) during his assignment in Scotland convinced Joe Tortorete that he should become an officer.

It was there that I decided to apply for OCS. I had CQ duty and I noticed that the Air Force practiced "rank discrimination" when it came time to getting some sleep. The OD [Officer of the Day] had a cot complete with sheets, pillow, and blanket—while I, a lowly staff sergeant, had nothing. After spending a miserable night trying to sleep curled up on a desktop, I decided RHIP was really true, and I had better try to get some. OCS seemed the best choice.

Graduating from Officer Candidate School in 1957, 2nd Lt. Joseph Tortorete served additional USAFSS tours in Texas, Alaska, Germany, Maryland, Pakistan and Washington, DC, before retiring in 1970. Tom Tennant's tour in Scotland ended in 1952.

I left the 37th RSM on 13 Aug 54, exactly 2 years after arriving, with my new bride, new TSgt. stripes and every intention to take my discharge and return to civilian life. Eighteen months later, however, I reenlisted in Sacramento, CA, as a SSgt., with a guaranteed assignment to Russian Language School and USAFSS. After Syracuse and a 19 month stay at the 6911th RSM, Darmstadt, I moved up to Rhein-Main. And the rest, as they say, is history.

Thomas Tennant and Scottish wife Margaret have been happily married since 1954. He began a USAFSS flying career as an airborne mission supervisor at Rhein-Main, Germany, during the summer of 1958, a career path that lasted a quarter century. When he retired in 1984, his squadron retired and presented to Chief Tennant his trusty 1960 standard Royal typewriter. They attempted to give him a G-175 airborne intercept receiver, but he declined to accept the receiver because he did not have an RC-135 recon jet to haul it around.

THT's Memories of Edzell DF Site

Reminiscing about the DF site at Edzell, Tom Tennant seems to remember every little detail about USAFSS operations at Edzell more than fifty years after being involved only peripherally with the site.

One of the first things I encountered as a new personnel sergeant in an unfamiliar command was that our unit was gaining a detachment, which was to be Det 1, 37th RSM, at RAF Station Edzell, near Montrose, Scotland. This no doubt was the same Det 101, 10th RSM, Stracathro, Angus, Scotland, but during my tenure the term Edzell was used almost exclusively,

Note: When Det 101 deployed to Scotland, the detachment was sometimes referred to as Stracathro, most likely due to the DF site itself being located close to Stracathro. Sgt. Tennant traveled to RAF Edzell to discuss personnel issues with detached team members.

I visited it once—the troops were billeted in an RAF barracks building, and the base still had a few Lincoln bombers left over from WW II. The Det was headed by TSgt. Murl G. Olson, a Morse op, and was 13 strong. I believe there were 4 other Morse ops, 5 20330-1's (Russians), 2 radio maint mechanics, and one other guy who I believe was a diesel mechanic/power-man, responsible for operating the auxiliary power units to support the DF site. Their [DF] net was tied directly to Chicksands; at that time Kirknewton had no DF capability. The other notable thing I remember is that most of the troops were married to young Scottish lasses, which was the prime occupational hazard for young single troops stationed in Scotland.

My recollection was that the DF site at Edzell was deactivated and moved to Kirknewton in early '54 after a hearability and technical survey. By that time, most of the original Det members were either gone or getting ready to leave, but the few who weren't had to have been pretty mad about the change. Edzell, I am told, was nearly a paradise, with little pressure, outside interference, commander's calls, training sessions, etc.

RELOCATING EDZELL DF SITE

George Montague was serving in Det 1, 37th RSM at RAF Edzell when the squadron relocated the DF system to RAF Kirknewton. The Kirknewton base was undergoing a renaissance when the DF team moved there from Edzell.

I guess the 37th was in operation almost a year when I arrived and things were very primitive. Operations was in tarpaper shacks down by the giant hangar, and we were living in all the old buildings. The building I was in ended up as the service club. The large building program was just starting about that time. When they closed the DF site up north and brought us back, I did not recognize the base.

Edzell was closed down about August-September '54 time frame. I have a couple of pictures that were taken when the DF site was being dismantled. When the site was closed, there was no loss of operation as a new DF unit was set up at Kirknewton. When we came off duty, we just got in a truck and drove down to Kirknewton and went to work there.

RAF Edzell—NSGA

On 6 July 1960, the U.S. Naval Security Group Activity activated "NSGA Edzell," a SIGINT intercept station, at RAF Edzell—former home of USAFSS direction finding detachment, Det 1, 10th RSM and Det 1, 37th RSM in the early 1950's.[178] The NSG returned RAF Edzell to the Ministry of Defence on 30 September 1997.[179]

37th RSM—New DF Station

As explained by George Montague, the DF station at RAF
Edzell was replaced with new direction finding equipment at RAF
Kirknewton.

*In fact, it was a completely new unit; it was the AN/TRD-
4. The hut had the usual DF equipment and 2 acquisition
positions. It also was larger—we could actually stand up
in it, and it had a built-in heater.*

Five decades later, Montague was saddened to learn that the
Kirknewton DF site had suffered a catastrophic fire.

Kirknewton DF—Fiery End

Bill Bowers, flight commander on duty in the SIGINT
compound at Kirknewton, was in the can doing his business—
literally—when he learned that the squadron DF shack was on fire.
At first, he believed someone was trying to hoodwink their flight
commander.

*One night my flight was working midshifts, and I had a
call of nature and was sitting on the porcelain throne
when one of my guys stuck his head in the door and yelled
"Hey Lt., the DF shack is on fire." Thinking this was
someone's idea of a joke, I told him to confirm it and find
out the severity and what had been done. He immediately
stuck his head back in and replied "That sumbitch is
burned down, and the firearms are going off, and the
operator called it in from the phone at the Officers Club."
(1/4 mile away)*

*Now this DF shack was about a 12 by 12 foot wooden
structure stuck way out at the end of a runway, so I had to
jump in my car and head out there right away. It was
snowing like hell, with about 8-10 inches on the ground.
My car was a little Austin-Healy Sprite. The route to the
DF shack had not been plowed, so I just followed the
tracks of the fire truck. They later said it looked like a
giant mole was rapidly burrowing through the snow.
Anyhow, once I got there and determined that the operator
was all right and the fire was under control, I talked to the
Fire Dept (local Scottish personnel, nonmilitary). It*

seemed they wanted to go inside the frame and put out all remaining embers.

We normally kept an M-1 with a loaded clip out there for their own protection. I asked the operator if the classified books were still in there, to which he said they were. I then asked him how many rounds of the ammo had gone off, to which he said about 2-3 as near as he could tell. I couldn't let the firemen in until I had confirmed the classified materiel had been destroyed. This could only be done by going in and poking around, myself. This I did with much trepidation, imagining more ammo going off as I am standing there. Fortunately, this didn't happen and the fire was subsequently extinguished.

Later investigations proved that someone had mistakenly put gasoline into a jerry can meant for kerosene for the heater. We had a green jerry can for kerosene for the heater and a red jerry can for gasoline for the generator. I can only assume that someone was color blind. We then got smart and wrote in large letters the words Kerosene Only and Gasoline Only.

The squadron ordered a replacement system, but it took a while to get the DF capability back online. Bowers believes that the DF shack burned in January 1963. By this time rumors were circulating that USAFSS would be terminating operations in Scotland.

6952nd Operations—Disappointment

A source knowledgeable about operational issues told the author that USAFSS and national intelligence authorities finally decided in 1964 to terminate operations in Scotland due to "technical reasons." A large mountain butte a few miles to the east-southeast was apparently filled with iron ore or some such metallic material that caused severe interference with primary intercept operations at the base. Officials really "wanted to make Kirknewton work because of its northern latitude, but they couldn't move the mountain." Reportedly, 6952nd Security Squadron had pretty much closed down by summer of 1964, although the base remained open for another year as a reduced staff wound up USAFSS operations.

6952ND SS DEACTIVATED

Capt. William Bowers was one of the last Americans who served with the 6952nd Security Squadron at RAF Kirknewton. He turned out the lights on 6952nd SS operations in 1966.

As the base got nearer to closing in '66 I kept absorbing more duties as attrition reduced the number of officers on base. I wrote the mission phase out plan in coordination with Laddie Marin at Chicksands, in which we transferred the mission to the 'Sands in two increments. It all went off smoothly, and it was really strange to walk around in an empty Ops building with all of the equipment moved out.

USAFSS officially closed and vacated RAF Kirknewton on 1 August 1966.[180] Signal reception issues had factored in the decision to close RAF Kirknewton; however, the advent of the FLR-9 antenna system that came online at Chicksands, Karamursel and San Vito also played a role. With the improved antenna system, the former 6952nd Security Squadron mission was readily accommodated at other USAFSS sites.

RAF Kirknewton—Post USAFSS

Out of curiosity, retired Chief Tom Tennant stopped by RAF Kirknewton in October 1991 while visiting wife Margaret's family in Edinburgh.

It had been basically abandoned for several years and was under caretaker status with a small cadre of about 12 RAF people shooing away visitors. I got to tour the entire area. All of the buildings that were built during my last year there [1954] and in the subsequent years were all deteriorating rapidly—the bowling alley, gym, NCO club, big PX, recreation center (none of which we had in my time), as well as the new barracks and Ops buildings. There were still a number of towers standing throughout the old runway area where our antenna farm was, but with no wires showing.

The caretakers told Tom Tennant that sometime in the '70's or early '80's, a U.S. Army special forces activity set up a training site there for a few years. The author can find no record of use of

RAF Kirknewton by an American organization after 1966; however, a UK Parliament record dated 23 February 2004 shows that the USAF handed the base back to the British Ministry of Defence on 26 September 1991.[181]

RAF Kirknewton was one of 42 sites/facilities included on a list "United States bases handed back to MoD since 1988," the earliest date for which information was available. Twenty-seven of the returned bases were USAF, thirteen were USN, and two were not defined. Interestingly, RAF Kirknewton is shown on the list as a hospital-type facility along with at least two inactive RAF hospitals that were leased to the USAF and USN for use as contingency hospitals during the Persian Gulf War (August 1990-March 1991). The USAF activated one of the hospitals—740-bed RAF Nocton Hall—and treated a limited number of casualties there in 1991,[182] but RAF Kirknewton appears to have remained only on standby during the war.

Unlike many former Ministry of Defence facilities that have been turned over to local government for redevelopment, the RAF Kirknewton facility appears to remain pretty much as the Air Force Security Service left it in 1966—unused and, due to lack of proper upkeep, in a deteriorating state. The 2175 Squadron Air Training Corps (Volunteer Gliding Schools) uses the facility, now called Kirknewton Airfield, to develop glider flying skills for air cadets.[183] The Livingston Model Aircraft Club also uses the facility as its flying site.[184] The 6950th Radio Group Mobile had been operating for a decade when the 6952nd Security Squadron was inactivated.

6950TH RGM ACTIVATED

In September 1956, the 6950th Security Group was inactivated, replaced by the 6950th Radio Group Mobile that stood up at RAF Chicksands. In turn, the 6952nd RSM reported to the 6950th RGM and the 6951st RSM was inactivated. The new 6950th RGM absorbed the mission and personnel of the 6951st. In a related "paper transfer," airmen who had performed second echelon analysis while assigned to the 6950th Security Group transferred to newly activated Detachment 1, 6901st Special Communications Group—addressed earlier in Chapter Four. Wayne Palmer, who reported to the 6951st RSM in 1955, remembers the "advance party of 6950th analysts who later became the 6901st Spec Comm Group."

Upon our arrival at Chicksands in the Fall of 1955, the 6950th (SG) was located in M Block and consisted almost entirely of 202x0's [analysts]—many on their second hitch. Some of the names I remember were Earl (the Pearl) Ramsey, Billy Bowers, Jerry Coleman, Ray Crawford, "Rip" Boyle and Billy J. Calloway.

They all went to Zweibrücken and converted the barracks at Turenne Kaserne into an Intelligence compound as Air Force tenants on a US Army post. It was not until the move was completed that they were formally designated the 6901st Spec Comm Group. At the same time, we at Chicksands woke up one morning and found out that our name had been changed to the 6950th Radio Group Mobile. We did not move anywhere or do anything special to earn this designation. I guess we were just in the right place at the right time.

Unbeknownst to Wayne Palmer, the analysts had transferred to Det 1, 6901st SCG when the 6950th Security Group was inactivated in September 1956. Those personnel relocated to Zweibrücken, Germany in late 1956. The author worked with TSgt.'s John P. "Rip" Boyle and Billy J. Calloway after they completed their tours at Zweibrücken and returned to the 6950th RGM in the late 1950's.

Contributed by Oscar DerManouelian

Col. William Rice, Francis Hollifield, Jimmy Sword, ?, Billy Calloway, Oscar DerManouelian, Kyle Abbott (kneeling), Intramural Basketball Champs, circa 1958

Trafalgar Square was (is) a famous tourist landmark in London.

Contributed by Bill Gray

Trafalgar Square, London, circa 1958

6950TH SW ACTIVATED

In another reorganization on 1 July 1963, the 6950th Radio Group Mobile became the 6950th Security Wing, and all USAFSS radio squadrons mobile became security squadrons, e.g., the 6952nd RSM became the 6952nd Security Squadron.

The chart that follows shows the lineage of the 10th RSM and 37th RSM (and successor units) that served in the United Kingdom for five decades (1950-1995).

Lineage of 10th RSM and 37th RSM (and successor units)	
Unit Designator	Action/Comments
10th RSM	Activated in Fall of 1949/Brooks AFB, TX
10th RSM	Deployed to RAF Chicksands, Eng, Nov '50
Det 101, (Det 1, 10th RSM)	Deployed fm Chicksands to Edzell, Scotland, in mid-1951
37th RSM	Activated in August 1951/Brooks AFB, TX
Det 102, (Det 2, 10th RSM)	Deployed fm Chicksands to Kirknewton, Scotland, in early 1952
37th RSM	Deployed to RAF Kirknewton, June 1952
Det 102, (Det 2, 10th RSM)	Inactivated/Replaced by 37th RSM in summer 1952
Det 1, 37th RSM	Replaced Det 101, RAF Edzell, Fall of 1952
6950th Scty Gp	Activated in 1953 at Brooks AFB
6950th Scty Gp	Relocated to RAF Chicksands in 1954.
Det 1, 37th RSM	Relocated to Kirknewton and deactivated in early 1954
6951st RSM	Replaced 10th RSM, 8 May 1955
6952nd RSM	Replaced 37th RSM, 8 May 1955
6950th RGM	Replaced 6950th Scty Gp, 1 Sept 1956
6951st RSM	Inactivated 1 Sept 1956; absorbed into 6950th RGM
OL-1, 6950th RGM	Activated at RAF Brize Norton, Eng, in 1959
Det 1, 6950th RGM	Replaced OL-1, 6950th RGM at Brize Norton
6950th Scty Wg	Replaced 6950th RGM, 1 July 1963;
Det 1, 6950th Scty Wg	Replaced Det 1, 6050th RGM at Brize Norton
6952nd Security Sq	Replaced 6952nd RSM, 1 July 1963
Det 1, 6950th Scty Wg	Moved fm Brize Norton to Upper Heyford in Jan-Feb 1965
Det 1, 6950th Scty Wg	Deactivated in Sept 1965; mission relocated back to Chicksands
6952nd Security Sq	Deactivated in 1966;
6950th Scty Gp	Replaced 6950th Scty Wg, 1967
Det 1, 6950th Scty Gp	Replaced 6913th Scty Gp at Bremerhaven in July 1967; deactivated 31 March 1968
6950th Security Sq	Replaced 6950th Scty Gp, 1 July 1978
6950th Electronic Scty Gp	Replaced 6950th Scty Sq, 1 Aug 1979
450th Intel Squadron	Replaced 6950th ESG, 1 Oct 1991
450th Intel Squadron	Inactivated at Chicksands, 30 Sept 1995 *
* British MoD assumed control of Chicksands this date.	

RAF Chicksands—Good Ole Days

Every American airman who served at RAF Chicksands no doubt has his or her favorite stories about the good ole days. The anecdotes that follow occurred during the late 1950's, but American service personnel who served tours in the United Kingdom anytime during the Cold War may see similarities to their own experiences. Chix alumni who served at the 'Sands in the 1956-1960 era most likely remember many of the events.

Burn Detail

Most airmen who ever served in a USAFSS field unit can relate to "Burn Detail," the process of destroying (burning) classified materials in the days before shredding machines. The author participated in a burn detail snafu on his first day in the operations compound at Chicksands in December 1956. Accompanied by the destruction certification officer, the author, a couple of other airmen and an NCO carried hundreds of oversized Kraft paper grocery bags stuffed with crumpled classified paper to a burn pit located within the fenced Ops compound. A dusting of wind-blown snow covered surrounding grounds.

We stacked the bags like cordwood (5-6 bags tall) in a circle surrounding the burn pit, stuffed the incinerator in the pit with burn bags, dropped a lit match into an opened bag in the incinerator and began feeding additional bags into a bellowing inferno. A wire mesh atop the smokestack was supposed to retain partially burned ashes within the incinerator. As the fire roared, fist-sized pieces of burning paper escaped from a newly developed hole in the mesh on the smokestack. Some fiery ashes fell on bags waiting to be stuffed into the incinerator, starting fires amongst the bags encircling the burn pit. Other smoldering ashes floated away in the breeze, landing outside the compound. At this point, the operations officer ordered a police detail of available men to scour Farmer Parrish's fields outside the compound to retrieve classified materials while others assisted in toning down the fire in the incinerator and completing burn detail. During a 21-year USAFSS career, I never participated in another burn detail.

It turns out that this was not the only burn detail mess to befall Chicksands operations. Retired MSgt. Ambrose Jackson recalled the day a burn bag took to the air enroute to the burn pit within the operations compound.

I was the Burn NCO on duty the day the burn bag blew away during a high wind and carried classified material over half of Bedfordshire. Every day before burn bags were delivered to the incinerator, the NCO in charge had to phone a certain officer in Group Operations to get final approval to burn. On the fateful day, the weather had been very windy and gusty, and I phoned the officer and told him about the bad winds, but he ordered me to go ahead with the burn. I had the phone operator, as always, inform each block in the tech site to deliver the bags to the incinerator, and some airmen were detailed to handle the burn procedure.

On this day, one of the men from a block lost his bag to a sudden gust of wind, and it literally exploded, blowing trash all over the place. Operations was notified immediately, and men were quickly send out to recover the paper. It was clinging to tree tops and across fields in all directions. USAFSS HQ in San Antonio was notified, and an investigation was ordered. The incident was finally hushed up, and it was officially declared that no compromise had occurred because the men had recovered enough material to fill a burn bag. For that reason, it was determined that all the material had been recovered.

Which begs the question; how did decision makers in Operations determine if weather conditions were suitable for burning classified materials? Former USAFSS NCO Frank O. Long, who had transferred from Darmstadt, Germany, to Chicksands in 1961, provided the answer in an email in 2001.

I worked in OPW (where you called to see if it was okay to burn—the wind not blowing towards the clothes line of the farm). Wonder how we knew? Light a cigarette and blow smoke to see which way it went or toss some loose grass in the air to see which way it blew—or if it was duty hours we would look at the flag at the HQ building. Then we would go back into the weather shop, pick up the phone and let you know if you could burn.

Foggy Ole England

"Pea soup fog" was coined in 1871 with regard to London's renowned fogs that often shut down the city for days.[185] Those who served at Chicksands during the 1950's recall pea soupers not only in London but at Chicksands as well. Precipitated by formations of static cooler air close to the ground (temperature inversion), England's dense fog conditions were exacerbated for centuries in cold weather by large amounts of smoke from soft coal fires. A pea souper in 1879 (Nov to March) brought four months of sunless gloom to Londoners,[186] and a resident of London created the term "smog" in 1905 to describe the menacing combination of natural fog and coal smoke.[187]

London's Great Smog of 1952 (5-9 December) resulted in the passage of the British Clean Air Act of 1956, creating zones where only smokeless fuels could be used.[188] Towns and villages around Chicksands were obviously outside the smokeless fuel zone since the local air was still laden with acrid, sulfuric smoke particles during heavy fogs in the late 1950's. The 1952 smog also produced a new nickname for London. Few American airmen visited London—they went to the "Big Smoke"—for entertainment.

Fog Alerts at Chicksands

During periods of intense fog, the Chicksands base commander often restricted single airmen to base, sometimes for two to three days at a time. Air policemen enforced the edict by turning back all airmen who did not live off base at the base gates. The fog tended to be worse at night, but there were days when visibility hovered around zero, even at midday. On pea soup foggy days—typically during the winter—the base commander would declare a "fog call" in mid-afternoon. Nonessential married dayworkers who had families off base were often permitted to go home early, and in severe conditions, married shift workers were advised to remain at home; single airmen living in the barracks had to work their shifts.

Cat's Eyes—Savior in Pea Soup Fog

Given foggy conditions in England, it is fitting that an Englishman invented the "cat's eye" road reflector in 1933,[189] and a row of cat's eyes marked center lines on most British roads long before their use became prevalent on roads all over the world. Americans who have driven on narrow roads in the UK are undoubtedly familiar with cat's eyes and may even owe their lives to those reflectors. However, there is no reflection if auto lights cannot penetrate dense fog, and the area along the Flit River that dissected Chicksands is especially susceptible to such heavy fogs in cold damp weather.

During the 1950's, shift workers who were on break would see dense fogs forming in the afternoon and rush off base ahead of a declared fog call. On one such occasion, the author left the base and made his way to Hitchin—driving his trusty right hand drive '52 Standard Vanguard. Arriving back at the Bottom Gate late at night, I found the fog so dense along the Flit River that the bridge was totally invisible. Afraid of smashing into the sides of the narrow bridge (or worse yet, into the river), I started the car in first gear at idle speed and steered through the open driver's door while walking along the left road curb, walking the car home to the parking lot. Robert Locknar, coworker and barracks mate, had his own pea soup fog encounter.

Author's Collection

Larry Tart's 1952 Vanguard, 1957
(Farmer Parrish's cows in background behind Nissen Hut)

Hot Date Cancelled by Fog

Our Dog Trick was on a three-day break in December 1958, and Bob Locknar had a hot date in Bedford when the base commander declared a fog call. Bob decided to bypass the system. Knowing the gate guard would not permit him to walk through the Top Gate and down Sandy Lane to the bus stop at the main road to Bedford, Bob modified his route. Donning his British "Sherlock Holmes" style trench coat, he crawled over the low cattle fence on the northern perimeter of the base and walked across Farmer Parrish's Brussels sprout field to Sandy Lane, out of sight of the gate guard, especially in the thick fog. Out of nowhere, the base sergeant of the guard drove alongside Locknar and returned him to the base. For that indiscretion, Bob received an Article 15 with the loss of one stripe and two weeks of restriction to base.

Quick-Draw Newkirk

Robert Locknar had a way of being in the wrong place at the wrong time. Bob and the author were Dog Trick Civair analysts in M Block, the first building on the right inside the 6950th RGM operations compound in the late 1950's. Our door to M Block was perhaps 25 yards from the 6950th guard shack at the entrance to Operations, and on slow shifts Bob and I often spent time inside the guard shack shooting the bull with our two USAFSS air policemen. The shack was about an 8' x 10' structure that was heated by an M-41 potbelly stove on which the AP's always had a hot pot of coffee. There was room for four persons in the shack, but with little spare room.

One slow midshift during a visit by Locknar and me in the guard shack, A1C Jim Newkirk and his AP sidekick practiced a little quick draw on each other—sans ammo clips, of course. They had stopped horsing around, when Newkirk suddenly had the urge for one more quick draw. Forgetting that he'd reloaded a clip in his clunky Colt .45, he drew the weapon and pulled the trigger. Tragedy struck, but Bob Locknar's guardian angel must have been peering down on that guard shack. Locknar was bending over to pour himself a cup of coffee when the .45 caliber bullet grazed one of his ribs and left gaping holes in the inside and outside walls of the shack. The bullet missed me by inches and would have caught Locknar squarely in the midriff, had he been standing upright.

Bob was in pain but not in shock. The four of us quickly decided that only Locknar and the two AP's were in the shack! During the investigation, I professed to have been walking from the snack bar within the compound to M Block when I heard the shot. The alibi amongst the others was that Newkirk's gun fell out of his holster as he was standing up, and that the .45 discharged when it hit the floor. Locknar was patched up and back to work in a matter of days, and the alibi fell apart even quicker. The Air Force OSI agent who investigated immediately recognized that the trajectory of the bullet had been parallel with the floor, not at the sharp angle that would have been apparent had the weapon discharged from floor level.

Given an unblemished record of several years as an air policeman, Jim Newkirk should have known the dangers of playing with weapons, but one had to feel sorry for him. Confronted by the OSI agent, he fessed up, was demoted to airman basic and served 30 days in the brig. Fortunately, Bob Locknar's wound was superficial.

Shootout at the Comm Center

The communicator who shot up G Block—the communications center—within months of Bob Locknar's being shot, was not as fortunate, but lucky nonetheless to suffer a nonfatal .45 wound. For a while, 6950th airmen believed they deserved combat pay just for showing up at work in the operations compound. A decorated Korean War paratroop veteran, the communicator may have been suffering post traumatic stress when he went on a shooting rampage in the comm center.

The communicator-crypto operator, who shall remain nameless, returned to base from a pub-crawling visit to Bedford, donned his fatigues, ate midnight chow in the mess hall and entered the operations compound with others reporting for duty on the midshift. He rang the door buzzer seeking admittance to the comm center where he was scheduled to work a mid. Admitted by a coworker who greeted him by name, the communicator grabbed a .45 caliber submachine gun ("grease gun" with a 30-round banana clip) from a gun rack inside the comm center door and emptied two clips into banks of teletype terminals. Coworkers—all uninjured—cleared the building through an emergency exit.

SSgt. Benjamin David, USAFSS air policeman on duty, rushed from the guard shack and hid behind bushes outside the main entrance door to the comm center, with his .45 automatic at the ready. Having heard lots of rapid fire followed by silence from within, he was prepared for the worst. One of the analysts walked out of M Block across the street from the comm center. Clueless to the comm center shooting foray, the analyst found it strange that Ben David was crouching in the shadows and waving as if to warn him to get down. Suddenly, the G Block main door burst open, and the attacker charged out, firing a carbine aimlessly in the air.

David brought the gunman down with a single .45 shot to the buttocks. The gunfight at Chicksands "corral" was over. The duty corpsman at the base dispensary transported the injured gunman to an off-base hospital. Air policeman Dick Ebersole guarded the gunman while he recovered in the hospital.

He only wanted to know who did the injury to him, and I had the hardest time telling him that I did not know anything about the case.

Former 6950th Airman Richard Brown has a vivid memory of the G Block shooting incident. He cleaned and maintained the weapons in the comm center. Suffering a serious, but non life-threatening wound, the gunman recovered and soon departed Chicksands. The final disposition of charges against him is unknown.

Communicator Suicide

A holdover from the days of mobile operations, a cache of weapons (.45 caliber pistols, M3 grease guns and M1 carbines) was maintained openly in USAFSS comm centers to safeguard unit cryptographic materials. In an unrelated tragedy sometime after the shooting incident, a staff sergeant communications shift supervisor (name withheld) stole a .45 pistol from G Block and committed suicide in his hotel room in London while on break. The task of cleaning that weapon also fell upon Richard Brown.

[He] took the .45 out of my desk in G Block and took it down to London, put it to his head and pulled the trigger. Got the .45 back from Scotland Yard six months later and never did clean all the dried blood off the piece.

The author is aware of no other shooting incidents at Chicksands, but a windstorm reportedly caused a casualty—maybe the first on-duty USAFSS death—in that same comm center at Chicksands in 1957.

G Block Knocked out of Action in Storm

During the wee hours of 3 November 1957, severe winds and rain toppled a giant tree within the 6950th RGM compound. Crashing on G Block, the tree sent a support beam tumbling into a row of teletype terminals, killing an airman on duty and shutting down secure telecommunications temporarily. The group relocated its communications function to J Block while the G Block facilities were rebuilt. Further details on this tragic death are unavailable.

Contributed by Richard Brown

Storm Damage to G Block (Comm Center), 3 Nov 1957

Retired MSgt. Brooks Northern reported to the 6950th RGM at Chicksands the night before the storm devastated the communications center.

> *I departed McGuire AFB aboard Flight 441 on 1 Nov '57, so probably arrived at Chicksands on November 2nd.*

A Russian linguist and seasoned globe-trotter who had served a tour in Japan, Northern traveled alone, arriving by train at Midland station, Bedford, about 10:00 p.m. The station master pointed Northern toward a bus stop from which a bus would take him to Chicksands. Carrying his luggage, he rode a green double-decker British bus to the base.

The bus left from Bedford, St. Peter's Square, up by the Granada. I think that bus left somewhere close to 11 p.m. That's the bus I caught after lugging my duffel bag and B-4 bag from the Midland Road train station.

Felt like I'd lugged those two bags a heckuva long way when I got to High Street. Thank goodness that bus went on base. Sandy Lane would have wiped me out. This happened on the night the tree fell on the comm center and killed that G.I.

I recall the tree incident but was on break in London when the storm struck. Weeks later, catching the 11 p.m. bus back to base from Bedford became a regular routine for Brooks Northern.

Record Store Romance—LP's and 45's Bring Love

Brooks Northern and Shirley Jeffs' chance meeting speaks volumes about the vast and sundry ways American airmen met, fell in love and married British brides during the Cold War. A chance visit to a record shop in Bedford soon after he arrived at Chicksands was all it took to hook Brooks on vinyl records—and bride-to-be Shirley Jeffs.

Shirley was "manageress" of the record shop at Clarabuts Electronics. After working my first cycle on Baker Flight, Wally Marshall, Noah J. Carter and a couple of other barracks mates were going to "show me London." We stopped by the Saracen's Head on our way to the train station and then someone wanted to stop at Clarabuts and see if a record they had ordered had come in. We stood in those little booths listening to various records that Shirley piped to us. I kept making eyes at Shirley and ... it was several months before I ever got to London.

In a soundproofed booth equipped with stereo headphones, a customer could listen to piped-in music from long-play and 45 RPM records before making purchasing decisions. The record shop approach to "try before you buy!" Brooks Northern listened to lots of records in one of Clarabuts' sound booths.

> *I did buy a few records from Shirley. She ordered a Tennessee Ernie Ford LP called "This Lusty Land" for me. I bought it mostly because his name was "Tennessee" Ernie and because I wanted a good excuse to visit her to check on "my" record.*

> *We had quite a few barracks parties in Noah J. Carter's cubicle. We chipped in for a case of beer and then listened to 45's on Noah's record player. Records and spilled beer would be all over the table, which was covered with a G.I. blanket. The next day, Noah would take all the sticky-with-beer 45's to the latrine and wash them like dishes in the sink. No idea why the labels didn't wash off the records.*

Unlike CD recordings today, the old LP and 45 recordings were nearly indestructible, although scratches on the vinyl records added unwanted pops and snaps to the music. The Saracen's Head was a popular pub on Market Square by the public parking lot in Bedford.

> *Everybody regularly tossed pennies, six penny pieces and a few shillings into a cigar box that Noah kept on the table. When the cigar box got full, we took off to The Saracen's Head for a few beers. I'm sure Sid appreciated being paid with all that small change. If I recall correctly, Sid's attractive daughter was a barmaid there, which no doubt added to the pub's popularity.*

The author also remembers well endowed, short, loveable Carol, another Saracen's Head barmaid, who added to the pub's ambience. Shirley Jeffs soon took her "Yank" friend Brooks Northern home to meet mum and dad.

Elstow Abbey—The Wedding

Wasting little time, Brooks popped the question, got the Jeffs parents' approval and selected an impressive village church, Elstow Abbey, for the wedding venue. Located in Elstow, a quaint village five miles outside Bedford, Elstow Abbey is a former monastery for Benedictine nuns—founded circa 1075 by a niece of William the Conqueror. The parish church was once part of the nunnery church. The next challenge was for Shirley to satisfy residence requirements to be married in the abbey. Since Shirley Jeffs lived in Bedford, she stayed with close friend Shirley Hunt's family in Elstow several times over a few weeks to be eligible to marry in the abbey. Brooks Northern reminisced about courting in Elstow.

We have very fond memories of walking from Shirley's home at Britannia Place up Ampthill Road and then along a walking path to attend evensong at Elstow Abbey as the church bells pealed and the tall grasses and wild flowers moved in the breezes. It was very idyllic. After evensong, we'd stop at The Red Lion for a drink and the vicar would often already be there. (Maybe we dawdled a bit as we walked across the cemetery.) The vicar, Rev. Peter Hartley, had been a POW who worked on the bridge over the River Kwai, as was Shirley's Uncle George.

Brooks Northern and Shirley Jeffs were married on 19 July 1958 at Elstow Abbey and celebrated their Golden Anniversary in '08. During his first year in England, Airman Northern caught the 11 p.m. bus from Bedford to Chicksands more times that he cares to remember.

11 p.m. Bus—Never a Dull Moment

Bus drivers and conductors on the Bedford to RAF Chicksands route earned their pay, especially on the last nightly trip to base (11 p.m.)—conveniently coinciding with closing time for local pubs (public houses as bars/saloons are known in the UK). During the 1950's, British pub hours were 10:00 a.m.-2:00 p.m. and 6:00-10:00 p.m. during winters, with hours extended to 10:30 p.m. in the summertime. "Last Orders, Please," was a common refrain at 10:00 p.m. As publicans announced thirty minutes later, "Time, Gentlemen, Please!" the double-decker bus that was bound for Chicksands would park at St. Peter's Square near the taxi stand by the Granada Cinema.

As driver and conductor left their bus at the square and lighted a fag, American airmen and a few Brits who lived enroute to the base found themselves seats on the bus. The driver and conductor took their places, and the bus departed the square at 11 p.m. sharp. The bus was often crowded, with stragglers standing in the aisle.

Airmen always complained about the early pub closing hours, but they had no problem getting "high" by 10:00 p.m. on British beers and ales served at room temperature. Some of the airmen could get downright rowdy. About 10:50 one night, a pub-crawling airman who had boarded the bus tired of waiting. He exited the bus, walked around the bus to the driver's door, started the bus and drove it to Chicksands, only to be arrested when the air policeman stopped him at the Top Gate.

There was bus service from Luton to Chicksands via the Bottom Gate in the 1951-1952 period, but it is unclear when the bus from Bedford began traveling down Sandy Lane to the base. According to Daniel D'Apolito, during his first tour at Chicksands (1951-1953), a bus from Bedford to Hitchin dropped airmen off at the Sandy Lane bus stop on highway A600, and he walked the lane to base many nights while dating future wife Jean.

One time I missed the bus. Jean lived on Palmerston St. about 8-10 blocks north of the taxi rank. As I approached St. Peter's church, the bus had left, so not wanting to spend money on a taxi to the base, I ran down to High St. (about 4-5 blocks away) in an attempt to catch the bus there. Well, when I got there the bus had pulled out and was gone. It so happened someone else had missed the bus, and we were trying to flag down a ride or a taxi. About that time two Bobbies saw us trying to catch a ride and stopped and questioned us. We told them we were trying to get back to the base and were short of money. So they told us to get in, and they took us back to the base.

On the way, they tried to run down jack rabbits running across the road and getting in the path of the car lights. They caught two and put them in the trunk and took us up to the gate at the top of Sandy Lane, told us Cheerio and headed back to town. Don't know if they ran down any more rabbits. Time frame was sometime in 1952.

Piddle Pause

The author recalls an unforgettable bus ride from Bedford in early 1957. Again, it was the 11:00 p.m. bus from St. Peter's Square to the base—it may have been payday night. Anyway, the double-decker had a full passenger load that night, and it seemed that most riders had stayed for "Last Orders, Please," at the Peacock, Saracen's Head, Silver Grill, King's Arms, Rose and Crown or other pubs.

Saracen's Head Pub and Silver Grill, Bedford, circa 1958

Enroute to base, one of the more disorderly passengers pulled the cord signaling the driver to stop at the next bus stop. When the bus stopped, the passenger asked the conductor to hold the bus a minute while he relieved himself beside the bus. Fortunately, all the passengers at this point were airmen. A couple of minutes later, others asked to stop the bus for a piddle pause. Accommodating, but at the same time wanting the trip to be over soonest, instead of stopping the bus, the conductor removed a wooden floorboard panel so the airmen could piddle as we drove merrily along road A600 to base. Being new in England and not accustomed to such shenanigans, that was my most memorable bus ride ever. Soon the proud owner of my first automobile, I rode the bus only infrequently thereafter.

Other Bus Memories

Discussing the bus journey between Bedford and Chicksands on an internet forum elicited comments from several Chix alumni from the 1950's, including Wayne Palmer.

Well Larry, now that you bring it up, I seem to recall a few of those "Late Nite Return Trips" to Chicksands on the last bus. We would, on occasion, sing a few off-color "shanties" as we tooled along past Cardington Camp. The one that seemed to be a favorite was "In Fourteen Hundred Ninety Two, Columbus and O'Malley."

Bill Chapman recalled prepping for a night in Bedford before riding the bus to town.

Many is the time after imbibing sufficient nickel-a-can beers in the BX snack bar to gird our loins for a night in Bedford as it were, we would reel out that gate with raincoat pockets overflowing with unopened cans of beer. Of course the gentlemanly sharing of one or two of those cans with the AP on duty would turn his eyes aside.

Then marching in cadence down the first hill singing cadences regarding the temperature of certain body parts of lady native Alaskans or continuing ad nauseam with bad verses following up: Ey Yi Yi Yi, in China they never eat chili, here comes the next verse, it's worse than the first. So waltz me around again, Willie.

The chorus lost its sound as the men trudged uphill along Sandy Lane to catch the bus to Bedford. The exuberance and songfest continued for Chapman's merry airmen on the return trip to base.

And then catching that last bus back to the 'Sands from Broadway at the top of the High Street in Bedford and flying down Sandy Lane. It became a contest between the driver's nerves and our insanity at the bottom of the hill where he had to turn a sharp left, and all of us brilliant young men would rush over to the right side of the upper deck to see if we could tip the bus just a little whilst making the turn, Oh the joy! We were gonna live forever, beer was a major food group, and Pall Malls were the staple of commerce.

Pall Mall cigarettes were # 1 with both the Americans and the British. Most likely, the author had the "honor" of policing up the beer cans that Bill Chapman's marauders had dumped along Sandy Lane during one of their trips to Bedford.

Policing Sandy Lane

The author was an avid basketball fan at Chicksands and attended away games as well as home games when work schedules permitted. An away game at RAF Alconbury in 1958 landed yours truly in the deepest official Air Force doo-doo that he endured in 21.5 years of active USAFSS service. Events leading up to my run-in with the "law" occurred during a rare weekend when our Dog Trick was on its long three-day break, permitting a few of us loyal Dog Trick fans to attend a championship game at Alconbury.

A basketball referee at the game between league leading Alconbury and Chicksands got perturbed because I gave him a hard time about his calls during the game. Beer was flowing profusely at the game, and at the final buzzer, the referee asked the Air Police to haul me away. They cited me for drunk and disorderly conduct. Willard Addington, one of our Chicks ballplayers, signed me out from the Provost Marshal's office on a hand receipt and drove my car back to Chicksands.

Bright and early on Monday morning, I discussed the situation with First Sgt. Gordon McConnell, who was himself known to put away a few brews at basketball and football games. MSgt. McConnell was an understanding older, balding World War II veteran with many longevity and combat hash marks on the sleeves of his uniform. He drove a pink and white block-long 1956 Packard Caribbean Convertible. He also had the most beautiful wife on base. Mrs. McConnell was the group commander's secretary. But I digress.

When I explained what had happened at the game, Sgt. McConnell said "Son, don't worry about it; if anything comes down from Alconbury, I will take care of it and the old man will never see it." A few days later, Sgt. Mac went on leave, and the D&D citation arrived from Alconbury. MSgt. McConnell's chief clerk, who was acting first sergeant, gave the citation to our commander, and the chi-chi hit the fan.

Awakened from a sound sleep after working a midshift, I was ordered to report to the commander in class A uniform immediately. The colonel was not amused. He offered me a choice: an Article 15 or a Summary Court Martial. I accepted the A-15 and his punishment, which he defined as two hours extra duty per day for two weeks. Because I was a shift worker, I could do the extra duty on my schedule by reporting to the chief clerk to receive an extra duty assignment. For several days, extra duty involved cleaning the offices of the colonel and his secretary—15 to 20 minutes work but two hours credit for each cleaning.

While on break, I wanted to go into Hitchin for the night, so I stopped in the orderly room to ask about doing my two hours extra duty during the day. The clerk checked with the commander who happened to be in the orderly room, and the colonel had just the job for me. On his drive to work that morning, he noticed an abundance of cigarette packs and beer cans lying along Sandy Lane, and he wanted the whole lane policed. He had the clerk call the mess hall and arrange for me to pick up a supply of empty gunny-type potato sacks to use as trash bags. He warned me that he was going to inspect it on the way home, and it had better be spotless.

I spent close to fours hours policing Sandy Lane that day from the Top Gate to the A600 Road to Bedford—more than a mile total. It sure was embarrassing when some of my drinking mates drove by and honked as I filled the gunny sacks with trash—three or four bagfuls. And some dependent wife who was waiting for the bus by A600 really added fuel to the fire when she told me how she thought it was terrible that the Air Force had me out there doing all the police-up work by myself. "The Air Force should have someone helping you." I neglected to explain to her that I was being punished. My first and last official Air Force punishment!

The Quickie

With so many fair British maidens anxious to meet young American males, I found it bizarre that some airmen would visit prostitutes, primarily in London although a few reportedly hung out in Bedford and Luton. Real "pros" in London could be spotted from afar, perched under a street light waiting to be picked up. A few airmen considered it a badge of honor to catch a train to the Big Smoke for a "quickie," and they would return from London, bragging about their quickie trysts.

With a wife and child back home in America, an anonymous young barracks mate of the author—"Bill"—was true blue to his wife; yet, he was fascinated with quickie stories that floated around the barracks. He was also compiling research notes for a book he hoped to publish some day. Curiosity finally got the best of him. "Bill" decided that he must experience a quickie in London—not for self-satisfaction—his story line was that he needed first-hand knowledge for the book he intended to write when he left the Air Force. He rode a train to King's Cross Station and took the Underground to Piccadilly Circus. Exiting the tube station by the Shaftesbury Memorial Fountain at Piccadilly Circus, "Bill" latched on to the first lady of the night he found on the corner. For a quid and a half (£1.50 = $4.20) plus another quid for a ten minute ride around a block at Piccadilly Circus, "Bill" experienced his quickie in the back of a London taxi. He took the next train from King's Cross to Hitchin, then a bus back to Chicksands. Mission complete! I never learned if "Bill" published his book.

Snack Bar Heist

On 16 July 1959, the author took an early discharge and returned to America. Missing life in Jolly Ole England, I reenlisted 52 days later for a guaranteed reassignment back to England. Returning to Chicksands in October 1959, I moved into Seco Hut # 503, immediately to the right of the base exchange and main snack bar. The band of brothers in 503 had a special relationship with Harry, an Irishman who worked the midnight shift in the snack bar six nights per week. Coming on duty at closing time (11 p.m.), Harry cleaned the facility and made donuts and rolls for sale the following day.

Late at night during a party in the barracks, it was not unusual for one of our barracks mates to visit Harry to mooch sandwiches made with snack bar ingredients. Harry kept the snack bar entrance doors locked from the inside but he would open them for those of us whom he knew. And we were welcome to help ourselves to bread and sandwich makings (ham, cheese and tuna salad, primarily)—all gratis. There was apparently no inventory mechanism for those items, and we often rewarded Harry with a pack of Pall Mall cigarettes. Life was good!

One night, a couple of our barracks buddies arrived from town somewhat hungry, and shall we say, a bit inebriated. Someone suggested that they visit Harry for a midnight snack. Not a good night for foraging in the snack bar pantry since it was Harry's night off. But that did not stop "Joe" and "Red." They kicked the snack bar entry doors off their hinges and returned to the barracks with a couple of loaves of bread, a bowl of tuna salad and large packs of ham and cheese for sandwiches.

Recognizing that a burglary had been committed, the rest of us in the barracks were no longer hungry. We convinced the bandits to return the bread and sandwich makings to their proper place in the snack bar. As they departed the snack bar, they stood the doors in place, giving the appearance that all was secure. The AP patrol did not even notice the break-in on their checks.

Sid, the British snack bar manager whom many considered to be a shyster, reported the burglary the next morning after the doors fell outward as he unlocked them. He inventoried goods on hand and determined that the only missing items were six cases of beer. Yeah, right! Quite obviously, Sid and his friends enjoyed those six cases of beer, but no one with knowledge of the facts was about to rat on him. And the provost marshal never determined who burglarized the snack bar. (Joe and Red, you are home free as the statute of limitations expired long ago.)

Flo's Ash Burgers

USAFSS personnel who worked shift work in 6950th Operations at Chicksands during the 1950's recall Flo, the middle-aged lady who worked the midnight shift in the operations snack bar. In many ways, Flo from Chicksands is reminiscent of Flo from Mel's Diner in the *Alice* TV series from the 1970's and 1980's. She did not say "Kiss my grits" like Flo from Mel's Diner, but our Flo at Chicksands would serve you a hamburger at 3 a.m. that was laden with ashes from the cigarette cinched in the corner of her mouth as she cooked. And if it was a few days before payday and you were short of cash—not to worry—Flo would feed you anyway. All of the airmen were her boys, and she treated them well.

Sam's 1952 Opel

Sam Ciocco was one of the author's barracks mates in Seco # 503, and we had been friends since arriving at Chicksands together in 1956. I purchased a 1952 Opel upon returning to the 'Sands in 1959, and Sam had borrowed the Opel on occasion when I had been working—I worked shift work and Sam worked straight days. The Opel ran well, but being a German car with a shortage of spare parts in England, a previous owner had jury-rigged a repair of the ignition system, bypassing the key-ignition with an ON-OFF toggle switch.

Perhaps the ignition key had simply been lost because a key was required to lock the doors, and there were no keys for the Opel when I purchased it. Thus, to operate the Opel, anyone could open the door, flip the toggle switch to ON and press the starter.

In late 1959, I parked the Opel at the Hitchin train station and caught a train to King's Cross Station—much faster, cheaper and safer than driving the 35 miles to London. Meanwhile, Sam Ciocco and Bill Lee rode a bus to Hitchin for a Friday night of merriment at the Woolpack Pub. (The Woolpack was a favorite watering hole for many Chix airmen, including the author.) By closing time, Sam and Bill had paired off with two Italian beauties (nurse aides on work visas) at nearby Arlesey Hospital. Several of us had befriended many of the nurse aides from various countries at Arlesey Pits (near the hospital)—an excavated water-filled clay quarry used unofficially as a swimming hole. Arlesey Pits has many precious memories for lots of Chicksands alumni!

Walking to Hitchin station where the ladies would board their train to Arlesey, Sam Ciocco noticed my Opel parked in front of Hitchin station. He decided to borrow it and drive their Italian signore home. They might get "lucky," and besides, Sam would return the Opel to the station before the author returned from London two days later. I never learned whether Sam and Bill scored that night, but they did deliver the gals to their hospital quarters without incident. Enroute back to the train station, Sam misjudged a curve and wrecked the Opel in a single-car accident. Fortunately, no one was injured but the Opel was a total loss.

Sam Ciocco told the investigating British bobby that he had borrowed the car from his American friend Larry Tart who was currently on vacation in London. The bobby turned the matter over to the Base Provost Marshal's Office at Chicksands. The provost marshal restricted Sam to base pending possible charges of stealing and wrecking Larry Tart's car. Sam Ciocco's dilemma— locate Larry Tart in London and head off a charge of auto theft. He managed to send word by an airman to me, and I hired a taxi from Hitchin to the base upon returning from London.

The air police sergeant of the guard interrogated me as soon as I set foot on base upon return from London. The AP's dropped all pending charges against Airman Ciocco after I confirmed that Sam had permission to use the Opel.

Entering our barracks, I found Sam Ciocco sitting on his cot with a sheepish smirk on his face. Sam showed me what remained of the 1952 Opel. He had salvaged the spare tire, and it lay on its side under his bunk. Smiling, Sam said, "Larry, how much do I owe you for the Opel that I bought from you?" Three hundred and seventy-five dollars and all he had to show for his money was a lousy spare tire!

Rocket Attack on Chicksands

Intercept operators serving at Chicksands in late 1957 remember monitoring Sputnik # 1, the Soviet satellite launched on 4 October 1957, but few know details about the "Russian rocket" found embedded on the Chicks' football field months later. An air policeman on routine patrol observed a strange looking object sticking out of the football turf at first dawn probably in May 1958. With tail fins, it looked like a rocket. Unrecognizable lettering stenciled on the device added to the mystery. Treating the object as a possible unexploded bomb, the AP desk sergeant informed the base officer of the day and posted a guard on it.

By now, Col. Lavelle, 6950th RGM commander, had arrived at his office and contacted 3rd Air Force HQ at RAF South Ruislip, London, and others on his contact roster. Airmen arriving on base for work were kept at bay by the guard as a crowd gathered. Someone observed a hammer and sickle and "CCCP" (U.S.S.R. in Russian) among indecipherable text on the strange object jutting out of the green grass, adding to ominous suspicions.

Meanwhile, two of Chicksands' finest officers and gentlemen— bachelor Lieutenants Raymond O'Neal and James Gessert—got nervous. Their idea of a practical joke had exceeded expectations and gotten out of hand. After investing a fortune to train O'Neal and Gessert as jet fighter pilots, the Air Force assigned them as intelligence officers (flight commanders on Baker and Dog Flights) in 6950th Operations. Jet jockeys at heart, they found little excitement in being in charge of a signals exploitation mission that they knew little about. O'Neal and Gessert expended much effort to scrounge metal pipe used for the missile and weld on tailfins. They added Cyrillic nomenclature data on the rocket as a coup de grâce.

Roger Sprague, a former Baker Flight Russian linguist who did the Russian lettering, recalls that the two lieutenants never dreamed that the prank would reach news headline proportions.

The idea came up at a trick party in Shefford one night. Lt. O'Neal asked me to write something for a fake rocket he and Gessert were building. Thinking it was the beer talking, I did and then pretty much forgot about it until the Monday morning when it appeared on the parade field, in a position where Col. Lavelle would see it when he came to work. See it he did, and panicked. Got on the phone to the BBC, 3rd Air Force, American Ambassador, and everyone else he could find numbers for.

As it became obvious that things were getting out of hand, O'Neal and Gessert, who had waited around for the fun, tried to get in his office to tell him they had done it. His response was "Get out. Can't you see I'm busy? Anything else I would believe from you two, but not this. This is the real thing." The bomb squad was summoned from I think, Alconbury, and determined it was a fake. At about that time, the American Ambassador arrived, and when told it was a fake, remarked that he thought it was a pretty clever practical joke. Probably the only thing that kept us all out of Leavenworth.

At this point, anger replaced fear in the colonel's mind, and he began to realize how many people had to have been involved. It was neatly painted and welded, and big enough to require a truck to haul it. The Russian wording was in Cyrillic, so a linguist must have been involved. Fortunately, he was never identified as the lieutenants said they had gotten it out of a Russian to English dictionary. No one bothered to check the grammar. He also realized that the regular air police patrols must have seen something, as it would have taken quite a while to dig a hole big enough to keep it upright. It was a piece of steel pipe about 12 feet long and a foot or so in diameter. He kept the AP midshift on duty to guard it, I suppose as a sort of punishment.

The linguist was not identified. It was rumored that the two lieutenants got letters of reprimand placed in their records, and were billed for materials used by the U.S. Air Force.

Thanks to the U.S. Ambassador's demeanor and sense of humor, Col. Lavelle was not as severe with punishment as he might have been otherwise. O'Neal and Gessert maintained their flying proficiency aboard fighters from RAF Wethersfield and Bentwaters. Living up to their college fraternity-brother reputations, they "buzzed" Chicksands on one of their training missions—for which they were also reprimanded.

Halt! Who Goes There?

Life was not all fun and games at Chicksands. In theory, a plan existed to arm everyone assigned to the base if defending the facility became necessary. When clearing into the unit, every USAFSS airman was assigned an M1 carbine that was stored in the armory located behind headquarters. Each airman received a weapon card identifying his carbine and was required to visit the armory and clean his weapon monthly. Ironically, the author vividly remembers cleaning his M1 and signing an armory roster monthly, but does not recall ever firing a weapon at Chicksands. Reportedly, there was a firing range on base.

During periods of international tension, the Air Force placed the base on increased readiness with armed airmen posted at select points along the base perimeter. On other occasions, higher headquarters declared practice alerts—again with airmen exchanging their weapons card for their M1 and an ammunition magazine to guard against "intruders." The use of armed perimeter guards in conjunction with alerts ended one dark, foggy night during the Suez War of 1956.

While guarding the north perimeter fence with his loaded carbine, a Seminole Indian named Joe (a nervous, perhaps over-zealous airman) heard movements within the adjacent field. Receiving no response after issuing a challenge, "Halt! Who goes there?" three times, Joe fired into the darkness, killing one of Farmer Parrish's cows. Increased readiness alerts did not end, but henceforth, airmen stood guard duty with an M1 sans ammunition.

Spy Base Boob Gets Reagan out of bed

An article from a Bedfordshire newspaper during the 1980's, "Spy base boob gets Reagan out of bed," addressed an incident in Chicksands' surveillance and warning center that resulted in a flash precedence Critic Report being sent to the White House.[190]

President Reagan was called out of bed in the middle of the night because of a 'foul up' at Chicksands which led Washington officials to believe that the balloon had gone up and nuclear war was imminent.

One lieutenant colonel and a senior civilian were posted immediately from the American spy base. Chicksands refused to confirm or deny the story but say that the postings of the two men were routine.

The reason for Reagan's disturbed night was a 'dummy run' exercise at the Bedfordshire base which listens to military and civil radio communications all over Northern and Eastern Europe, including Russia.

But the exercise commander failed to inform others that this was purely a practice and there was panic when it was thought to be the real thing.

A former USAFSS/ESC senior NCO recently said he traveled to Chicksands in mid-1985 to investigate the incident. Intent on sending a bogus message to exercise their system, an analyst had inadvertently transmitted a valid message—with far reaching implications alluded to in the British news report.

The SMOKE SCREEN program that Air Force traffic analysts in field units used to exercise the Critic Reporting process had built-in safeguards to prevent inadvertent release of a practice Critic Report. Unfortunately, SMOKE SCREEN did not address issues involved in the reported incident—at least it did not prior to the mid-1980's.

Chicksands Original SIGINT Compound

Officially called Technical Site A by the British, the SIGINT operations compound that Air Force Security Service used at Chicksands prior to 1964 consisted of thirteen separate buildings identified as Blocks A through M. Enclosed in a chain link cyclone fence topped with strands of barbed wire, twelve of the structures (Blocks A-L) existed when USAFSS arrived in 1950, and the U.S. Air Force added Block M in 1954. The security access gate was set up in the southeast area of the compound.

Within Tech Site A, Block G sat on the left just inside the compound. Looking north from the security gate, M Block was in the southeast corner of the compound to the right of G Block. Farther inside the compound, Blocks F, E and D were situated north of M Block along the compound's eastern fence, and Blocks C, L and B were established to the west of Block D on the northern edge of the compound.

Continuing counterclockwise, Block A was in the southwest corner of the compound (south of Block B). In turn, Blocks K and J were located along the southern edge of the compound—to the left of G Block. Finally, Blocks I and H were built pretty much in the compound's center (surrounded by the other blocks). There were also a couple of Nissen huts within the compound, as well as the operations snack bar, euphemistically called "Flo's Diner" in the late 1950's.

Chicksands Operations Compound—1950's

Depending on the period when USAFSS operations personnel arrived at Chicksands, they have different recollections of where functions were conducted in the compound since some parts of the mission shifted from one block to another over time. Dan D'Apolito, who later cross-trained to traffic analysis, was a Morse intercept operator during 1951. He recalls that 10th RSM intercept operations were in G Block, which later became the squadron communications center.

When I first got there in Jan '51, G Block was an intercept block. When you came in the door, there was an office room on the left which contained the block chief plus a voice intercept position. On your right when I got there, I believe there were about five Morse positions, and as people came, we soon filled up the block with various assignments. Then shortly, we moved to J Block, and when I left J and K Blocks were intercept positions.

C block was eventually a weather intercept block, but back in '51 the U.S. Navy and pre-6901st [second echelon analysis] people were in that block. Weather was copied in our [air and air defense] blocks. I remember the analysts came from E block. Before I left in '54, they opened L block as intercept.

I Block and H Block were the Honcho blocks. I Block was the Identification block with the RDF operator [plotter] and mission supervisor. We didn't have an S&W supervisor in the blocks. When I returned in '60, we [surveillance and warning center analysts] were in an intercept block, in a partitioned room off part of [the] intercept block. Can't recall the block letter.

Wayne Palmer, a retired USAFSS traffic analyst, remembers that the S&W Center moved to F Block sometime in 1957. Bill Gray, another retired traffic analyst, linked IBM keypunch operations to A block during the late 1950's.

I once worked in "A Block." Jim Wooten and I, and several others were placed there to keypunch on IBM cards technical details of work produced by collection operators. If we punched 2,000 cards, we could leave work for the day. Jim would always finish well before any of the rest of us, and immediately catch the bus to town. Our IBM-card results were placed on the G Block teletype circuit to the 6901st in Zweibrücken.

"I Block" was, as Dap indicated, where the honchos worked. I clearly recall Chuck Shaver, Max Hawkes and Lt.'s O'Neal and Gessert (of Russian rocket fame) working there, communicating with the other blocks by intercom. That's where the antenna patch panel was located, so operators could call them and switch antennas. It was one of those blocks which had a "blast door" in front of the entrance—to protect from bombs or shrapnel, I suppose.

During 1957, the author made many trips to I Block to obtain Lt. Gessert's signature on outgoing Spot Reports that I in turn delivered to G Block—the comm center from 1952 forward according to Ernie Tippie.

When I first arrived at Chicksands in the fall of 1952, I was assigned to Tech Services as a 30470 radio repairman. We were in the first building on the right as you came in the gate to the site [F block]. As I recall, on the left hand side of the drive as you came into the site, they built a Quonset hut later which housed the new IBM equipment. Behind that was another building which housed the teletype equipment [G Block]. A MSgt. by the name of Swindell was in charge of that block.

All of the antennas terminated in a central building in the center of the site. The terminations from the antenna field were in a lean-to on the outside of the building. It had a poor roof and the rain would come in and disrupt the signals from the antennas. The emergency generators were across the drive. The snack shack was just to the east of the central building with the antenna terminations.

Retired CMSgt. James Swindell was inducted posthumously into AIA's Hall of Honor in 2006, in large measure, for his role in implementing a highly acclaimed communications capability in G Block in the early 1950's. Regarding missions performed in other blocks, a communications security team monitored UK-based U.S. Air Force communications at intercept positions within H Block.

Chicksands Ops Compound—Early 1960's

Retired Lt. Col. William C. Grayson, who served two tours at Chicksands and published the book, *"Chicksands, A Millennium of History"* in 1992, shared the following overview of USAFSS "block" operations at Chicksands, circa 1960 and beyond.

I might flunk the test just now on which blocks were used for what. I do remember that in 1960, a new exploitation officer arrived and set to work on improving reporting timeliness. The exploitation officer and his branch (OED) was in F Block. For reporting timeliness improvement, the flight commander was relocated from I Block (yes, where the mission supe and antenna patch panel were) to E Block, where the guy we called T/E [traffic exploitation] controller and all the 202's were.

That move saved time in carrying 3-part message forms from E to I for signature by a flight commander, who was seeing reports for the first time, and then over to the comm center in G Block.

H Block was maintenance. Block A was TRANSEC, which had pony circuits that duplicated all the message traffic from and to all the 3rd Air Force tactical wings in the UK. These were manually scanned for plaintext transmission of classified messages.

B was weather; C and L were Morse; and D was IBM keypunch. J and K were non-Morse [printer] collection.

Block L also housed the voice intercept section—the author worked there in 1959-60. These were the work locations for personnel within 6950th RGM operations during the early 1960's—until the unit (by then the 6950th Security Wing) moved into its newly built operations complex (Building # 600) on "The Hill" west of Tech Site A in 1964. The list that follows is a snapshot of block usage at Chicksands in 1960.

Chicksands—SIGINT Compound * Early 1960's	
Building	**Use**
Block A	COMSEC and TRANSEC
Block B	Weather intercept
Block C	Morse intercept
Block D	IBM Keypunch
Block E	Flight Commander, S&W Center and shift analysts
Block F	Traffic Exploitation (Analysis and Reporting day workers)
Block G	Criticomm Telecommunications Center
Block H	Maintenance (Tech Services)
Block I	Mission Supervisor, Traffic ID and antenna patch panel
Block J	Non-Morse (Printer) intercept
Block K	Non-Morse (Printer) intercept
Block L	Morse intercept and voice intercept
Block M	Operations Officer and Mission Management
* 6950th Security Wing relocated Ops to Building 600 in 1964	

Seco Hut Barracks Area behind NCO Club, 1958

Chicksands' "Elephant Cage" Antenna

Sylvania Electronic Systems began installing a circularly disposed antenna array (AN/FLR-9) system at Chicksands in 1962 while concurrently building a similar system at San Vito, Italy. Part of the "Iron Horse," the contractor tested the FLR-9 systems at Chicksands and San Vito, Italy, in tandem in 1963-early 1964. A description of the FLR-9 is provided in Chapter Five.

The FLR-9, together with a new SIGINT operations building, was located northwest of Tech Site A—Chicksands' original SIGINT compound in a field that formerly contained most of the original tall wooden World War II-era antenna masts. Wayne Wetterman, a retired USAFSS Morse/printer intercept operator, was one of the original cadre of 33 airmen who operated the 6950th's FLR-9 system. After completing training at Keesler AFB in two groups in the spring of 1963, the men commenced work at Chicksands—seven operators, analysts and maintainers per shift, plus an officer, NCOIC and others on Easy Shift.

CMSgt. Peter Grozdanich headed the FLR-9 project and Capt. Edward Naylor was the officer in charge. The 33-man FLR-9 team was affectionately known as "Grozdanich's Gorillas." They supported all the final testing, with official certification of the FLR-9 system occurring in November 1963. The 6950th Security Wing went operational with the FLR-9 in 1964.[191]

FLR-9 "Elephant Cage", Chicksands, circa 1990

Chicksands' FLR-9 is history but a WW II-era 240 feet high antenna still stands tall on the station.

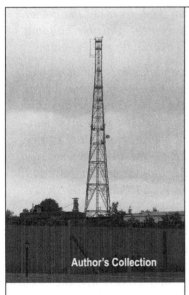

The Elephant Cage antenna became the best known landmark in the Bedfordshire area and is still a point of discussion with local Brits who could view it readily from roads that bypassed the base. Many were sad to see it removed in 1996; however, the FLR-9 was surplus to the need of the British Ministry of Defense that assumed control of the base from the U.S. Air Force in 1995. One of the 240 feet tall antenna masts that was originally installed in 1940 remains in the heart of the former Tech Site A complex on base today.

One of five original 240 feet antennas, erected in 1940

BLDG 600—NEW OPS BUILDING

Work commenced on a new operations building—Building 600 on a hill northwest of the old 6950th Operations compound at Chicksands in late 1960 or early 1961 and was completed in the fall of 1962. Construction of the new Ops building and the FLR-9 antenna system proceeded in parallel, and both became operational together as a single new intercept and DF system in mid-1964.

Clyde Orr, a former senior USAFSS electronic maintenance NCO, supervised bringing the new equipment on line.

I was stationed at Chicksands from Sept '62 to Sept '66. The new Ops building was just being completed when I got there. I worked in Mat-M [Maintenance] as a 30474 and was assigned the task of installing all new equipment racks and operator positions in the new building.

Sylvania technicians arrived about the same time to begin installing the FLR-9 equipment. My crew and I worked along with them during the day, then some of us were hired to work nights fabricating and running antenna cables. I worked after duty hours with Sylvania at a rate of $1.25 per hour—good money in 1962. I walked the tunnel from the Ops building to the central antenna building many times. The tunnel was just over 3000 feet in length.

It took about nine months to complete the installation. We started the big move of all the equipment in the summer of '63. During the last phase, the E&I [Engineering and Installation] Team arrived, and I worked with them until the task was finished. We were operational within a very short time frame, but the FLR-9 had to be tested and proven before it was ready. This took several months as I recall. I think it was sometime in '64 that it was signed over to us as fully operational.

After Operations moved to Building 600, the World War II-era blocks were recycled. Receiving a new coat of paint, some continued in support roles, while others were demolished. Block F became the Base Education Office and classrooms; the Security Police moved into H Block; G ended up as the Base Disaster Preparation Center; and D served as a Wood Craft Shop.

By 1973, all Tech Site buildings had been assigned building numbers instead of block letters, and three former blocks (A, B and L) were used to house the 6900th Security Squadron that moved from Frankfurt, Germany. Several of the WW II buildings still exist today as renovated structures that look very different than they did when last used operationally decades ago.

Welcome to Chicksands—Sponsor's Letter

Air Force Security Service prided itself in being one big happy family, and part of that comradeship derived from the command's personalized "Sponsor" program. Under the program, a member of a gaining unit sponsored each incoming airman and officer—writing a welcome letter to the new unit member well in advance of the member's arrival on station. Receiving background data on incoming personnel (rank, field/job, marital status, children's ages, etc.), the sponsor provided the new member an overview of the new member's duty station and helped the new member get settled upon arrival on station. While completing training at Goodfellow AFB in December 1971, Jeff Ewing received a typical welcoming letter from his sponsor at Chicksands.

Welcome to the Showcase of the USAFSS in Europe, RAF Chicksands. I have been chosen to be your sponsor for your stay here and will try to acquaint you with the base, its activities and the surrounding area.

A little about the work, and then I'll go into the base itself. You will be working shift work: four swings, one day break, four mids, four days, and then the best part of the cycle—three days of break. After the third cycle, you will fall into the routine; then you will only know what day of the cycle it is. The three days of break give you ample time to travel around the country or just catch up on sleep.

The base is small, even smaller than Goodbuddy. We are located about 45 miles from London—about an hour and a half by car or one hour by train. The base is quite pretty; hence the name "Showcase of Europe." We have a BX that is quite small and not very good, but there are three fantastic BX's located at Mildenhall, Lakenheath, and South Ruislip that you can easily get to. If you think the BX at Goodfellow is bad, wait till you get here.

There is an eight lane bowling alley on base, which is always in use. They have all kinds of leagues, and if you are a bowler, then you have it made. The athletic program is quite good. There is an intramural and a varsity program. Each flight usually participates in the intramural league. The base varsity teams compete with other base teams in the UK and the rest of Europe, so if you are a jock, you will really enjoy the sports program.

There is a theater on base, but the shows are far from recent. I got here in August and I am still seeing the shows that were shown at Goodfellow in February and March. The theaters, or cinemas as the Blokes call them, in the English communities are quite good. There is an Airmens Club that costs a buck a month to belong to. It is better than the one at Goodfellow. They have a wide range of entertainment, ranging from dancing and floor shows to strip shows. It is a good place to meet the British girls. I have never seen so many girls, and do they have nice legs. But watch out, they will soak you for drinks.

The barrack life isn't too bad, and then again, it isn't too good. You will be living two to a room, which is great as it beats open bay living that I had at Goodfellow. Presently, some of the barracks are being fixed up and shouldn't be too bad once everything is done. Just recently, they started cleaning details, which everybody hates. You will find out more about that once you get here.

The base is really hipped up on haircuts, shoe shines and saluting officers in your civvies. You will be pulling details up at work, in the squadron area and in the barracks. So you can see the situation.

That's about all I can tell you about the base. Like I said, there isn't much I can tell you that would not sound like a put on. Lets face it—the life at Chicksands isn't going to be all that great, no matter what they told you at your briefing. Keep a smile on your face.

Of course, this was a letter from one first-termer young airman to another unmarried airman, and it did not address family issues and schools. Former Airman Ewing remembers "how much the letter deflated my expectations (a good thing)."

> *The day-to-day life of a first-termer assigned to the operations area turned out to be far from ideal, but it beat the hell out of field stripping a M16 or trying to get some sleep by counting RPG detonations instead of sheep.*

With the Vietnam War going full bore in the late 1960's-early 1970's, many airmen enlisted in the Air Force as an alternative to being drafted in the Army with almost assured combat duty in Vietnam. Conversely, while serving at Chicksands many USAFSS airmen volunteered for a consecutive overseas tour in Vietnam, and 18 Air Force Security Service members paid the ultimate price while supporting the Vietnam conflict.

Author's Collection

Dorm that replaced Nissen and Seco Huts, July 2000

USAF Chicksands—Development Milestones

Airmen who served at RAF Chicksands during the 1950's never enjoyed the amenities found on base from the early 1960's forward. By the early 1970's, Chicksands was indeed one of the "showcase bases" in Europe—as depicted in the list that follows, a bit of Americana in the heart of the British countryside.

Chicksands—Significant USAF Milestones

Date	Event
November 1950	USAFSS arrives at RAF Chicksands
December 1950	Base exchange and snack bar
December 1950	NCO club
1951	Base chapel
1951	Class VI liquor store
1951	Officers club
1951	Base library
Circa 1952	USO service club
1952	Basketball (Chicksands Chicks) (17-0 against British teams); joined USAF league in 1953. UK Champs in 1955
1953	Chicksands Chicks football
1953 or 1954	Chicksands Chicks baseball
Circa 1954	Commissary
Circa 1955	Bowling alley
1955 or 1956	Chicksands Chicks soccer (USAF & RAF leagues)
1957	Base gymnasium opened
1957	BX service station (tax-free, rationed gasoline)
1959	New NCO club
1959	Airmens club opened in former NCO club
1964	Moved Operations to Building 600
1964	FLR-9 declared operational
Circa 1965	A few multistory barracks replace some Nissen and Seco huts; more new barracks built later
Circa 1965	New theater dedicated near NCO club and gym
Circa 1965	First family housing units and dependent school
?	New 6950th headquarters building built
Before Oct 1976	New commissary operational
1977	New BX, barber shop and class VI store
?	New chapel
30 Sept 1995	RAF Chicksands officially returned to British

All Good Things Must End

Within American Intelligence circles, RAF Chicksands developed a reputation as one of the most beautiful military bases in the world—a sought after tour in the SIGINT community. With

excellent family housing and grade schools on base, plus modern
base exchange, commissary, chapel, clubs and other recreation
facilities, the base was a dream assignment for married career
airmen.

At the same time, with the abundance of lovely, young and
readily available English lasses, Chicksands was seventh heaven
for single airmen. But as the saying goes, "All Good Things Must
End." With the implosion of the Soviet Union in 1991,
Chicksands' days as a U.S. intelligence gathering facility were
numbered. Soon after the East German government abandoned the
Berlin Wall in 1989, the Air Force Electronic Security Command
began dismantling its traditional SIGINT posts in Europe.
Returned to the British Ministry of Defence in September 1995,
Chicksands was the last of the Cold War Air Force SIGINT sites
to shut down.

ESC/AFIC/AIA Base Closures in Europe at End of Cold War		
Unit	Location	Closing Date
Det 1, 6910th ESW	Lindsey AS, Wiesbaden, Ger.	September 1990
6916th ESS	Athens, Greece	December 1990
6914th ESS	Mehlingen Annex, Sembach, Germany	Early 1990's
6952nd ESS	RAF Alconbury, England	1991?
6913th ESS	Augsburg, Germany	13 March 1991
6919th ESS	Sembach, Germany	31 July 1991
690th ESG	Berlin, Germany	1 July 1992
6911th ESS	Metro Tango, Hahn, Ger.	1 April 1993
6931st ESS	Iraklion AS, Crete	30 Sept 1993
6917th ESG	San Vito AS, Brindisi, Italy	31 March 1993
450th Intel Sqdn	RAF Chicksands, England	30 Sept 1995

Rumors abounded throughout the early 1990's regarding the
status of U.S. Air Force operations at Chicksands. There was also
speculation that the stature of the station—most modern HF
SIGINT facility in Europe—would save Chicksands from the
government "bean counters'" post-Cold War scalpel. Ultimately,
the end of the Cold War brought about the closure of American
operations at Chicksands as part of the "peace dividend."

Under the headline, "Shock closure of Chicksands," the *Hitchin Comet* newspaper announced the closure in February 1994.[192]

> *RAF Chicksands is to close as a United States Air Force base in September next year. The shock news was announced on Thursday—and it puts a question mark over the future of the 180 British workers employed there.*
>
> *The base has a population of around 3,600 people made up of about 1,500 military personnel, 80 U.S. civilians and dependents—and it plays an important role in the local economy.*
>
> *Worried Beds County Council arranged an urgent meeting with the Ministry of Defence to discuss the fate of the base near Shefford. County planning officer Michael Gwilliam met with MoD land agent Barry Sygrove on Monday to talk about the future of the 537-acre site.*
>
> *Mr. Gwilliam said, "Bedfordshire County Council is very saddened by the announcement of the end of the American presence at Chicksands. Over the 45 years of their residence, our American friends have become a valued part of the community and they will be missed. Only last year, we were assured that there were no proposals to change the function or size of the base. We now, however, have to assess the implications on local employment and businesses, and to consider how best the excellent facilities at the base might be used in the future."*

Another British newspaper announced the closure, effective 30 September 1995, and described Chicksands as "Little America."

> *The base resembles a small U.S. town complete with its own church, grocery and department stores, petrol station, garage, fire and police station and school. Recreation facilities include a cinema, leisure centre, library, gymnasium, bowling alley, tennis courts, softball diamonds, soccer, rugby and American football pitches.*
>
> *It has been home to the 774th Air Base Group, the Air Defence Intelligence Agency's 450th Intelligence Squadron and the Department of Defense Joint Operations Center Chicksands.*

Reportedly, there was indecisiveness in the U.S. intelligence community concerning disposition of the 450th Intelligence Squadron at the end of the Cold War. Some wanted to retain AIA operations at Chicksands, others wanted to use satellite and remoting technology to assume the 450th IS mission elsewhere. In the end, those who controlled intelligence budgets refused to continue funding American operations at Chicksands.

TURNING OUT LIGHTS AT CHICKSANDS

Retired Air Force Lt. Colonel Paul Gifford had a key role in discontinuing AIA SIGINT operations at Chicksands. In 2007, he discussed with the author the closedown of the 450th Intelligence Squadron at the base.

> *I closed the 6917ESG [Electronic Security Group] at San Vito in June 1993, then went to Chicksands, arriving in July 1993. They didn't tell me I was to close it, but within three months the word came to close it. We closed the AIA side around July 1994, but NSA kept their side open until around 1995 or so. . . . .*
>
> *I'm not sure Chicks[ands] closed because the Brits wanted it, [or] more because it was so expensive for us.*

Contributed by Yvonne Jones

450th Intelligence Squadron hosted a reunion for
RAF Chicksands WW II Veterans at the Priory in 1993.

When then Major Gifford joined the 450th IS at Chicksands as operations officer in mid-1993, all indications were that Chicksands had been saved from post-Cold War fund cutbacks. However, word soon arrived that American forces would be evacuating the base on an expedited schedule—reportedly at the request of Britain's Ministry of Defence. The United States returned RAF Chicksands to British MoD control on 30 September 1995.

Sad Goodbyes

With an American father and British mother from Bedford, Kirk Carter was born and spent most of his adult life in Bedfordshire. In January 2000, he expressed sadness attached to the closure of Chicksands in 1995.

> *My family was at Chicksands from the '50's to its closure. My father, Ken Carter, was first stationed there in the '50's where he met my mother Belle Cook in Bedford. Later, he stayed and worked there as a civilian. Many of you from the '80's would have known my brother Glenn Carter at the bowling center, and Debbie Carter at the commissary. My father saw the last year at Chicksands and passed away that same year. We brought him back home here to Fort Dodge, Iowa, to rest.*

In discussing a "Welcome Back Yanks" reunion then scheduled for July 2000, Kirk Carter had mixed emotions regarding the reunion.

> *I am not sure about returning for the reunion. I was there at the end, and it was like seeing an old friend leave for good. It was so quiet! No traffic, no lights, just the sound of the flag pole rope tapping on the pole in the night breeze. The gas pumps were gone, the BX closed and empty. it was a very sad sight. It had been my second home since 1961, and now it has gone! Who knows, I may change my mind. My best wishes to all of you who served there. Kirk.*

DISC—Defence Intelligence and Security Centre

The Ministry of Defence wasted no time assigning a new mission to the station once the United States returned RAF

Chicksands to British control. Moving its Intelligence Corps HQ and Defence Intelligence and Security School to the Bedfordshire base by Shefford from Ashford, Kent, the MoD created the Defence Intelligence and Security Centre at Chicksands.[193] An article, "What goes on at Chicksands," that was posted on a Shefford website in 1999 provides an overview of Chicksands' new mission.[194]

When the Americans left Chicksands in 1995, there was much local speculation on who or what would take over the site. What has formed up is a new organisation called the Defence Intelligence and Security Centre, or DISC for short.

DISC is a Ministry of Defence training organisation. We do all the military intelligence and security training for the Royal Navy, Army and Royal Air Force and MoD civilians. To give you a feel for the range of courses, we have young service recruits learning Arabic and Russian for up to 75 weeks, we have brigadiers learning how to be Defence Attachés for 3 weeks, we have Norwegians learning the skills of information gathering in the Balkans—we do these courses for NATO—and we have mixed civilian/military audiences attending seminars on worldwide risk of conflict. DISC is a sort of university as well as a highly technical, specialist school.

Our permanent staff is about 500 with 350 servicemen and 150 civilians. The student population is around 6,000 so far and growing each year. Chicksands is also the home of the Army's Intelligence Corps, which celebrates its 60th Anniversary next year. The Corps was first formed during the Boer War, reformed in the First World War and reformed for the third time in 1940, this time for good.

A MoD annual report ending 1 April 2004 discussed the DISC mission, staffing and expenditures for the 2003-2004 fiscal year.[195]

The Defence Intelligence and Security Centre trains the Armed Forces and other intelligence agencies in intelligence and security disciplines, and conduct after capture. It also contributes advice on appropriate intelligence and security policy matters, and maintains an operational capability. The centre was launched as a Defence agency on 1 October 1996.

The annual report listed a staff of 470 members (310 service personnel and 160 civilians) and net operating costs of £27,051,000. In many ways, primary missions at Chicksands and Goodfellow AFB, Texas, are quite similar today—intelligence, security and information support training for the British MoD and the U.S. Defense Department, respectively.

As a multiservice centre Chicksands is now considered a military camp, not an RAF station. The Bottom Gate is permanently closed, and the sign at Road A600 and Sandy Lane that leads to the Top Gate reads simply, "Chicksands." Building 600—former American SIGINT compound—is now DISC's primary training and operational facility.

Sign at Intersection A600 and Sandy Lane, 2005

Defence Intelligence Corps Headquarters

Commanded by a Royal Army Brigadier, the Intelligence Corps "provides specialist intelligence and security capabilities in support of military operations."[196] Primary Corps functions are: "Signals Intelligence (SIGINT), Imagery Intelligence (IMINT), Human Intelligence (HUMINT), Operational Intelligence (OPINTEL) and Counterintelligence (CI)."

Intelligence Corps tasks include: "Intelligence Collection, Intelligence Management, Intelligence Production, and Field Security Advice." Combat intelligence, security intelligence protective security, photographic interpretation, the study of foreign armies and interrogation also fall within the domain of the Intelligence Corps.

Decision to Relocate DISC to Chicksands

Brigadier Chris G. Holtom was the second Commandant of Chicksands' Defence Intelligence and Security Centre. He discussed the decision to relocate the DISC to Chicksands with the author in 2007.

My predecessor, Brig. Mick Laurie, was the key figure in the decision to move to Chicksands. I was Commandant DISS [Defence Intelligence and Security School] (Ashford) at the time and played a small part in a not very difficult decision!

I visited Chicksands first in September 1995. We had just visited RAF Newton near Nottingham, which was another possible site for DISC. It was a wind swept airfield in the middle of nowhere interesting, and we were quite depressed so you can imagine coming to Chicksands was something of a contrast. I remember vividly that as we drove over the brow of the hill from the guardroom and saw the Priory and its park on the right hand side in the distance, the three of us looked at each other and said "Wow, this is where we have to come to." When I approached Brigadier Laurie that same night and gave him my first impression, he said that he had already made up his mind like us and that he could not care less about the investment appraisal that had yet to be done!

First Impressions and Surprises

To Brigadiers Laurie and Holtom, their initial visit to Chicksands constituted love at first sight, but many surprises lay ahead.

Apart from the obvious WOW factor, I spent some time looking around the PX and Commissary (Bldg 357 and the one adjacent opposite the church) as I saw the DISS and

Intelligence Corps training being in these buildings if we put some windows in and an atrium. I also walked around the Priory which was by that time in relatively poor condition—thinking how on earth will we get the money to do this up to use, let alone how will we manage to maintain it. Again, Brig. Mick Laurie must take all the credit for being so robust on the decision to use the Priory as the Officers Mess and to get it properly restored.

Priory and Walled Gardens (south view), circa 2000

The first of many pleasant surprises was the attitude of the local people. They could not have been more welcoming from the Lord Lieutenant (Sam Whitbread), Sir Stanley Odell—who played a major part in the creation of the Friends of the Priory—Sarah and Richard Osborn (family owners of the Priory), the local council and people in Shefford and the surrounding villages. Some of the employees who stayed on after the US left were also absolute stalwarts in holding the place together in the pioneering days when we had no budget but had to keep the place running.

The outgoing USAF personnel were more than helpful leaving all kinds of stuff for us. The problem was we were not due to assemble at Chicksands until April 1997, which meant that there was some uncertainty over the future of the base at the critical time the USAF was leaving. For example, they sold the machinery in the bowling alley thinking that the place would be demolished for a housing estate. When they heard that a fellow military agency was to form up there later, they were mortified.

I cannot recollect any horrors other than to learn that the grounds maintenance budget was one fifth of what the USAF had to maintain the place. In fact, the lack of a sensible running cost budget plagued my whole tour there, and I was determined to establish a proper budget before I left. As it happened, luck smiled on us and we were the first military unit to outsource the maintenance budget to a private contractor under a trial scheme, and my successor was able to spend it on new accommodation, and you will be glad to hear, on the Priory, orangery and greenhouse restoration!

Upon Brigadier Laurie's departure, Brigadier Holtom assumed command of the DISC and remained the Commandant at Chicksands until his retirement in December 2000.

Y2K REUNION AT CHICKSANDS

Delving into Chicksands' history, Brigadier Holtom decided in 1998 to commemorate the 50th anniversary of the U.S. Air Force Security Service arrival at the station with a "Welcome Back

Yanks" reunion. He discussed the reunion in a reunion programme cover letter provided to reunion attendees in July 2000.

The Chicksands US Reunion
11-15 July 2000
Programme of Events

Late in 1997, I found the Bedford website where veterans of Chicksands exchanged messages. Having read the messages, it became obvious that Chicksands was held in deep affection by many people who had been posted here. It was this that prompted me to offer to open the camp to any of you who may be interested. As you know, a great many are interested, so here we are at the reunion that has been 19 months in the planning.

None of this would have been possible without a small band of volunteers in the USA who took on the huge task of coordinating so many people to come back to Chicksands from several parts of the world. Thanks are due to our sponsors and my own staff, all of whom have busy jobs as well. This point is, we made it.

We are marking the contribution of the many veterans of Chicksands to the successful conclusion of the Cold War. It could have turned out very differently, but for the diligence and innovation of those who served here and elsewhere for 45 years. Conditions were less than perfect—some of the 10th RSM veterans have admitted to me that they burned the fence around their hut just to keep warm! Their very generous gift of the FLR-9 scale model more than makes up for an old fence!

RAF Chicksands was a historic example, of co-operation between the US and the UK. This reunion seals that bond and opens new ways to sustain our relationship.

Chris Holtom
Commandant Chicksands.

Brigadier Holtom and his staff devoted an entire work week (Monday-Saturday, 10-15 July 2000) to hosting the Chicksands US Reunion.

Programme of Reunion Events	
Date	Event
Monday, 10 July	Registration on base; Book into events and special outside trips
Tuesday, 11 July	Golf at Beadlow; BBQ at midday; Re-dedication of WO Gibbs Memorial at church; Concert supper on Priory lawn
Wednesday, 12 July	Rededication of Chicksands memorial; Group photograph; Chicksands Pageant; Beating of Retreat; Formal dinner/dance
Thursday, 13 July	Opening of US Museum; Opening of nature trail; Barn dance and supper
Friday, 14 July	Visits to Duxford, US military cemetery, Bletchley Park and other outside trips
Saturday, 15 July	Chicksands Open [House] Day—Craft Fair, Victorian Fair, Museum and Priory Tours

Brigadier Holtom commented on the reunion in an email exchange with the author in 2007.

I was amazed at the common feeling of a bond that the US veterans had for Chicksands. We too now feel this bond. It is one of the good places in the world, and you have to be quite insensitive not to feel something for this place. The reunion was a delight from start to finish. I particularly remember the awful weather on the first day when we were rescuing sodden figures tramping down Sandy Lane and breathing some life back into them in the old cinema with some weak English tea.

Nobody complained, there was a real sense of self help and can do, just as it must have been when the 10th RSM advance party arrived on a foggy day in 1950. Ed Wiggins described those early days to me and in some senses, I felt that our experiences at the start of DISC were much the same. I was made to realise that the reunion was an important duty that I had to see through when during the early preparations I was in contact by email with veterans from all over the world from late 1998 and learned that three of my correspondents had died during the preparation for the reunion.

It was this that prompted me to create some sort of museum and memorial. The response to the museum idea was overwhelming, and in the space of 9 months we had collected a substantial archive and inherited our own team of local ex-pat Americans from the Bedford area.

Finally, I can report that the reunion did a great deal to unite the camp. We were a new Defence organisation with Army, Navy, Marines and Royal Air Force together. The common cause of the reunion was the single event that created DISC as an entity, and the spirit exhibited by the veterans kind of soaked into the new generation entrusted with the care of this special place. Thank you all for that— your soul lives on.

Chicksands—Brigadier Holtom's Perspective

The Chicksands Commandant offered additional personal comments on his tenure at the camp.

Being Commandant of such a unique and historic establishment was clearly the highlight of my career. It was made the better by the fact that we were the new team, we had few staff, no money and few ideas—all of which combined to make it a place where initiative could prosper. I was blessed with some quite excellent people, many of whom remain lifelong friends.

I remember when the lake flooded for the first time, and I declared that one Thursday the camp was free to volunteer to help clear the trees out, expecting 10 or some people to turn out. We got over 200 including students on basic training courses and their instructors, and we all got completely covered in mud, but we fixed the problem in a few hours—there being no budget to clear lakes!

I also remember the first day the Priory opened, and the Duke of Edinburgh came to stay the night in my rather nasty modern house at the back of the Priory. The Priory was not finished; the kitchens were still under construction, but the chefs somehow managed to produce an excellent meal amongst the dust and rubble. Luckily, the Duke had spent some time with the Navy contingent at pre-dinner drinks, and he was content before the meal started. So by the end of it I believe he was at least intrigued, and he clearly enjoyed himself. He has been back to visit since, which is a good sign!

Doing up the walled garden was also memorable. I remember putting a spade in by the wall and saying we will have a long border just here little realising that it would take 18 months to complete. Perhaps I became too engaged in the walled garden but it had its uses. I was up there most evenings dressed in scruffy clothes mowing the lawns. (We had no budget for the walled garden!) Few of the students recognised me and assumed I was the gardener. As a result, I gained a good feeling as to the real points of tension in this strange Tri-Service establishment based on the overheard conversations and exchanges in the garden!

Needless to say, loyalty to their Commandant and esprit de corps were quite obvious during the reunion. One of the most personable and dynamic individuals the author has ever met, Brigadier Holtom had his imprimatur on all associated reunion activities—making sure the guests' stay at Chicksands were enjoyable and memorable. As their Commandant, the brigadier set the example for his charges on base, and everyone on duty went out of their way to make their American visitors feel welcome and comfortable.

Going Home—Fond Memories

To the author (Chicksands veteran 1956-60), the most memorable part of the reunion was being able to live in quarters on base—going back to old Security Service roots, so to speak. The Commandant opened excess billets on station for reunion guests, and I was fortunate to stay in a room in base housing where American families lived five years earlier. This arrangement was easy on the wallet (£10 sterling daily, B&B). Moreover, living on base was convenient and brought back fond memories. The WW II-era Nissen huts with potbellied stoves and centralized latrines of the 1950's and 1960's had been replaced, and breakfast was British bangers, beans and eggs instead of American "SOS." However, the Junior Ranks Mess where breakfast was served is a modern iteration of the "chow hall" that served Americans at Chicksands from 1950-1995—and RAF WAAF during the 1940's.

Getting to Chicksands was half the fun! Even after forty years the author managed to find his way from Heathrow Airport to the base in a rental car without getting lost. Arriving after midnight, Chicksands' "Accommodation Cell" offered a hearty welcome. A security guard roused Private Atwood—a 21-ish blue-eyed, ponytailed blonde receptionist—out of bed. She escorted the author to his quarters and carried his heavy suitcase up the stairs to his quarters. Kinda embarrassing for a slender British lady private to lug around the baggage, but she was the proper hostess and insisted!

The highlight of the planned events was the wreath-laying and rededication of the Chicksands Memorial Wall honoring Cold War MIA's and KIA's. The ceremony included a military parade with a smartly dressed British military marching band, British Army, Royal Navy and RAF marching troops and a USAF honor guard.

Thursday was highlighted by the grand opening of the American Room in the Chicksands Museums of Defence Intelligence. By removing some historical British Intelligence memorabilia from display in the museum until additional space becomes available, Brigadier Holtom created the "Commemorative USAF Room" in the museum. The room pays tribute to the U.S. Air Force's 45 years at Chicksands with a series of displays and period-specific photographs of USAFSS activities at Chicksands from 1950 to 1995. The USAF displays include a scale model of the FLR-9 system and a typical late 1950's vintage intercept position with SP-600 and R-390 receivers, manned by a USAFSS Morse intercept operator mannequin with a traffic analyst looking over his shoulder. There is also a collection of photographs of Chicksands Fighting Chicks sports teams, USAFSS airmen involved in various activities and early American activities on base—all contributed by former Chicksands alumni.

Some 350 Americans made the pilgrimage to Chicksands for the Y2K Reunion. Going "home" to Chicksands was itself special, and sharing camaraderie with comrades from five decades earlier and making new friends was icing on the cake. Noteworthy spontaneous outings included a wonderful lunch at the Greyhound Pub in Haynes and a small gathering for dinner at the Green Man Pub outside Shefford. Both still serve excellent English fare. The Black Swan Pub in Shefford was also still well kempt. The Chicksands Millennium Reunion was truly a once-in-a-lifetime opportunity with fond memories that the author will cherish forever.

Contributed by Bill Gray

Black Swan Pub, Shefford, Beds., July 2000

Sharing Reunion Experience

Jeff Ewing, who served a tour at Chicksands as a single airman in the mid-1970's, was so elated after attending the Y2K Reunion that he shared his memories in an internet forum in late July 2000. Hoping to capture "some of the essence of the reunion experience for those who were unable to attend" and "provide some entertainment for all readers without offending anyone," Jeff Ewing summarized his reunion experience in a multipart report.

England 25 Years Later

Ewing arrived in England the Friday before the reunion (8 July) and spent three days in London. He stayed in a small hotel in Paddington—EXPENSIVE, but convenient—near Underground-rail stations and lots of tourist attractions. London seemed twice as crowded as 25 years ago, but Piccadilly Circus and Leicester

Square were much cleaner that in the past. A "Party in the Park" (Hyde Park in Paddington) drew 100,000 people on Sunday to see Elton John, Christina Aguilera and others. "Cell phone use is now the national sport." McDonald's, Burger King and KFC are easy to find, and the Hard Rock Café is still very crowded—American tourists are everywhere.

Jeff Ewing had forgotten the length of summer days in England. "Sunrise was about 4:30 a.m. and there was still a trace of light at 10:30 p.m." He passed through St. John's Wood on the way to The Olde Swiss Cottage Pub, a regular stop (as was The End of the World Pub in Chelsea) on his visits to London 25 years earlier. He rented a car at a Hertz outlet at Marble Arch and headed north on Watling Street—not exactly a prudent move on Monday morning. "All those who rented cars seemed to have the same three adjustment problems: a tendency to hit the curb with the passenger side front wheel, trying to look up to the right for the rearview mirror, and opening the passenger car door instead of the driver's door when returning to the car." Chicksands had never looked better when Jeff arrived at the Top Gate about midday.

Chicksands 25 Years Later

According to Jeff Ewing, a major reason he returned to Chicksands for the reunion was that "after not seeing the base for 25 years, it had begun to lose its 'concreteness' in my mind." Explaining that Chicksands still exists, he took the reader on a virtual tour of the base as he found it in July 2000.

All six (A thru F) of the dorms are still standing although "D" and "E" have been radically retrofitted (by the USAF) with balconies and outside entrances to each room. What they did was turn the old central hallway into individual bathrooms; you share a bath with the room directly across the hall.

The area around the commissary is quite different, and initially I thought the British had constructed a lot of new buildings. Then I remembered that Dennis Stiffler had written to me about this in early 1976. Digging out his letter he said: "the base is really going through some changes. There is a brand new BX between Baker Dorm and the commissary parking lot. New chapel and Class VI store right next to each other on the old baseball diamond. New tennis courts, new ball diamond. They built a handball court onto the gym."

The commissary and recreation center (both with additions since 1974) and the new BX are now classrooms. Some of the shops and the chapel Dennis referred to are still in operation. The tiny bowling alley beside the commissary is now a day-care center. The library, the theatre and the NCO Club (appropriately in use as the Warrant Officers and Sergeants Mess) look much the same, and they expect to start showing movies again later this summer.

Going up the road the supply and transportation area looks the same, and the old BX and Class VI buildings are standing. All the older little buildings are gone: laundry, American Express, Stars & Stripes, education center, Clothing Issue and Rod & Gun—the concrete floor of the barber shop is a BBQ area.

In the huge parking lot beside "E" dorm (where the British insurance salesmen used to sit in their cars and where I once bought an ill-fated Harley Sportster), the USAF built a very large bowling alley. When I asked the sergeant major if the trainees did a lot of bowling, she explained that when we closed the base: "you took your kit." Which means we stripped out the pin-setting machines and destroyed the alleys, leaving them with a shell. We did the same to the base theatre, stripping out the seats and the projection equipment.

The chow hall is much the same although it is now called the Junior Ranks Mess. This is where we came for breakfast. But there was no SOS, no peanut butter, and no biscuits (American definition). That was not as sad as standing in the NCO Annex parking lot and seeing no NCO Annex. It is gone and apparently has been gone for a long time. The bus shelter is there, the dumpster area walls are there, the delivery drive is there, the sidewalk is there; but no club. However, there was a bright spot for those of us who like to pretend we are still 21 years of age.

Down where the old commissary warehouse used to be they have a junior ranks pub that is very nice. Pool tables, dartboards, food, and best of all—a sound and video system that plays VH1 Classic all day.

Contributed by Bill Gray

Chicksands Base Chapel, circa 1958

While the clinic looks much the same, the old chapel is gone. Most of the mystery buildings in this area are still standing, with their function just as much a mystery to me as it was in 1974. Fire station, post office and gas station buildings are still standing but have been modified for some other purpose. Building 250 looks the same and is still used as HQ.

The new Intelligence Museum is nearby and most of the mystery buildings in this area remain mystery buildings. I believe that the Security Police complex was back there somewhere. There is now some strange combination of hog farm and bat guano factory just outside the base perimeter in this area. On bad days I imagine everyone longs for the old 1970's aroma of rotting Brussels sprouts. Building 600 still sits up on the hill but instead of having to compete for parking spaces up there, they now use a part of the parking lot for camper storage. Times do change.

The Priory looks wonderful and we were told that they had just completed a major restoration. I'm a poor one to ask about the Priory in 1974 because I never went there— that was officer country and nothing good ever came from wandering over in that direction. In fact, I never realized that there was a second family housing complex in back of the Priory until my last week on base when I needed to borrow a car (from someone who lived there) to take a WAF to a movie in Luton.

There's a small "city" back there. The other family housing area looked just fine although seeing the now unused dependent school was sad—I remember many a University of Maryland European Extension class in that building. Apparently the British families send their kids to the Bedfordshire schools.

We are indebted to Jeff Ewing for his comparison of facilities at Chicksands in 1974 and 2000. The mystery buildings that Jeff mentions are original structures built during World War II and used by USAFSS during the 1950's and 1960's—old 6950th HQ, armory, base supply, personnel office, etc.

The Reunion as Enjoyed by Jeff Ewing

Prior to flying to England for the reunion, Jeff Ewing dug Air Force memorabilia out of his old duffel bag to try "to get in the spirit of the occasion." He found a copy of orders dated September 1974, sending him home to America. Returning to Chicksands for the reunion represented going full circle. He found only a few of his mid-1970's comrades at the reunion—Mike Simmons whom Jeff had trained with at Goodfellow and served with on Baker Flight at Chicksands, Tom and Marilyn Ciszkowski (Able Flight) and Gary Graves (Dawg Flight). Jeff also roamed the base with Joe Lynch, who was at Chicksands during the early 1960's in something called "TRANSEC." Not only did Joe fail to find anyone else who had worked in TRANSEC, "he failed to find anyone who even knew what TRANSEC was."

Jeff heaped high praise on Brigadier Holtom and his staff, who made everyone feel welcome. Joe, Mike and Jeff designated Warrant Officer Hayley Smith as their favorite British soldier— she is the star of the ENIGMA video in the Intelligence Museum.

They found her "very helpful, very informative, and just fun to talk with." She radically improved Jeff's image of warrant officers. He also enjoyed talking to Holly Lamb in the Intelligence Museum so much that he toured the exhibits twice. And Tom Ciszkowski and Jeff were in awe of the physical conditioning and beer drinking ability of the female British sergeant standing near them in the NCO Club Tuesday night—"Impressive, most impressive!"

Ewing provided a day by day accounting of events during the reunion, commencing when he arrived at the Top Gate Monday.

I was directed to the base theatre where British personnel were assigning rooms, collecting money, and providing general orientation. I was assigned a 2nd floor room on the back side of "D" dorm, interesting coincidence because my last contact with Chicksands had been a phone call in late 1974 to a WAF in "D" dorm. "D" was also the haunted dorm. Used by the communications squadron when I first came to Chicksands, they left in 1973 and the place sat vacant for over a year. At night the only lights were the red exit signs; a very spooky place.

Colonel George (remember him) also had a room on the 2nd floor. If you had asked me in 1974 what was most likely in July 2000—that I would lead the first manned space flight to Mars or that I would return to Chicksands and stay in "D" Dorm with Colonel George—I would have asked you what color Martian I should bring back.

The weather on Monday was terrible, rainy and cold. You could not really walk around so I drove around the base a couple times and then went back to the theatre to socialize with anybody who drifted in. That was where I first met TRANSEC Joe, who soon headed off with a group to London to see Phantom of the Opera. I had signed up for the "Pub Crawl" and at about 7:30 a group of us got on a bus and headed over toward Old Warden.

Tuesday was cloudy and cold, but thankfully no rain. Ewing's commentary continues.

I don't remember July weather at Chicksands being this bad. After breakfast in the chow hall d/b/a [doing business as] the Junior Ranks Mess, I rode with TRANSEC Joe into Bedford. Our mission was to find mailing materials so he could ship his warm weather clothes back to Houston. I kept my warm weather clothes. They were very useful; I wore them under my cold weather clothes. For me the "layered look" was definitely in all week.

The balloon hangars are still at RAF Cardington although the base has that closed look. I told Joe about the day in 1972 when the Goodyear Blimp tried to dock there and they had too few people on the mooring ropes—the blimp dragged them across the field until it hit a house and deflated. Then it draped itself over several other nearby houses. Anyone remember this?

Bedford looks great; they now have an indoor mall called the Harpur Centre. We then drove back to the base for a lunch BBQ. It was supposed to be outside (as was the concert that night) but weather conditions moved things into the NCO Club d/b/a the WO and Sgt.'s Mess.

Mike made his first reunion appearance at the BBQ. That afternoon we walked around the base—taking Holly's tour of the Intelligence Museum and seeing a screening of the museum's ENIGMA video (staring Hayley—roll credits please). Elsewhere on the base Marilyn and Tom were renewing their wedding vows (they had first met at Chicksands), creating yet another day of the year for Tom to try to remember as their wedding anniversary. That evening we had a great "big band" sound dinner concert at the NCO club. Someone even thought to park a 1965 Mustang and a 1967 Camaro just outside the club entrance.

WEDNESDAY: Here comes the sun, at least for a little while. If you don't like the weather wait around a little and it will change. VERY impressive ceremony this morning for the rededication of the memorial wall, located between the old commissary and the river. There was a military band, individual formations of RAF and British Army trainees, and a host of dignitaries. Royal Navy trainees lined both sides of the procession from the road to the wall.

Congratulations to the quick thinking RAF trainee who broke ranks to catch the fainting female trainee in front of him. That sent the sergeants into the ranks to pull out anyone who was looking unsteady, one from the RAF and two from the Army formation. The Royal Navy stood fast and completed the ceremony with their full complement.

I missed the group photo on the Priory lawn but I could still claim to be in it. The photographer (trained by Francis Gary Powers?) took the photo while standing somewhere in Upper Gravenhurst. Identification of specific individuals is a little difficult. That afternoon there was a Medieval Pageant on the Priory grounds, tours and excellent living history presentations. The restored Priory is a national treasure.

Instead of attending the formal dinner that evening, I drove to Hitchin to visit the cottage where I lived in 1973. Built in 1460, I was not surprised to find it virtually unchanged, as was the Gosmore village green directly across the street. The old Kinks album "Village Green Preservation Society" flashed through my mind as soon as I saw it.

Thursday brought the official opening of the USAF element in the Intelligence Museum. Jeff Ewing found the large crowd and temperature in the museum too stifling, so he "made for the door," and spent the rest of the day at the pub and roaming the base. He later attended a plenary meeting at the base theatre and the barn dance and closing address at the WO/Sgt.'s Mess. Although guests were permitted two more nights in base quarters, this was really the closing of the reunion. Jeff went on the all-day bus tour to Bletchley Park and Stratford on Friday and checked out from billeting at Chicksands on Saturday—after one last stop by the USAF Room in the Intelligence Museum, where "the exhibits play up the human-interest angle very well."

Ghosts—Ewing Reminisces

Jeff Ewing titled the final part of his reunion commentary, "Ghosts"—recollections, some good and some bad, that came to mind as he traipsed around Chicksands and its surroundings for five days. One involved a fellow motorcycle enthusiast at the base who had died in a head-on collision outside Shefford in May 1972. Jeff's second ghost brought back memories of a WAF he called "C" with whom he had shared the cottage in Hitchin. The third ghost reminded him of a close friend from Chicksands who had died in a car accident back in the States in 1974.

Ghost "A," another WAF he met just three months before leaving Chicksands, haunted him after he departed in 1974. To impress Ghost A, Ewing got out of the Air Force early, returned to college and completed his degree. "If I had not known her, I would still be drifting somewhere." Finally there was "T," a 17-year old Air Force dependent at Chicksands whose mother "was none too keen on her daughter associating with us 'airmen' types." Ghost T visited the reunion one morning as Jeff walked past a point where she had gotten into trouble with her mother for smiling at him during a chance passing on the sidewalk.

This was a "moment" I had totally forgotten and it made a very nice gift to take back home—worth the trip.

Undoubtedly, all of the Chix alumni came face to face with their ghosts from the past during their reunion visit to Chicksands.

CHICKSANDS FIVE YEARS LATER

The author and wife Diane visited Chicksands in July 2005— on-base guests at a reunion of RAF veterans who had served at Chicksands during WW II. A couple of these veterans had participated in the opening of RAF Station Chicksands in 1940. Except for some new construction along Churchill Drive in the vicinity of the Junior Ranks Mess, camp facilities at Chicksands in 2005 appeared to the author to be pretty much the same as they had been during the reunion in July 2000. As stated by retired Brigadier Holtom in 2007, the camp continues to flourish as a British MoD facility.

In my current life as a consultant to the oil and gas industry, I also do some work for the Ministry of Defence as hobby stuff. This takes me back to Chicksands where I keep a low profile and try to help in those areas of training that will always need attention—analysis, collective intelligence training and the art of creating useful databases.

Indeed, I am there next week on just such a mission finding that I can extract money from the government for a good cause more effectively than I could when I was serving! I can report that Chicksands gets stronger, better and more appreciated by its incumbents all the time.

The Friends [of Chicksands] flourish, the Priory has just been refurbished again, and the avenue of trees up to the memorial wall now look as if they belong. When you veterans arrived in 2000, they had been there only two months, and we were hoping they would not die. None did.

A "Google Earth" satellite image of Chicksands shows the camp's modern-day facilities.[197] The circular clearing where the FLR-9 antenna was located is evident in the northwest (top left) quadrant of the satellite image. Other rather easily recognizable landmarks include the River Flit that bisects the base (east to west), the Priory north of the river and Chicksands Avenue that traverses north-south from the Top Gate across the River Flit to the Bottom Gate. This concludes our post-World War II USAFSS history for Europe and the Middle East. Volume III of *Freedom Through Vigilance* addresses Air Force Security Service history in Alaska and the Far East.

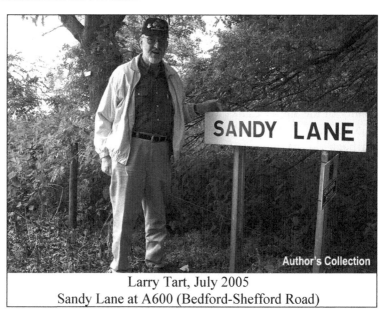

Larry Tart, July 2005
Sandy Lane at A600 (Bedford-Shefford Road)

APPENDIX A—ACRONYMS & ABBREVIATIONS

Acronym/Abbrev	Meaning
-0	203xx-0 was a Polish linguist
-1	203xx-1 or 208xx-1 was a Russian linguist
-2	203xx-2 or 208xx-2 was a Chinese linguist
-9	203xx-9 or 208xx-9 was a Korean linguist
1A8	airborne cryptologic linguist
1N2	communications signals intelligence specialist
1N3	cryptologic linguist
1N4	signals intelligence analyst
1N5	electronic signals intelligence specialist
1N6	electronic systems security assessment specialist
2-T	two-tour promotion program
291	crypto/comms system operator
292	Morse intercept operator
293	Morse radio operator
294	special signals operator/analyst
201	cryptologic analyst
202	radio traffic analyst
203	linguist
204	air intelligence analyst
205	special signals operator/analyst (replaced 294)
206	photo interpreter
207	Morse intercept operator (replaced 292)
208	voice intercept operator
3-D	consecutive tour promotion program
301	radio/electronic maintenance technician
304	ground comms maintenance technician
306	electronic/comms maintenance technician
8031	COMINT Staff Officer Course
8034	SIGINT Officer Course
A-2	Air Force Intelligence
A-3	Air Force Operations
A&R	analysis and reporting
A1C	airman first class (E-4)
A2C	airman second class (E-3)
A3C	airman third class (E-2)
AA	airborne analyst
AAA	antiaircraft artillery
AAC	U.S. Army Air Corps, forerunner of USAF
AACS	Airways and Air Communications Service

AAF	U.S. Army Air Forces
AAFJOG	Army Air Force Joint Operating Group
AB	airman basic (E-1)
ABCCC	Airborne Battlefield Command & Control Center
ABW	air base wing
AC	aircraft commander
AC&W	aircraft control and warning
ACRP	airborne comms intelligence recon platform
ACS/I	Assistant Chief of Staff/Intelligence
Adm.	Admiral
admiral	USAFSS airborne mission supervisor/Europe
ADVON	advance echelon
AETC	Air Education and Training Command
AEW	air expeditionary wing
AFB	air force base
AFCC	Air Force Communications Command
AFCCO	Air Force Center for Cryptologic Operations
AFCD	Air Force Cryptologic Depot
AFCENTCOM	Air Force Central Command
AFCERT	Air Force Computer Emergency Response Team
AFCS	Air Force Communications Service
AFCSC	Air Force Cryptologic Support Center
AFCYBER	Air Force Cyber Command
AFEWC	Air Force Electronic Warfare Center
AFIC	Air Force Intelligence Command
AFIOC	Air Force Information Operations Center
AFISRA	Air Force Intelligence, Surveillance and Reconnaissance Agency
AFIT	Air Force Institute of Technology
AFIWC	Air Force Information Warfare Center
AFLC	Air Force Logistics Command
AFMC	Air Force Materiel Command
AFOUA	Air Force Outstanding Unit Award
AFR	Air Force Reserves
AFRTS	Armed Forces Radio and Television Service
AFSA	Armed Forces Security Agency (became NSA)
AFSAC	Air Force Special Activities Center
AFSC	Air Force Systems Command
AFSCC	Air Force Special Communications Center
AFSG	Air Force Security Group
AFSOC	Air Force Special Operations Command
AFSS	U.S. Air Force Security Service
AFSSO	Air Force Special Security Office
AFTAC	Air Force Technical Application Center

AG-22	data entry keyboard
AIA	Air Intelligence Agency
AIT	American Institute in Taiwan
aka	also known as
AKL	light cargo ship
ALK	voice intercept training
ALS	Army Language School, Monterey
AM	Air Medal
AMC	Air Mobility Command
AMS	airborne mission supervisor
AMT	airborne maintenance technician
ANG	Air National Guard
ANGB	Air National Guard Base
AN/CRD-2	direction finding set
AN/GRC-26	radio teletype
AN/MSR-1	comms intercept van
AO	aeronautical orders
AOB	air order of battle
AP	Associated Press or air policeman
APN-59	airborne search radar
APN-81	airborne search radar
APN-99	airborne Doppler radar
APO	Army Post Office (overseas)
AQM-34	remotely controlled airborne vehicle (drone)
AR	army regulation
ARC-106	digital secure airborne data system
ARCENT	Army Central Command
ARDF	airborne radio direction-finding
ARVN	Army, Republic of Vietnam
ASA	Army Security Agency
ASAPAC	Army Security Agency Pacific
ASRP	airborne signals intelligence recon platform
ATC	Air Training Command
AWACS	airborne warning and control system
AZK	airborne voice intercept training
B&B	bed and breakfast
back-ender	recon crew specialist on recon mission
Bahnhof	train station (German)
bat	airborne intercept operator in 6988th SS
BEE, Project	See DANCER, Project
Blue Sky	project name, RC-47 in Korea; later Rice Bowl
BND	Bundesnachrichtendienst, Foreign Intelligence Service (Germany)
BOQ	bachelor officer quarters
BUFF	B-52 bomber

ACRONYM LIST

BUIC	Back-up Intercept Control
BX	base exchange (PX in Army)
C/A	cryptanalysis
C2	command and control
C3	command, control and communications
C3CM	command, control and comms countermeasures
C4I	command, control, communications, computer and information
CAA	Civil Aeronautics Authority
CALSU	Combat Airlift Support Unit
CAP	combat air patrol
Capt.	captain
CARS/DGS	Contingency Airborne Reconnaissance System/Deployable Ground System
CBPO	consolidated base personnel office
CC	commander
CDG	Comms Depot Group
CENTCOM	U.S. Central Command
CENTAF	Central Command Air Force
CESD	Continental Electronic Security Division
CI	counterintelligence
CIA	Central Intelligence Agency
CIC	Counterintelligence Corps
CINC	commander in chief
CINCPAC	Commander in Chief, Pacific Command
CMSAF	Chief Master Sergeant of the AF
CMSgt.	chief master sergeant (E-9)
CO	commanding officer
COC	combat operations center
COIC	combat operations intelligence center
COIN	counterinsurgency
Col.	colonel
Combat Apple	RC-135M Rivet Card mission in SEA
Combat Cougar	EC-47 ARDF program
Combat Cross	EC-47 ARDF program
Comfy	USAFSS-sponsored program
Comfy Echo	contingency airborne SIGINT system
Comfy Gator	C-130 remote intercept platform
Comfy Levi	replaced Comfy Echo
COMINT	communications intelligence
Commando Forge	EC-47 ARDF program
Commando Lance	C-130 ACRP missions in SEA
Commando Royal	C-130 ACRP missions (local)
Commando Solo	EC-130E Rivet Rider (PSYOP) aircraft
Compass Bright	intercept receiver on U-2

Compass Call	C3CM C-130 aircraft
Compass Dart	EC-47 ARDF program
Compass EARS	Emergency Airborne Reaction System (mobile S&WC)
Compass Flag	remote intercept system
Compass Jade	TADIL data correlation system
COMPUSEC	computer security
COMSEC	communications security
CONOP	concept of operations
Cotton Candy	RC-135A Rivet Brass mission
Cpl.	corporal
CQ	charge of quarters
CRB	Cam Ranh Bay
CRC	control and reporting center
Creek Grass	USAFE project name, C-130A-II and B-II
CRITIC	most urgent intelligence report
CRITICOMM	critical intelligence communications
CSAF	Chief of Staff, USAF
CSF	communications security flight
CSGD	Comms Security Group Depot
CSO	computer security officer
CSOC	consolidated security operations center
CSS	communications security squadron
CV	vice commander
CW	continuous wave (Morse code)
CWO	chief warrant officer
D-Day	planned/scheduled date
DAF	Department of the Air Force
DANCER, Project	ARVN personnel used as linguists
DC	District of Columbia
DC-6	commercial version of USAF C-118
DCGS	Distributed Common Ground System
DCS/Intelligence	deputy chief of staff for intelligence
DCS/Ops/Operations	deputy chief of staff for operations
DEFSMAC	Defense Special Missile and Astronautics Center
DEROS	date of estimated return from overseas
Desert Shield	deployment to Saudi Arabia in August 1990 to protect country
Desert Storm	First Persian Gulf War (Aug '90-Feb '91) against Iraq
Desert Strike	field training exercise
Det	detachment
DEW Line	Distant Early Warning Line
DF	direction-finding
DFC	Distinguished Flying Cross

DGIF	deployable ground intercept facility
DGS	distributed ground system (also deployable ground station)
DIRNSA	Director, National Security Agency
DISC	Defence Intelligence and Security Centre (UK)
DISS	Defence Intelligence and Security School (UK)
DLAB	Defense language aptitude battery
DLI	Defense Language Institute
DLIEC	DLI East Coast
DLIWC	DLI West Coast (Monterey, CA)
DMZ	demilitarized zone
DNIF	duty not to include flying
DO	directorate of operations/operations officer
DOA	analysis section in operations
DOI	directorate of operations and intelligence
DOR	operations production section
DOT	operations training section
DOV	Ops standardization & evaluation (Stan/Eval)
DOW	area specialist office
DOZ	directorate of space activities
DoD	Department of Defense
DP	directorate of personnel
DPMO	Defense Department POW/MIA Office
DR	discrepancy report
Dream Boat	project name for USAFE RB-50 ACRP's
Drill Press	EC-47 SIGINT mission in SEA
DRU	direct reporting unit
DRV	Democratic Republic of Vietnam
DSCP	downlink signal collection platform
DSO	direct support operator
DSU	direct support unit
Eagle Pull	emergency evacuation of Phnom Penh, Cambodia, 12 April 1975
EC	electronic combat
ECS	electronic combat squadron
EESD	European Electronic Security Division
ELINT	electronic intelligence
ELSEC	electronic emissions security
ELT	emergency locator transmitter
EOB	electronic order of battle
ERU	emergency reaction unit
ESC	Electronic Security Command
ESD	Electronic Security Division
ESE	Electronic Security Europe
ESG	electronic security group

ESP	Electronic Security Pacific
ESR	European Security Region
ESS	electronic security squadron
ESSA	electronic security systems assessment (replaced COMSEC)
ESSAC-CON	ESSA Central-Continental
ESSAC-EUR	ESSA Central-Europe
ESSAC-PAC	ESSA Central-Pacific
EST	Electronic Security Tactical
ESW	electronic security wing
ETO	European Theater of Operations
EUCOM	European Command
EWO	electronic warfare officer
FAA	Federal Aviation Administration
FASTC	Foreign Aerospace Science & Technology Center
FEAF	Far East Air Forces
ferret	reconnaissance mission
FLASH precedence	most urgent precedence
FLR-9	HF circular disposed array antenna/DF system
FLR-12	VHF/UHF antenna
FPO	Fleet Post Office (overseas)
Frequent Wind	emergency evacuation, Saigon, 29-30 April '75
FRG	Federal Republic of Germany (West Germany)
front-ender	cockpit (flight) crew member on recon mission
FSA	Field Station Augsburg
FSI	Foreign Service Institute
FTC	Foreign Technology Center
FTD	Foreign Technology Division
FTV	Freedom Through Vigilance
FTVA	Freedom Through Vigilance Association
G-1186	digital secure airborne data system
G-2	Intelligence (Army)
G-3	Operations (Army)
G.I.	government issue; slang for military person
GCHQ	Government Communications Headquarters, UK
GCI	ground-controlled intercept
GDR	German Democratic Republic (East Germany)
Gen.	general
GHRS	God rest his/her soul
GMS	ground mission supervisor
GMT	Greenwich Mean Time (aka Zulu time)
GNP	gross national product
GOT	Gulf of Tonkin
GP	group

GRC-137	digital secure ground-to-air data system
GRC-26	direction finding system
GRSOC	Ft. Gordon Regional SIGINT Operations Center
GRU	Soviet army intelligence
GVN	government of Vietnam
GWOT	global war on terrorism
H-1 van	45-foot multipurpose USAFSS enclosed trailer/van
Hawkeye	EC-47 prototype ARDF in SEA
HF	high frequency
HO-17 hut	portable shelter
HO-28 hut	portable shelter
HQ	headquarters
HUMINT	human intelligence
HVCCO	Handle Via COMINT Channels Only
I-NOSC	Integrated Network Ops and Security Center
ICAO	International Civil Aviation Organization
ICBM	intercontinental ballistic missile
ICE	integrated control enabler
ICJ	International Court of Justice
ID	identification
IED	improvised explosive device
IFEL	Institute of Far Eastern Languages
IFF	identification friend or foe
IG	inspector general
IG	intelligence group
IIO	information integration officer
IL-28	Soviet medium jet bomber
IMINT	imagery intelligence
IN	Intelligence
INF	intermediate range nuclear forces
INSCOM	Intelligence and Security Command (Army)
INYSB (AF/INYSB)	SIGINT branch, U.S. Air Force HQ
IO	information operations
IOG	information operations group
IOS	information operations squadron
IOW	information operations wing
IRO	instructor radio operator
Iron Horse	automated display of air surveillance tracking
IPF	integrated processing facility
IRAN	inspection and replacement as necessary
IS	intelligence squadron
ISR	intelligence, surveillance and reconnaissance
ISS	intelligence support squadron
IW	intelligence wing (also information warfare)

IWAS	information warfare aggressor squadron
J-2	Joint Service Intelligence
JAMMAT-USAFG	Joint American Military Mission for Aid to Turkey-U.S. Air Force Group
JASDF	Japan Air Self-Defense Force
JC2WC	Joint Command and Control Warfare Center
JCS	Joint Chiefs of Staff
JCSB	Joint Commission Support Branch
JEWC	Joint Electronic Warfare Center
JFCC-Space	Joint Functional Component Command-Space
JFEX	joint expeditionary forces experiment
JRC (JCS/JRC)	Joint Reconnaissance Center
JTF-FA	Joint Task Force-Full Accounting
JUSMAAG	Joint U.S. Military Advisory Assistance Group
JUSMAG	Joint U.S. Military Advisory Group
KC	tanker type aircraft
KGB	Soviet secret police
KIA	killed in action
KP	kitchen police
KRSOC	Kunia Regional SIGINT Operations Center
KY-3	secure telephone
KY-8/KY-28	secure voice radio
LG	Logistics
Linebacker I and II	bombing campaigns over North Vietnam
LRA/LRAA	Long Range Aviation/Long Range Air Army
LST	landing ship for tanks (amphibious)
Lt.	lieutenant
LTV	Ling-Temco-Vought
M/T	Metro Tango (Hahn, Germany)
-MA	208xx-MA was a Russian linguist
MAAG	military air advisory group
MAC	Military Airlift Command
MACV	Military Assistance Command, Vietnam
Maj.	major
MAJCOM	major command
MARS	Military Affiliated Radio Station
MATS	Military Air Transport Service
Mayaguez Incident	Khmer Rouge seizure of SS Mayaguez, 1975
-MB	208xx-MB was a Chinese linguist
-MC	208xx-MC was a French linguist
MC-88	military typewriter (ALL UPPER CASE)
MCOC	Misawa Cryptologic Operations Center
-MD	208xx-MD was a Vietnamese linguist
-ME	208xx-ME was an Albanian linguist
MEPS	Military Entrance Processing Station

-MF	208xx-MF was an Arabic linguist
-MG	208xx-MG was a Polish linguist
-MH	208xx-MH was a Bulgarian linguist
-MI	208xx-MI was a Korean linguist
MI	Military Intelligence
MIA	missing in action
-MJ	208xx-MJ was a German linguist
-MK	208xx-MK was a Spanish linguist
-ML	208xx-ML was a Romanian linguist
-MM	208xx-MM was a Serbo-Croatian linguist
MM	Monkey Mountain (by Da Nang, Vietnam)
-MN	208xx-MN was a Czechoslovakian linguist
-MO	208xx-MO was a Hungarian linguist
MoD	Ministry of Defence (UK)
MOD 28	teletype/data entry terminal
MOD 35	teletype/data entry terminal
MOS	military occupational specialty
-MP	208xx-MP was a Persian (Farsi) linguist
MP	military police
-MR	208xx-MR was a Hebrew linguist
MRSOC	Medina Regional SIGINT Operation Center
MSgt.	master sergeant (E-7)
MSOC	Misawa Security Operations Center
-MV	208xx-MV - Vietnamese linguist (short course)
MVD	Soviet Ministry of Internal Security
NAAFI	Navy, Army and Air Force Institutes (British military shoppette)
NAIC	National Air Intelligence Center
NAS	naval air station
NASIC	National Air and Space Intelligence Center
NATO	North Atlantic Treaty Organization
NCO	noncommissioned officer
NCOIC	noncommissioned officer in charge
Nisei	2nd generation Japanese-American
NKP	Nakhon Phanom RTAFB
NLF	national liberation front
NNWC	Naval Network Warfare Command
NOSC	network operations and security center
NSA	National Security Agency
NSAM	National Security Action Memorandum
NSC	National Security Council
NSCID	NSC Intelligence Directive
NSG/NSGA	Naval Security Group (Activity)
NSOC	National SIGINT Operations Center
NVP	National Vigilance Park at Ft. Meade, MD

NWW	network warfare wing
O-2	small observation aircraft
O&M	organization and maintenance
OB	order of battle
OCB	Operations Coordinating Board; part of the NSC
OIC	officer in charge
OJT	on-the-job training
OL	operating location
Olympic Fire	U-2 remote mission in Key West
Olympic Game	U-2 remote mission in Korea
Olympic Torch	U-2 remote mission in Thailand
ONC	operational navigation chart
OPINTEL	operational intelligence
OPSEC	operations security
Ops NCOIC	NCO in charge of operations
ORD	operational readiness document
Org chart	organizational chart
OSD	Office of Secretary of Defense
OSIA	On-Site Inspection Agency
OSNAZ	Soviet signals intelligence
OT&E	operational testing and evaluation
OTS	Officer Training School
PACAF	Pacific Air Forces
PACOM	Pacific Command
PAL	pathological and anatomical laboratory
pan	panoramic display receiver
PANG	Pennsylvania Air National Guard
PARPRO	Peacetime Aerial Reconnaissance Program
PAVN	People's Army of Vietnam
PBS	pilot billet suffix (callsign)
PCS	permanent change of station
PDJ	Plaine de Jarres, Laos
PESD	Pacific Electronic Security Division
Pfc.	private first class
PHOTINT	photo intelligence
Phyllis Ann	EC-47 ARDF program
PIO	public information officer
PMFR	post mission flight report
PMI	preventive maintenance inspections
POE	port of embarkation
POW	prisoner of war
POW's/MIA's	prisoners of war and missing in action persons
PPI	planned position indicator
PROCERT	proficiency certification
PSR	Pacific Security Region

PSYOP	psychological operations
PVO	protivo-vozhdushnaya oborona (Russian) antiaircraft air defense
PX	post exchange (BX in Air Force)
QAF	Quality Air Force
QU-22B	Beech Bonanza remoting platform
Queen Bee	RB-50/C-130B-II ACRP mission
R&R duty	rest and relaxation
R/T	radiotelephone
RAF	British Royal Air Force
raven	electronic warfare officer on recon aircraft
RB	recon-configured bomber
RBN	radio beacon
RC	recon-configured transport aircraft
RFI	radio frequency interference
RGM	radio group mobile
R.I.	radio intercept
Rice Bowl	project name for RC-47 operations in Korea; earlier called Blue Sky
RIRAK	Remote Intercept Recovery at Kelly
Rivet Brass	RC-135A aircraft project name
Rivet Card	RC-135M project name
Rivet Gym	College Eye EC-121 aircraft
Rivet Joint	RC-135V/W project name
Rivet Rider	C-130E Commando Solo aircraft
Rivet Top	EC-121 command and control prototype
Rivet Victor	project name for C-130A-II and B-II ACRP
RJ	Rivet Joint RC-135 ASRP
RMK/BRJ	Raymond, Morrison, Knudsen-Brown, Root and Jones conglomerate (contractor)
ROE	rules of engagement
ROK	Republic of Korea
ROKAF	Republic of Korea Air Force
RPM	revolutions per minute
RRFS	radio research field station
RRSOU	radio research special operation unit
RRU	radio research unit
RS	reconnaissance squadron
RSD	radio security detachment
RSS	radio security squadron/radio security section
RSM	radio squadron mobile
RSM (G)	radio squadron mobile (Germany)
RSM (J)	radio squadron mobile (Japan)
RSOC	regional SIGINT operations center
RTAFB	Royal Thai Air Force Base

RTASS	remote tactical SIGINT system
RTP	radio technical regiment (Russian "Polk")
RU-6 Beaver	single-engine Army ARDF aircraft
RVN	Republic of Vietnam
RVNAF	Republic of Vietnam Air Force
S-141	"Little John" hut or shelter
S&T	scientific and technical
S&TI	scientific and technical intelligence
S&WC	surveillance and warning center
SA-2	Guideline surface-to-air missile
SA-3	Goa surface-to-air missile
SA-4	Ganef surface-to-air missile
SAC	Strategic Air Command
sailor	covername, recon crew member in Europe
SALT	Strategic Arms Limitation Talks/Treaty
SAM	surface-to-air missile
SAO	Special Access Only
SAR	search and rescue
SC	Maintenance
SCC	special communications center
SCG	special communications group
SCI	Secret Compartmented Information
SCR-399	HF intercept radio
SDU	signal display unit
SEA	Southeast Asia
Senior Book	COMINT collection system
Senior Ruby	ELINT collection system
Senior Spear	COMINT collection system
Sentinel Bright	voice intercept training system
SESD	Space Electronic Security Division
SFG	security forces group
SFOR	stabilization force
SG	security group or support group
Sgt.	sergeant (E-4 in Air Force)
SI	Special Intelligence (SIGINT)
SID	Signal Intelligence Division
SIGINT	signals intelligence
Silver Dawn	C-130B-II mission
S.I.S.	Signal Intelligence Service
SLK	Shu Lin Kou
SMSgt.	senior master sergeant (E-8)
SOA	special operating agency
SOFP	Special Operations Flight Program
SOP	standard operating procedure
SOS	distress signal (also special Ops squadron)

Sour Grapes	RC-47 exploratory missions in SEA
SOUTHAF	Southern Command Air Force
SOUTHCOM	Southern Command
SOW	special operations wing
SQ/Sqdn	squadron
SP-600	intercept receiver
SPCS	space control squadron
SrA.	senior airman (E-4 in U.S. Air Force)
SRIC	signal radio intelligence company
SRO	senior ranking officer
SRS	strategic reconnaissance squadron
SS-4	surface-to-surface missile
SS	security squadron or support squadron
SS (M)	Security Squadron (Mobile)
SSA	Signal Security Agency
SSgt.	staff sergeant (E-5 in U.S. Air Force)
SSM	surface-to-surface missile
SSO	special security office
Sun Valley	project name for C-130A-II and B-II ACRP's
SW	security wing
T-29	trainer/passenger aircraft
T-54	Soviet army tank
T/A	traffic analysis
T/E	traffic exploitation
T/I	traffic identification
TAC	Tactical Air Command
TACAIR	tactical air
TACAN	tactical air navigation beacon-transponder
TACC	tactical air control center
TACC-NS	Tactical Air Control Center-Northern Sector
TACREP	tactical report
TADIL	tactical digital information link
TASS	official Soviet news agency
TC-8	DF system
TC-9	intercept system
TCG	tactical control group
TDY	temporary duty
Teaball	air warning tip-off project in SEA
TELINT	telemetry intelligence
TEMPEST	compromising emanations
TEWS	tactical electronic warfare squadron
TFA	Task Force Alpha
TFW	tactical fighter wing
TGIF	transportable ground intercept facility
TI (also DI)	training instructor (drill instructor)

TIBS	tactical information broadcast service
TO&E	table of organization and equipment
TPW-2	Olympic Torch U-2 flight control center
TQM	Total Quality Management
TR-1	Improved U-2 remoting aircraft
TRANSEC	transmission security
TRD	thermal heat device (infrared)
TRG	training group
TRS	training squadron
TRW	training wing
TSgt.	technical sergeant (E-6 in U.S. Air Force)
TSN	Tan Son Nhut Air Base
TTG	technical training group
TTP	tactics, techniques and procedures
TTY	teletype
TUSLOG	The U.S. Logistics Group
TWCC	Teaball Weapons Control Center
U-2	high-altitude recon aircraft
U202	COMSEC traffic analyst
U.S./USA	United States/United States of America
UHF	ultra high frequency
UN	United Nations
UPI	United Press International
URC-53	digital secure data system
USA-13	Scott AFB USAFSS DF site
USA-51	6950th/Chicksands designator
USA-512	6916th SS/Rhein-Main designator
USA-512J	6916th SS/Athens designator
USA-60	6937th Comm Gp/Pakistan
USAREUR	U.S. Army Europe
USAF	United States Air Force/U.S. Air Force
USAFE	United States Air Forces, Europe
USAFR	USAF Reserves
USAFSS	United States Air Force Security Service
USAFSS/DOR	USAFSS HQ Airborne Operations
USAFSS/TAD	USAFSS HQ Airborne Operations
USASA	U.S. Army Security Agency
USASAAL	U.S. ASA Alaska
USCIB	United States Communications Intelligence Board
USG	United States Government
USMC	U.S. Marine Corps
USSR	Union of Soviet Socialist Republics
USSTRATCOM	U.S. Strategic Command
V-2	German WW II rocket

V-E Day	Victory in Europe Day, WW II
V-J Day	Victory over Japan Day, WW II
VC	Viet Cong
VFW	Veterans of Foreign Wars
VHF	very high frequency
VIP	very important person
VOQ	visiting officer quarters
VPAF	Vietnamese People's Air Force
VPTS	voice processing training system
WAAF	Women's Auxiliary Air Force (British)
WAC	Women in the Army
WAF	Women in the Air Force
WAVE	Women in the Navy
WD	war department
Willy	project name for first USAFSS foray into Korea
WOJG	warrant officer junior grade
WORMS	We openly resist military stupidity
WPC	warrior preparation center
WW I	World War I
WW II	World War II
Y Service	British COMINT Service
ZI	Zone of Interior (Continental United States)
ZSU-4	Soviet antiaircraft artillery gun

APPENDIX B—USAFSS UNIT LOCATIONS

Location	Unit Identifier	Dates
Linz, Austria	Det 1, 12th RSM	1951-54
	OL 1, 12th RSM	1954-55
	Det 1, 6912th RSM	1955-57
Vienna, Austria	Flt F, 12th RSM	1953-54
	Det 4, 12th RSM	1954-55
	Det 3, 6912th RSM	1955
Brize Norton, England	OL 1, 6950th RGM	1959-61
	Det 1, 6950th RGM	1961-63
	Det 1, 6950th SG	1963-65
Burtonwood, England	6972d Comm Scty Flt	1951-53
	Flt A, 31st CSS	1953
	Det 1, 31st CSS	1954
	6931st Comm Scty Sq	1955-56
	Det 1, 6931st CSS	1955-56
	6931st Comm Scty Flt	1956-61
Bushy Park, England	31st Comm Scty Sq	1953-54
	Det 2, 31st CSS	1953-55
	Det 2, 6931st CSS	1955-56
Chicksands, England	10th RSM	1950-55
	6906th Scty Flt	1952-55
	6951st RSM	1955-56
	6950th RGM	1956-63
	Det 1, 6901st SCG	1956
	6950th Scty Wg	1963-67
	6950th Scty Gp	1967-78
	6900th Scty Sq	1973-75
	6950th Scty Sq	1974
	6950th AB Sq	1974-78
	Det 1, 6950th SG	1977
	Det 1, 6950th SS	1978
Mildenhall, England	6931st Comm Scty Sq	1959-61
	Det 1, 6936th CDG	1961-64
	Det 1, AFCD	1964-69
	Det 1, 6985th SS	1970-73
	Det 1, 6949th SS	1974
	6954th Scty Sq	1974
Orford RSC, England	Det 1, Eur Scty Rgn	1971-72
Upper Heyford, England	Det 1, 6985th SS	1967-70
West Drayton, England	Flt F, 6910th SG	1953
	Det 1, 6950th SG	1953-54

Kirknewton, Scotland	Det 102, 10th RSM	1952
	37th RSM	1952-55
	6952d RSM	1955-63
	6952d Scty Sq	1963-66
Stracathro, Scotland	Det 101, 10th RSM	1952-53
Vittel, France	2d RSM	1945-49
Augsburg, Germany	OL CC, 6910th SG	1971-72
	6910th Scty Gp	1972-74
	OL DA, 6913th SS	1975-76
	OL F0, 6970th ABG	1975
	OL FU, 6950th SG	1976
	OL FU, 6913th SS	1976-77
Bad Aibling, Germany	OL F1, 6970th SG	1971
	OL F1, 6970th ABG	1972-75
	Det 72, 6950th SG	1976-78
	OL FT, Det 1, HQ AFSS	1978
Berlin, Germany	Flt A, 2d RSM	1954
(Tempelhof Airport)	Det 1, 85th RSM	1954-55
	Det 1, 6914th RSM	1955-56
	Det 1, 6910th RGM	1956-59
	6912th RSM	1959-63
	6912th Scty Sq	1963
Bingen, Germany	6912th RSM	1955-59
Bremerhaven, Germany	41st RSM	1951-55
	6913th RSM	1955-63
	Det 2, 6913th RSM	1956-58
	6913th Scty Sq	1963-67
	Det 1, 6950th SW	1967
	OL 1, 6950th SG	1967-68
Darmstadt, Germany	2d RSM	1949-55
	Det 21, 2d RSM	1950-51
	Det 22, 2d RSM	1950-51
	Det 25, 2d RSM	1951
	6910th Scty Gp	1952-56
	85th RSM	1953-54
	6911th RSM	1955-56
	6911th RGM	1956-61
	6910th RGM	1961-63
	6910th Scty Wg	1962-70
	6910th Spt Sq	1963-65
	6911th Scty Sq (M)	1963-72
	6910th Spt Gp	1965-70
	6910th Scty Gp	1970-72
	OL JH, 6910th SG	1972
Eckstein, Germany	OL AA, 6910th SG	1971-72
	OL JA, 6910th SG	1972-73
	Det 1, 6910th SG	1973-74
	6913th Scty Sq	1974

Fassberg, Germany	Det 1, 41st RSM	1954-55
	Det 1, 6913th RSM	1955-56
Frankfurt, Germany	31st Comm Scty Sq	1954-55
	6900th Scty Wg	1954-61
	6931st Comm Scty Sq	1955-56
	6931st Comm Scty Flt	1956
	Eur Scty Rgn	1961-72
	6900th Spt Gp	1963-72
	Det 1, HQ USAFSS	1963-64
	Det 2, 6901st SCG	1963-64
		1965-66
	OL 1, 6970th SG	1966-70
	OL AA, 6970th SG	1970-71
	OL FA, 6970th SG	1971-75
	OL FA, 6970th ABG	1972
	OL AB, HQ USAFSS	1972-73
	6900th Scty Sq	1972-73
	OL FA, 6950th SG	1975-78
	OL FA, Det 1, HQ AFSS	1978
Grunstadt, Germany	85th RSM	1954-55
	6914th RSM	1955-56
	6910th RGM	1956-59
Hahn AB, Germany	OL HA, 6911th SS (M)	1975
	6911th Scty Sq (M)	1975
Hof, Germany	Det 2, 12th RSM	1955
	Det 2, 6912th RSM	1955-57
	Det 5, 6910th RGM	1957-59
	6915th RSM	1959-63
	6915th Scty Sq	1963-64
	6915th SG	1964-71
	OL BB, 6910th SG	1971
Kassel, Germany	Det 2, 85th RSM	1954-56
	Det 2, 6910th RGM	1956-57
Landsberg AB, Germany	12th RSM	1951-55
	6900th Scty Wg	1953-54
	6910th Scty Gp	1953-56
	Det 2, 6912th RSM	1954-55
	Det 6, 12th RSM	1954-55
	6901st Spec Comm Gp	1955-56
	Det 1, 6912th RSM	1955-56
	6905th Comm Sq	1955-57
	6912th RSM	1955-59
Landshut, Germany	Det 1, 6912th RSM	1956-57
	Det 4, 6910th RGM	1957-59
	OL 1, 6910th RGM	1959-61
	Det 1, 6910th RGM	1961
	Det 1, 6910th SW	1963-64

Lindsey AS, Germany	Det 5, AFCD	1966-73
	OL 6, 6970th SG	1968-70
	OL FF, 6970th ABG	1970-75
	OL AC, HQ USAFSS	1972-73
	OL CA, AFSCC	1972-75
	OL MB, AFCD	1973
	OL KB, AFCOMSECCEN	1973-75
Munich, Germany	Det 1, 6901st SCG	1963-66
	Det 3, 6910th SW	1966-67
	OL 1, 6910th SW	1967-70
	OL 14, 6970th SG	1968-70
	OL 2, Eur Scty Rgn	1970
	OL NN, 6970th SG	1970-71
	OL BB, Eur Scty Rgn	1970-71
	OL FN, 6970th SG	1971-72
	OL BB, 6900th ABS	1971-72
	OL JB, 6910th SG	1972-73
	OL FN, 6970th ABG	1972-75
	Det 71, 6950th SG	1976-78
	OL F0, Det 1, HQ AFSS	1978
Ramstein AB, Germany	OL QA, 6970th ABG	1972-75
	OL CG, 6960th ABS	1973-76
	OL AB, HQ USAFSS	1973-78
	OL KB, AFCOMSECCEN	1975
	OL QA, 6950th SG	1976-77
	OL HC, 6911th SS (M)	1976-79
	Det 1, HQ USAFSS	1978
	OL RM, Det 1, HQ AFSS	1979
Rhein-Main AB, Germany	6910th Scty Gp	1956
	Det 1, 6911th RGM	1956-59
	6937th Scty Flt	1958
	Det 1, 6900th SW	1959-60
	6916th RSM	1960-63
	6916th Scty Sq	1963-73
	6911th Scty Sq (M)	1972-75
	OL DB, 6916th SS	1973-74
	OL HC, 6911th SS(M)	1975
	OL QA, 6970th ABG	1975
Rothwesten, Germany	Det 23, 2d RSM	1950-52
	OL FF, 6910th SG	1971-72
Schleissheim, Germany	Det 2, 12th RSM	1951-53
Sembach, Germany	Flt A, 85th RSM	1953-54
	85th RSM*	1954-55
* Deployed to Sembach in	6914th RSM	1955-56
May 1954, 85th RSM	6910th RGM	1956-61
Operations located at	OL AX, HQ USAFSS	1973-75
Grunstadt, Germany.	OL GR, 6960th ABS	1974-75
	OL HB, 6911th SS (M)	1975-79
	Det 3, 6911th SS	1979

Stuttgart, Germany	OL GG, 6970th SG	1970-71
	OL FG, 6970th SG	1971-72
	OL FG, 6970th ABG	1972-75
	Det 70, 6950th SG	1976-78
	OL FG, Det 1, HQ AFSS	1978
	OL 7, 6970th SG	1978-79
Wasserkuppe, Germany	Flt A, 6910th SG	1953-54
	Flt B, 2d RSM	1954
	Flt 0, 12th RSM	1954
	Det 3, 85th RSM	1954-55
	Det 3, 6910th RGM	1956-57
Wiesbaden, Germany	15th Radio Scty Section	1949-50
	Det D, 136th CSS	1950-53
(Wiesbaden, Camp Pieri,	6910th Scty Gp	1951-53
and Freudenberg Annex	Det 4, 6972d CSF	1953
were in the same	Flt D, 31st CSS	1953-54
geographic location.)	Det 3, 31st CSS	1954-55
	Det 3, 6931st CSS	1955-56
	Det 3, 6912th RSM	1956-57
	Det 6, 6910th RGM	1957-63
	Det 2, 6910th SW	1963-69
	OL 3, Eur Scty Rgn	1969
Zweibrücken, Germany	6905th Comm Sq	1956-57
	6901st Spec Comm Gp	1956-68
	OL 2, 6970th SG	1966-67
	OL 1, Eur Scty Rgn	1966-68
Athenai Apt, Athens,	OL 2, Eur Scty Rgn	1967-68
Greece	OL 2, 6916th SS	1968
	Det 1, 6916th SS	1968
	6916th Scty Sq	1973
Iraklion, Crete	Det 2, 34th RSM	1954-55
	6938th RSM*	1955-58
* 6930th RGM, Wheelus,	6930th RGM*	1958-63
Libya, exchanged unit	6931st Scty Gp	1963-73
designators with 6938th	6931st Scty Sq	1974
RSM, Crete, in 1958.	6931st AB Sq	1974-78
San Vito, Italy	6917th RSM	1960-61
	6917th RGM	1961-63
	6917th Scty Gp	1963-78
	6917th Scty Sq	1974
	6917th AB Sq	1974-78
Pepperell AFB,	Det 4, 36th CSS	1953-55
Newfoundland	6986th Comm Scty Flt	1955-56
	Det 10, 6982d RSM	1956
	Det 7, 6936th CSS	1956
	6986th Scty Flt	1956-58
Red Cliff AC&W Site,	Det 10, 6982d RSM	1955-56
Newfoundland		

1021

Karachi, Pakistan	OL 2, 6937th CG	1960-61
	Det 2, 6937th CG	1961-65
Peshawar, Pakistan	Comm Flt, Provisional	1958
	6937th Scty Flt, Prov	1958
	6937th Comm Flt	1958
	6937th Comm Gp	1958-70
Wheelus Field, Tripoli,	34th RSM	1951-55
Libya	6930th Scty Gp	1953-56
	Det 4, 31st CSS	1953-55
	Det 2, 34th RSM	1954
	6934th RSM	1955-56
	Det 4, 6931st CSS	1955-56
	6930th RGM*	1956-58
	6938th RSM*	1958-60
Adana, Turkey	OL 2, 6933d RGM	1959-60
	Det 1, 6916th RSM	1960-63
	Det 1, 6916th SS	1963-64
Ankara, Turkey	Det 1, 75th RSM*	1953
	Det 1, 14th RSM	1953
* Unit began operations as	Flt A, 34th RSM	1953-54
Project PENN in the Joint	Det 1, 34th RSM	1954-55
American Military Mission	6933d RSM	1955-56
for Aid to Turkey	6933d RGM	1956-57
(JAMMAT) area in Ankara	OL 8, 6970th SG	1968-70
in late 1951.	OL 1W, 6970th SG	1970-71
	OL FH, 6970th SG	1971-72
	OL FH, 6970th ABG	1972-75
	OL FH, 6933d SG	1976-77
	OL FH, 6917th SG	1977-78
	OL FH, Det 1, HQ AFSS	1973
Diyarbakir, Turkey	Det 3, 34th RSM	1955
	Det 4, 6933d RSM	1955-56
	Det 4, 6933d RGM	1956-58
	6935th RSM	1958-63
Incirlik AB, Turkey	Det 1, 6933d SG	1970-71
Karamursel, Turkey	6933d RGM	1957-62
	6933d Spt Gp	1962-69
* TUSLOG Det 94-1	6933d Scty Wg	1962-70
	6933d Scty Gp	1970-77
** TUSLOG Det 94-2	6933d SS*	1974-77
	6933d ABS**	1974-77
Samsun, Turkey	OL 1, Flt A, 34th RSM	1953-54
	OL 1, Det 1, 34th RSM	1955-55
* TUSLOG Det 3-2	Det 2, 6933d RSM	1955-56
	Det 2, 6933d RGM	1956-58
	6932d RSM	1958-63
	6932d Scty Sq	1963-64
	6932d SG*	1964-70

Sue, Turkey	Det 3, 6933d RGM	1955-58
Sinop, Turkey * TUSLOG Det 204	6934th SS*	1970-77
Trabzon, Turkey * TUSLOG Det 3-1	OL 2, Flt A, 34th RSM	1953-54
	OL 2, Det 1, 34th RSM	1954-55
	Det 1, 6933d RSM	1955-56
	Det 1, 6933d RGM	1956-58
	6939th RSM*	1958-63
	6939th Scty Sq	1963-70
Andersen AFB, Guam	Det 2, 6926th RSM	1956
Midway Island	Det 8, 6926th RSM	1955-56
Wake Island	Det 3, 6926th RSM	1955-56
Ashiya AB, Japan	Det 12, 1st RSM	1950-52
	15th RSM	1951-55
	6922d RSM	1955-56
	6922d RGM	1956-59
Camp Zama, Japan	OL 10, 6970th SG	1968-70
	OL JJ, 6970th SG	1970-71
	OL FJ, 6970th SG	1971-72
	OL FJ, 6970th ABG	1972-75
	Det 74, 6921st SW	1976
	Det 74, 6920th SW	1978
	OL FJ, 6920th SS	1978
Chitose AB, Hokkaido, Japan	Flt A, 6920th SG	1953-54
	Det 7, 6926th RSM	1955-56
Fuchu AB, Japan	32d Comm Scty Sq	1956
	6932d Comm Scty Flt	1956-58
	Det 2, 6920th SW	1957-58
	6988th Scty Flt	1953-59
	6988th RSM	1959-63
	Det 1, 6988th RSM	1963
	Det 1, 6988th SS	1963-69
Fukaura, Japan	Det 4, 6921st RGM	1956
Hakata ADM, Japan	6918th RSM	1958-63
	6918th Scty Sq	1963-72
Johnson AB, Japan	1st RSM	1949-53
	6920th Scty Gp	1951-54
	Flt B, 6920th SG	1953-54
	Flt C, 6920th SG	1953-54
Kamiseya City, Japan	Det 2, 6988th RSM	1961-62
	OL FX, 6970th ABG	1974-75
	OL FX, 6921st SW	1976
	OL FX, 6920th SW	1977
Makubetsu, Japan	OL 1, 6986th RSM	1961
	Det 1, 6986th RSM	1961-62
	Det 1, 6986th RGM	1962-63
	Det 1, 6986th SG	1963-64

Misawa AB, Japan	Det 11, 1st RSM	1951-53
	Flt B, 1st RSM	1952-54
	1st RSM	1953-55
	6921st RSM	1955-56
	6921st RGM	1956-62
	6989th RSM	1958-63
	6989th Spt Sq	1958-63
	6921st SW	1962-70
	6989th Scty Sq	1963-64
	6989th Spt Sq	1964-69
	6921st Spt Sq	1969-70
	6921st Scty Gp	1970-72
	6920th AB Sq	1972
	6921st Scty Wg	1972-76
	6920th ABG	1972-78
	6920th Scty Gp	1974-78
	6920th Scty Wg	1976-78
	6920th Civil Engr Sq	1977-78
	6920th ABG	1977-78
	6920thScty Sq	1978
Nagoya, Japan	Det 1, 32d CSS	1953-55
	Det 1, 6932d CSS	1955-56
Nemuro, Japan	Det 1, 1st RSM	1954-55
	Det 1, 6921st RGM	1955-57
Obu AB, Japan	Det 3, 6922d RGM	1956-57
Okushiri Shima, Japan	Det 3, 1st RSM	1954-55
	Det 3, 6921st RGM	1956-57
Shiroi AB, Japan	Flt E, 6920th SG	1953-54
	Flt A, 84th RSM	1953-54
	84th RSM	1954-55
	6920th Scty Gp	1954-55
	6920th Scty Wg	1955-58
	6902d Spec Comm Gp	1955-59
	6924th RSM	1955-56
	Det 1, 6926th PSM	1955-56
	6926th RSM	1955-56
	6903d Comm Sq	1956-57
	Det 4, 6921st RGM	1956-57
Tachikawa AB, Japan	OL 2, 6988th RSM	1961
	Det 3, 6988th SS	1961-65
Tokyo, Japan	6971st Comm Scty Flt	1950-53
	32d Comm Scty Sq	1953-56
	6932d Comm Scty Sq	1955-56
	6932d Comm Scty Flt	1955-58

Wakkanai, Japan	Det 12, 1st RSM	1951-52
	Flt A,1st RSM	1952-54
	Ops B, Det 11, 1st RSM	1952-55
	Det 2,1st RSM	1953-55
	Det 2, 6921st RSM	1955-58
	Det 2, 6921st RGM	1956-58
	6986th RSM	1958-62
	6986th RGM	1962-63
	6986th Scty Gp	1963-72
Yamato AS, Japan	OL 2, 6920th SW	1961-62
	Det 1, Pac Scty Rgn	1961-64
Yokosuka, Japan	6905th Scty Flt	1952
Yokota, Japan	Det 1, 6924th RSM	1955-56
	Det 1, 6903d Comm Sq	1956-57
	Det 1, 6920th SW	1957-58
	OL 1, 6988th Scty Flt	1958-59
	Det 1, 6988th RSM	1959-63
	6988th RSM	1963
	6988th Scty Sq	1963-72
Osan AB, Korea	Det, 15th RSM	1953-58
	6929th RSM	1958-63
	6929th Scty Sq	1963-64
	Det 1, 6922d SW	1964-70
	OL 1, 6988th SS	1969-70
	6903d Scty Sq	1970
	Det 1, Pac Scty Rgn	1970
	OL AA, 6988th SS	1970-71
	OL EA, 6988th SS	1971-72
Osan Ni, Korea	Det 2, 32d CSS	1953-55
	Det 1, 6922 RGM	1956-58
Paengnyong-do, Korea	Det 3, 15th RSM	1953-55
	Det 2, 6922d RGM	1956-58
Pyong'taek, Korea	Det 6, 6926th RSM	1955-56
	OL BB, 6903d SS	1971
	OL DB, 6903d SS	1971-72
Seoul, Korea	Det, 1st RSM	1951-52
	Det, 15th RSM	1952-53
Taegu, Korea	Det, 1st RSM*	1950-51
* Det C, 1st RSM, Jan '51	Det 1, 15th RSM	1952-55
Naha AB, Okinawa	Det 3, 32d CSS	1953-55
	Det 3, 6932d CSS	1955-56
Onna Point, Okinawa	6927th Scty Flt	1956
	6927th RSM	1956-63
	6927th Scty Sq	1963-65
	6927th Scty Gp	1965-71
Sobe City, Okinawa	Det 2, 6927th SG	1965-67

Kadena AB, Okinawa	Det 1, 29th RSM	1955
	6927th Scty Flt	1955-56
	6927th RSM	1956
	6902d Spec Comm Gp	1959
	6922d RGM	1959-62
	OL 1, Kadena AB	1961
	Det 1, 6927th RSM	1961-63
	6922d Scty Wg	1962-65
	Det 1, 6927th SG	1963-71
	6990th Scty Sq	1967-71
	OL 3, 6927th SG	1968-70
	6990th Scty Gp	1971-74
	6905th Scty Sq	1972-75
	6990th Scty Sq	1974
	6928th Scty Sq	1974-76
Torii Station, Okinawa	OL 1, 6927th SG	1967-68
	OL 5, 6970th SG	1968-70
	6971st Spt Sq	1970-71
	OL RR, 6970th SG	1971
	OL FR, 6970th SG	1971-72
Yontan, Okinawa	Det 152, 15th RSM	1952-53
	Det 2, 15th RSM	1953
	Flt C, 15th RSM	1953
	Flt A, 29th RSM	1953-54
	Det 1, 6929th RSM	1953-55
	Det 5, 6926th RSM	1955-56
	6927th Scty Flt	1955-56
Clark AB, Philippines	29th RSM	1952-55
	Det 3, 29th RSM	1954-55
	6925th RSM	1955-56
	Det 4, 6926th RSM	1955-56
	Det 1, 6932d CSS	1955-56
	6925th RGM	1956-58
	Det 2, 6925th RGM	1957
	6925th RSM	1958-62
	6925th RGM	1962-65
	6926th Scty Sq (M)	1963-74
	6922d Spt Sq	1965-70
	6922d Scty Wg	1965-70
	Det 4, AFCD	1966-70
	6922d Scty Gp	1970-74
	6922d Scty Sq	1974
San Miguel, Philippines	Det 1, 6925th RGM	1962
Tarumpitao, Philippines	Det 2, 29th RSM	1954-55
	Det 2, 6925th RSM	1955
Chiayi AB, Taiwan	OL 3, 6987th RSM	1960-61
	Det 3, 6987th RGM	1961-63
	Det 3, 6987th SG	1963-67

Nan-Szu-Pu, Taiwan	Det 3, 29th RSM	1954-55
	Det 1, 6925th RGM	1955-58
Shu Lin Kou AS, Taiwan	6987th RSM	1958-62
	6987th RGM	1962-63
	6987th Scty Gp	1963-77
	6987th Scty Sq	1974-77
	6987th AB Sq	1974-77
Taichung, Taiwan	OL 2, 6987th RSM	1960-61
	Det 2, 6987th RGM	1961-63
	Det 2, 6987th SG	1963-67
	OL 2, 6987th SG	1967-70
Taipei City, Taiwan	OL 1, 6987th RSM	1960-61
	Det 1, 6987th RGM	1961-63
	Det 1, 6987th SG	1963-67
	OL 1, 6987th SG	1967-70
	OL 12, 6970th SG	1968-70
	OL 4, 6987th SG	1969-70
	OL LL, 6970th SG	1970-71
	OL DO, 6987th SG	1970-72
	OL FL, 6970th SG	1971-72
	OL FL, 6970th ABG	1972-75
	OL FL, 6987th SG	1976-77
	OL FL, 6922d SS	1977
Bangkok Cy, Thailand	Det 3, 6923d RSM	1962-63
	6923d Scty Sq	1963
	Det 3, 6925th SG	1963-65
	Det 3, 6922d SW	1965-67
	OL 11, 6970th SG	1968-70
	OL KK, 6970th SG	1970-71
	OL FK, 6970th SG	1971-72
	OL FK, 6970th ABG	1972-75
	OL FK, 6924th SS	1976
	OL FK, 6922d SS	1976-78
Ko Kha AFS, Thailand	6300 Spt Sq	1971-72
	6300 Aerospace Spt Sq	1972-75
Korat Royal Thai Air Base, Thailand	Det 7, 6922d SW	1966-70
	OL 1, 6990th SS	1968-70
	OL BA, 6990th SS	1972-73
	OL BA, 6908th SS	1973-74
Nakhon Phanom, Thailand	Det 3, 6994th SS	1969-72
	OL AA, 6990th SS	1971
	6908th Scty Sq	1971-75
	OL NA, 6994th SS	1974
	6994th Scty Sq	1972-74
Ramasun Station, Thailand	6924th Scty Sq	1971-76
	6908th Scty Sq	1975
Ubon AFD, Thailand	Det 2, 6923d RSM*	1962-63
* Unit activated on paper,	6994th Scty Sq	1974
but not staffed.	Det 3, 6994th SS	1972-74

Udorn, Thailand	Det 4, 6922d SW	1965
	Det 4, Pac Scty Rgn	1965-71
Cam Ranh Bay, South Vletnam	OL 1, 6994th SS	1968-69
	OL 2, 6990th SS	1969-70
	Det 1, 6990th SS	1970-71
DaNang, South Vietnam	Team 1A, 6922d RSM	1962
	Det 1, 6923d RSM	1962-63
	Det 2, 6925th RGM	1963-65
	Det 2, 6922d SW	1965
	6924th Scty Sq	1965-71
	Det 2, 6994th SS	1970-73
Monkey Mountain, South Vietnam	Ops Site, 6924th SS	1962-69
	OL 1, 6924th SS	1969-70
	Monkey Mtn Ops Branch	1970-71
	OL AA, 6924th SS	1971-73
Nha Trang Field, Vietnam	Det 1, 6994th SS	1966-69
Phu Cat AB, Vietnam	Det 1, 6994th SS	1969-71
Pleiku Airport, Vietnam	Det 2, 6994th SS	1966-70
Tan Son Nhut AB, South Vietnam	6923d RSM	1962
	6923d Scty Sq	1962-63
	Det 5, 6922d SW	1965
	6994th Scty Sq	1966-72
	OL 4, 6970th SG	1967-70
	OL 1, Pac Scty Rgn	1968-70
	OL DO, 6970th SG	1970-71
	OL AA, Pac Scty Rgn	1970-71
	OL FD, 6970th SG	1971-72
	OL FD, 6970th ABG	1972-73
	OL LA, 6994th SS	1972-73
Adak, Alaska	Flt A, 3d RSM	1950-54
	Det 1, 6981st SG	1964-67
Eielson AFB, Alaska	OL 1, 6981st RGM	1960-61
	Det 1, 6981st RGM	1961-62
	6985th RSM	1962-63
	6985th Scty Sq	1963
Ladd AFB, Alaska	Det 1 , 6985th CSF	1955-56
Naknek AFB (King Salmon Airport), Alaska	Det 3, 3d RSM	1951-55
	Det 2, 6981st RGM	1955-57
Nome, Alaska	Flt B, 3d RSM	1950-53
	Det 2, 3d RSM	1953
Northeast Cape, Alaska	Det 2, 3d RSM	1953-55
	Det 1, 6981st RSM	1955-60
	6980th RSM	1960-63
	6980th Scty Sq	1963-67
Point Barrow, Alaska	Det 4, 6981st RGM	1956-58

Elmendorf AFB, Alaska	3d RSM	1950-55
	Det 2, 3d RSM	1950-55
	6973d Comm Scty Flt	1951-53
	Det I, 36th CSS	1953-54
	Det 8, 36th CSS	1954-55
	6985th Comm Scty Flt	1955-58
	6981st RSM	1955-56
	Det 10, 6926th RSM	1955-56
	6981st RGM	1956-63
	6981st Scty Gp	1963-74
	OL 4, 6960th SG	1968
	Det 2, 6960 Spt Gp	1968-71
	Det 1, AFCOMSECCEN	1972-75
	6981st Scty Sq	1974
	OL FF, 6981st SS	1977
Shemya AFB, Alaska	Det 9, 6926th RSM	1955-56
	Det 3, 6981st RGM	1956-60
	6984th RSM	1960-63
	6984th Scty Sq	1963-74
	OL FW, 6970th ABG	1974-75
	Det 1, 6981st SS	1974
	OL FW, 6981st SS	1976
Wildwood Army Installation, Alaska	OL 2, 6981st RGM	1958-60
	Det 2, 6981st SG	1958-64
	Det 2, 6981st RGM	1961
Beale AFB, California	Det 2, 6949th SS	1966-69
	OL 1, 6949th SS	1969
McClellan AFB, California	Det J, 136th RSS	1950-51
	Det 9, 136th CSS	1951-53
	Flt F, 36th CSS	1953-54
	Det 6, 36th CSS	1954-55
	Det 5, 6936th CSS	1955-56
	Det 1, 6982d RSM	1956-59
	Det 2, AFSCC	1959-68
March AFB, California	Det 1, 26th RSM	1953
	26th RSM	1953-55
	Det 7, 36th CSS	1953-55
	Det 6, 6936th CSS	1955-56
	6983d RSM	1955-57
	USAFSS School	1956-57
	6941st Spt Sq	1957-58
	6940th TTG	1957-58
	6942d School Sq	1957-58
	6943d Student Sq	1957-58
Mather AFB, California	Det 1, 8th RSM	1954-55

Ottawa, Canada	Det 1, 6961st CS	1958-60
	OL 17, 6970th SG	1968-69
Buckley ANGB, Aurora, Colorado	OL 2, 6970th SG	1970
	OL DB, 6970th SG	1970-71
	OL FB, 6970th SG	1971-72
	OL FB, 6970th ABG	1972-75
	Det 73, 6970th ABG	1976
Corry Field, Florida * OL LA, USAF School of Applied Cryptologic Sciences	OL 1, 6940th TTG	1967-70
	OL AA, 6940th TTG	1970-73
	OL LA, *	1973-75
	6945th School Sq	1975-78
Cudjoe Key, Florida * 6947th RSM, 1 Jun '63	OL 1 (aka ERU-1)*	1962-63
	6947th SS	1963-70
Eglin AFB, Florida	Det 5, AFSCC	1967-70
	OL CF, HQ AFEWC	1975
	OL GJ, 6960th ABS	1977
Homestead AFB, Florida	Det 1, 6947th SS	1968-70
	6947th Scty Sq	1970
Key West Naval Air Station, Florida	6947th Scty Sq	1963-70
	OL 1, 6947th SS	1970
	OL BB, 6947th SS	1970
MacDill AFB, Florida *** Det 3, AFSCC moved from MacDill to Orlando AFB on 30 June 1960.**	Det C, 136th RSS	1950-51
	Det 3, 136th CSS	1951-53
	Flt B, 36th CSS	1953-54
	Det 2, 36th CSS	1954-55
	Det 2, 6936th CSS	1955-56
	Det 10, 6982d RSM	1956-59
	Det 3, AFSCC*	1959-60
	Det 1, 6945th RSM Prov.	1962
	Det 1, 6945th RSM	1962-63
	Det 1, 6947th SS	1963-70
	OL QB, 6970th ABG	1975
Orlando AFB, Florida	Det 3, AFSCC	1960-68
Pensacola, Florida	Det 2, 6940th TTG	1963-64
Wheeler AFB, Hawaii	6920th Scty Wg	1958-62
	Pac Scty Rgn	1962-72
	Det 4, 6960th SG	1970-71
	6902d Spt Sq	1970-71
	OL AG, HQ USAFSS	1973
	Det 4, 6961st Spt Sq	1971-72
Brunswick NAS, Maine	Det 8, 8th RSM	1954-55
	Det 8, 6982d RSM	1955-57
Baltimore, Maryland	Det 1, 6949th SS	1965-67

Hickam AFB, Hawaii	Det E, 136th RSS	1949-51
	Det 5, 136th CSS	1951-53
	Flt F, 32d CSS	1953-54
	6975th Comm Scty Flt	1953
	Det 4, 32d CSS	1954-56
	Det 1, 6902d SCG	1955-57
	Det 1, 6920th SW	1955
	Det 4, 6932d CSS	1955-56
	Det 1, 6932d CSF	1956-57
	6928th Scty Flt	1958-59
	6928th Comm Scty Flt	1959-60
	Det 1, 6985th COMSEC Depot Gp	1960-63
	Det 2, Pac Scty Rgn	1962-67
	Det 2, 6936th COMSEC Depot Gp	1963
	Det 2, AFCD	1964-67
	OL KA, AFCOMSECCEN	1972-78
	OL AG, HQ USAFSS	1973-78
	OL GG, 6960th ABS	1973-78
	OL CE, HQ AFEWC	1974-78
	OL FB, 6970th ABG	1977-78
	Det 2, HQ USAFSS	1978
Fort George G. Meade, Maryland	Det 3, 136th CSS	1943-53
	Det 1, 136th CSS	1944-53
	Det 4, 136th CSS	1944-53
	Det 5, 136th CSS	1944-53
	Det 6, 136th CSS	1944-53
	Det 7, 136th CSS	1944-53
	Det 3, 6969th Spt Sq	1954-55
	6971st Spt Sq	1955-62
	Det 1, 6970th Spt Sq	1957
	6970th Spt Gp	1957-72
	OL BB, 6948th SS (M)	1971-73
	6970th ABG	1972
	OL EB, 6948th SS (M)	1973-77
	6971st Scty Sq	1976
	6972d Scty Sq	1976
	6973d Scty Sq	1976
	6974th Scty Sq	1976
	Det 1, 6948th SS (M)	1977
	Det 3, HQ USAFSS	1979
Suitland Hall, Suitland, Maryland	6972d Spt Sq	1955-62
	6973d Spt Sq	1955-56

Fort Devens, Mass.	Det 4, 6960th SG	1962-66
	Det 1, 6940th TTG	1966-68
* OL LB, USAF School of	OL 2, 6940th TTG	1968-70
Applied Cryptologic	OL BB, 6940th TTG	1970-73
Sciences	OL LB, *	1973-78
Hanscom Field, Mass.	Det 1, 6960th SG	1961-67
	OL 1, 6960th SG	1967-70
	OL AA, 6960th SG	1970-71
Westover AFB, Mass.	Det 4, AFSCC	1965-68
Kinross AFB, Michigan	Det 6, 8th RSM	1954-55
	Det 6, 6982d RSM	1955-57
Keesler AFB, Mississippi	OL 3, 6960th SG	1961
	Det 3, 6960th SG	1961-66
* OL LD, USAF School of	OL GA, 6960th SG	1971
Applied Cryptologic	OL GA, 6960th ABS	1971-74
Sciences	OL LD, *	1974-78
	OL GK, 6960th ABS	1978
Malmstrom AFB, Montana	Det 3, 6982d RSM	1956-57
Offutt AFB, Nebraska	Det 1, 6940th SW	1963-65
	6949th Scty Sq	1965-75
* OL LE, USAF School of	Det 6, AFSCC	1970-75
Applied Cryptologic	OL 1, 6948th SS (M)	1970
Sciences	OL AA, 6948th SS (M)	1970
	OL 1, 6948th SS (M)	1970
	OL AA, 6948th SS (M)	1970-73
	OL EA, 6948th SS (M)	1973-78
	6944th Scty Wg	1974-79
	Det 6, AFEWC	1975-78
	OL AH, HQ USAFSS	1976-79
	OL CG, AFEWC	1978
	OL FE, 6944th SW	1978-79
	OL LE, *	1978
	6949th Scty Sq	1979
	OL FE, 6949th SS	1979
Griffiss AFB, New York	OL 2, 6960th SG	1961
	Det 2, 6960th SG	1961-64
	Det 5, 6960th SG	1965-67
	OL 2, 6960th SG	1967-70
Lockport AFS, New York	Det 7, 6982d RSM	1955-57
Montauk AFS, New York	Det 9, 8th RSM	1954-55
Shawnee, New York	Det 7, 8th RSM	1954-55
Suffolk County AFB, NY	Det 9, 6982d RSM	1955-57
Ellsworth AFB, SD	Det 4, 6982d RSM	1955-57

Brooks AFB, Texas	HQ&HQ Sq USAFSS	1949-51
	8th RSM	1949-55
	136th Radio Scty Sq	1949-51
	3d RSM	1949-50
	10th RSM	1949-50
	Det J, 136th RSS	1950
	12th RSM	1950-51
	Det B, HQ&HQ Sq AFSS	1950
	6923d Pers Proc Sq	1950-53
	Det B, 3d RSM	1950
	Det 9, 136th CSS	1950-53
	Det 10, 136th CSS	1950-53
	Det 11, 136th CSS	1950-53
	Det 12, 136th CSS	1950-53
	Det 13, 136th CSS	1950-53
	Det 14, 136th CSS	1950-53
	Det 15, 136th CSS	1950-53
	HQ USAFSS	1951-53
	136th Comm Scty Sq	1951-53
	6960th SG	1951-53
	26th RSM	1951-53
	41st RSM	1951
	34th RSM	1951
	37th RSM	1951-52
	15th RSM	1951
	HQ Sq Sec, USAFSS	1951-53
	6910th Scty Gp	1951
	Det 13, 1st RSM	1951-52
	14th RSM	1951-53
	6961st Comm Sq	1952-53
	29th RSM	1952
	Det 1, 6923d PPS	1952-54
	Det 2, 6923d PPS	1952-54
	Det 3, 6923d PPS	1952-54
	6963d Air Police Sq	1953
	6962d Comm Scty Cen	1953
	6961st Spec Comm Cen	1953
	6950th Scty Gp	1953-56
	Det 1, 36th CSS	1953-55
	75th RSM	1953
	84th RSM	1953-55
	6982d RSM	1955-59
	Det 1, 6936th CSS	1955-56
	Det 1, AFSCC	1959-70
	Det 6, 6960th SG	1970-71
	Det 6, 6960th ABS	1971-72
	6906th Scty Sq	1972-75
	OL EE, 6948th SS (M)	1975-77
	6906th Scty Sq	1977

Kelly AFB, Texas	26th RSM	1951-53
	Det 1, 6960th SG	1952
	Det 4, 6923d PPS	1952-54
	HQ USAFSS	1953-79
	AF Spec Comm Cen	1953-75
	136th Comm Scty Sq	1953
	36th Comm Scty Sq	1953-55
	6960th Spt Gp	1953-55
	6961st Comm Sq	1953-63
	6963d Air Police Sq	1953-66
* 6940th Tech Training Wg	USAFSS School *	1953-56
	85th RSM	1953-54
	AF Comm Sec Cen	1953-56
	6962d Supply Sq	1953-61
	6965th Spt Sq	1953-56
	6901st Spec Comm Cen	1953
	6902d Comm Scty Cen	1953
	6923d Pers Proc Sq	1953
	6966th Tech Tng Sq	1954-56
	6936th Comm Scty Sq	1955-60
	6960th Spt Gp	1955-71
	6926th RSM	1955
	6966th Student Sq	1956-57
	HQ Sq Sec, HQ AFSS	1956-57
	6936th CSEC Depot Gp	1960-64
	6946th Student Sq	1962-63
	6946th School Sq	1962-64
	Det 1, 6940th TTW	1963-64
	HQ AFCD	1964
	Det 1, 6960th SG	1968-71
	6960th AB Sq	1971
	OL 5, 6960th SG	1968
	OL 1, Eur Scty Rgn	1968-70
	OL M, Eur Scty Rgn	1970-71
	6961st Spt Sq	1971-79
	OL BA, 6900th ABS	1971-72
	Det 1, 6961st SS (MET)	1971-72
	AF COM SEC CEN	1972
	OL GB, 6960th ABS	1972-75
	6964th Computer Svc Sq	1972
	6948th Scty Sq (M)	1973
	6962d Mgt Engr Flt	1973
	OL ED, 6948th SS (M)	1973
	6955th Scty Gp	1974-75
	6926th Scty Sq (M)	1974
	AFEWC	1975
	OL TA, 6944th SW	1976-79
	OL HE, 6911th SS (M)	1977-78
	OL TA, 6949th SS	1979

Medina Annex, Lackland AFB, Texas	6993d Scty Sq OL DB, 6906th SS	1967 1977
Goodfellow AFB, Texas * USAF School of Applied Cryptologic Sciences	USAFSS School 6966th Tech Tng Sq 6966th Student Sq 6941st Student Sq 6942d Student Sq 6943d Student Sq 6944th Student Sq 6940th AB Wg 6940th TTG 6940th Tech Tng Wg 6945th Scty Sq 6942d School Sq 6943d School Sq 6944th School Sq 6941st School Sq 6940th A.B Gp 6940th Tech Tng Sq 6948th Scty Sq (M) 6940th Scty Wg 6940th Spt Gp Det 3, 6960th SG USAF Disp./Hospital Det 3, 6961st SS (MET) USAF School of * USAF Clinic, Goodfellow OL GL, 6960th ABS	1953-58 1954-56 1956-57 1958-63 1958-63 1958-63 1958-63 1958-60 1958-60 1965-73 1960-63 1961-65 1963-75 1963-72 1963-72 1963-78 1963-64 1972-78 1963-65 1963-73 1963-78 1964-72 1970-71 1971-75 1971-72 1973 1975 1978
Hill AFB, Ogden, Utah	6984th Comm Scty Flt 6985th CSEC Depot Sq Det 3, AFCD OL MA, AFCD	1958-60 1960-63 1965-73 1973
Arlington Hall Station, Virginia	HQ&HQ Sq USAFSS 136th Radio Scty Det Det A, HQ&HQ Sq AFSS 6969th Armed Forces Spt Sq 6969th Spt Sq 6970th Spt Gp 6974th Spt Sq	1948-49 1949 1949-49 1950-50 1950-53 1953-55 1955-57 1960-64
Washington, DC	36th Comm Scty Sq Det 1, 6969th Spt Sq Flt C (SSO), 6969th SS Det 1 (NSA), 6969th SS Det 2, 6969th Spt Sq Det 1, 6970th SG OL 3, 6970th SG	1942-55 1953 1953 1953-55 1954-55 1965 1965-68

Fort Myer, Virginia	6973d Spt Sq	1956-58
Vint Hill Farms Station, Virginia	8th RSM	1947-49 1949
Langley AFB, Virginia	Det H, 136th RSM	1950-51
	Det 8, 136th CSS	1951-53
	Flt C, 36th CSS	1953-54
	Det 3, 36th CSS	1954-55
	Det 3, 6936th CSS	1955-56
	Det 11, 6982d RSM	1956-59
	Det 4, AFSCC	1959-65
	OL 3, 6960th SG	1968-70
	OL CC, 6960th SG	1970-71
	OL CD, AFSCC	1974-75
	OL AE, HQ USAFSS (USAFSS/CR Langley)	1975
	OL GH, 6960th ABS	1976-78
McChord AFB, Washington	Det 2, 136th CSS	1944-53
	Det 5, 36th CSS	1953-55
	Det 2, 8th RSM	1954-55
	Det 2, 6982d RSM	1955-57
	Det 4, 6936th CSS	1955-56
Osceola AFS, Wisconsin	Det 5, 8th RSM	1954-55
	Det 5, 6982d RSM	1955-57

APPENDIX C—2ND RSM
SPECIAL INSPECTION, MAY 1944

*********EXTRACT COPY***********EXTRACT COPY********

HEADQUARTERS OF THE ARMY AIR FORCES
WASHINGTON 25, DC

Office of
The Field Air Inspector,
National Guard Armory
Tampa, Florida

6 May 1944

SUBJECT: Report of Special Inspection of the 2d Radio
Squadron Mobile (German), MacDill Field, Florida

TO: Commanding General, Army Air Forces,
Washington, 25, D. C.,
Attention: The Air Inspector

AUTHORITY

1. This special inspection was conducted at MacDill Field, Florida, 1 May 1944, by Major Thomas Eistrat, Air Corps, Pursuant to request of the AC/AS Training, HQ AAF under authority of AAF regulation 120-1.

3. The background of the 2d Radio Squadron Mobile (German), is as follows:

    a.   The 139th Signal Radio Intelligence Company was activated at MacDill Field, Fla., 14 Feb 1943 with a cadre of 13 enlisted men transferred from the 402d Signal Company Aviation.

4.

    a.   In November 1943, the unit was designated as a (German) unit and training along the new lines was undertaken.

    b.   The 139th and 952d Radio Intelligence Companies were reorganized in March 1944 to form the 2d and 4th Radio Squadrons, Mobile, German. The 954th Signal Radio Intelligence Company was disbanded and personnel transferred to the 2d and 4th Radio Squadrons, Mobile, German. On 16 March 1944, the 139th Sig Rad Intelligence Company was reorganized under T/O & E 1-1027, 25 January 1944, as the 2d Radio Squadron Mobile.

IV. RECOMMENDATIONS

5. That the 2d Radio Squadron Mobile (German) be immediately transferred to the European Theater for further training.

For the Field Air Inspector:

THOMAS EISTRAT
Major, Air Corps
Field Air Inspector

APPENDIX D—REORGANIZATION OF 2ND RSM, DECEMBER 1945

HEADQUARTERS
U.S. FORCES, EUROPEAN THEATER

(MAIN) APO 757
13 December 1945

AG 322 GCT-AGO

SUBJECT: Reorganization of Second Army Air Forces Radio Squadron

TO: Commanding General, U.S. Air Forces in Europe

1. It is requested that your headquarters take the necessary action to reorganize the Second Army Air Forces Radio Squadron Mobile at strength of 17 Officers and 285 enlisted men composed of the following columns, current edition Table of Organization and Equipment 1-1027, one each of columns 5, 6, 7, 8, 9, 11, 12, 15, 18, 19, 22, 26, and three each of column 24.

2. Additional personnel required by this action will be obtained from sources made available to you. Personnel reported surplus will be reported to your headquarters for disposition.

3. Unit morning report will contain the appropriate remarks prescribed in Section IV, AR 345-400, dated 1 May 1944.

4. Upon completion of reorganization, this headquarters request that subject unit be transferred to Headquarters, Army Security Agency.

5. Twenty-six copies of orders issued will be furnished this headquarters.

Auth: War Department Cable WX-65712 dated 29 November 1945.

BY COMMAND OF GENERAL McNARNEY

T.W. GUPTILL
Capt., AGD
Assistant Adjutant G.

Dist: G-3
        G-4
        AG Opns) O & E
        AG Records
        HQ ASA (Attn Col. Cook)

APPENDIX E—ORDERS, TRANSFER OF 2ND RSM TO USAF, FEB 1949

HEADQUARTERS
US ARMY   APO 66 Unit 1

GENERAL ORDERS   10 February 1949
NUMBER   2
            EXTRACT   EXTRACT

DEPARTMENTAL TRANSFER OF 2D RADIO SQUADRON MOBILE

1.   Confirming verbal orders of the Commanding Officer, effective 1 February 1949, 2d Radio Squadron Mobile, APO 66 Unit 1, US Army, is transferred from the Department of the Army to the Department of the Air Force and is further assigned to the United States Air Force Security Service. Department of the Army personnel currently assigned to this unit are hereby assigned to the Department of the Air Force for further assignment with that unit.

No change in status, duty assignment or departmental status of personnel is involved.

2.   All equipment authorized this unit by Table of Equipment and Emergency Modification List will accompany unit on transfer. Authorized items of equipment will be requisitioned through Theater Air Force Channels. Non-authorized or special items will be requisitioned direct from Headquarters, United States Air Force Security Service.

3.   AUTHORITY: Letter, Departments of the Army and the Air Force, file AGAO-1 370.5 (28 January 1949) and AFOOR 370.5 (101 Frank), Subject: "Transfer of First, Second and Eighth Radio Squadrons, Mobile and 136th Radio Security Detachment," dated 28 January 1949 as amended; Cable WX-83764, Headquarters, Department of the Army, dated 4 February 1949; Cable XF-531 Army Security Agency (60), dated 9 February 1949; Verbal instructions, Major Callaway, OPOT Division, Headquarters, European Command, o/a 5 February 1949.

BY ORDER OF MAJOR SCHAUERS:

OFFICIAL: THOMAS L GALE
                          CAPT   AGD
                          ADJUTANT

APPENDIX F—2ND RSM MOVEMENT DIRECTIVE, FEB 1949

MOVEMENT DIRECTIVE

Commanding Officer
2d Radio Squadron Mobile
APO 66, US Army

1. Pursuant to authority contained in AFSS 12, 9 Feb 49 Ecgot SX-1649, HQ EUCOM, 24 Feb 49, and EUCOM Circular 142, 26 Oct 1948, it is desired that you take without delay the action for which you are responsible to move the 2d Radio Squadron Mobile from Herzo Base, Herzogenaurach, Germany, to Darmstadt, Germany.

2. Date of Movement: Effective on or about 26 Feb 1949.

3. Change of Station: This movement will constitute a PERMANENT change of station.

4. Allowances of Clothing & Equipment to Accompany Unit Movement:
   a. Clothing and individual equipment as prescribed in EUCOM Circular 151, cs.
   b. All items of organizational equipment currently in possession of subject unit that is authorized under appropriate columns of T/O & E 32-1027.

5. Method of Movement: Movement will be effected by vehicles organically assigned to the 2d Radio Squadron Mobile.

6. Other Instructions: Map coordinates of Darmstadt, Germany: 49° 52'N 8° 40'E.

   b. Movement of dependents to Darmstadt will be contingent upon availability of quarters thereat and approval of the Commanding Officer thereof.
   c. APO 175, C/O Postmaster, New York, will service unit at new destination.

No per diem is authorized for this movement.

BY COMMAND OF LIEUTENANT GENERAL CANNON:

TEL: WIESBADEN 7401

Capt. Samson 7401
Organization Sec
25 Feb 1949

APPENDIX G-1—2ND RSM OFFICER ASSIGNMENTS, AUG 1949

HEADQUARTERS
2D RADIO SQUADRON MOBILE
APO 175   US ARMY

SPECIAL ORDERS)   11 August 1949
NUMBER   70)

1. Fol named officers this HQ are trfd fr DA to DAF UP JAARAR 1-1-2, 1947. Aprop Cs of indiv recs will be made to reflect new departmental status.

NAME	RANK	AFSN	EFF DATE
WYATT E. HINES	1ST LT	AO1633276	25 Jul 49
CARL J. KOEHLER	1ST LT	AO1646799	6 Jul 49

2. Fol duties are directed for officers this orgn:

CAPT GORDON H. J. FLEISCH Operations Officer (0503) Prim Dy
AO660642   USAF   Deputy Squadron Commander
                          Intelligence Officer
                          Security Officer
                          Summary Court Officer

CAPT CAMPBELL Y. JACKSON Staff Liaison Officer (0503) Prim Dy
AO431357   USAF   (HQ USAFE DCS/Int)

1ST LT ARTHUR W. BANNE   Detachment Commander (0503) Prim Dy
AO590288   USAF

1ST LT WILLIAM F. FAIRCHILD D/F Officer (0503) Prim Dy
AO868447   USAF   Asst Supply Officer

1ST LT WYATT E. HINES   CW Intercept Officer (0503) Prim dy
AO1633276   USAF   Historical Officer

1ST LT CARL J. KOEHLER   Executive Officer (0503) Prim Dy
AO164799   USAF   Adjutant
                          Personnel Officer
                          Classification & Assignment Officer
                          Personal Affairs Officer
                          Civilian Personnel Officer
                          Medical Section Admin Officer
                          Postal Officer

APPENDIX G-2—2ND RSM OFFICER ASSIGNMENTS, AUG 1949

2d Rad Sq Mob, APO 175, SO 70, 11 August 1949

1ST LT CARL J. KOEHLER
Certifying Officer
Claims Officer
Recruiting Officer
Savings Bond & Insurance Officer
Class "A" Finance Agent
Unit Fund Council

1ST LT JOHN D. MCMAS
C1643988   SIG C
Motor Transport Officer (0600) Prim Dy
Supply Officer
Ground Safety Officer
Photographic Officer
VD Control Officer

1ST LT EDWARD R. MURRAY
AO1638149   USAF
Traffic Officer (9605) Prim Dy
Cryptographic Security Officer
Signal Center Officer
Top-Secret Control Officer

1ST LT JOHN V. LERSKY
AO1635435   USAF
Communications Officer (0200) Prim Dy
Mess Officer
T/I & E Officer
Ground Training Officer
Special Service Officer
Voting Officer
Unit Fund Council

BY ORDER OF CAPTAIN PRYOR:

OFFICIAL:

CARL J. KOEHLER
1ST LT   USAF
Adjutant

APPENDIX H—EVOLUTION OF TURKISH-AMERICAN ALLIANCE AND TUSLOG

A growing Turkish-American alliance began shortly after World War II. With the Soviet Union demanding territorial concessions from Turkey and instigating communist guerrilla actions against Greece, U.S. President Harry Truman proposed assistance to those two countries—the "Truman Doctrine." In 1947, Congress appropriated $100 million for Turkey, and the Joint American Military Mission for Aid to Turkey (JAMMAT) was created.

Under JAMMAT, by 1948 the U.S. Air Force was helping the Turkish Air Force acquire American aircraft and build or modernize Turkish air bases. Many of the bases built with American aid later hosted USAFSS intercept facilities. With Turkey being admitted to the North Atlantic Treaty Organization (NATO) alliance in 1952, JAMMAT eventually evolved into "The United States Logistics Group" (TUSLOG) with headquarters in Ankara. The U.S. presence in Turkey grew rapidly, and by 1966, the number of Department of Defense personnel on duty in Turkey reached 30,000, many of whom were U.S. military engaged in signals intelligence gathering at several intercept sites.

The TUSLOG acronym provided a shield for obscuring the presence of sensitive U.S. military entities in Turkey, with all military units being referenced in open communications by a TUSLOG identification instead of the organization's true unit designator. TUSLOG got its start when U.S. Air Forces Europe (USAFE) assumed responsibility for logistic support for all U.S. forces in Turkey in April 1953. USAFE delegated that responsibility to its 7206th Air Base Squadron at Hellenikon Air Base, Athens, Greece, with that squadron activating Detachment 1, 7206th ABS at Ankara, Turkey, on 1 April 1954.

On 15 May 1955, Seventeenth Air Force, Wheelus Air Base, Libya, activated the 7217th Support Group in Ankara, with this group assuming the title, Headquarters TUSLOG. With Detachment 1, 7206th ABS being discontinued, the 7217th SG activated the 7217th Air Base Squadron (TUSLOG, Detachment 1). Subsequently, HQ TUSLOG assigned a TUSLOG designator to all U.S. military units and civilian components in Turkey. The TUSLOG unit designator system was discontinued in 1982.

Index

INDEX

INDEX

NOTES

1   Public Law 624, 81st Congress, July 1950, extended commitments of active duty personnel for one year.

2   Air Force history; chronology Kitty Hawk to WW II, http://www.airforcehistory.hq.af.mil/PopTopics/kitty.htm.

3   Air Force Magazine, May 2002, pg. 37.

4   As part of the command, control and communications countermeasures (C3CM) mission, a signals intelligence unit may selectively intercept and exploit a detected signal, jam the intercepted signal, deceive the enemy by surreptitiously injecting false information into the intercepted signal, and/or fool ("spoof") the enemy by transmitting inaccurate data for the enemy to intercept.

5   Pagination for the main part of Volume II starts at page 545; last page in Chapter Three (Volume I) was 544.

6   Berlin Airlift; http://www.usafe.af.mil/berlin/quickfax.htm.

7   Some SIS/ASA history at Herzo Base; http://www.asa-alpiners.com/herzo.htm.

8   The Morse radio operator course was moved to Keesler AFB, Mississippi, later in 1949.

9   Trick was a military term for crew or shift in units where multiple "tricks" worked shift-work 24/7.

10   T/O & E 1-1027, dated 19 Jan 1945

11   Special Orders # 33, 2d RSM, dtd 31 May 1949.

12   Special Orders # 56 (corrected copy), 2d RSM, dtd 15 July 1949.

13   Rothwesten has a storied Luftwaffe heritage. In 1935, the Nazis clandestinely built Rothwesten Reichsfliegerhorst in a heavily wooded area north of Kassel. The treaty ending World War I expressly forbid Germany to possess an air force, but Air Marshal Herman Goering established Germany's first post-WW I pilot flying school at Rothwesten, and many Luftwaffe pilots were Rothwesten alumni.

14   The Army Language School moved to the Presidio of Monterey, California, in 1946, at which time the school activated its Russian language program.

15   TSgt. Schrock was NCOIC of the Intercept Section. SSgt. George T. Sherman, Sgt.'s William L. Reid and Clifford O. Losignont, and Cpl.'s Stanley P. Moore and Edward A. Thompson were assigned to the new Control Section; 2nd RSM Unit History, February 1950, Section X, Personnel.

16   Ibid.

17   http://en.wikipedia.org/wiki/Bremerhaven.

[18] http://en.wikipedia.org/wiki/German_aircraft_carrier_Graf_Zeppelin.

[19] Letter Order 7-1, 2nd RSM, APO 175, dtd 4 July 1950.

[20] Letter Order 7-5, 2nd RSM, APO 175, dtd 14 July 1950.

[21] Letter Order 8-11, 2nd RSM, APO 175, dtd 25 Aug 1950.

[22] Letter Order 8-16, 2nd RSM, APO 175, dtd 30 Aug 1950.

[23] Other airmen who arrived in Det D in Berlin in 1951 included: Pfc. Wiley V. Davis, Sgt. Ronald A. Kluge, Cpl. Gordon L. Marlow, Cpl. Robert D. Allen.

[24] Berlin Tempelhof Air Base special menu for Thanksgiving 1952 listed all personnel assigned to Detachment D, 2nd Radio Squadron Mobile: 1st Lt. Kenneth F. Pearsall, TSgt. Darral H. Hanson, SSgt.'s Robert D. Allen, Jack W. Dukes, Richard L. Frandsen, Ronald W. Moilanen, John T. Stanton, John L. Stief, A1C's Alfred H. Allee, Patrick L. Alston, William J. Arsenualt, Leslie H. Brown, James K. Day, Wiley V. Davis, John P. Freeman, Robert M. Howland, Francis W. Lynn, Wayne E. Mann, Bobby J. Matlock, Thomas D. McClelland, Melvin C. Miles, Paul E. Raver, Donald D. Smith, Martin E. Sullivan, Donald D. Zumwalt and A2C's Joseph G. Arnold, Allan Mann and Joseph C. Weaver.

[25] "The Price of Vigilance," by Larry Tart and Robert Keefe; published 2001 by Ballantine Books.

[26] General Order # 6, HQ USAFSS, dtd 19 January 1951.

[27] Unit History, 2nd RSM, January 1950.

[28] SO # 151, 2nd RSM, dtd 18 June 1951 awarded additional AFS to 11 airmen, APO 174, Linz, Austria.

[29] 2nd RSM veteran Paul Lafitte recalls Det A, 2nd RSM commanded by 1st Lt. Francis X. Miller being at Linz, Austria, in the late 1950's, suggesting the detachment moved to Linz before Feb 1951.

[30] SO # 43, 2nd RSM, dtd 20 March 1951 transferred MSgt. Joseph E. Arnaud from Darmstadt to Det 25, 2nd RSM at APO 61, Landsberg, Germany.

[31] GO # 8, 2nd RSM, dtd 6 April 1951.

[32] Unit History, 12th RSM, 1 Jan 1951-31 Mar 1951.

[33] Unit History, 12th RSM, 1 Apr 1951-30 Jun 1951.

[34] GO # 8, 2nd RSM, 6 Apr 1951.

[35] GO # 12, 12th RSM, 1 Aug 1951.

[36] GO # 15, 12th RSM, 17 Aug 1951.

[37] SO # 172, 2nd RSM, dtd 9 Aug 1951.

[38] http://en.wikipedia.org/wiki/Johnny_Cash_-_Biography.

[39] Per Keith Barkley, the first group of 41st RSM traffic analysts included: Barkley, Robert Baker, Joseph Bevins, Frank Holt, Raymond Whitner, Archie Cochran Frank Hargis and Warren Cloer.

[40] There is no record of a Col. Stroot being assigned to the 41st RSM.

[41] Phone discussion with author in July 2006.

[42] USAFSS reassigned A1C Larry R. Tart and A2C's Douglas R. Craig, Mervyn E. Eastberg, Hermon A. Eddy and Ronald L. Teker from the 6950th RGM/Chicksands to the 6913th RSM in Aug 1960; 6950th RGM SO D-234, dtd 10 Aug 1960.

[43] A Continuing Legacy: USAFSS to AIA, Brief History (1948-2003); AIA History Office, 2003.

[44] Ibid.

[45] SO # 1, HQ 6910th Security Group, APO 633, USAF, dtd 10 Sept 51.

[46] Other 6910th traffic analysis officers named by Duane Russell included: Capt.'s James Ray, Paul Lewis, Dean Binkley, Rondeau Johnson, Joe Mundorff, James Rosati, and Lt.'s Bottom, Ollie Cover, Renaldo Hamilton, Hector Quintanilla, Vogeli, and civilians Bob Machinist and Mary Ryan.

[47] U.S. Army Intelligence history; http://www.army.mil/cmh-pg/books/Lineage/mi/ch7.htm.

[48] SO # 50, HQ 6910th Security Group, APO 633, USAF, dtd 8 May 1953.

[49] A Continuing Legacy: USAFSS to AIA, Brief History (1948-2003); AIA History Office, 2003.

[50] SO # 107, HQ 6910th Security Group, APO 61, NY, dtd 2 October 1953.

[51] NSA HISTORY Call: K-SQ-RAD-85-HI, Reel: 47729, Frame: 138.

[52] Det 2, this organization, APO 178-A, Kaufbeuren, Germany, SO 125, 12th RSM, dtd 26 Jun 53.

[53] Det 2, this organization, APO 130, Sembach, Germany, SO 195, 12th RSM, APO 61, dtd 21 Oct 53.

[54] Reassigned to Det 2, this org, APO 114, Hof, Germany, SO 12, 12th RSM, APO 61, dtd 2 Feb 55.

[55] Declassified USAFSS abstract of 85th RSM history.

[56] Origin and history of 6914th RSM; http://6914thradiosquadronmobile.fortunecity.com/#.

[57] Letter Order # 269, 6900th SW, dtd 19 July 1954.

[58] Letter Order # 389, 6900th SW, dtd 3 Nov 1954.

[59] Letter Order # 253, 6900th SW, dtd 2 July 1954.

[60] Letter Order # 135, 6900th SW, dtd 21 Apr 1955.

[61] Letter Order # 184, 6900th SW, dtd 31 May 1955.

[62] http://www.raymack.com/HomePage/USAFSS/mexchristmas.html.

[63] Ibid.

[64] http://www.6912th.org/history.htm.

[65] SO # 94, 6912th RSM, APO 252. NY, NY, dtd 10 July 1956.

[66] SO # 124, 6912th RSM, APO 252, NY, NY, dtd 23 Sept 1957. 6910th was at APO 130/Sembach.

[67] Det 4, 6910th RGM became OL-1, 6910th RGM in 1959, Det 1, 6910th RGM in 1961 and Det 1, 6910th Security Wing 1963-1964.

68 http://www.6912th.org/history.htm..
69 A Continuing Legacy: USAFSS to AIA, Brief History (1948-2003); AIA History Office, 2003.
70 Ibid.
71 http://community-2.webtv.net/GLOBEMASTER1/ DET26912thRADIOSQ/.
72 GO # 51, EUCOM, dtd 2 June 1949; 2nd Lt. David R. Kingsley, navigator of B-17 "Opissonya," gave his parachute to fellow crewmember. See http://www.arlingtoncemetery.net/kingsley.htm.
73 Det 1, 603rd AC&WS became Det 1, 602nd AC&WS in July 1956; http://community-2.webtv.net/wild-willy/DET26912thRSMHOF/page2.html.
74 Hof memories; http://community-2.webtv.net/wild-willy/DET26912thRSMHOF/page2.html.
75 Email and phone exchanges with Nathan Britt in 2006.
76 Hof memories; http://community-2.webtv.net/wild-willy/DET26912thRSMHOF/page2.html.
77 Kreuzberg Kaserne in WW II; renamed Turenne Kaserne by French Occupation Forces in 1945; renamed Kreuzberg Kaserne again in 1965.
78 http://www.electricianeducation.com/biography/Zweibrücken.htm.
79 In late 1962 or early 1963, COMA-41F became OPN-AW when 6901st office symbols changed.
80 Air Force Magazine, May 1979, pg 96-97.
81 Air Force Magazine, May 1977, pg 133-134.
82 Air Force Magazine, May 1979, pg 96-97.
83 http://www.6901st.org/history6901st.htm.
84 A Continuing Legacy: USAFSS to AIA, Brief History (1948-2003); AIA History Office, 2003.
85 Ibid.
86 Ibid.
87 Ibid.
88 Ibid.
89 Commencing in the 1960's, nickname "Comfy" was used to identify new USAFSS systems/projects. The command nickname changed to "Prism" on 20 February 1992.
90 Named for Col. Levi Goldfarb, well known USAF/INY staff legend and proponent of the system.
91 Hagy and the author flew recon missions together from Rhein-Main AB, Germany, during the late 1960's.
92 The name of each air mission in USAFE began with the nickname "Creek."
93 7405th Support Sqdn activated 10 May 1955, GO # 32, HQ USAFE, dtd 3 May 1955.

94 Aviation Week and Space Technology Magazine; dtd 9 Oct 2000, pg. 103.
95 German newspaper article; http://www.tagesspiegel.de/politik/archiv/28.03.2001/ak-be-bl-447902.html.
96 First production model S&WC accepted in 1978; http://www.rl.af.mil/History/1970s/1978.html.
97 SIGINT overview by Jeffrey T. Richelson; http://www.euronet.nl/~rembert/echelon/usic08.htm.
98 DeRousse and the author flew recon missions together from Rhein-Main AB in the 1969-1973 period.
99 http://www.globalsecurity.org/military/facility/einsiedlerhof.htm.
100 In July 1981, the 6911th ESG was redesignated the 6911th Electronic Security Squadron.
101 Email from Jim Kimmett, July 2006.
102 Email from Brian McHugh on Metro Tango website, 13 Nov 2003.
103 A Continuing Legacy: USAFSS to AIA, Brief History (1948-2003); AIA History Office, 2003.
104 Unofficial unit list provided by USAFSS veteran Frank Clark.
105 http://world-information.org/wio/infostructure/100437611746/100438659207/?ic=100446325897.
106 Ibid.
107 Former USAFSS TSgt. and retired Army ASA WO-2 Richard Garrant remembers the date; his birthday.
108 A Continuing Legacy: USAFSS to AIA, Brief History (1948-2003); AIA History Office, 2003.
109 Unofficial history of Eckstein border site; http://members.tripod.com/~Rimbacher/history.html.
110 Ibid.
111 Discussion with author in 2006.
112 Ibid.
113 Date provided by former SSgt. James Riley Jr. who relocated to Det 4, 6911th in August 1980.
114 A Continuing Legacy: USAFSS to AIA, Brief History (1948-2003); AIA History Office, 2003.
115 Ibid.
116 Don Watson's 6911th RGM website; http://www.donmar.org/6911rgm/
117 A Continuing Legacy: USAFSS to AIA, Brief History (1948-2003); AIA History Office, 2003.
118 A Continuing Legacy: USAFSS to AIA, Brief History (1948-2003); AIA History Office, 2003.
119 Ibid.
120 Unofficial unit list provided by USAFSS veteran Frank Clark.

[121] A Continuing Legacy: USAFSS to AIA, Brief History (1948-2003); AIA History Office, 2003.

[122] Ibid.

[123] A brief history of Sembach Air Base; http://www.sembachveterans.org/sabhistory.htm.

[124] A Continuing Legacy: USAFSS to AIA, Brief History (1948-2003); AIA History Office, 2003.

[125] Ibid.

[126] Ibid.

[127] A Continuing Legacy: USAFSS to AIA, Brief History (1948-2003); AIA History Office, 2003.

[128] Ibid.

[129] Americans, Germans bid fond farewell—U.S. leaving Augsburg; Stars & Stripes, 21 June 1998.

[130] Stars and Stripes, European Edition, 7 October 2003.

[131] Comms relay facility worries residents of German town; Stars & Stripes, 1 April 2004.

[132] Local Trng Area 6910 (Dagger Complex); http://www.globalsecurity.org/military/facility/dagger.htm.

[133] Declassified abstract of USAFSS history.

[134] VFW Magazine, Feb 1998, article "Cold War on NATO's Southern Flank: Facing Down The Soviets."

[135] History of Project Penn; http://www.gwu.edu/~nsarchiv/news/20050318/complaint_final.pdf.

[136] SRH-244, 8th RSM Unit History, 21 Nov 47 to 28 Feb 54.

[137] Email discussion with T. Garland, 8 Aug 2005.

[138] http://www.trabzonairstation.com/veryoldpostings.htm.

[139] Sgt. Barthel's short assignment to Det 1, 14th RSM was most likely an administrative error.

[140] Carson King was assigned to Flt A, 34th RSM at Ankara in 1954; Internet FTVA Sign-in, 8/14/2003.

[141] 6930th RGM overview; http://www.gordon.army.mil/MPD/RSO/Enotes/2005/2005jun.htm.

[142] Commander's Welcome to Karamursel Pamphlet, TUSLOG Det 95, dtd 15 November 1970.

[143] Willy Pardue's description of Karamursel in 1957; http://www.geocities.com/r8wilt/tuslog.htm.

[144] Deacon Allor's memories of Turkey; http://www.merhabaturkey.com/1ALLORindex.html.

[145] Diyarbakir/Pirinclik FPS-17 operations; http://www.globalsecurity.org/space/facility/pirinclik.htm.

[146] Ibid.

[147] Ibid.

NOTES

[148] American Espionage and the Soviet Target, Jeffrey Richelson, 1987 and The Puzzle Palace, James Bamford, 1982.

[149] The U.S.-Turkish Alliance in Disarray; World Affairs, Winter 2005; Michael M. Gunter.

[150] Ibid.

[151] Iraklion Air Station background; http://pws.prserv.net/varney/ias/.

[152] USAFE info on Iraklion Air Station; http://en.wikipedia.org/wiki/Iraklion_Air_Station.

[153] USAFSS unit awards; Spokesman listing by unit; date unknown.

[154] Letter Order 247, 6900th SW, dtd 22 July 1955 and LTRO 379, dtd 9 Dec 1955.

[155] Unofficial unit list provided by USAFSS veteran Frank Clark.

[156] U.S. Is Dismantling Peshawar Spy Base; Washington Post; 10 April 1969.

[157] USAF Communications Station, Peshawar; Msg # A-550, J.W. Spain, dtd 6 October 1969.

[158] UPI special item # 1831, dateline Badaber, dtd 9 January 1970.

[159] Tortorete, who shared his USAFSS experiences with the author, passed away 2 February 2009.

[160] Email from Flight Lt. Salma Malik, 19 Dec 2004.

[161] SO # 39, 6910th RGM, dtd 28 Jan 1959.

[162] Bruno Calo' unofficial history of San Vito on San Vito internet forum, 21 June

[163] Technical Manual TM 32-5985-217-15 for AN/FLR-9(V7/V8), Dept of Army, June 1976.

[164] http://www.fas.org/irp/program/collect/an-flr-9.htm.

[165] "Comfy" was an unclassified code name for USAFSS programs, i.e., Comfy Cloud, Comfy Levi, etc.

[166] Movement Order 4062A, dated 12 September 1950.

[167] Table of Organization and Equipment 1-2232T, dtd 31 July listed authorized equipment and personnel, with each squadron having its own vehicles, mechanics, drivers, generators, field stoves, cooks, etc.

[168] Built in the 12th Century, the Priory is alleged to be haunted by Rosata's ghost, "A legend of a 'naughty nun' is supposed to account for the multiple hauntings at Chicksands Priory. A nun called Berta Rosata apparently became pregnant after a love affair with a monk. This was considered to be such a heinous crime that she was walled up alive in the cellars and forced to watch her lover being beheaded before the last brick was placed. Berta's ghost reappears on the 17th of each month whenever the moon is full." http://www.galaxy.bedfordshire.gov.uk/webingres/bedfordshire/vlib/0.digitised_resources/chicksands_news_ghosts_nun.htm

[169] Special Order # 211, 2nd RSM, dtd 30 Nov 1950.

[170] Some Seco huts at Chicksands had five side panels and four dividers.

171 1958 Chicks Soccer Team: Standing from left: Harry Wilson (coach), John Patterson, Emmett Toon, Jeff Pearcy, Kenneth Barr, Larry Tart, Jim Gertz, ?. Kneeling from left: ?, TSgt. Moss, Kenneth Hammer, Bill Obitz, Herbert Merten and Capt. LaChance (Team OIC).

172 Special Order No. 59, 10th RSM (USAFSS), 8 May 1955; IAW GO 13, HQ USAFSS, dtd 7 Mar 55.

173 Unofficial unit list provided by USAFSS veteran Frank Clark. DF site was probably near inactive, former RAF Stracathro, but USAFSS airmen billeted at RAF Edzell.

174 37th RSM history in Scotsman (final issue of RAF Kirknewton base newspaper); 23 Oct 1965.

175 USAFSS Ltr Order No. 55, 1 May 1952; Shipment 5690-A, 37th RSM PCS to APO 124, NY, NY.

176 37th RSM was organized under TO&E 1-2232T, 31 July 1950.

177 Basketball in the East of Scotland; http://www.lothianba.org.uk/history.htm.

178 U.S. Navy (Edzell) Tartan created 6 July 1985; http://members.aol.com/ewalker01/brechin/Page39.html.

179 http://www.publications.parliament.uk/pa/cm200304/cmhansrd/vo040223/text/40223w14.htm.

180 USAFSS closed RAF Kirknewton 1 Aug '66; http://www.staff.ncl.ac.uk/d.f.j.wood/thesis_files/5-6.pdf.

181 http://www.publications.parliament.uk/pa/cm200304/cmhansrd/vo040223/text/40223w14.htm.

182 USAF use of RAF Nocton Hall; http://raf-lincolnshire.info/noctonhall/noctonhall.htm.

183 Volunteer Glider School at Kirknewton; http://www.2175atc.co.uk/gliding.html.

184 Livingston Model Aircraft Club flying site; http://www.lmac-site.com/.

185 http://en.wikipedia.org/wiki/Pea_soup.

186 http://www.epa.gov/history/topics/perspect/london.htm.

187 http://en.wikipedia.org/wiki/Smog.

188 http://www.portfolio.mvm.ed.ac.uk/studentwebs/session4/27/greatsmog52.htm.

189 Invented by Percy Shaw in Yorkshire, England. http://en.wikipedia.org/wiki/Cat's_eye_(road).

190 Spy base boob gets Reagan out of bed; http://www.philipjohnston.com/news/reagan.htm.

191 Email feedback from Wayne Wetterman in 2007.

192 Hitchin Comet (Hitchin, Hertfordshire) news article dated 2-3-94.

193 Intelligence Corps History; http://www.army.mod.uk/intelligencecorps/.

[194] http://www.sheffordtown.co.uk/newsline/autumn99/
edition18_13.htm.
[195] MoD Annual Rept 2003-04; http://192.5.30.131/publications/
performance2003/supdoc_agencies.htm.
[196] Intelligence Corps History; http://www.army.mod.uk/
intelligencecorps/.
[197] Chicksands; http://maps.google.com/maps?ll=52.042580,-
0.388298&spn=0.052674,0.080887&t=k.

CPSIA information can be obtained at www.ICGtesting.com
Printed in the USA
LVOW01s1740160915

454443LV00029B/846/P